The Changing Demography
of Spanish Americans

Work Is the Lure

The Changing Demography of Spanish Americans

A. J. JAFFE

Graduate School of Business
Columbia University
New York, New York

RUTH M. CULLEN

Office of Planning and Evaluation
U.S. Office of Personnel Management
Washington, D.C.

THOMAS D. BOSWELL

Department of Geography
University of Miami
Coral Gables, Florida 33124

With a Foreword by Joseph P. Fitzpatrick

ACADEMIC PRESS
A Subsidiary of Harcourt Brace Jovanovich, Publishers
New York   London   Toronto   Sydney   San Francisco

This is a volume in

STUDIES IN POPULATION

A complete list of titles in this series appears at the end of this volume.

ACADEMIC PRESS, INC.
111 Fifth Avenue, New York, New York 10003

United Kingdom Edition published by
ACADEMIC PRESS, INC. (LONDON) LTD.
24/28 Oval Road, London NW1 7DX

Library of Congress Cataloging in Publication Data

Jaffe, A. J.   Date
    The changing demography of Spanish Americans.

    (Studies in population)
    Bibliography: p.
    1. Hispanic Americans——Social conditions.
2. Hispanic Americans——Economic conditions.
3. United States——Economic conditions——1971–
4. United States——Social conditions——1960–
I. Cullen, Ruth M., joint author. II. Boswell,
Thomas D., joint author. III. Title. IV. Series.
E184.S75J32   305.8'68   80–1101
ISBN 0–12–379580–X

PRINTED IN THE UNITED STATES OF AMERICA

80 81 82 83   9 8 7 6 5 4 3 2 1

Contents

1

Introduction   1

2

The Natural Cycle of an Ethnic Group— Some Theoretical Considerations   9

3
The Findings—A Summary

4
Demographic Convergence

5
The Hispanos

6
The Mexican Americans

Foreword

This study by A. J. Jaffe, Ruth Cullen, and Thomas Boswell is, without a doubt, the most intensive analysis of a body of census data ever published. It is remarkable from many points of view. It focuses on one large and increasingly important segment of the U.S. population, the Hispanics. They are growing rapidly while the rate of growth of the total population of the United States is declining almost to zero population growth. The Hispanics will constitute a significant part of the population in the next century. It is important to know as much as we can about them. The present book provides us with a substantial increase in insight and understanding.

The study has an important theoretical focus: the use of demographic indicators to determine the extent to which the Hispanics are merging into the general population of the United States. With the emphasis on Chicano Power, Puerto Rican Power, the preoccupation with Cuban refugees in the United States, and with the emphasis on bilingual and bicultural educational programs, the fear has been raised more than once that the Hispanics are developing into a segregated block with little relationship to the larger society and population. It is in relation to this problem and this argument that the book is most significant. Using the variables of intermarriage (Hispanics with non-Hispanic whites), retention of the Spanish language, and levels of fertility, Jaffe, Cullen, and Boswell find that a "demographic convergence" is definitely taking place. To the extent to which the demographic variables indicate it, the Hispanics are becoming part of the mainstream of U.S. life, in much the same way that previous newcomers did. This finding is seriously challenged by many of the Hispanic groups, which are understandably concerned about the loss of their culture. But the demographic evidence is there; and Jaffe, Cullen, and Boswell have analyzed it with great care and competence. It will be important to study the extent to which Hispanic culture continues to be viable despite the evidence of demographic convergence. If this occurs, it will be a new phenomenon in the experience of newcomers to American life.

With reference to the Puerto Ricans, the book is significant in its relationship to another publication, the Report of the United States Commission on Civil Rights, *Puerto Ricans in the United States: An Uncertain Future* (1976). The general tone of the commission's report is gloomy; it does not present a very promising picture of Puerto Rican progress when measured by socioeconomic variables. However, when selected variables are held constant, as in this study, the picture of Puerto Rican progress is much more promising. This is particularly clear when the data about second-generation Puerto Ricans are analyzed in contrast to that of the first generation. Level of education also appears to be a discriminating variable: High school graduates become assimilated more often than those who are less educated.

This book is essential for demographers and for anyone who is working in race and ethnicity. The data are 1970 Census data. Nevertheless, it is not the particular date of the census that is important, but rather the process that the skillful demographic analysis reveals. There appears to be an irresistible pressure in the United States toward intermarriage, the adoption of the English language, and diminishing fertility as education and socioeconomic levels increase. The demographic convergence, which is so evident, probably reflects a cultural convergence as well. We owe a genuine debt of thanks to the authors of this volume for a new and significant insight into the Hispanic experience in the United States.

JOSEPH P. FITZPATRICK
Department of Sociology
Fordham University

Preface

This study is divided into two main parts. In the first we describe the theoretical aspects of our study and the broader findings that pertain to all the Spanish-origin people who live in the United States. The second part consists of separate chapters for each of the five groups analyzed.

In carrying through this study we relied exclusively on data already collected, almost all by the U.S. Census Bureau; most of these data are as of 1970, as there are comparatively few data for earlier dates and even less for the post-1970 period. If we had collected new information as part of this analysis, not only would the cost have been significantly greater but also the study design and the types of findings would have differed to some extent. How different and in what ways we cannot say; we can only say that our findings in part result from the format and design imposed by the available data.

This restriction had several observable results. First, since we were dependent on the U.S. Census, the specific Spanish-American groups that we could study were defined, essentially, by Census Bureau personnel. The five groups analyzed are Mexican, Puerto Rican, Cuban, Hispano, and Central and South American as one composite group. Such other potential groups as Santo Dominicans, Colombians, Argentinians, and so on, could not be included individually because of the lack of basic data. Brazilian-origin people were omitted, since they are not Spanish Americans.

A second restriction forced by the available data is the depth of the possible analysis. For example, the Census Bureau collects no information on the attitudes of one population group—Spanish or non-Spanish—to another; therefore, this aspect could not be studied. We can, however, refer to the literature for studies on this topic. In general, we attempted to resolve the problem of the lack of in-depth information by making inferences from the available data. We have not hesitated to imply and to suggest the possible factors underlying some of the observed results based on census data. For example, among the Puerto Ricans living outside of New York there are more adult men than there are women; in New York there is an excess of women. Furthermore, Puerto Rican men earn more outside New York. Hence we infer migration, probably out of New York, for economic reasons, although we have no data to test our inference.

A third restriction is the nature and amount of analysis possible for each group. The several chapters in Part II are of varying length, because of the amounts of data available.

Finally, we alert readers that we have not distinguished the Spanish Americans according to the Census Bureau's "color or race." Almost all the Spanish Americans reported themselves as "white" at the time of the 1970 Census; accordingly, we treat them as white in our analysis.

Acknowledgments

Various people helped considerably in the preparation of this study, and we wish to thank all of them. However, the authors alone assume responsibility for the findings and interpretations presented. Of the three authors, Thomas Boswell participated during the first year, after which he left for the University of Florida at Gainsville. Ruth Cullen replaced him and continued on to the end of the study.

Fray Angelico Chavez gave us much information about the Hispanos. Larry Adcock of the University of New Mexico supplied otherwise unavailable statistics for the Spanish-American population of New Mexico. Robert Cuba Jones gave us important insights into the Mexican people, both those living in the United States and those living in the Republic of Mexico. Pnina Grinberg carried out the multitude of computer tabulations needed for this study. Barbara Rios supplied the photographs for the jacket and the frontispiece.

Others who assisted us with advice, comments, and so on, include Robert Lewis of Columbia University; Roberto Rios of Columbia University and Lehman College; John Macisco and Mary Powers of Fordham University; and Lincoln Day and Zaida Carleton. Amy Davey was of inestimable assistance in the preparation of the final manuscript. And to any whom we may have inadvertently omitted, our apologies.

We thank the National Institute of Child Health and Human Development of the Department of Health, Education and Welfare and Earl Huyck for supporting our work. Finally, our many thanks go to Vera Rubin, Lambros Comitas, and the Research Institute for the Study of Man, under whose auspices the research was conducted.

The Changing Demography
of Spanish Americans

1

Introduction[1]

THE NATURE OF THE PUBLIC INTEREST

The Spanish Americans became a newsworthy topic in the national American press and thinking only during the last several decades. Before then, interest was localized. For example, New York City newspapers emphasized the Puerto Ricans, since many had migrated there since World War II. The Mexican Americans had always been of interest to the media in the southwestern states. After the Castro revolution and the migration of many Cubans to Florida, this group became of interest in Miami. In short, increasing numbers and increasing visibility of any particular group focuses attention on them in the area in which they are most visible. Overall, however, in past years there has been comparatively little concern with Spanish Americans *in toto*.

During the 1960s public opinion began to focus on the neglected, disadvantaged, and discriminated-against elements in our society. Perhaps the efforts of the black population to achieve some measure of equality, whether at the public drinking fountain or washroom or at the job, spearheaded this movement. Other groups, including women, Native Americans, and Spanish Americans, joined the fray. In 1964 Congress passed the Civil Rights Act; Title VII made discrimination in employment illegal. This was followed by a host of legislative and administrative actions designed to provide, as a minimum, equal

[1] This study was supported by Grant No. NIH–NICHD 72–2795 from the Department of Health, Education and Welfare, National Institute of Child Health and Human Development.

employment opportunities for these several groups. The flavor of these actions is well illustrated by the following:

> The purpose of the provisions in this part is to set forth the interpretations and guidelines of the Office of Federal Contract Compliance regarding the implementation of Executive Order 11246 as amended, for promoting and insuring equal employment opportunities for all persons, employed or seeking employment with Government contractors and subcontractors or with contractors and subcontractors performing under federally assisted construction contracts, without regard to religion or national origin. . . .[2]

and:

> An employer may acquire the Race/Ethnic identification information necessary for this section either by visual surveys of the work force, or from post-employment records. . . .
>
> The concept of race as used by the Equal Employment Opportunity Commission does not denote clearcut scientific definitions of race/ethnicity. For the purposes of this report an employee may be included in the group to which he or she appears to belong, identifies with, or is regarded in the community as belonging to. However, no person should be counted in more than one race/ethnic category.
>
> The five race/ethnic categories are defined as follows . . .
>
> 1. White (not of Hispanic origin): All persons having origins in any of the original peoples of Europe, North Africa, the Middle East or the Indian subcontinent.
>
> 2. Black (not of Hispanic origin): All persons having origins in any of the black racial groups.
>
> 3. Hispanic: All persons of Mexican, Puerto Rican, Cuban, Central or South American, or other Spanish culture or origin, regardless of race.
>
> 4. Asian or Pacific Islanders: All persons having origins in any of the original peoples of the Far East, Southeast Asia, or the Pacific Islands. This area includes, for example, China, Japan, Korea, the Philippine Islands, and Samoa.
>
> 5. American Indian or Alaskan Native. All persons having origins in any of the original peoples of North America.[3]

It is evident that the Spanish Americans were included as a group being discriminated against. However, these people are not defined precisely; for example, sometimes they are described by their place of

---

[2] Equal Employment Opportunity, U.S., Department of Labor, *Federal Register,* vol. 38, no. 13, 19 January 1973, pt. 60–50.

[3] *Ibid.,* vol. 40, no. 114, 12 June 1975, pt. 1602. Revised in May 1977. See U.S. Department of Commerce, Office of Federal Statistical Policies and Standards, Directive No. 15. The revisions do not affect the definition of Hispanic persons.

birth or by their ancestors' place of birth, and somtimes by commonly employed terms such as "Mexican" or "Cuban." In any event, such legislation and resulting judicial administrative actions give the appearance that the Spanish Americans are one group, although local newspapers continue to accentuate local versions of Spanish Americans. These various antidiscrimination measures treat all Spanish Americans as one group, with little or no differentiation.

Another movement that made headway in the 1960s—at least it made newspaper headlines—and contributed to public interest in the Spanish Americans was that of advocating a lower birth rate. Against this background it was observed that the crude birth rates of Mexican Americans in the Southwest and of Puerto Ricans in New York City were higher than that of the general population. This, in turn, led to inquiries about the demographic characteristics of the Spanish Americans. In reality how high was their birth rate, and why? What are possible trends in fertility and related demographic characteristics?

These two major movements apparently were interrelated, at least as far as could be determined by casual observation. The Spanish Americans were poorer than the general white population, and fewer were in the higher paying and higher status jobs. And they had higher fertility. Perhaps there is a connection between these observations, and perhaps if the Spanish Americans could be brought into the nation's economic mainstream, their fertility would decrease and their demographic characteristics would approach those of the general white population. It is in light of this type of thinking that we embarked upon our study of the demographic and economic characteristics, and longtime changes therein, of the Spanish Americans.

THE DIFFERENT SPANISH-AMERICAN GROUPS

It is clear that in the United States there are a large number of very different groups rather than a single, monolithic "Spanish American." Furthermore, the members of these various groups recognize themselves as different, and they have very different demographic and economic characteristics. Therefore, in our study we have examined five groups individually, and nowhere do we speak of "Spanish Americans" as a group. As we shall see, these groups are too different to be lumped together into a monolithic whole.

These five groups are of the following origins: Mexican, Puerto Rican, Cuban, Central and South American, and the Hispanos. There is nothing arbitrary about this selection; they are simply those groups for which we could obtain data from the U.S. decennial censuses, particularly that of 1970. Since our analysis is based primarily upon such census data—we did not collect any data from special surveys—we are forced to adopt the census designations. (For detailed information on the census data, see Appendix A.) We realize further that each of these groups is highly diverse, but we cannot go beyond the census statistics. At this point we should define these five groups in general terms as follows:

1. *Self-identification*: The 1970 Census permitted people to designate themselves as one of the five origin groups if they so desired; this was done on the 5% sample.
2. *Country of birth of person or his or her parents:* On the 15% sample of the census there was no self-identification. But for this sample, country of birth of the foreign born and country of birth of the person's parents were asked. Hence, it was possible to distinguish those born in Mexico or Puerto Rico, for example, from those born on the U.S. mainland and who had one or both parents born in one or another of the countries of origin.

We combined those individuals who were included in these two definitions in order to maximize our Mexican-, Puerto Rican–, and Cuban-origin populations. For those of Central and South American origin, the census question on self-identification was in error, and the data for this group were taken only from country of birth information. The Hispano population was delineated by abstracting the natives of native parentage from the group that had designated itself as "Other Spanish."

IS RELIGION A COMMON DENOMINATOR?

Most of the Spanish Americans, but not all, are of the Roman Catholic religion, at least nominally. This statement alone, however, does not reveal the possible influences of religion on the demographic and related factors that we are studying. We assume that religion has, or had in the past, some undetermined influence on these factors. Furthermore, we have the impression that the specific type of Catholicism varies from one Spanish-American group to another. Such variations in religion presumably have differential influences on the subjects of our interests. Because we think that this topic is important, we raise it. We can, however, say no more on it, because we have no data and the subject is far too broad for inclusion in our study. Further research, we suspect, will indicate that some of the sociodemographic-economic differences observed in 1970 can be traced to differing religious influences, particularly in the past.

THE FRAMEWORK OF THIS STUDY

It is well known that many persons in these five groups are poor, have inadequate housing and food and little education, and are, or were, discriminated against in employment. Census statistics are not needed to prove these points, as, for example, equal employment opportunity legislation was enacted about a decade before the 1970 Census data became available. Furthermore, the situation of the 1970s is history. The social scene is always changing; the lessons of the past have value only insofar as they help illuminate the future, for we can be certain that the social situation a generation or two in the future will be different from the past. Accordingly, if social programs are to be introduced—and they require a number of years to implement—they should be aimed at what the situation is likely to be in the future and not at what it was at some past date.

We are taking a dynamic approach, based on the history of the changes that are, apparently, occurring in the demographic and economic characteristics of each of these groups. Our major questions may be stated as follows:

1. How rapidly, if at all, are the demographic and economic characteristics of these several groups changing?
2. How closely do they seem to be approaching the characteristics of the non-Spanish white population among whom they live?
3. What are the forces, if any, that are apparently moving the characteristics of these people to approach (or not to approach) those of the non-Spanish white?

The answers to these questions will provide us with a look into the future a generation hence.

Since we are primarily concerned with the demographic changes which are taking place, we are only secondarily interested in the absolute numbers of Spanish Americans who were living in the United States in the late 1970s. We realize that the numbers game—how many?—is emphasized by the media and some spokesmen for ethnic groups. They do so on the mistaken assumption that increased federal funds will become available if their numbers can be increased. Our feelings are (a) all absolute numbers are partly fiction rather than fact; and (b) our study was not undertaken in order to allocate federal monies; hence our secondary interest in absolute numbers.

THE PROBLEM OF MEASURING CHANGE

Change over time in the demographic characteristics of a population may occur in several ways. To begin, the group characteristics can change if, for example, selective emigration occurs, as when retired persons return to the original home country. Or there may be selective immigration, such as college students who come to the United States to study and remain here. Entry or withdrawal from an ethnic class can occur without foreign migration. A person of one ethnicity may change his name and claim to be a member of a different ethnic group. Or, the child whose parents are of differing ethnicity may decide to consider himself as one or the other, or perhaps just "American." Clearly, there are several ways by which selective entry or withdrawal may come about.

Second, the characteristics of an ethnic group are affected as the distribution by phase of the generation cycle shifts over time. For example, the foreign-born members may have little schooling, and their United States-born children much more schooling. Initially, when the foreign-born component constitutes a large portion of the total population, the population will appear to be largely unschooled. If a generation or two later the native element predominates, the group will appear to be, as it really is, much better educated.

Third, as the individual's life cycle changes, the group's characteristics may change. For example, persons enter the labor force as youth and obtain lower-level jobs; as they grow older and achieve more work experience, many rise on the occupational ladder. If, initially, the labor force is composed predominantly of young persons, the group will be seen to hold less desirable jobs. If a decade later there are many more older persons in the labor force, the group will appear to have climbed the occupational ladder. In reality, it will have done so via the life cycle.

Finally, the person may change. A high school dropout may return to school and become a college graduate; or a worker in a part of the country where wage rates are relatively lower, may move to a section where wages are significantly higher and immediately earn more, even though he or she has not changed occupation or type of work.

No data, longitudinal or otherwise, exist that will permit the complete untangling of this intricate web. The best that can be done is to describe the group's characteristics at various times; to note which characteristics are changing in unison; to analyze age, sex, and nativity groups individually (i.e., component analysis); and then to infer the probable pattern of changes. If the inferences are reasonably correct, then there is a basis for estimating the future demographic characteristics with a fair degree of confidence.

— 2

The Natural Life Cycle
of an Ethnic Group:
Some Theoretical Considerations

Ethnic or minority or nationality groups emerge, or are created, as distinguishable entities, continue for a few or many generations, and then generally disappear. This natural life cycle takes place over a period of at least a century, and very often several centuries and perhaps millennia. We suspect that it happens to all groups, although there may be an occasional and rare exception.

Because of the slow rate with which groups pass through this cycle, it is often thought that they are immutable and unchanging entities. One is likely to see little change during the course of a lifetime and, indeed, may be more impressed by the apparent stability than by the slow and gradual changes that are occurring. This change is the central theme that we are addressing in this section.

In arriving at this hypothesis we admit to having been significantly, but not exclusively, influenced by the history of the United States. As we read this history we see that a number of groups, as, for example, the Hessians at the time of the American Revolution, the early colonial seventeenth-century Dutch, or the pre–Civil War German immigrants, have all more or less disappeared as separate entities; they have merged into the general population.[1] We believe that this same process has been going on throughout the world, but at greatly varying rates.

---

[1] See, for example, the excellent study by Ira Rosenwaike, *Population History of New York City* (Syracuse: Syracuse University Press, 1972). For an excellent summary of much of the English literature on ethnicity, see Leo Grebler, Joan W. Moore, and Ralph C. Guzman, *The Mexican-American People: The Nation's Second Largest Minority* (New York: Free Press, 1970), p.566ff. We see no need to repeat the literature survey in our report.

Perhaps this process has been unusually rapid in the United States, but not unique.

DEFINITION

There is no agreed-upon definition of *ethnicity, nationality,* or *minority groups,* and we are not proposing one. Indeed, we are not even attempting to distinguish among these three terms. In the United States, groups that are so designated in popular parlance are generally relatively small in numbers and have, or are supposed to have, characteristics that are different from the main body of the population that is supposedly more nearly homogeneous. The equal employment opportunity legislation, previously quoted, named some of these groups in line with popular thinking. We are sure that other groups could have been named if so desired and if census data about them were available. This last point is particularly important, since reality and legitimacy tend to be ascribed to those groups that have been specifically counted by the census. For example, we sometimes think of the WASPs as a separate group in the United States. However, because they have never been enumerated by the census, they have not been designated as an ethnic group.

Presumably a definition of ethnicity would involve at least the following three elements:[2]

1. Generally, the members of such a group think of themselves as being somehow different from other groups and in turn are so regarded.
2. An ethnic group is often usually a numerically smaller group, that is, smaller than the "majority," whom we tend not to consider as an ethnic group. At least this is the situation in the United States, although not necessarily world wide.
3. The group has either migrated, voluntarily or involuntarily, to an

---

[2] Charles Wagley and Marvin Harris in *Minorities in the New World* (New York: Columbia University Press, 1958) include, in addition to these characteristics, that minority and/or ethnic groups are generally subject to prejudice and discrimination because of their supposedly special characteristics, for example, language and religion.

For the most part, sociologists tend to emphasize the subordinate position of minorities, which implies some form of discriminatory behavior on the part of the majority or dominant group. This does not mean that an ethnic group *per se* is automatically a minority, if one posits discrimination and prejudice as a defining characteristic. See, for example, George E. Simpson and J. Milton Yinger, *Racial and Cultural Minorities,* 3d ed. (New York: Harper & Row, 1965).

area away from its homeland or has been overrun in its own homeland by an invading group.

Any definition that attempted to be all-inclusive would have to be more complicated. Let us consider some of these ramifications. To be a member of an ethnic group presumably a person ought to think of himself as a member of such a group. The strength of allegiance, however, varies tremendously from one person to another. Some will openly boast of their ethnicity—they could be labeled "professional ethnics." Others will admit to such affiliation only under pressure, and still others will deny their ethnicity. Are those who deny affiliation not members of the particular ethnic group?

The latter question, in turn, is related to how these persons are considered by others. If their neighbors and society, including members of other ethnic groups, consider them to be members of ethnic group Z, they will be so considered, even though they may deny it until death. Indeed, in light of the way their neighbors look upon them, they may ultimately look upon themselves as members of that group, but probably with minimum effort of self-identification. Furthermore, even if they reluctantly admit the identification, they may not consider themselves to be different in any way from those who are not members of ethnic group Z. On the other hand, if they have a strong allegiance to their group, they are likely to think of themselves as different from others.

Another complication arises from the often strong relationship between ethnic groups and economic class. As we saw, many of the Spanish Americans in the United States are in the lower economic classes. We may ask how U.S. society regards Spanish Americans who are in the upper economic classes. We suspect that the rich and well-educated Spanish American is considered by his neighbors and by society to be totally different from his poverty-stricken countrymen; the two are not to be lumped together. Lewis *et al.* have developed this point at considerable length with regard to the nationalities in the Soviet Union;[3] class distinctions cannot be separated from nationality distinctions. We believe the same holds true in the United States and throughout the world.

Religion can be used as an ethnic identifier, although this also poses problems. On the one hand, we see, for example, that Mexican and Irish Catholics would consider themselves different from each other; a common religion is not sufficient to make them into one ethnic group.

---

[3] Robert A. Lewis, Richard H. Rowland, and Ralph S. Clem, *Nationality and Population Change in Russia and the USSR* (New York: Praeger Publishers, 1976).

On the other hand, there is evidence that increasing education blurs religious distinctions. Two Ph.D.'s of different religions may not even be aware of that distinction. The common experiences of their schooling may negate any possibly differing tendencies due to religious origin.

Perhaps the overriding element in all discussions of ethnicity or minority status is the great heterogeneity of the members of each group, a topic to be discussed subsequently. Only if all members were completely homogeneous in their characteristics might we be able to speak positively about different ethnic groups.

SOME ILLUSTRATIONS

We may illustrate as follows. The Mexicans who migrated to the United States are considered to be an ethnic group. The same people living in Mexico would not consider themselves to be different and to comprise an ethnic group.

The Hispanos originally settled in the Southwest in the seventeenth and eighteenth centuries; many were the migrants from Spain who had stopped off temporarily in the present-day country of Mexico. Prior to the mid-nineteenth century, they were the dominant European-origin group in the Southwest, mainly in what is now the state of New Mexico; except for some American Indians, few others were living there. However, we must note that many of these Indians had migrated to the Southwest from northern and eastern areas of the modern United States not long before the Hispanos arrived there. Indeed, some may have migrated during the early period of the Hispano settlement. In 1848 the United States took possession of this area, and the Hispanos and Indians each became ethnic groups.[4]

The most recent case of the creation of an "instant" ethnic group is that of the South Vietnamese in the United States. As long as they lived in Vietnam, we did not consider them to be an ethnic group. After several plane loads arrived in the United States together with the attendant media publicity, the Vietnamese became an ethnic group overnight and eventually will be identified separately in the census. In the early 1960s the Cubans also became an "instant" ethnic group in the United States.

Elsewhere in the world we see this general picture repeated. For ex-

---

[4] For further details see Caroline Zeleny, *Relations between the Spanish Americans and Anglo Americans in New Mexico* (1944; reprint ed., New York: Arno Press, 1974). See also Gordon C. Baldwin, *Indians of the Southwest* (New York: Capricorn Books, 1973).

ample, in Central Asia today there are a number of groups who have been designated as "nationalities" by the Soviet government. Let us consider only four: the Kirghiz, Uzbeks, Turkomans, and Kazaks. Originally, these were only a few of a number of indistinguishable groups of people—tribes—living under their own local feudal "lords." Perhaps the main point of differentiation were the feudal rulers. The Russian armies conquered this territory in the nineteenth century, and it was subsequently inherited by the Soviet government. Throughout the czarist period, there had been problems with these various tribes who had no particular liking for their Russian conquerors. Finally, the Soviet government officially "recognized" these tribes by consolidating them into the limited number of groupings now called "nationalities" and by considering them as nominally "independent" units within the Union of Soviet Socialist Republics.

The Ukrainians are another example of a created ethnic group or nationality. Several centuries ago they were part of the Russian people and were not differentiated from the latter. The Poles conquered the population segment that later became the Ukrainians and influenced them slightly, so that the latter began to think of themselves as a distinct group. When the czars regained possession of this population, the Ukrainians who considered themselves not to be Russian, became a separate nationality.

The several Arab states now in existence were largely created by the European powers in the post–World War I period. Previously there had been a number of groups, tribes in some instances, living under the domination of the Ottoman empire. When the Europeans became involved, they drew various boundary lines, and the world found that there were Lebanese, Jordanians, Syrians, and so on. From the outsiders' point of view, it would appear that these nationalities, ethnic groups, or whatever they may be called, were simply created by drawing boundary lines. From the viewpoint of the people living in these geographic areas, they still distinguish separate groups among themselves, such as Shiite versus Sunnite Moslem.

The entire history of the eastern Mediterranean and Southwest Asia illustrates the emergence and disappearance of what we now consider separate groups. Several millennia ago there were the Babylonians, Assyrians, Scythians, Cimmerians, Turks, Armenians, Medes, Hebrews, Phoenicians, and numerous other groups, each of which has been given a name by Herodotus or present-day historians. These groups emerged by splitting off from other groups, and most of them eventually disappeared as separate entities. For example, if there are any descendants of the Scythians living today, they are Russians, Ukrainians, Turks, or

Western Hemisphere citizens whose ancestors had migrated from Europe.

In what is now China there had been various groups: the Ch'u, Han, Wei, Yen, and many others. Eventually many of these peoples co-alesced into the "Chinese" population. Indeed, the Chinese are proud of their ability to absorb other tribes or peoples. Nevertheless, even the last quarter of the twentieth century, there are numerous "national minorities" within the borders of China. These recognized minorities constitute perhaps 5% of the total population.[5]

An interesting and detailed account of the life cycle of one of these groups is *Chinese Jews of Kaifeng-Fu* by J. Preuss.[6] Hebrew traders from the time of King Solomon, if not earlier, had migrated to China, where they participated in the Silk Route trade and perhaps elsewhere. At some early date Jews had already established a community in Kaifeng in Honan province. By 1605, when they first came to the attention of Westerners, they were already racially Chinese as a result of intermarriages in previous centuries. They spoke Chinese and, apparently, had taken on most Chinese characteristics, except for religion. By the early part of the twentieth century, they had completely disappeared. A Jewish visitor in 1932 reported that "although the Chinese Jews of Kaifeng knew nothing of Judaism any longer and realized that they were Chinese, completely assimilated, there was pride in the knowledge that they sprang from an ancient people who were different from the Chinese people around them."[7]

Even a casual reading of the histories of these various groups throughout the world reveals that most had become separately iden-tified groups as a result of migration—every known population has come from some place else to its present residence—or through con-quest by a militarily superior group who incorporated them. As a result of the ensuing contacts, the original groups became amalgamated or otherwise changed so that they disappeared. Undoubtedly a very small number of such "ethnic" or "nationality" groups have continued to ex-ist for the last several millennia or longer. Most of them have faded from the world scene or have been so greatly changed that they are unrecognizable. This is what we mean by the *natural life cycle*. As we

---

[5] See Leo A. Orleans, *Every Fifth Child* (Stanford: Stanford University Press, 1972), chap. 5, "National Minorities."

[6] Published by the Museum Haartiz in Tel Aviv, 1961.

[7] *Ibid.*, pp. 28, 29. It has been suggested that as late as the 1970s there are some "Jewish" Chinese people. However, racially they are Chinese and do not follow any Jewish relgious traditions or forms. Rabbi Anson Laytner, "Chinese Jews Survive," *The National Jewish Monthly*, vol. 79, no. 4 (December 1979): p. 6ff.

shall see subsequently, we believe this cycle is operating today on the five Spanish-American groups who are living in the United States.

ALL POPULATIONS ARE HETEROGENEOUS

The essential problems in distinguishing an ethnic or minority group from the majority are that (a) all populations have heterogeneous rather than homogeneous characteristics; and (b) all characteristics and their distributions are changing continuously. In statistical terms we can depict the situation as follows. For simplicity let us consider two characteristics, X and Y, which can be physical, social, cultural, economic, or any other. All members of a group are not identical: Some are rich and others poor; some are illiterate and others have Ph.D.'s, and so on. If the characteristic is plotted, presumably a normal bell-shaped curve or a reasonable approximation thereof will appear, as shown in Figure 2.1.

With reference to both characteristics, some members of the minority group will have the characteristics of some members of the majority group. Only the average values of the characteristics distinguish the two groups. For example, let us assume that the minority population averaged 10 years of formal schooling and the majority, 13 years. Yet both groups contain some people who have no schooling and others who have Ph.D.'s or M.D.'s. Furthermore, over time the average for the minority may coincide with that of the majority.

It is clear that we cannot depict the majority group precisely because all the members of the group are not identical. We can only say that (a) the average values of their various characteristics differ from the average values of other groups; (b) the members have a feeling of belonging to their group; and (c) the group has the power to discriminate against other groups.

If we cannot depict precisely the dominant group, it follows that we cannot depict other groups and cannot define the exact boundaries of the several groups. Hence, we are left with vague groupings. Only when there are physical or other highly visible characteristics are the groups distinguishable. One such highly visible characteristic might be religion, insofar as people can be observed to follow specified religious principles. However, if a member of a religious group does not follow the accepted rules, by, for example, working on the specified day of rest, his religious position is not clearly visible. Again we are left with rather vague ethnic groupings.

Let us now return to a previous observation—that minority groups

Characteristic X

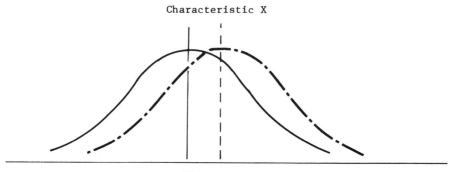

Means

Characteristic Y

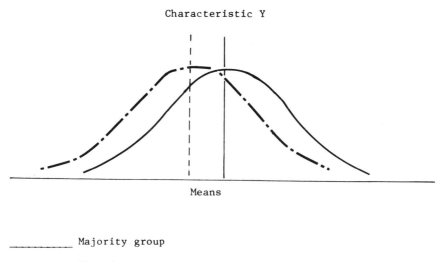

Means

_____ Majority group

– – – – – Minority group

FIGURE 2.1. *Theoretical distribution of characteristics in majority and minority groups.*

often appear after migration away from the homeland and into territory occupied by another group or after invasion of their homeland and conquest by a militarily superior people. In either event, people who originally thought of themselves as different come into contact, and interbreeding follows. The resulting offspring may or may not have a feeling of belonging to one or the other group. In addition to interbreeding, some members of the minority group may take on the values and characteristics of the majority. In short, the demarcation between the two groups becomes more and more blurred. As this blurring occurs, the average values of the various characteristics approach each other, and the power of one group to discriminate against another may be lessened.

This process went on in many parts of Latin America as the Spaniards met the Indians. In Mexico the blurring of the lines led to the recognition of the "Mexican" people as a blend of the two. There still are some Indians in Mexico, of course, since some of the original population have not taken on Spanish characteristics. Indeed, in Mexico and elsewhere in Latin America, the people called Indians are generally those who speak an Indian language rather than Spanish, wear Indian rather than European clothing, and live in rural areas. Despite the survival of physical differences between the European and the Indian in many instances, the ethnic group differences have become blurred where the original Indian population has taken on Spanish or European characteristics.

The ethnic group has completed its natural life cycle, and it is time for a new ethnic group to arise.

THE MELTING POT VERSUS THE RAGOUT

This process of blurring is neither assimilation nor the melting pot, according to our way of thinking. As for assimilation, we do not know what it means. As for the melting pot, this concept implies that people become identical in a number of respects. As we have seen, people are not identical even among the dominant group. Unlike different metals that can be melted and mixed to produce a uniform alloy, people can never be fused into one indistinguishable group.

Rather, if one must coin a popular name, we should say that this process, the natural life cycle, results in a ragout. Every ragout—beef, lamb, fish, and so on—has much commonalty in the liquid and seasoning. Yet each also has visibly different ingredients; the eater can always distinguish between the meat, potatoes, and carrots.

For the five Spanish-American groups we are studying, we are concentrating exclusively on their measurable demographic and economic characteristics. Because of lack of data, we can say nothing about their psychological or cultural characteristics. We shall only describe the manner and extent to which members of these groups are—or are not—taking on the measurable characteristics of the non-Spanish white majority population.

DETERRENTS TO THE COMPLETION OF THE LIFE CYCLE

One powerful deterrent is isolation, a lack of contact and communication. If a group is sufficiently isolated, it may continue largely unchanged for an untold period of time. Such small groups have been reported to exist in various parts of the world: descendants of the ancient Mayas in remote areas of Mexico and tribes in the mountains of the Philippines, in parts of New Guinea, in the Amazon valley, and perhaps elsewhere. Once contact with the outside world, especially the modern world, is established, the characteristics of the group begin to change.

Cultural reinforcement is another deterrent. We believe that this is the case with those people of Mexican descent who are living in the United States. This group may not be changing as rapidly as are other groups, because of the constant influx of migrants from Mexico. The migrants keep the Spanish language alive and continue to reintroduce elements of the Mexican culture to the Mexican-American population. Hence, those Mexican Americans who are taking on the measureable characteristics of the non-Spanish white population are replaced by immigrants who bring in the traditional values and characteristics. A complete cessation of immigration would result in the Mexican-American population changing at a faster rate than it is now doing.

Solé refers to this element simply as "Strengthening of the group by immigration."

> In the Southwest and California immigration has played a decisive role. Even today, it continues to be an extremely important source of linguistic renewal, although to a lesser extent. In addition, geographical continuity and transportation facilities make for frequent journeys, and close links are maintained with Mexico through radio, cinema and television. As for the Puerto Rican nucleus in the Northeast, the easy accessibility of the Island by air is an important point of contact, and in Florida, a continuing stream of Latin Americans is another source of renewal, apart from the fact that the problem of Cuban–United States relations has still to be solved.[8]

The Hispano population illustrates this point. There are no immigrants to reintroduce the Hispano culture. As long as these people

---

[8] Carlos A. Solé, "Spanish Spoken Here," Americas, 28 (April 1976) p. 6.

lived in relative isolation, which was the case into the first part of the twentieth century, they could continue to maintain those characteristics that had distinguished them from the non-Spanish white population. Now that they have entered the mainstream of Anglo culture, they seem to be disappearing as a separate recognizable ethnic group.

Finally, we note that within any particular group there may be a number of people who are tradition oriented and who will make every effort to retain their separate identity. Presumably there are many psychological and other factors that influence them to do so. Whatever the reasons may be, a small nucleus may continue to exist indefinitely as a distinct ethnic entity. An example are the Samaritans, whose history goes back over 2000 years. There are some, perhaps 500 or so, still living in Israel, and they continue many, if not all, aspects of their traditional life. But 500 people can hardly be considered a full-fledged ethnic group.[9]

A third factor that helps a group maintain its separate ethnic identity is legal recognition of such status, having its own geographic and political territory and/or rights, and speaking its own language. In the United States, for example, those American Indians—the Native Americans—who live on reservations are in this position. As long as they live on and are part of reservations, they continue to receive certain rights, privileges, and economic benefits from the federal government. Presumably, they will continue to remain ethnics indefinitely, or at least as long as they believe that they benefit from such status.[10]

The federal government has also granted funds to Native American organizations whose members live off reservations. Thus, for example, the American Indian Community House, Incorporated, in New York City received a grant from the U.S. Department of Health, Education and Welfare "to locate and determine the needs of the 10,000 Indian

---

[9] *Facts About Israel, 1969* (Tel Aviv: Ministry for Foreign Affairs, 1969), p. 166.

[10] An example of this relationship, or perhaps a reverse example, is provided by the following, from the *New York Times*, 4 October 1976.

The power of the Bureau of Indian Affairs to restrict the definition of Indian to members of Federally recognized tribes is being challenged in U.S. District Court. . . . The case may have far reaching effects. . . since most of Michigan's 20,000 Indians are Ottawas who do not live on reservations and are not federally recognized as a tribe—a situation similar to that of many nonreservation Indians across the nation. . . . A policeman charges that he was denied a bureau post as a criminal investigator . . . because he is non-Indian according to the Government's definition. . . . The suit asks that he be treated as an Indian and that he be paid damages for the difference between what he earns and what he would have earned had he been given the job.

people living in New York City according to the Census."[11] Obviously such governmental action helps to maintain ethnic identity.

A fourth factor may be physical racial characteristics. Pronounced differences in skin color and other physical characteristics do not facilitate the convergence of separate groups. Black Americans are the best example of such a group.

---

[11] From a two-page statement describing the activities of this organization, available at the House, 10 East 38th Street, New York City 10016.

3

The Findings: A Summary

We shall bring together in this chapter summary data for the five groups we have studied, with emphasis on the factors that contribute to demographic and social change.[1] Obviously, the situation as of 1970 and earlier will be touched upon, but we are seeking and emphasizing the dynamic aspects that are changing the observed 1970 characteristics. In addition, we are interested in comparing the several groups to determine how and why they are the same or different.

First, we shall briefly review the history of these several descent groups: when they first came to the United States, the types of immigrants, and so on. Partly because of their diverse historical backgrounds, there are differences among these groups in the United States in the 1970s. Next, we shall note their geographical distribution within the United States and touch upon the possible implications of such geographical patterns. Finally, three major areas will be examined as follows: (a) levels of education and school attendance; (b) fertility; and (c) selected economic characteristics.

The approximate number of people at the time of the 1970 Census of population were Mexican origin, 4.5 million; Hispano, .85 million; Puerto Rican, 1.5 million; Cuban origin, .5 million; Central and South American origin, .5 million.

---

[1] Considerably more detail for each descent group is given in the individual chapters in Part II.

THE CHANGING SCENE IN THE UNITED STATES

The entire socioeconomic scene in the United States has been changing dramatically over our entire history. Whether the rate of change was more rapid during the twentieth century than it had been previously, we leave to historians to decide. It suffices to say that change has been, is, and will continue to be an integral part of our lives. Furthermore, this change involves all aspects of life: social, cultural, economic, political, technological, attitudinal. It also involves all segments of the population. Perhaps there are small groups of people who have not perceptibly changed their way of life in the last several decades. They are, however, probably only minute isolated pockets which, for unique historical reasons, have remained outside the mainstream of American life.

The Spanish-American groups in the United States are part of this changing scene. They have changed and will change in a manner paralleling that of the general society. The United States moved from a rural and agrarian economy and mode of life to a highly urbanized and technologically sophisticated nonagricultural economy and its concomitant way of life. The Spanish Americans have done likewise. With each passing decade, they are being brought closer to the mainstream of social change and economic development of the larger society until eventually there will be a merging.

Their measurable demographic and economic characteristics—those with which we are concerned in this study—are also changing in accordance with national transformations and trends. The extent of education has increased dramatically; fertility had decreased; large numbers of women have entered the urban labor force. The rates at which these changes are occurring have varied from one group to another, but all changes have been significant. With improving American attitudes toward minority groups, encouraged by the governmental laws previously referred to, these groups are gradually entering the main economic stream and are obtaining jobs in a variety of occupations from which they were virtually absent not many decades ago.

We are not implying that all the Spanish Americans are economically as well off as the non-Spanish white U.S. population. The differences among the Spanish Americans are great. Our analysis, however, shows that they are gradually moving so that in another generation or two they will be almost indistinguishable from the general U.S. population. Their measurable demographic and economic characteristics will closely resemble those of the non-Spanish whites.

Such amalgamation is expedited by intermarriage with the non-

Spanish population (to be discussed in Chapter 4). There is a considerable amount now occuring with every prospect of more in the future. Such intermarriage and the vast increase in schooling, in turn, are related to the greater use of the English rather than the Spanish language. In short, all the social and economic changes visible in the latter half of the twentieth century in the United States are bringing about a closer resemblance between the Spanish Americans and the non-Spanish whites.

In this respect the Spanish-American odyssey resembles that of the various nationality groups in the Soviet Union, as depicted by Lewis et al.[2] The rates of demographic and economic change have varied from one nationality to another. As of 1970 some groups have more closely resembled the dominant Russians than have other groups. Change is taking place, however, and the nationalities are mixing geographically and, to some extent, by intermarriage. Of course, the histories and changes in these Soviet nationalities do not match precisely the histories and changes of the several Spanish-American groups in the United States. However, there are sufficient parallels, so that we can speak with confidence of generalized processes at work.

BACKGROUNDS

By definition all the Spanish groups are, or are the descendants of, immigrants to what is now the United States. The Hispanos are the earliest, and the Cubans and Central and South Americans the most recent.

HISPANOS

Soon after Cortés conquered the Aztecs, the Spanish began to explore northward into the present-day United States. By the end of the sixteenth century, the first attempts at permanent settlement had been made in what is now New Mexico. The original settlers were a collection of poor Spanish peasants, Indians and mixed population who emigrated from the modern country of Mexico, then called New Spain, and some religious and aristocratic Spanish conquistadores. Obviously, the Spanish settlers had to travel via New Spain, as there was no direct travel from Europe to present-day New Mexico at that time. Other Spaniards, Indians, and mestizos continued to move northward from

---

[2] Lewis, Rowland, and Clem, *Nationality and Population Change.*

New Spain during the seventeenth, eighteenth, and nineteenth centuries until New Mexico was taken over by the United States in 1848, when the northward migration largely ceased.

During this period numbers of local Indians of mixed aboriginal ancestry were absorbed. Eventually, some of these mixed bloods—genizaros—formed their own communities, which were distinct from both the Spanish and Indian settlements. In effect, a new ethnic group had come into being during the course of the Spanish settlement.

Also, during these centuries, wanderers from the United States and from Europe arrived as traders, soldiers of fortune, and adventurers. Some of these men remained and intermarried within the local population.[3]

The culture of the Hispanos was basically seventeenth- and eighteenth-century Spanish, together with some Indian influences of that same period. Once the United States possessed the area, large numbers of Anglos moved in, and the descendants of the settlers became a minority, an ethnic group. Also, considerable intermarriage with Anglos occurred. From the mid-nineteenth century to the present, the Hispano culture was influenced considerably by that of the Anglos or the non-Spanish U.S. whites. No longer were there new immigrants from Spain who continued to bring Spanish cultural patterns to the Hispanos. Even the few nineteenth- and twentieth-century Spanish immigrants who did arrive, however, brought the Spanish culture of the nineteenth and twentieth centuries, which was already different in many respects from the earlier Spanish culture from which the original settlers had come. Clearly, once the United States gained control, there was little to perpetuate the original Spanish culture. Only those forces that were operating within the Hispano population itself could continue the original culture. These indigenous forces themselves were subject to influence and change by the larger Anglo population.

Finally, we note that the Hispanos are natives of native parentage, most of whose ancestors have been in the United States for a number of generations.

MEXICAN DESCENT

The present-day Mexican population is the product of immigration from present-day Mexico, largely during the twentieth century. A few had arrived in the late nineteenth century, but, according to the best in-

---

[3] See, for example, Zeleny, Spanish Americans and Anglo Americans; Fray Angelico Chavez, My Penitente Land, Reflections on Spanish New Mexico (Albuquerque: University of New Mexico Press, 1973). Fray Angelico Chavez, "Genizaros," in Handbook of the North American Indians.

formation available, a large majority arrived after the turn of the century.[4] These people differed from the Hispanos insofar as twentieth-century Mexican society and culture differ from those of the seventeenth- and eighteenth-century Spanish culture. True, both groups spoke Spanish, were Roman Catholics (although the nature of the Catholicism differed), were of mixed Indian and other European blood, and were largely agriculturalists at the poverty level. Beyond these factors there is considerable question of how similar they were. Indeed, today, if asked, the inhabitants of the southwestern states will distinguish themselves as being Hispanos of early settlement or newly arrived Mexicans.

Following the Mexican revolution of 1910, great emphasis was placed on creating a "Mexican" who was different from both his Spanish forefather and his Indian foremother. Indeed, the twentieth-century Mexican citizen is different from his ancestors and has created an identifiable Mexican culture, society, and nation.

Large-scale immigration, both legal and illegal, has continued from Mexico into the United States during much of the twentieth century. These immigrants have continued to bring their customs with them and hence have reinforced the Mexican culture of those members already living in the United States. For example, use of the Spanish language is still prevalent in the last quarter of the twentieth century, although it is probable that many more Mexicans today are bilingual, as compared with earlier periods. Attitudes toward women, schooling, education, family size, and so on, tend to be influenced by the culture south of the Rio Grande. As we shall see, Mexican-American culture is changing, but, in our opinion, at a slower rate than that of other groups who are not reinforced culturally.

The bulk of the twentieth-century Mexican immigrants have little, if any, education, tend to be untrained in modern skills and occupations, and are very poor. Since these characteristics apply to the total Mexican population, we cannot say positively whether the immigrants are a cross section or a selected group of all Mexican nationals. In any event, many bring these attributes with them and therefore are disadvantaged.

Finally, we note that since many Mexican-origin people have been in the United States for almost a century, there are substantial numbers who are natives of native parentage. Our best estimate is that in 1970 about half were third and subsequent generation natives (i.e., their parents had been born in the United States), about one in three was a

---

[4] See also Appendix B.

native whose parents migrated from Mexico, and about one in five was born in Mexico.

PUERTO RICAN DESCENT

The island of Puerto Rico was a territory of the United States from the time of the Spanish-American War in 1898 until 1952, when it achieved Commonwealth status. Under Spanish rule, it was poor and largely underdeveloped, many of its inhabitants were illiterate, and, of course, it was largely agricultural. Various U.S. influences affected the island and its people from 1898 onward. For example, at one time attempts were made to operate the schools with English as the "official" language. During the Great Depression of the 1930s, federal relief programs were introduced, and there was considerable activity under Governor Rexford G. Tugwell to improve living conditions. These measures introduced additional North American influences to the island.

Prior to World War II there was little migration to the mainland. Following the war, with inexpensive air transportation and job opportunities on the mainland available, especially in the New York area, many Puerto Ricans migrated northward. During the peak years net out-migration exceeded the volume of natural increase. Many were from rural areas, were poor, had few occupational skills except for farm labor, and had little education. They were disadvantaged and entered the kinds of urban jobs commonly held by disadvantaged workers. By about the mid-1950s, migration slowed down, and since that time there have been some years in which migration from the mainland to the island exceeded that from the island.

What is most important from the viewpoint of this study is that in the generation since large-scale migration began, large numbers of Puerto Rican–origin children were born on the mainland and thus came under non-Spanish cultural influences. Furthermore, the island population itself underwent a vast transformation from largely rural to largely urban, from little schooled to significantly more schooled, from farm laborer to urban worker. As a result, the island migrants during the 1960s, and especially the 1970s, are very different from the earlier migrants, and the culture they bring with them is a blend of the Spanish and the North American non-Spanish.

This transformation of the island itself was brought about partly by the large numbers of Puerto Ricans who returned to the island and by the vast back-and-forth movements. We may say that the island's transformation away from its original Spanish culture was reinforced culturally through these back-and-forth and return movements.

We may speak of the mainland population as continuing to be culturally reinforced from the island, through both migration and extensive visiting and other movement between the island and the mainland. This cultural reinforcement contains, however, many aspects of New York City culture brought to the island and subsequently returned to New York; it is no longer a pure or original Spanish island culture.

Since most of the migration has occurred since World War II, there are very few mainland-born persons whose parents were also born on the mainland.

CUBAN DESCENT

In large measure, Fidel Castro can be thanked for this population. Migration from Cuba was minimal prior to his advent, and therefore the Cuban-American population is about 20 years old. Unlike the Mexican and Puerto Rican migrants, the Cubans were mainly middle and upper class. They were not a cross section of the population living in Cuba. Hence, they brought with them the Cuban middle-class culture, which in many respects is similar to the middle-class culture and values of the U.S. population. For example, the Cuban migrants were fairly well educated—many professionals were included in their ranks—and they were an urban population, skilled in urban occupations. Furthermore, many of them knew English upon arrival and could fit into the North American scene more easily.

CENTRAL AND SOUTH AMERICAN DESCENT

The majority of this group has come to the United States since about 1960. This group includes everyone from Guatemala south to Chile and Argentina and includes the Dominican Republic; Portuguese Brazil is excluded. Because of this geographic diversity we cannot really speak of a common cultural heritage. At one end, the Guatemalan immigrants tend to resemble those from Mexico. At the other end, those from southern South America tend to resemble those from European countries; indeed, there are large numbers descended from Italian, German, Yugoslavian, and other non-Spanish Europeans.

This group seems to be from the middle and upper classes; they definitely are not a cross section of the Central and South American population. Furthermore, many came to the United States originally to study and subsequently remained here. Accordingly, as a group they are fairly well educated, are urban, and are skilled in modern urban occupations; they resemble the Cubans.

Although immigrants from Central and South America continued to come to the United States in the 1970s, we can hardly speak of cultural reinforcement. The original cultures are too diverse, and there are not enough immigrants from any one culture to have much impact. Furthermore, there is reason to think that the most recent migrants are coming from countries different from the home countries of earlier migrants. We have not done a country-by-country analysis, however.

Since the arrival of the migrants has been so recent, there are very few natives whose parents were also born in the United States.

THEIR GEOGRAPHIC DISTRIBUTION WITHIN THE UNITED STATES

The several groups distributed themselves within the United States with minimum overlapping. The Hispanos are largely concentrated in New Mexico, Colorado, and California. The Mexican Americans are largely concentrated in Texas, Arizona, and California and, to a lesser extent, are found in Colorado, New Mexico, and Illinois.

The Puerto Rican–origin people are largely in New York City and adjacent areas of New Jersey; minor settlements are found in Illinois and California. The Cuban-descent population is concentrated in Florida, with minor settlements in the New York metropolitan area and California. Persons of Central and South American origin are found largely in New York and California.

Substantial overlapping is found only in California and New York. Other states that contain many members of any one group tend to have only small pockets of other Spanish-American groups.

This spatial separation may have several consequences that, in turn, may affect the demographic and social characteristics analyzed in our study. Unfortunately, we have no way of drawing direct connections between the spatial and the other characteristics.

To begin, there is probably a minimum of competition, both economic and social, among the members of the five groups. To compete for jobs, for example, people must live adjacent to each other.

Second, the economic, social, and demographic characteristics of a population will take on some of the characteristics that may be unique to a particular part of the United States. For example, there are differences in wage rates between the Florida and New York labor markets—New York pays higher rates—so that we can expect some differences betweeen the earnings of Cubans and of Puerto Ricans. Obviously, no analysis can tell us what part of any observed differences between any two Spanish-American groups is due to their geographic separation; we can only speculate.

Finally, we suspect that the inability of the Spanish-American groups to develop a single cohesive power group is largely due to their geographic separation. The problems faced by the Mexicans in Texas are different from those faced by Puerto Ricans in New York City. Each wages its own political battle.

SCHOOLING AND EDUCATION

In U.S. society in the twentieth century, formal education is an important force for change. The various ethnic populations take on the visible characteristics of the majority or dominant society among which they live according to the amount of formal schooling they have. We cannot overemphasize this point. Members of an ethnic group who are college graduates tend to resemble all other college graduates, including non-Spanish white college graduates. At lesser levels of schooling there are also pronounced tendencies for the members of different groups to resemble each other. Conversely, if a group wishes to maintain its own characteristics that are different from those of others, it can most nearly accomplish this if its members have a minimum of education, as among the Amish, for example. Clearly, ethnicity and class tend to merge; at the upper educational levels, the ethnic demarcation lines are blurred.

We do not contend that education makes originally different groups similar in all respects. This is impossible. We are simply stating that with increased schooling the visible and measurable characteristics of the several groups tend to become more nearly similar. In the discussions of fertility and economic characteristics that follow, the influence of schooling will become apparent. Further evidence of the influence of schooling is presented in Chapter 4 on "Demographic Convergence."

NATIVE VERSUS FOREIGN BORN

Native persons generally have received more formal education than their foreign-born parents or grandparents have. This is most clearly evident in the younger age groups. (See Appendix Tables G–1 to G–5 for full detail.) The importance of place of birth is that the educational level of the native Spanish-American population is an indicator of their socioeconomic status in future decades. Over the next several decades, the U.S. born will become an ever larger proportion of each group. For example, in 1970 the Puerto Rican population living on the mainland was predominantly island born and had less schooling than the general population. In another several decades, the mainland born will out- number the island born; since the mainland born have more schooling, the general level of education of the entire Puerto Rican population will be raised significantly. Furthermore, we know that the native groups are exposed to the U.S. public school systems; therefore, we may assume that differences in educational attainment represent a mix of educational—or cultural—desire on the part of the young people, together with differential educational opportunities provided by the various states.

YEARS OF SCHOOLING COMPLETED AS OF 1970

The large differences in educational attainment indicate that there are basic background variations among the several Spanish-American groups. These backgrounds are different because of a variety of historical factors, including differential selectivity among the im- migrants in past decades. There is reason to believe that the lesser schooled predominated among twentieth-century migrants from Puerto Rico and Mexico, whereas the more educated predominated among migrants from Cuba, Central and South America, and Spain. The Hispanos have not been affected by twentieth-century migration movements.

Completion of High School. The clearest way to discern the differ- ence is to note the proportions of each group of those born in the United States who had completed 4 or more years of high school and the proportions who had gone to college. Among all U.S. white persons aged 20–24, over 80% had completed high school. This proportion was matched by the natives of Cuban origin and of Central and South American origin.

Among the U.S. or mainland born of Mexican and Puerto Rican origin, almost 60% had finished high school. Of the Hispanos, close to 70% were high school graduates (Table 3.1; see also Appendix Tables G–1 to G–5).

There is virtually no difference between men and women in the pro- portions of those who completed 12 or more years of school.

Among the immigrants, a lot fewer had completed 12 years or more of schooling. This is to be expected, since many arrived as almost- illiterate adults and subsequently had received little if any education in the United States. This is particularly the situation for the Mexicans and Puerto Ricans; less than 4 in 10 of the migrants were high school

TABLE 3.1
Percentages Who Completed High School, by Descent, Age, Sex, and Nativity, as of 1970

	MEN Age (1970)			WOMEN Age (1970)		
	55 and over	20 to 24	Change	55 and over	20 to 24	Change
Non-Spanish white	34	82	+48	37	82	+45
Mexican descent						
Native	9	56	+47	9	53	+44
Foreign born	9	38	+29	9	32	+23
Puerto Rican descent						
Mainland born	12	59	+47	16	64	+48
Island born	12	37	+25	10	37	+27
Hispanos	19	68	+47	23	67	+44
Cuban descent						
Native	15	82	+67	20	81	+61
Foreign born	41	70	+29	25	66	+41
Central and South American descent						
Native	58	83	+25	51	84	+33
Foreign born	43	66	+22	36	41	+5

(or equivalent) graduates. On the other hand, those migrants who arrived as young children went to school in mainland United States and may have had as much schooling as those born in the United States.

The immigrants with the most schooling are those from Cuba and Central and South America.

Entry into College. For the proportion of high school graduates who enter college, we find that among the U.S. white population aged 25–29 (by this age almost everyone who will ever enter college has done so) 55% of the men and 48% of the women had entered college and completed at least 1 year. The U.S.-born of Cuban and Central and South American origin had about the same proportions. At the bottom of the educational hierarchy are those of Mexican and Puerto Rican origin and the Hispanos, among whom hardly one in three entered college. Men are much more likely to enter college than are women, although the proportions of high school graduates is about the same for both sexes.

Completing Four Years of College. As for completing college, only among the Central and South Americans did proportions as large as

TABLE 3.2

Percentages Who Completed College, by Descent, Age, Sex, and Nativity, as of 1970

	MEN Age (1970)			WOMEN Age (1970)		
	55 and over	25 to 29	Change	55 and over	25 to 29	Change
Non-Spanish white	8	22	+14	6	15	+9
Mexican descent						
Native	1	4	+3	1	3	+2
Foreign born	2	3	+1	1	2	+1
Puerto Rican descent						
Mainland born	1	8	+7	1	6	+5
Island born	2	3	+1	1	2	+1
Hispanos	4	8	+4	3	5	+2
Cuban descent						
Native	1	16	+15	4	17	+13
Foreign born	15	15	0	5	8	+3
Central and South American descent						
Native	16	28*	+12	5	19*	+14
Foreign born	14	20*	+6	5	10*	+5

*Age 25 to 34.

those among the U.S. non-Spanish white graduate (Table 3.2). The Cubans were not far behind. Among the Hispanos and those of Mexican and Puerto Rican descent, however, very few had completed college.

In summary, we see that the Cubans and Central and South Americans have almost the same educational advantages as do the non-Spanish whites. The Mexicans and Puerto Ricans, as groups, have the largest proportion of those with little schooling and thus contain the largest proportions of "disadvantaged." The Hispanos are approximately in the center, not well off and not "greatly disadvantaged."

INCREASED SCHOOLING OVER THE YEARS

All groups experienced vast increases in the amount of education received over the last couple of generations. We may compare those aged 20–24 years in 1970 with those aged 55 and over. The younger cohort was of high-school-completion age during the late 1960s; the older cohort was of high-school-completion age about the time of World War I or during the 1920s (Tables 3.1 and 3.2).

The proportions who completed 12 years or more of school increased greatly for all groups, including the non-Spanish whites. For example, among native men of Mexican descent who were aged 55 and over, only about 9% had finished high school. Among their male descendants aged 20–24, 56% had at least this much education. Among the mainland-born Puerto Rican men the proportions rose from 9% to 56% and among Hispano men, from 19% to 68%. Similar increases are observed for women.

College completion also increased over the years (Table 3.2), but not as dramatically as did high school completion.

The events associated with World War II and its aftermath seem to have given impetus to increases in education. This conclusion is based on the answers to the following questions:

1. In what time period did 50% of a school-age cohort first achieve completion of elementary school, presumably around age 14?
2. In what time period did 50% of a school-age cohort first achieve completion of high school, presumably around age 18?
3. In what time period did 25% of a school-age cohort first enter college, presumably around age 20 (allowing for some late entries)?

The Cubans, Central and South Americans, Hispanos, and U.S. whites completed elementary school either before World War I or shortly thereafter (Table 3.3). The Mexican and Puerto Rican populations achieved this shortly before or about the time of World War II; this is 20–25 years after the first category achieved this much education.

The same pattern is found for high school completion. Before World War II, many Central and South Americans and U.S. whites completed high school (Table 3.4). Persons of Cuban origin reached this level of education at about the time of World War II, and the Mexicans, Puerto Ricans, and Hispanos, for the most part, in the 1950s and 1960s. As of 1970 the foreign-born Mexican and the island-born Puerto Rican populations had not yet reached the 50% mark for high school graduation.

Essentially the same pattern is found for entry into college. Indeed, as of 1970 the Mexican and Puerto Rican groups had not yet achieved this level, that is, 25% entering college. The Hispanos, Cuban, Central and South Americans, and U.S. whites had reached this level by the time of World War II or soon thereafter (Table 3.5).

In summary, the differences among the five groups in the achievement of education are long-standing. The populations that were more

TABLE 3.3

Period in Which 50% of School-Age Cohort Achieved Completion of Elementary School

---

After World War II

Mexican origin, foreign born; men, women

Around World War II

Mexican origin, native; men, women
Puerto Rican origin, born on Island; women

Interwar years

Puerto Rican origin, born on Mainland; men, women
Puerto Rican origin, born on Island; men
Hispanos; men
Cuban origin, native; men

Prior to World War I

Hispanos; women
Cuban origin, native; women
Cuban origin, foreign born; men, women
Central and South American origin, native; men, women
Central and South American origin, foreign born; men, women
U.S. WHITE; MEN, WOMEN

TABLE 3.4

Period in Which 50% of School-Age Cohort Achieved Completion of High School

---

Not Achieved as of 1970

Mexican origin, foreign born; men, women
Puerto Rican origin, born on Island; men, women

After World War II

Mexican origin, native; men, women
Puerto Rican origin, born on Mainland; men, women
Hispanos; men, women
Cuban origin, foreign born; women

Around World War II

Cuban origin, native; men, women
Cuban origin, foreign born; men
Central and South American origin, foreign born; women

Interwar years

Central and South American origin, foreign born; men
U.S. WHITE; MEN, WOMEN

Prior to World War I

Central and South American origin, native; men, women

34

TABLE 3.5
Period in Which 25% of School-Age Cohort Achieved Entry into College

---

Not Achieved as of 1970

Mexican origin, native; men, women
Mexican origin, foreign born; men, women
Puerto Rican origin, born on Mainland; men, women
Puerto Rican origin, born on Island; men, women
Hispanos; women

After World War II

Hispanos; men
Cuban origin, native; women
Cuban origin, foreign born; women
Central and South American, foreign born; women
U.S. WHITE; WOMEN

Around World War II

Cuban origin, native; men
Central and South American origin, native; women
U.S. WHITE; MEN

Interwar years

Cuban origin, foreign born; men
Central and South American origin, foreign born; men

Prior to World War I

Central and South American origin, native; men

---

schooled before World War I are more schooled in 1970. If the previously lesser schooled are catching up, it is at a slow rate.

SCHOOL ATTENDANCE, 1970

We saw that there had been large increases in the amount of schooling received and that those adults who had been born in the United States had more years of schooling than did those born abroad. What about the future? One possible indication is derived from examination of school attendance rates. If the population under 20 years of age is attending school at about the same rate as is the non-Spanish white, then we can anticipate the time when the several Spanish-American groups may have about the same number of years of education as the non-Spanish white. Of course, school attendance rates must also take into consideration the rate of progress through the school system. For example, a 16-year-old who is in seventh grade is lagging and may never catch up.

Let us first look at persons aged 15–18, the high school age, in 1970; these persons will be of college age during the 1970s. The standardized percentages[5] attending school were as follows:

Group	Percentage
Non-Spanish white	87
Mexican descent	76
Puerto Rican descent	68
Cuban descent	82
Hispanos	77
Central and South American descent	83

All the Spanish-American groups lag behind the non-Spanish white, however, the Cubans and Central and South Americans differ the least.

The Puerto Rican descent group falls behind the most, with a school attendance rate of only 68% as compared with 87% for non-Spanish whites. As we shall see subsequently, much of this lag occurs in New York City, where school attendance for this group is unusually low.[6]

The Mexicans and Hispanos fall about 10 percentage points behind the non-Spanish whites, well above those of Puerto Rican descent.

The younger people, 7–14 years of age, were of elementary school age in 1970 and will be of college age in the early 1980s. The standardized school attendance rates are considerably higher for this age group as follows:

Group	Percentage
Non-Spanish white	97
Mexican descent	95
Puerto Rican descent	87
Cuban descent	89
Hispanos	93
Central and South American descent	94

[5] Standardized on the basis of the 1970 distribution of the non-Spanish white population by single years of age between the ages of 15 and 18 inclusive.

For detailed data on school attendance, see Appendix Table G–7.

[6] Detailed study of the New York City school system and other factors specific to this city are outside the scope of the present study.

The Mexicans, Hispanos, and Central and South Americans fall slightly behind the non-Spanish white group. The Puerto Ricans and Cubans, however, lag much more.

Next, let us examine the rates of progress through the school system for the total population aged 7–19 years. On the basis of the age of the person who is attending school, this person can be allocated to: below the modal grade in school for his age, at the modal grade, or above the modal grade.[7] These calculations provide the following figures:

Group	Total (%)	Below mode (%)	At mode (%)	Above mode (%)
Non-Spanish white	100.0	6.8	91.0	2.2
Mexican descent	100.0	19.4	78.2	2.4
Puerto Rican descent	100.0	18.6	75.5	5.9
Cuban descent	100.0	13.6	82.4	4.0
Hispanos	100.0	11.7	85.3	3.0
Central and South American descent	100.0	13.1	82.0	4.9

Among those attending school, the Cubans, Hispanos, and Central and South Americans are progressing almost as rapidly as are the non-Spanish whites. All three groups have larger proportions that are below the modal grade, but they also have somewhat higher proportions than do the non-Spanish whites of students above the mode.

Those of Mexican descent have many more below the mode and about the same percentage above the modal grade as do the non-Spanish whites.

The Puerto Rican student population contains large proportions below the mode, but also has larger proportions above the modal grade than are found among the non-Spanish whites.

Perhaps for all five groups, and especially for the Puerto Ricans, the lower attendance rates resulting from dropouts account for the higher proportions above the modal grade. If the more academically successful students are the ones who remain in school, we can expect a somewhat larger proportion to be above the modal grade.

From all the preceding information we may infer that in the next generation—say by the year 2000—the Cubans and Central and South Americans will continue to be the most schooled. They will be followed

---

[7] See U.S. Bureau of the Census, Census of Population: 1960, School Enrollment, PC (2)–5A, (Washington D.C.: Government Printing Office, 1973), p. ix.

by the Hispanos. Those of Mexican and Puerto Rican descent will continue to be the least schooled among these five Spanish-American
groups.

SCHOOLING AND THE USE OF THE ENGLISH LANGUAGE

The use of the English rather than the Spanish language in the home
is related to higher school attainment. Which may be cause and which
effect is difficult to say. There is a tendency for persons who grew up in
homes where Spanish was spoken to continue to speak Spanish at
home when adults and to have fewer years of formal schooling. On the
other hand, large numbers who spoke Spanish at home when children
do achieve more years of schooling and do switch to the English
language. What do we know at this time of writing?

The following table shows the proportions of U.S. born persons
whose parents were foreign-born and who reported in the 1970 Census
that English was their mother tongue (language spoken in home during
childhood).

Group	Age	
	Under 14 (%)	25–44 (%)
Mexican	7	4
Puerto Rican	10	9
Cuban	13	19
Central and South American	32	38

The groups that achieved the most education, as we saw previously,
are the Cuban and Central and South Americans. Apparently there is
some tendency for those who spoke English at home when children to
go further in school.[8]

However, the relationship between the proportion using English
mother tongue (the use of English when a child at home) and the
number of years of school completed is low. Other population groups,
such as the Japanese, Chinese, and Greek (native of foreign parentage,
age 25–44) also spoke English as their mother tongue to the same extent
as did the Spanish Americans, yet, by and large, the former completed

---

[8] Why some spoke English as mother tongue and others did not is a separate question
calling for its own investigation.

more years of formal schooling than did the Spanish Americans.[9] Clearly, another factor that we can only call "socioeconomic–cultural" influences the extent of formal schooling at least as much, if not more than, mother tongue. This is a topic for a separate study as well.

Some time between childhood and adulthood, many formerly Spanish–speaking persons switch to English. Our best estimate is that some 4 in 10 of U.S.-born Spanish Americans switch from Spanish mother tongue to English as the language "now usually spoken at home."[10]

Those who do speak English now are more likely to have finished high school (as of 1971, 1972) and to have gone to college. Does further schooling result in switching to English at home, or is it the other way around?

SOME POSSIBLE EFFECTS OF MIGRATION

To some extent the educational differences observed among the several Spanish-American groups may reflect past differences in the types of persons who migrated from these countries to the United States. Migration is almost always selective; rarely does a true cross section of an entire population migrate. For example, among the immigrants from Central and South America up to 1970 there are proportionately many more professional and other white-collar persons than there are among those who migrated from Mexico.

Now we also know that the children of more-schooled parents achieve more schooling. Hence selective migration in the past, insofar

---

[9] The specific figures for natives of foreign parentage, aged 25–44 are

Ethnic group	English mother tongue (%)	Men			Women		
		12 + (%)	a	b	12 + (%)	a	b
Mexican	4	39	37	34	35	33	37
Puerto Rican	9	51	36	40	50	22	42
Cuban	19	71	50	49	54	42	35
Central and South American	38	71	59	52	75	45	54
Japanese	9	88	52	58	91	41	44
Chinese	15	87	70	64	89	57	52
Greek	19	81	62	62	83	39	48

Note: Column a is percentage of high school graduates who entered college, and Column b is percentage of college entrants who completed 4 or more years.

[10] Estimated from data in U.S., Bureau of the Census, *Population Characteristics*, ser. P–20, no. 213, *Persons of Spanish Origin in the United States: November 1969* (Washington, D.C.: Government Printing Office, 1971).

as it brought in persons of higher socioeconomic levels from one country and of lower socioeconomic levels from another, probably influenced the extent of education of their U.S.-born children and contributed to the differential extent of schooling that we observed among the U.S.-born.

FERTILITY

It is commonly believed that the Spanish Americans have high fertility—high, that is, in comparison with the U.S. non-Spanish white population and very high in comparison with the idea of zero population growth. Even such a reputable magazine as *Americas*, published by the General Secretariat of the Organization of American States, contained the article "Spanish Spoken Here,"[11] which opens with: "At the beginning of World War II there were about two million people in the United States whose native tongue was Spanish. . . . At present, according to the 1970 Census data and other government surveys, there are at least twelve million Spanish speakers in the United States." Although the writer acknowledges that immigration played a part, the implication is of a high birth rate that produces very large population increases. Incidentally, the 1970 Census reports about 7,800,000 persons whose mother tongue is Spanish;[12] perhaps "population increase" is proceeding at a slower rate than Solé implies.

Casual "sidewalk" inspection does indicate a high Spanish-American birth rate. We estimate that the average annual number of births per 1000 Spanish-American population between 1965 and 1969 was approaching 30. In comparison, the U.S. white population as a whole had a birth rate of 17. Somewhat closer inspection reveals that there are significant differences among the several groups. The estimated crude birth rates (average annual births, 1965–1969, per 1000) were Mexican, 27; Puerto Rican, 30; Cuban, 16; Hispano, 27; and Central and South American, 25.[13] Hence, it appears that with the ex-

---

[11] Solé, "Spanish Spoken Here."

[12] U.S., Bureau of the Census, PC(1)–D1, *U.S. Summary*, Table 193, 1973.

[13] In comparison with Latin America, these rates are not high. In Mexico the reported rate was 43 (1965–1970); in Central America: Costa Rica, 31 (1972); El Salvador, 41 (1972); Guatemala, 43 (1973); in South America: Argentina, 21 (1968); Chile, 28 (1971); Colombia, 45 (1965–1970); Ecuador, 45 (1965–1970); Peru, 42 (1965–1970); Venezuela, 41 (1965–1970). There is good reason to believe that these rates were underreported and that the actual birth rates were higher. On the island of Puerto Rico the reported rate was 23 in 1973. Data from U.S. Bureau of the Census, *Statistical Abstract of the United States, 1975* (Washington, D.C.: Government Printing Office, 1975), p. 839.

ception of the Cubans, the groups have rates that are 50% or more above those for the total U.S. white population.

Careful analysis, on the other hand, indicates that Spanish-American fertility is actually much closer to that of the U.S. non-Spanish white population than the above crude birth rates seem to suggest. After taking into account the age and sex composition of each group, its education level, marital status, and the employment status of the women,[14] and calculating the average number of children ever born alive per 100 women aged 15–44 (as of 1970), we have

Group	Fertility	Index
U.S. non-Spanish white	158	100
Mexican descent	196	124
Puerto Rican descent	166	105
Cuban descent	121	77
Hispano	181	115
Central and South American descent	134	85

The Mexican-American rate is only 24% above that of the non-Spanish whites, and the Hispano, is but 15% above. Puerto Rican fertility is very close to that of the non-Spanish whites, and Cuban and Central and South American fertility rates are well below. Clearly, there is very great disparity among the five descent groups. Therefore, let us now turn our attention to the factors that influence the fertility rate and note how they were operating in the latter half of the twentieth century.

CHANGES OVER THE LAST CENTURY

For the two groups, the Hispanos and those who reported Mexican descent, we have estimates of the course of fertility since the mid-nineteenth century. The general picture portrayed is of (a) higher fertility for these two groups than was found in the U.S. non-Spanish white population; (b) comparatively little, if any, decrease until about 1960; and (c) significant decrease between 1960 and 1970.

For both groups the child–woman ratio (children under 5 years of age, adjusted for child mortality, per 100 women aged 15–44) is available for the past century or longer. For the earlier dates only

---

[14] See Appendix C.

estimates are available, and no precise changes can be depicted; for the later dates, from mid-twentieth century on, the figures are more precise.

These ratios of children to women are as follows for the Hispanos:

Date	Variation in child–woman ratio	
1850	80 to 90	(Bernalillo County, New Mexico, only)
1910	80 to 90	
1950	80 to 90	
1960	80 to 90	
1970	65	

Fertility seems to have remained largely unchanged during the century or more preceding 1960. It is possible that in the mid-nineteenth century the ratio was closer to 90, whereas by 1960 it may have been closer to 80. However, the available information is too imprecise to detect such a small change, if it did occur.

The sharpest drop in fertility occurred between 1960 and 1970. This was to have been expected, since the 1960s was the decade in which the more-schooled women became an important element among all Hispano women in the reproductive ages. We noted previously that only after World War II, say around 1950, did half the young women complete high school. Hence, since 1950 more high school graduates entered the reproductive ages. Approximately a half generation later, 15 years or so, they became numerically important enough to affect the child–woman ratio. And, as we noted, the more schooling, the lower the fertility rate is.

Substantially the same picture appears for Mexican-origin women. The child–woman ratios adjusted for child mortality are

Date	Variation in child–woman ratio	
1850, 1860	80 to 90	(San Antonio, Texas, only)
1930	80 to 90	
1950	80 to 90	
1960	80 to 90	
1970	60	
1976–1978 average	58	

If there was any decrease between the mid-nineteenth and twentieth centuries, it was slight. Then, during the 1960s there was a decline as the native Mexican-origin women who had completed high school became a numerically important part of all women in the reproductive ages. However, the foreign-born Mexican women, who constitute a substantial portion of all Mexican-origin women in the United States, continue to be little educated, and they continue to migrate to the United States, with the result that the child–woman ratio changed little between 1970 and the late 1970s.

With respect to the Puerto Rican–origin women, we have no long-time fertility history for them. However, since greater numbers of them are completing high school, we infer that their fertility also has decreased.

Women of Cuban and Central and South American origin have been in the United States for too short a period of time to permit any long-term analysis.

THE INFLUENTIAL FACTORS

Age Composition. The average number of children ever born increases as the cohort of women increase in age during the childbearing years: the older the women, the more children they are likely to have. Therefore, in the following analysis (and in Table 3.6 and Figure 3.1) all groups have been given the same age distribution between 15 and 44 years, that is, they have been standardized on the U.S. non-Spanish white population. Hence we can compare the several groups and know that our results are due to differences in characteristics—education, the type of group, and so on—rather than to possible differences in age composition.

Marital status. Women who are married and living with their husbands have considerably more children than do never married, widowed, and divorced women. Considering the nature of the society in which we live, this is to be expected; the Spanish Americans are no different from the non-Spanish U.S. white women. In general, being married and living with husband results in an increase of one-third to one-half in the average number of children ever born (Table 3.6).[15]

These increases result after standardizing all the groups for employment status and years of schooling, in addition to age. We may legitimately compare the several groups. Thus, for example, the standardized rate of 227 for the Mexican-descent women who are married, spouse present, indicates that this population has significantly higher

---

[15] Further details on the influence of each characteristic together with the joint influence are given in the separate chapters devoted to each group.

TABLE 3.6

Standardized Average Number of Children Born Alive per 100 Women Aged 15–44, by Descent, 1970

	Total	Marital status		Employment		Years schooling	
		Married spouse present	All other	Employed	Not employed	Under 12 years	12+ years
MEXICAN							
Total U.S.	196	227	137	170	220	262	168
Foreign born, total	186	219	123	164	205	251	164
Native, total	198	229	139	172	223	267	168
Residence							
Inside SMSAs	193	224	136	167	217	256	166
Foreign born, total	185	217	123	164	204	246	164
Native, total	196	226	139	168	220	262	166
Outside SMSAs	210	243	139	185	232	286	181
Foreign born, total	190	226	119	166	208	284	164
Native, total	212	246	136	187	230	288	181
5 Southwest states	197	228	138	170	221	262	169
Foreign born, total	189	222	125	168	207	253	167
Native, total	199	230	140	171	223	267	168
Residence							
Inside SMSAs	194	225	138	168	214	255	167
Outside SMSAs	211	244	139	185	232	284	182
All other states	192	221	128	168	212	265	164
Foreign born, total	172	204	112	150	192	243	156
Native, total	197	226	130	173	217	273	165
HISPANO	181	214	136	162	210	244	166
CUBAN							
Total U.S.	121	144	74	101	136	127	103
Inside central cities	117	139	75	96	134	124	99
Outside central cities	124	148	73	107	137	129	117
Foreign born	119	143	71	97	136	121	106
Living in U.S. 1965	121	148	80	98	140	130	111
Not living U.S. 1965	113	134	61	93	129	123	92
CENTRAL & SOUTH AMERICA*	134	158	84	118	147	139	118
PUERTO RICAN							
Total U.S.	166	191	150	136	195	227	150
Island born	169	192	153	138	198	234	154
Living Mainland 1965	173	194	153	140	199	234	155
Not living Mainland 1965	166	187	139	130	198	245	150
Mainland born	156	180	125	134	176	197	139
New York City	156	179	148	124	186	217	145
Island born	162	184	149	127	195	225	150
Mainland born	148	169	129	122	169	192	130

*Foreign born and native of foreign parentage.

44

TABLE 3.6 (cont.)

	Total	Marital status		Employment		Years schooling	
		Married spouse present	All other	Employed	Not employed	Under 12 years	12+ years
Remainder U.S.	177	192	152	149	204	249	158
Island born	178	202	165	150	205	253	160
Mainland born	164	196	111	144	180	206	148
ISLAND OF PUERTO RICO							
Total	175	208	108	149	196	206	144
Urban	163	190	109	139	183	177	142
Rural	183	219	106	156	204	220	147
NON-SPANISH WHITE							
Total U.S.	158	184	108	136	177	196	146
Inside SMSAs	156	182	105	133	175	193	144
Outside SMSAs	165	190	119	146	182	205	155
5 Southwest states	154	176	116	135	170	195	140
Inside SMSAs	153	175	113	133	169	192	139
Outside SMSAs	163	183	131	151	174	208	152
New Jersey and New York							
Inside SMSAs	139	168	82	110	163	161	128
NON-SPANISH NEGRO							
Total U.S.	206	233	175	186	224	257	167
Inside SMSAs	200	227	173	179	220	250	164
Outside SMSAs	233	262	190	216	238	289	191

fertility than has the Cuban-descent group, with a rate of 144, or the Puerto Rican–descent group, with a rate of 191. As would be expected, the rates for the marital-status characteristic parallel those for the total groups. Those of Mexican descent have the highest rates, followed by the Hispanos, Puerto Ricans, Central and South Americans, and Cubans, in this order.

Although marital status is clearly related to fertility at any one time, we cannot explain changes in fertility as due to changes in marital composition. There really is little difference in marital composition among the several groups with which we are concerned (see Appendix Tables G–18 to G–28), indeed not enough difference to account for the large differences in fertility.[16] Furthermore, the marital composition of any

[16] For example, among both Mexican and Cuban women aged 20–44 in 1970, 73% were married and living with their husbands. Yet the average number of children ever born was about 60% higher among the Mexican women, as we saw above and in Table 3.6.

population changes very little over time. We can say with confidence that any possible future changes in marriage patterns will be too slight to have a visible and measurable effect upon fertility. Therefore, we can rule out changes in marital status as a dynamic factor leading to changes in fertility in future decades.

Employment Status.[17] It is well known that the fertility of employed women is significantly lower than that of women who are unemployed or are not in the labor force. The Spanish-American women are no exception. We see, for example, that Mexican women who were employed averaged 1.7 children, whereas those not employed averaged 2.2 children ever born (Table 3.6). In each Spanish-American group, as well as in the non-Spanish white U.S. population, being employed is directly related to a smaller number of children ever born.

In general, being employed is associated with a decrease of 20–30% in the number of children ever born. The smallest decrease was observed among those of Central and South American descent, and the largest was among women of Puerto Rican descent. These fertility rates have been standardized so that each population group has the same age, marital status, and educational composition. Hence the fertility rates are directly comparable among the several groups, and we can compare the percentage decreases resulting from employment.

There is considerable variation among the several groups in the employment of women, as we shall see. Therefore, differences in the proportions employed are related to differences in fertility at any one moment of time. From the viewpoint of change over time and the future, however, it is most significant that employment is not a stationary variable, as marital status is. It is highly likely that in the future larger proportions of these women will be employed, if the labor market will have jobs for them. Hence we can expect that fertility will also change and is likely to decrease in those groups that had the highest fertility in 1970: the Mexicans, Hispanos, and Puerto Ricans. For example, in 1970, 37% of Mexican women aged 20–44 were employed, as compared with 52% of Cuban women. By 1980 and certainly by 1990, if jobs will be available, we expect employment among Mexican women to increase above 50%, and that of Cuban women to above 60%. Fertility will decrease as employment increases. We project this pattern, although we claim no causal relationship between

---

[17] For present purposes we have dichotomized the women into two groups: those employed at the time of the 1970 Census and those not employed, including those not in the labor force.

employment and fertility. Rather, we hold that those factors that lead to increased employment also lead to decreased fertility.

One factor directly related to increased employment is increased schooling. For example, among Mexican-descent women aged 25–29, of those who had not finished high school, 29% were employed, as compared with 50% of the women who had finished high school. Among Cuban women the corresponding percentages employed were 47 and 54. As we saw previously, over the last several decades there were significant increases in the number of years of schooling completed, and we expect further increases in the next generation. Accordingly, we expect increases in employment of women to follow suit. Such increases will be accompanied by decreases in fertility, especially among the present high-fertility populations.

Of course, increased schooling is not the only element leading to higher employment rates. We have reason to believe that the entire U.S. labor force is becoming more "feminized," that is, more and more women will be participating in the labor force.[18] The Spanish-American women will not be an exception. Of course, a generation hence, there may still be significant differences in the participation rates of the several groups, but the rates will be well above those observed in 1970 for women of all five groups.

Education. Increases in the number of years spent in school lead to decreases in fertility. This has been observed among virtually all populations ever studied, including the Spanish Americans.[19] Indeed, among those who completed high school only the Mexican and Hispano women have fertility rates above those of the non-Spanish white women; the Puerto Ricans have virtually the same fertility, and those of Cuban and Central and South American descent have rates significantly lower (Figure 3.1).

These rates were standardized for age, marital status, and employment on the basis of all non-Spanish white women in the United States in 1970. Hence, we are saying that the Puerto Rican women, for example, who were of the same age and had the same marital and employment status as non-Spanish white women and had completed 12 or more years of schooling had virtually the same number of children ever born as had the latter. Even the Mexican and Hispano women who

---

[18] A. J. Jaffe and Jeanne Clare Ridley, "Lifetime Employment of Women in the United States," *Industrial Gerontology* (Winter 1976): 25–36.

[19] Ajax de Smyrna, "The Zhopa Principle," *New York Statistician* 23 (January–February 1972): 1.

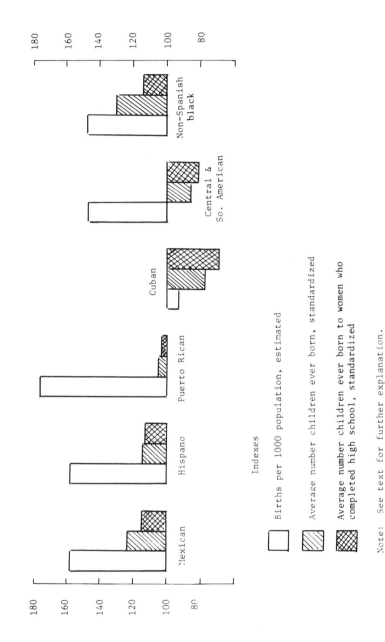

FIGURE 3.1. *Birthrate and number of children, by ethnicity of mothers, 1970 (non-Spanish) white women equal 100).*

48

were high school graduates had rates only some 15% above that of the non-Spanish whites.

The value of schooling as a dynamic engine of change is that all groups are completing more years of schooling as time passes. Furthermore, schooling is a factor amenable to social influence. On the one hand, to the extent that people believe that schooling is desirable they will attempt to have their children receive more schooling. On the other hand, to the extent that the government provides, or fails to provide, schools and related facilities, more or fewer children go to school and complete more or fewer years of education. In short, a society can achieve lowered fertility by promoting education.

Increased schooling is not necessarily the cause of lowered fertility. Rather, it operates both directly and indirectly upon fertility. The indirect effects include, for example, increases in the labor force participation rates of women, as we saw previously. Most importantly, it produces new social values and personal attitudes, a different way of life. Increased schooling, for example, helps to advance the feminist movement, and all of these influences result in lower fertility.

Continuously increasing numbers of years of education will not necessarily lead to ever-decreasing fertility. There seems to be some level—or perhaps two or three steps—above which further schooling may have comparatively little influence. In the United States in the latter part of the twentieth century, this level seems to be completion of high school. The woman who had graduated from high school is very different in many respects, including fertility, from her "dropout sister." Completion of a 4-year college and perhaps receipt of a graduate degree represent additional steps, each of which contributes further influence. Perhaps some day a bachelor's degree will represent the same level of importance for the majority of women as does high school graduation in the post–World War II period. In any event, we believe that continuous increases in numbers of years of schooling will not necessarily lead to ever-decreasing fertility rates.

NO INFLUENCE OF FAMILY INCOME

Once we have controlled for age, marital status, education, and employment, family income appears to have no additional influence. Within any subuniverse that we have controlled for the above factors, women living in families with high and low incomes have reasonably similar average numbers of childeren ever born.

TABLE 3.7

Percentage of Women Aged 35–44 Years Who Had Given Birth to Six or More Children, and Percentage These Children Are of All Children, by Type of Spanish Origin, and for Non-Spanish White Women: U.S. 1970

Schooling	Mexican descent		Puerto Rican descent		Cuban descent		Hispano		Non-Spanish white	
	% women	% children	% women	% children	% women	% children	% women	% children	% women	% children
0–7 years	39.9	65.5	23.1	46.9	2.1	8.1	34.1	61.5	16.0	39.2
8–11 years	26.4	47.5	13.2	30.3	2.5	8.8	25.7	48.4	12.5	27.5
–12 years	34.5	59.1	18.8	40.4	2.3	8.5	28.8	53.5	13.1	29.3
12 years	14.7	32.2	5.9	15.8	2.3	7.9	14.0	31.4	7.5	35.0
13+ years	9.9	25.0	4.7	13.2	1.7	6.2	10.5	26.5	5.3	14.1
12+ years	13.7	30.9	5.6	15.2	2.1	7.2	13.1	30.3	6.8	28.8
Total	29.6	54.2	15.7	35.8	2.2	7.9	22.2	45.5	8.8	29.0

THE "BIG PRODUCERS"

Much of the higher birth rate of the Mexican, Hispano, and Puerto Rican women is due to the small proportions who have large numbers of children. Among Mexican-origin women, for example, aged 35–44, about 30% had 6 children or more ever born, which accounts for over half of the total children that this age cohort had. Among all non-Spanish white women in the United States, slightly less than 1 woman in 10 had 6 or more children ever born, and these constituted 30 children of every 100 born to all women aged 35–44 (Table 3.7). This same general pattern appears among all ethnic groups. Clearly, if the potentially "big producers" changed their reproductive behavior, total fertility for the ethnic group would fall considerably.

Education plays an important part. With increased schooling there are fewer women who had six or more children ever born. This holds for every group except the Cubans, among whom practically no women, regardless of how little schooling they had, had given birth to six or more children.

Summary. With the exception of the Cuban-descent women, the other Spanish-American groups do have higher birth rates than the non-Spanish white women in the United States. These higher rates, however, occur because relatively few women had many children and because these groups, demographically, have a mix of characteristics that are conducive to a higher birth rate. They contain more younger women, more who are less educated, and more who are economically poorer, as we shall see.

These demographic characteristics are not immutable, however; they are constantly changing. Indeed, many Spanish-American women have already acquired, or closely approached, the demographic and economic characteristics of the non-Spanish white women. In so doing, their fertility has tended to converge to that of the latter. In the future we expect increasing convergence, as will be seen in Chapter 4.

THE ECONOMIC PICTURE

The Spanish Americans are among the economically poorer segments of U.S. society. The Native Americans and the blacks are the only major groups that are poorer than the Spanish Americans. This fact is well known and requires no elaboration on our part. Indeed, their lower economic position is one of the reasons these people come under the protection of the equal employment opportunity laws. Accordingly, in this section we shall only briefly summarize their economic conditions as of 1970, show the great divergencies among the five groups, and, then, indicate the role of formal schooling in raising economic levels.

It must be noted that it is difficult to compare the several economic criteria for the five groups with those for the non-Spanish white population because of the regional diversity that was noted previously. The various Spanish-American groups live in different parts of the United States, and wage rates, as well as labor-market conditions, including industrial and occupational compositions, differ from one part of the country to another. For example, let us examine Florida, where many Cubans live. This state contains more light industry than do many other states, and light industries pay lower wages. The average hourly earnings of all production workers in Florida in 1969 was $2.89, whereas the average for the total United States was $3.36. Hence Cubans employed in manufacturing in Florida may receive 47 cents less per hour than if they worked elsewhere; indeed, if they had worked in Michigan, they may have averaged $3.97 per hour, or $1.08 more than in Florida. Accordingly, once we have said that the Spanish Americans are poorer than the average non-Spanish white, further refinement is possible only by making a detailed study that takes into account occupation, industry, and state.[20] Such a detailed analysis is beyond the scope of our study.

FAMILY INCOME [21]

Average (or median) family income in 1969 ranged from a high of $8900 for those of Central or South American descent and $8700 for those of Cuban descent to a low of $6200 for those of Puerto Rican descent (Table 3.8). For comparative purposes, note that family income averaged $10,100 for the non-Spanish white.

---

[20] An indication of the regional variation in earnings is provided in S. E. Baldwin and R. S. Daski, "Occupational Pay Differences among Metropolitan Areas," *Monthly Labor Review* 99 (May 1976): 29 ff. For example, in the category "office clerical jobs," the range of earnings varied from a low (index number; national average equals 100) of 80 in San Antonio, Texas, to a high of 116 in Beaumont–Port Arthur–Orange metropolitan area. Skilled maintenance workers' earnings varied from a low of 72 in Greenville, South Carolina, to a high of 117 in San Francisco–Oakland. The pay for unskilled plant workers varied from 62 in San Antonio to 126 in Akron.

[21] This is the total money income from all sources including benefit and welfare payments, interest, and so on. Families are designated by ethnicity of head. Unrelated persons living alone are excluded.

TABLE 3.8
Median Family Income by Number of Earners in Family, by Ethnic Group: 1969

		Number earners		
Group	Total	0	1	2 or more
Non-Spanish white	$10,100	2,970	8,780	12,350
Mexican	6,960	1,800	5,750	9,080
Puerto Rican descent	6,230	2,430	5,860	9,900
Hispano	7,860	1,920	6,700	9,650
Cuban descent	8,690	1,520	6,560	10,490
Central and South American descent	8,920	1,880	7,160	10,940

Source: Public Use Sample (PUS) tabulation.

Families having under $3000 may be considered as the poorest of the poor. About 1 in 10 families was in this category among the non-Spanish whites, Cubans, and Central and South Americans. Among the Puerto Ricans, 1 in 5 was as poor.

Before investigating other aspects of family income, we note that the ranking of average income is the reverse of that of fertility and parallels that of education, as follows:

Descent	Median family income	Fertility	Years schooling completed, women aged 20–24 in 1970
Central and South American	Highest	2	Highest
Cuban	2	Lowest	2
Hispano	3	3	3
Mexican	4	Tied for highest	Lowest
Puerto Rican	Lowest	Tied for highest	4

Those of Cuban and Central and South American origin have the higher income and education and the lower fertility. Those of Mexican and Puerto Rican descent have the lower income and schooling and the higher fertility. The Hispanos are in the center. Clearly, these factors are interrelated and must have a bearing on each other.

Family income is the total of all incomes received by the several members of a family; the more members who have income, the higher the family income will be. Accordingly, let us examine 1969 family income in conjunction with the number of workers in a family (Table 3.8). If there were no earners, family income generally averaged around $2000; most of this money came from benefit and welfare payments. If there was one earner in the family, total family income increased considerably and was highest if there were two or more earners. Among those of Central and South American origin, income averaged about $11,000 if there were two or more earners. For the other ethnic groups, income averaged over $9000 when there were two or more earners.

It is clear that there are large differences among the groups in the number of earners per family (Appendix Table G–36). Three in five of the Cuban families had two or more earners, whereas among those of Puerto Rican descent, only slightly more than one in three had this number. We can estimate the effect of the number of workers on family income by noting:

1. The observed maximum difference was some $2700, which is the difference between median family income of the Central and South Americans versus the Puerto Ricans.
2. If all had the same number of earners, the difference would have been reduced to something over $1000. If the Puerto Ricans had contained fewer families having no earners and more families having two or more earners, their average family income would have been between $1000 and $1500 higher.

In summary, it appears that half or more of the variation in average family income among the five groups can be accounted for by differences in the number of earners.

LABOR FORCE PARTICIPATION

Women. The second earner in a family is likely to be the wife, although sometimes a child, parent, or other relative is the second worker. Most families contain a husband and wife, and in most cases the husband is an earner; hence if there is a second earner, it is probably the wife.

It would seem that among the Central and South Americans and Cubans, half of the women aged 16 and over were in the labor force in 1970 (Figure 3.2); this means that many wives worked in 1969. Among the Puerto Rican and Mexican populations, however, only about one-third of the women were in the labor force; apparently fewer wives

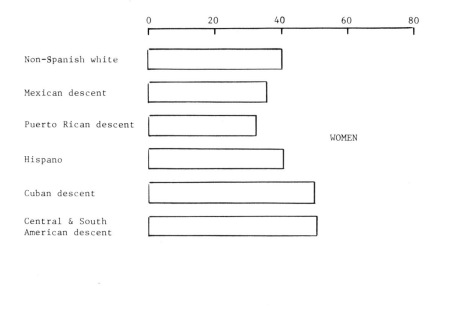

WOMEN

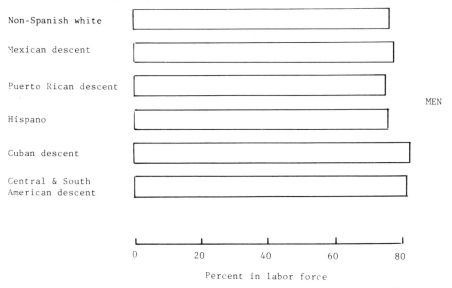

MEN

Percent in labor force

FIGURE 3.2. *Percentage of women and men aged 16 and over in the labor force, by ethnic group, 1970.*

were in the labor force. The Hispano women were in the center. Again we see another parallel with fertility.

Furthermore, as we shall see, of women who completed high school, proportions significantly larger than those of women with less education were in the labor force. Here we see the indirect effect of schooling upon fertility.

Men. Among men there are relatively few differences between the several ethnic groups. Three-quarters or more of all the men were in the labor force in 1970.

INDIVIDUAL EARNINGS

Family income is derived in large measure from the wages, salaries, and self-employment earnings of its individual members. Hence let us study these earnings. In 1969 median earnings for men ranged from a high of $6140 for men of Central and South American descent to a low of $4970 for those of Mexican descent (Table 3.9). All of the Spanish-American groups averaged less than did the non-Spanish white men.

Among women, those of Puerto Rican, Cuban, and Central and South American descent had average earnings above those of non-Spanish white women. The Mexican and Hispano women earned less money in 1969.

The influence of increased education on earnings is clearly evident. Among both women and men, those who had completed college earned two or more times the amount earned by persons who had not completed high school.

Let us relate these individual earnings to family income by assuming husband and wife families in which both are employed; let us also assume that the educational levels of husband and wife are similar. We then have the following hypothetical average family earnings:

| | Schooling of husband and wife | |
Group	Under 12 years ($)	16 or more years ($)
Non-Spanish white	8080	17,620
Mexican descent	6130	14,580
Puerto Rican descent	8250	15,910
Hispano	6540	15,330
Cuban descent	7900	13,140
Central and South American descent	8140	15,020

TABLE 3.9
Earnings by Years of Schooling and Sex, for Groups, 1969

| | Men | | | | | Women | | | | |
| | Years of schooling | | | | | Years of schooling | | | | |
	Total	Under 12 years	12 years	13-15 years	16+ years	Total	Under 12 years	12 years	13-15 years	16+ years
Non-Spanish white	$7290	5850	7730	7920	11620	$3090	2230	3400	2870	6000
Mexican descent	4970	4460	6070	6310	8990	2100	1670	2930	2940	5590
Puerto Rican descent	5430	5080	5960	5920	9820	3420	3170	3880	4060	6090
Hispano	5800	4940	6610	6380	9620	2350	1600	2950	2820	5710
Cuban descent	5710	4980	5810	6640	8590	3260	2920	3470	3570	4550
Central and So. Amer. descent	6140	5050	6530	6630	10360	3470	3090	3960	3600	4660

We thus complete our picture by noting that increased schooling leads to increased labor force participation and average earnings on the part of women. As for the men, increased education also leads to increased average earnings. Hence increased schooling results in larger family incomes and lower fertility. We are not saying that no other factors influence fertility but only that extent of schooling is of great importance, both directly and indirectly.

OCCUPATIONAL COMPOSITION

The type of job that a person has is highly dependent upon the extent of his or her schooling. Other factors play a part, including age—older men (or women) generally earn more than do young persons when they first enter the labor force—industry, and part of the country in which one lives. Of all these factors, the single most important is education. In anticipation of the evidence to be presented in the following discussion, we now state that college graduates have the higher level occupations and that there is very little difference among the college graduates of the several Spanish-American groups.

If we consider all members of each group, we find the majority of the Mexican and Puerto Rican men to be in the lower-level jobs (Table 3.10). This is largely because many of them have too little schooling to satisfy the requirements of the U.S. job market in the latter half of the twentieth century. The Cuban men and those from Central and South America have occupational structures only slightly below that of the non-Spanish white men. Among women, all the Spanish-American groups occupationally tend to be below the non-Spanish white women.

A summary measure of the occupational hierarchy is provided by means of the Census Bureau's Socio-Economic Status (SES) scores.[22] The larger the score for a population, the higher on the occupational ladder it is. The several groups score as follows:

Group	Men	Women
Non-Spanish white	60	64
Central and South American descent	59	57
Cuban descent	57	56
Hispano	53	58
Puerto Rican descent	50	56
Mexican descent	46	52

[22] U.S., Bureau of the Census, "Methodology and Scores of Socioeconomic Status," Working Paper No. 15, Washington D.C., 1963.

TABLE 3.10

Broad Occupational Groupings by Sex and Ethnicity, Population Aged 16 and over: 1970 (Percentage distribution)

	Mexican	Puerto Rican	Hispano	Cuban	Central & South American	Non-Spanish white
MEN						
Total	100.0	100.0	100.0	100.0	100.0	100.0
White collar	18.6	23.2	30.5	37.4	40.4	42.7
Upper	9.6	8.8	16.5	20.6	24.5	27.4
Lower	9.0	14.4	14.0	16.8	15.9	15.3
Craftsmen	20.5	15.5	21.9	18.0	18.9	21.7
All other	60.9	61.4	47.6	44.5	40.8	35.6
WOMEN						
Total	100.0	100.0	100.0	100.0	100.0	100.0
White collar	39.6	42.9	53.7	41.5	45.4	65.4
Upper	8.5	8.9	13.7	10.9	12.6	20.5
Lower	31.1	34.0	40.0	30.6	32.8	44.9
Craftsmen	2.4	2.4	1.6	2.6	2.1	1.9
All other	58.0	54.7	44.8	56.0	52.4	32.8

From the preceding we see that among men, those of Central and South American and Cuban descent score quite high and the Hispanos are in the center and are followed by the Puerto Ricans. Those of Mexican origin have the lowest jobs on the occupational ladder. Among women, the first four Spanish-American groups are very similar; the Mexican-descent women are further down the ladder.

Longtime Changes. There was considerable movement up the occupational ladder during the last several decades for the men of Mexican and Hispano origin but only slight movement for those of Puerto Rican origin (Figure 3.3). (The other two groups have lived in the United States for too short a time to have longtime changes.) Indeed, the upward movement was relatively greater for these first two groups than it was for the total U.S. white males, whose SES scores increased from 44 to only 60 during 1930–1970.

Perhaps one of the reasons why the Mexican-origin men experienced the greatest increase was simply their movement out of agriculture. Simple mobility from farm to nonfarm laborer in itself raises socioeconomic status, since the latter earn more than do farm workers. In 1930 one-third of them were farm laborers, and another third, nonfarm laborers. Since 1930 there was a large-scale out-movement from agriculture among all groups, including those of Mexican origin.

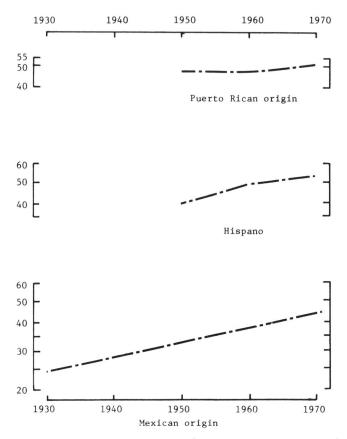

FIGURE 3.3. *Socioeconomic status scores for men, Puerto Rican and Hispano 1950–1970 and Mexican origin 1930–1970.*

Schooling and Occupational Status. The number of years of formal schooling completed is of extreme importance in determining one's position on the occupational ladder. This is so, partly because the better jobs require more training and partly because employers tend to prefer more-schooled workers for the higher paying and more prestigious jobs. Accordingly, those who have not finished high school have the lower level jobs, and the college graduates, the better ones.

Let us consider as having better jobs those who are professionals (but excluding the semiprofessional) and those managers who are employees. (The self-employed managers often are proprietors of small retail shops and cannot be considered as having climbed high on the occupational ladder.) Among persons who completed 16 or more years of schooling, we find the following proportions in these better jobs:

Group	Men (%)	Women (%)
Non-Spanish white	75	80
Mexican descent	74	79
Puerto Rican descent	72	78
Hispano	76	80
Cuban descent	60	44
Central and South American descent	72	60

Among persons who have not finished high school, there are very few in these better jobs; persons who are high school graduates or have some college education occupy an intermediate position on the occupational ladder.[23]

Among all of the Spanish-American groups with the exception of the Cubans, the occupational position of college graduates compares favorably with that of the non-Spanish whites. We suspect, but have no proof, that English-language problems may be hampering some of the Cubans and members of other groups in obtaining jobs commensurate with their level of schooling.

As will be recalled, the Mexicans, Puerto Ricans, and Hispanos had less schooling than did the other groups or the non-Spanish whites. Hence, upon taking all levels of schooling into account, we now see an important reason why they have lower-level jobs. If these groups had as much education as do the non-Spanish whites, they would be significantly higher on the occupational ladder.

We also saw that the younger members of these several groups are receiving significantly more schooling than did their parents. Hence, we can expect them to have better jobs than their parents had. Therefore, generation by generation, as the level of schooling of the Spanish Americans approaches that of the non-Spanish whites, we can expect their occupational structure also to approach that of the non-Spanish whites. But we also saw that school attendance rates for teenagers of Mexican and Puerto Rican descent and the Hispanos still lag significantly behind those for the non-Spanish whites. Hence, we can expect that the future occupational structures of these groups will continue to lag behind those of the non-Spanish whites until these groups achieve the same levels of schooling as do the latter.

One further point bears investigation. We noted previously that at each educational level the Spanish Americans earned less than did the

---

[23] For full details, see Appendix Tables G–1 to G–7.

non-Spanish whites. Nevertheless, their occupational structures tend to be similar at each educational level. We also noted that there are a variety of reasons for accounting for differences in earnings—region of the country, industry of employment, discrimination, and so on. We have no further explanations of why earnings do not keep pace with occupational position.

_4_ Demographic Convergence

Three measures of demographic, and perhaps social, convergence are available: outmarriage, the use of English language at home, and the absence of a Spanish surname. Each of these factors, in turn, will be related to fertility levels as measured by the average number of children ever born. Finally, we have a measure of one factor that seems to impede convergence, namely, living in a high-fertility neighborhood.

In anticipation of the findings that follow, we state here simply that the first three factors seem to be increasing and leading to demographic convergence. Furthermore, all three—outmarriage, use of English language, and lack of Spanish surname—are related to lower fertility. On the other hand, living in a high-fertility community per se seems to be conducive to higher fertility.

OUTMARRIAGE

Research concerned with the so-called assimilation of immigrant groups into the so-called main stream of American life has frequently used the extent of intermarriage as an indicator of the degree of adjustment made by these people to the dominant society. The inference is that persons from an ethnic group who marry into the native white American population presumably take on the social and demographic characteristics of that population. Thus, consistently high rates of outmarriage would mean the eventual disappearance of the distinctive characteristics of an ethnic group, and of the group itself.

Accordingly, we present some findings with respect to, first, the extent to which Spanish Americans married in or out of their ethnic group and, second, the fertility of women who married husbands of the same versus different ethnicity, by age and education of wives.

We may summarize our findings[1] as follows:

1. Most outmarriages were to non-Spanish whites.
2. In general, the highest rates of outmarriage were among the high school graduates and those who had gone on to college.
3. There were no age differences; roughly the same proportions of younger as of older persons married out.
4. The Hispanos had the highest rate of outmarriage, followed by the Cubans, then the Puerto Ricans, with the Mexicans last. (Outmarriage could not be determined for those of Central and South American origin.)
5. The natives of every group tended to marry other natives, regardless of level of schooling.
6. In general, higher proportions of those married more than once married out of the group, primarily to non-Spanish whites. The rate of outmarriage was highest among the better educated natives who married more than once.
7. In general, outmarriage resulted in lower fertility after controlling for age and education of wife.

FACTORS RELATED TO OUTMARRIAGE

Since outmarriage can result in demographic convergence, important questions with regard to the future of Spanish origin groups in the United States are

1. Has the rate of outmarriage increased over time, that is, are young people of Spanish origin marrying out with greater frequency than did their parents?
2. Are those who marry out drawn from selective groups within the Spanish-origin populations?
3. What is the ethnic background of the spouse, that is, do those who marry out marry into another Spanish-origin group or do they marry non-Spanish whites?

---

[1] These findings were obtained from a special Public Use Sample (PUS) tabulation for husbands and wives who were living together at the time of the 1970 Census enumeration. Hence we have no information about the possible extent of outmarriage among separated, widowed, or divorced persons.

The following analysis is limited to native women, since we can assume that they grew up and married in the United States. As for the foreign-born or the island-born Puerto Ricans, we do not know whether they married in the United States or in the home country. If they married in the United States, they could be studied in the same way as the natives can be. However, if they arrived in the United States already married, it is idle to speak of outmarriage.

Whom Did They Marry? In general, the large majority of outmarriages were to non-Spanish white spouses. Native women who married out, married men of the following descent groups:

	Wives			
Husbands	Mexican descent (%)	Puerto Rican descent (%)	Hispano (%)	Cuban descent (%)
Other Spanish	9	6	57	19
Non-Spanish white	84	76	41	64
Non-Spanish other	7	18	2	17

The Hispanos seem to be an exception. However, their marriages to other Spanish persons were mostly to husbands who reported themselves of Mexican origin. Since there is some merging of identity between the two groups, such marriages may not be considered as outmarriages by the Hispano women.

Marriage to other Spanish persons may be considered as marriage within the Spanish culture. Marriage to non-Spanish whites, on the other hand, clearly implies a dilution of the traditional Spanish culture. Just how "non-Spanish" the wife becomes or how "Spanish" the husband becomes, we do not know. We can only infer that each takes on some of the spouse's culture. In any event, if this melding of the cultures continues long enough, the groups as distinguishable entities eventually disappear.

This melding may be particularly true of the children of such marriages. They can claim affinity to either the mother's or the father's culture. However, considering that they attend English-language schools and live in a society that is predominantly non-Spanish, we suspect that they will gradually meld into the larger, non-Spanish society. This will certainly be the case if we consider several generations of outmarriage. The grandchildren of a 1970 outmarriage may be only one-quarter Spanish, and the great-grandchildren, one-eighth. By the year 2000 there will be large numbers who will be able to claim only one-sixteenth Spanish "blood." We think it unlikely that these persons will continue to claim close identity with a Spanish culture, especially if they do not speak or use the Spanish language.

The Extent of Outmarriage. In light of the preceding observation that the large majority of outmarriages are with non-Spanish whites, we have combined marriage within the specific group with marriages to spouses who reported other Spanish origin. Hence, outmarriage is defined in the following data as marriage to non-Spanish. The proportions of native wives who had married out are

Group	Percentage
Mexican descent	16
Puerto Rican descent	33
Hispano	39
Cuban descent	46

Age and Schooling. There are no consistent differences in rates of outmarriage by age for the three groups that could be studied: the Mexicans, Puerto Ricans, and Hispanos (Table 4.1).

As for schooling, however, women who had completed high school were much more likely to have married a non-Spanish husband than were those who had not completed high school. Indeed, two to three times as many of the more schooled were likely to marry out, and this pattern is found for all four groups. Among women of Mexican descent, for example, only 1 in 10 of the lesser schooled married out, whereas among high school graduates, 3 in 10 married out. The highest rate is observed among the Hispano women who completed high school; over half of them married non-Spanish husbands.

Those who marry out also tend to marry persons with the same education. Among Mexicans, for example, 69% of wives and 65% of husbands who married out had spouses with the same education, compared with 60% of marriages within the same ethnicity. Among Hispanos, 69% of wives and 75% of husbands who married out were married to spouses with the same education, compared with 59% of marriages where both partners were Hispanos.

That better-educated persons of Spanish origin have higher rates of outmarriage than do their lesser-schooled counterparts raises other questions. Do the better educated have high rates of outmarriage

TABLE 4.1

Percentage of Native Wives Who Married Husbands of Same Ethnicity, by Ethnic Group, Age, and Schooling: 1970

Wife's age and husband's ethnicity	Wife's ethnicity and years of schooling											
	Mexican			Puerto Rican[b]			Hispano			Cuban		
	-12 years	12+ years	total	-12 years	12+ years	total	-12 years	12+ years	total	-12 years	12+ years	total
Under 35												
Same as wife's[a]	89	70	81	83	59	70	75	48	60	NA	NA	NA
Non-Spanish	11	30	19	17	41	30	25	52	40	NA	NA	NA
Total	100	100	100	100	100	100	100	100	100	NA	NA	NA
35 and over												
Same as wife's[a]	92	63	87	71	49	61	73	44	63	NA	NA	NA
Non-Spanish	8	37	13	29	51	39	27	56	37	NA	NA	NA
Total	100	100	100	100	100	100	100	100	100	NA	NA	NA
All ages												
Same as wife's[a]	91	68	84	79	56	67	74	47	61	63	49	54
Non-Spanish	9	32	16	21	44	33	26	53	39	37	51	46
Total	100	100	100	100	100	100	100	100	100	100	100	100

[a] Includes husbands who are of other Spanish American ethnicity.

[b] Born on the Mainland.

regardless of nativity? To what extent do individuals tend to marry those of the same nativity as themselves?

Nativity and Repeat Marriages. With regard to nativity, it is clear that native persons in each of the four groups tended to marry other native stock, of the same or different ethnicity. U.S.-born persons, by and large, married spouses who were also U.S. born. For example, among native Mexican-origin wives we find the following proportions married to native husbands:

Wives	Percentage
Under 12 years of schooling	
Married once	82
Married more than once	84
12 or more years of schooling	
Married once	81
Married more than once	87

The preceding also illustrates that neither extent of schooling nor number of times married seems to affect the affinity of native for native.

Repeat marriages result in more outmarriage. Among the lesser and the better educated, the proportion of native stock who married persons of the same nativity but of different ethnicity increased with repeat marriage. Among lesser-educated Hispano wives, for example, 36% of those who were married once had married out, compared with 53% of those who married more than once. Among the better educated, 82% of repeat marriages were to husbands of different ethnicity (Table 4.2).

OUTMARRIAGE AND FERTILITY

We already noted that fertility is significantly lower among women who completed high school than it is among those who did not do so. We conclude that outmarriage appears to be as important as education in reducing fertility, and higher levels of schooling together with marriage out of the group resulted in further reduction in the fertility of these women (Table 4.3).[2] Since the greater proportion of out-marriages

---

[2] Of the 24 comparisons in Table 4.3, there are only three exceptions to this pattern: Puerto Rican women aged 35–44 and having 12 or more years of schooling, Cuban women aged 35–44 and having under 12 years of schooling, and Cuban women aged

TABLE 4.2
Percentages of First and Subsequent Marriages of Spanish-Origin Groups, by Nativity and Education: 1970

	Under 12 years schooling		12 or more years schooling	
	Married once %	Married more than once %	Married once %	Married more than once %
MEXICAN ORIGIN				
Native wives, husbands:				
Native, same ethnicity	74	65	63	43
Native, different ethnicity	8	19	28	44
Foreign born, same ethnicity	17	5	7	10
Foreign born, different ethnicity	1	2	2	4
PUERTO RICAN-ORIGIN				
Mainland-born wives, husbands:				
Mainland born	38	18	31	13
Native, different ethnicity	18	50	40	71
Island born	42	32	25	13
Foreign born, different ethnicity	2	0	4	3
CUBAN ORIGIN				
Native wives, husbands:				
Native, same ethnicity	32	20	19	14
Native, different ethnicity	41	40	54	71
Foreign born, same ethnicity	18	20	23	14
Foreign born, different ethnicity	9	20	4	0
HISPANO				
Hispano wives, husbands:				
Hispano	62	45	39	16
Native, different ethnicity	30	44	53	75
Foreign born, Spanish ethnicity	3	2	2	2
Foreign born, non-Spanish ethnicity	6	9	6	7

were to non-Spanish whites, we conclude that the values held by native non-Spanish white Americans favoring lower fertility have an impact even on the lesser-educated Spanish-origin women who married out.

Although we have no information from the U.S. Census on religious affiliation, the great majority of Spanish Americans are at least nominally Catholic, which may help to explain the higher fertility among these women (except Cubans), since Catholicism has been associated with higher fertility levels. In the case of outmarriage, we

---

15–24 and having 12 years or more of schooling. In all three instances, there were fewer than 100 women in the sample so that this divergence from pattern may be attributable to the small number of cases and may not indicate a truly different pattern.

TABLE 4.3

Children Ever Born per 100 Women by Type of Spanish Origin, by Age, Years of Schooling Completed, and Outmarriage: 1970

Ethnicity, years of schooling, and age	Married in	Married out	Married out as % of married in
MEXICAN			
Under 12 years schooling			
15-24 years	181	150	82
25-34 years	373	285	76
35-44 years	503	335	67
12 years and over schooling			
15-24 years	103	73	71
25-34 years	248	207	83
35-44 years	369	295	80
PUERTO RICAN			
Under 12 years schooling			
15-24 years	169	133*	79
25-34 years	293	244*	83
35-44 years	376	275*	73
12 years and over schooling			
15-24 years	101	64*	63
25-34 years	221	185	84
35-44 years	259	267*	106
CUBAN			
Under 12 years schooling			
15-24 years	115*	100*	87
25-34 years	211	153*	73
35-44 years	205	328*	160
12 years and over schooling			
15-24 years	59*	69*	117
25-34 years	185	148*	80
35-44 years	217	182*	84
HISPANO			
Under 12 years schooling			
15-24 years	163	128*	79
25-34 years	347	252	73
35-44 years	404	324	80
12 years and over schooling			
15-24 years	100	79	79
25-34 years	216	189	80
35-44 years	320	272	85

* Rates are based on fewer than 100 women.

have no information about either the ethnicity or religious background of the non-Spanish spouse. The question arises: If outmarriage is to Catholics of non-Spanish ethnicity (e.g., Italian), would values favoring larger numbers of children still be an important influence? We think not. Research indicates that when age and education are held constant, Catholics have practically the same fertility as do non-Catholics.[3] We therefore have no reason to conclude that religion would be an important element, even if non-Spanish spouses have the same religious background.

Since both education and outmarriage result in lower fertility, can we reach any conclusions of whether one factor has a greater impact than has the other, or is it the combined effect of both higher levels of schooling and outmarriage that accounts for the lower fertility of these women? In order to answer this question, we standardized for age the children-ever-born rates by education of woman and type of marriage for each Spanish-origin group (Table 4.4). On the basis of the age-standardized rates, we can conclude that outmarriage affected the fertility of the lesser-schooled women to about the same degree as it did the better educated.

Whereas outmarriage does appear to have an impact on fertility independent of education, fertility levels of lesser-schooled women who married out, nevertheless, are higher than are those for better-educated women who married within the same ethnicity. For example, among Mexican-origin women who had not completed high school but had married out, the average number of children ever born per woman (standardized for age) was 2.4. On the other hand, Mexican women who were high school graduates and had married Mexican husbands averaged only 2.1 children. It is the combination of higher educational attainment and outmarriage that has the greatest impact on fertility. We suspect that the type of woman who is likely to marry out of her ethnic group is also the type (or has the characteristics) who is likely to complete high school and to have fewer children. The two demographic characteristics are interrelated and have some unknown but basic factors in common.

ENGLISH SPOKEN HERE

To the extent that the Spanish Americans are giving up the Spanish language for English, they are acquiring some of the characteristics of the non-Spanish population and can be said to be converging. To some

---

[3] See, for example, Charles F. Westoff, "The Yield of the Imperfect: The 1970 National Fertility Study," *Demography* 12 (November 1975): 573–580.

TABLE 4.4

Standardized Rates of Children Ever Born per 100 Spanish-Origin Women Aged 15–44, by Education and Inmarriage or Outmarriage: 1970

Ethnicity and years of schooling completed	Married in	Married out	Married out as % of married in
MEXICAN			
Under 12 years schooling	330	244	74
12 years and over schooling	213	169	79
PUERTO RICAN			
Under 12 years schooling	264	208*	79
12 years and over schooling	179	152*	85
CUBAN			
Under 12 years schooling	171	178*	104
12 years and over schooling	139	122*	88
HISPANO			
Under 12 years schooling	289	221	76
12 years and over schooling	189	160	85

*Rates are based on fewer than 100 women

extent, at least, they are substituting non-Spanish culture for the Spanish. Fray Angelico Chavez has emphasized this point when writing of the Hispanos, "when the old language of Cervantes is no more, it can only mean the end."[4]

By the mid-1970s about 1 in 4 persons of Spanish origin spoke English only and another 2 in 5 usually spoke English but had Spanish as their second language. Close to two-thirds have already shifted to English, if we can assume that the ancestral language of virtually all Spanish-origin people was Spanish. Only about 1 in 10 spoke Spanish exclusively, and another 1 in 4 usually spoke Spanish but also spoke English as his second language.[5]

The transition point from Spanish to English is more likely to occur among the second generation born in the United States than among

---

[4] Chavez, *My Penitente Land*, p. 272.

[5] Estimated from U.S., Bureau of the Census, *Language Usage in the United States: July 1975*, Series P–23, no. 60. Washington, D.C.: Government Printing Office, 1976.

their parents or foreign-born grandparents. Among the latter at the time of the 1970 Census practically all reported Spanish as the language spoken at home as a child. Large numbers continued to speak Spanish at home, so that their children were also raised in Spanish-speaking homes. Many of these children, however, as a result of attending English-language schools and living in an English-speaking environment, used English in their own homes and raised their children—the second generation born in the United States—in English-speaking homes. Hence, in order to measure the language changeover, if such is occurring, we must study those who are natives of native parentage. The Hispanos consititute the only group for which data (1970) are available for study.[6]

Even these 1970 Census data include some changeover—an unknown amount. The question asked was "What language, other than English, was spoken in this person's home when he was a child?" A number of persons who had been raised in homes where both Spanish and English were spoken must have checked "Spanish." Probably the only Hispanos who reported English as the childhood language were those living in homes where only English was spoken.

Although the majority of the Hispanos were raised in homes where Spanish was spoken as either the first or second language, over the years more are growing up in homes where English may be the only language used. Of children under age 5, 1 in 4 is in a family using English; among persons aged 45 and over, most of whom were born before World War I, only 1 in 20 grew up in a family where English was spoken. Among these older persons, many must have switched to the use of English as either a first or second language. This can be attested to easily by any visitor to New Mexico, who will find that virtually everyone of Spanish origin speaks English.

---

[6] There are large numbers of Mexican-origin people who are natives of native parentage. Because of the manner in which the Census Bureau collected the information on language spoken at home when a child, language information is available only for the natives of foreign parentage. Since we expect to find the large majority of this first U.S.-born generation to be speaking the language of their foreign-born parents, there is no point is studying this group.

The estimates for the Hispanos were derived from a special PUS tabulation of the Spanish-surname population living in New Mexico and Colorado. The foreign-born and natives of foreign parentage were omitted. The remaining natives of native parentage are largely Hispanos. Hispanos having non-Spanish surnames were excluded, and these people are more likely to have had English as a childhood language. Hence, the estimates of English-speaking persons as presented in the text are minimized.

Children who were raised in English-speaking homes were more likely to have received more education. Of all persons aged 25 and over, 28% of those raised in homes where Spanish had been spoken completed high school. On the other hand, of those raised in homes where English was spoken, 58% finished high school.

We may infer that persons raised in homes where English was spoken had parents who had more schooling than did the average person. We infer this, since we know that the children of more-schooled parents also tend to receive more schooling. Hence, we infer that there is an intergenerational "cause" and "effect." Hispano parents who had more education tended to use English at home; their children, having been raised in homes where English was spoken and having more-schooled parents, receive more education in their turn. The cumulative effect over the next generation and longer will be to have more children raised in homes where English is spoken exclusively as a result of the increased schooling. These children, in turn, will obtain still more schooling, and the cycle will keep repeating.

The language that was spoken at home when the woman was a child is also related to her subsequent fertility. Among all women aged 35–44 we find that having been raised in an English-speaking home results in a decrease of about 15–20% in the number of children ever born. Further decrease is attributable to increased schooling, and we have as follows:

Homes	Number of children
Spanish-speaking	
Under 12 years of schooling	4.8
12 or more years of schooling	3.6
English-speaking	
Under 12 years of schooling	3.9
12 or more years of schooling	3.1

We must also note that the use of the English language appears to be associated with outmarriage. The majority of such outmarriages are with non-Spanish whites, for most of whom English is the mother tongue. Thus we see a pattern: more schooling, more outmarriage, more use of English, and lower fertility.

Finally, we note that many persons who were raised in Spanish-speaking homes, as adults use English as their current language (i.e., the language usually spoken in the home at the time of the census inquiry). Of close to 7 million persons who reported Spanish as the language used in their homes as children, over 2 million, or 1 in 3, apparently switched to English as the language currently used at home.[7] We suspect that these people have had more schooling than have those who continued to use Spanish at home. Thus, we see a gradual diminution in the use of the Spanish language. Each succeeding generation is likely to contain more English-speaking members. Unless continued immigration replenishes the supply of Spanish speakers, that language will gradually fade away.

SPANISH VERSUS NON-SPANISH SURNAMES

The existence of a non-Spanish surname generally, but not always, indicates outmarriage. A number of Latin Americans who have immigrated to the United States were of non-Spanish European ancestry and brought non-Spanish surnames with them. Other persons with Spanish surnames may have anglicized them; *Rios* can be changed to *Rivers*, *Sierra* to *Mountain*, *Blanco* to *White*, *Caballero* to *Knight*, and so on. Nevertheless, the large-scale prevalence of non-Spanish surnames would indicate outmarriage at some time in the past and the possibility of demographic convergence.

Among those who reported themselves as Hispanos, one in three has a non-Spanish surname, and among those reported as of Mexican descent, one in six.[8] It is not possible to determine whether there are any longtime trends in the prevalence of the two types of surname, and we do not know if more Mexican or Hispano people had non-Spanish surnames in 1970 than they had in previous decades. We can only speculate as follows. If in the past persons having non-Spanish surnames blended into the non-Spanish population (as they well could have done) and gave up their Spanish identity, then there could have been considerable increase in the prevalence of non-Spanish surnames that would not have shown up in the statistics. All persons who did not classify themselves as of Spanish-American origin would have been lost to our analysis. Therefore, to the extent that convergence is occurring and that some Hispanos and Mexican Americans are becoming Anglos, a non-Spanish surname may be an inadequate indicator of convergence.

---

[7] Census Bureau, *Persons of Spanish Origin, 1969*, Table A.

[8] The 1970 Census designed Spanish surname only for residents of Arizona, California, Colorado, New Mexico, and Texas. Since comparatively few members of the other three Spanish-American groups live in this area, we must limit the analysis to the Mexicans and Hispanos.

SCHOOLING AND SURNAMES

There appears to be a significant difference between the Hispano population having Spanish surnames and that having non-Spanish surnames (assuming that the census designation of Spanish surname is reasonably correct). Those having Spanish surnames have received significantly less schooling; fewer have graduated from high school and fewer have gone to college (Table 4.5). It is likely that the type of name is related to language spoken at home when a child; those having non-Spanish surnames tended to come from English-speaking homes, we infer. However, we have no statistics actually to tie the two together.

Further exploration of the statistics on extent of schooling indicates that among Hispanos having Spanish surnames, males received significantly more schooling than did females. However, of those who had non-Spanish surnames, the same proportions of men and women graduated from high school. More non-Spanish-surname men than women had gone on to college, but this sex difference is true for the total U.S. non-Spanish white population also.

These different patterns of education by sex suggest that the early family environment of the Spanish-surname population was different from that of the non-Spanish-surname population. The female was regarded differently. This difference, we suggest, applies to Hispano women who married Anglo men and thus acquired non-Spanish names;

TABLE 4.5

Level of Schooling Completed for Hispanos and Natives of Mexican Descent, by Age, Sex, and Type of Surname: 1970

	Spanish surname				Non-Spanish surname			
	% completed high school		% entered college		% completed high school		% entered college	
	Men	Women	Men	Women	Men	Women	Men	Women
HISPANO								
Total	41	33	15	7	53	55	25	16
20 to 24 years	65	58	22	17	72	74	35	22
25 to 34 years	53	38	19	5	71	66	33	19
35 to 44 years	38	32	17	6	56	58	26	18
45 and over	26	16	8	3	31	36	13	9
MEXICAN								
Total	34	28	12	6	42	44	18	11
20 to 24 years	54	50	18	13	63	60	27	18
25 to 34 years	45	37	16	7	50	55	20	14
35 to 44 years	29	22	11	4	36	35	18	8
45 and over	14	10	5	2	20	22	7	4

their early home environment was somehow different from those who married Spanish-surnamed men. Furthermore, there is a relationship between type of surname and the fertility of women, as we shall see in the following sections.

The natives of Mexican descent have the same pattern; more of those having non-Spanish surnames completed high school, and more entered college (Table 4.5). The general level of schooling completed was lower for these people than it was for the Hispanos, but the pattern is the same.

As with the Hispanos, among native Mexican Americans having Spanish surnames, more men than women had completed high school. Among those having non-Spanish surnames, the same proportions of each sex completed high school. This suggests that the home life and environment of the two surname groups are different and that the attitudes toward education of women are more favorable among the non-Spanish surnamed.

However, significantly more men than women enter college, regardless of surname. In this respect, both those of Mexican descent and Hispanos are similar to the general U.S. society.

SURNAMES AND FERTILITY

Having a non-Spanish surname also resulted in lower fertility, as is shown for women aged 35–44 who were married and living with their husbands as follows:

	Average number of children per woman	
Surname	Hispano	Native Mexicans
Spanish		
Under 12 years of schooling	5.0	5.0
12 or more years of schooling	4.1	3.6
Non-Spanish		
Under 12 years of schooling	4.1	4.6
12 or more years of schooling	3.0	3.1

Both more education and a non-Spanish surname result in lower fertility. Each contributes around a 20% decrease.

SUMMARY

We see that the factors of education, inmarriage or outmarriage, language spoken in home when a child, type of surname, and level of fertility are all inextricably involved with one another. As we see it, the extent of education permeates all other variables, and for that reason we ascribe considerable importance to schooling as the "engine of change." Furthermore, all of the above factors seem to indicate a changing society—one whose demographic characteristics at least are becoming similar to that of the general U.S. non-Spanish society. Demographic convergence is occurring.

AN IMPEDIMENT: RESIDENCE IN A
HIGH-FERTILITY NEIGHBORHOOD

People live in groups. Each group develops its own culture, mores, and behavior patterns that govern the beliefs and practices of its members. And, each person within the group influences the others and in turn is influenced by them. These are basic principles. Fertility is not likely to be an exception. In groups or societies where most women have many children, each individual considers such to be the proper behavior and will have many children if she can. In societies where few children are the rule, each woman will attempt to limit her fertility. There are always individual exceptions, of course, and societies and cultures change over time. Nevertheless, these principles lead to the conclusion that if an individual, woman, or family is to adopt a changed form of reproductive behavior, not only the individual but also the group of which the person or family is a member must adopt a changed form of behavior. The group influences the individual's fertility.

In the case of the Mexican-origin women (the only Spanish-American group that we could study), we hypothesized that those who reside in high-fertility neighborhoods are more likely to retain the high fertility pattern of Mexican society—that is, high relative to the non-Spanish white fertility patterns. Our analysis reveals that this is the case for the native Mexican women (Table 4.6) who were married and living with their husbands. We compared 12 groupings developed from three age categories, two employment categories, and two years-of-schooling categories. In each case, fertility in the higher fertility area was above

TABLE 4.6

Average Number of Children Ever Born per Woman, Mexican-Origin Women Born in the United States: U.S. 1970

	Married spouse present			
	Under 12 years schooling		12 and more years schooling	
	Neighborhood birth rate		Neighborhood birth rate	
Age	Low	High	Low	High
Employed 1969				
15 to 24 years	1.57	1.67	.60	.88
25 to 34 years	3.51	3.91	1.92	2.25
35 to 44 years	3.80	5.00	3.02	3.22
Not employed 1969				
15 to 24 years	1.73	2.04	1.30	1.38
25 to 34 years	3.68	4.13	2.76	2.92
35 to 44 years	4.49	5.65	3.59	3.67

	All other marital status			
	Under 12 years schooling		12 and more years schooling	
	Neighborhood birth rate		Neighborhood birth rate	
	Low	High	Low	High
Employed 1969				
15 to 24 years	.29	.18	.17	.15
25 to 34 years	2.09	2.26	.83	.96
35 to 44 years	3.34	3.47	2.04	2.17
Not employed 1969				
15 to 24 years	.15	..14	.30	.18
25 to 34 years	2.98	2.24	2.23	(2.67)
35 to 44 years	4.20	4.49	(3.05)	(4.00)

Note: When there were fewer than 25 women in the cell, the rate is enclosed in parentheses.

that in the corresponding lower fertility area.[9] It is clear that the neighborhood influences affect the individual's behavior.

These results cannot be purely statistical artifacts, since we omitted the neighborhoods in which over 50% of the population reported Spanish language. In the neighborhoods that we studied, there were enough non-Mexicans so that the neighborhood fertility level could not be interpreted as due only to "Mexican influence."

Note that we controlled for age, schooling, employment, and marital status—the four factors that have been shown to influence Mexican fertility. Apparently, the type of neighborhood further influences fertility. From this we deduce that so long as Mexican-origin women continue to live in higher-birth-rate neighborhoods, their fertility will continue to be higher, despite increased schooling and their employment. Unfortunately, we have no information on whether there has been movement over the last several decades out of the—presumably—originally high-fertility Mexican ghettos. Hence we are unable to appraise the possible influence of the neighborhood on Mexican fertility in the decades ahead. We can suggest only that the more the population mingles with others who have lower fertility, the more Mexican fertility will decrease in the future.

SOME IMPLICATIONS

Given these findings, what can be said of the future of Spanish-origin groups with regard to their continued cultural distinctiveness? To the extent that marriage into the dominant group, that is, non-Spanish whites, implies taking on the demographic and social behavior of native non-Spanish white Americans, including lower fertility, the findings presented here seem to point toward the eventual demographic absorption of Spanish Americans into the dominant American cultural patterns, except as new immigrants replenish the stock. Undoubtedly, the rate of demographic conversion will differ for each group and will be affected by factors that could not be examined in this report. Continuation of residence in predominantly high-birth-rate neighborhoods, especially if they are Spanish-American ghettos, will retard this process of demographic absorption but will not stop it.

---

[9] For the combined group of women other than married with spouse present (widowed, divorced, separated, and never married), there is no relationship of fertility to type of neighborhood. We suspect that this is because of the marital heterogeneity of this other group and the relatively few cases available for study, a factor that increases the size of the sampling error.

In future generations, as the native stock form even greater proportions of persons of Spanish origin and achieve higher levels of education, they can be expected to marry out with greater frequency and to have lower fertility than had the parent generations. If this is so, and in the absence of any great changes in existing immigration laws (and migration patterns among the Puerto Ricans), it will most likely be the foreign born and natives with low levels of educational attainment who will form the bulk of Spanish cultural groups in the United States. This is likely to be the case for the Mexican-origin group, since the migrants from Mexico are predominantly little schooled and have high fertility.

As for the Cubans and Central and South American-origin population, both the migrants and the natives are more schooled, so that outmarriage is likely to loom large in the future, and consequently there will be low (or lower) fertility.

With regard to the Puerto Rican-origin population, the increasing amount of schooling being given on the island will probably result in more-schooled future migrants. Hence, outmarriage is likely to loom larger, together with lower fertility.

The Hispanos already seem to be disappearing as a distinctive cultural group, as Fray Angelico Chavez has suggested.[10]

In general, the Spanish Americans appear to be following in the footsteps of the older immigrant groups who preceded them. Nevertheless, this process of integration, wholly or partly, into the white non-Spanish U.S. population is slow moving and will take several generations.

---

[10] Chavez, *My Penitente Land.*

5

The Hispanos

INTRODUCTION

The forebears of the twentieth-century Hispanos were living in what is now the United States well before the pilgrims landed on Plymouth Rock. Their subsequent history—demographic, political, and cultural—thus has its roots in an environment quite different from that from which the twentieth-century Mexican-American population has come. Let us, therefore, very briefly review this early period from the time of Cortés to the mid-nineteenth century, when the United States absorbed the southwest territory where the Hispanos lived.

Some clarification of nomenclature is advisable at this point in order to appreciate the history of the Hispanos. The land that Cortés had conquered by 1521 was named New Spain by the conquerors, and the capital city was called Mexico. By the middle of the sixteenth century, Spanish explorers had gone northward into what is now the southwestern United States; when Spain claimed these lands, they were referred to as New Mexico, or sometimes as Northern New Spain. Apparently Spain laid claim to lands as far east as the Mississippi River, as far west as the Pacific Ocean, and to some indefinite line in the north. During the sixteenth and seventeenth centuries, so little was known about the geography of western North America that virtually all land claims had to be indefinite.

After the war of independence in 1821, the inhabitants of New Spain changed the name of their country to Mexico. By this time the northern area overlapping present-day northern Mexico and the southwestern United States had been subdivided into several areas: San Luis Potosi, which included much of present-day Texas; Nuevo Mexico, which included parts of modern Texas, Oklahoma, Kansas, and most of New Mexico and Colorado; and Nueva California, which included parts of New Mexico, Colorado, Wyoming, and all of California, Nevada, Arizona, and Utah.[1]

When the United States took possession of these southwestern territories, the name New Mexico was given to what is today the state of that name, together with parts of Colorado and Arizona. In 1861 part was incorporated into the Colorado Territory, and in 1863 part became the Arizona Territory. Hence in 1863 the present state of New Mexico received its present boundaries.

THE GEOGRAPHY

The earliest settlers, aside from the indigenous Indians, were Spaniards who carried with them sixteenth- and seventeenth-century Spanish culture, Indians, and mestizos from the present country of Mexico. Apparently they first followed the Rio Grande, which carried most of them through present-day southern Texas and into central and northern New Mexico and southern Colorado. Very few initially settled in the other southwestern areas. In 1598 Don Juan de Oñate led a group of settlers and founded San Gabriel de los Espanoles about 48 kilometers north of present-day Santa Fe, New Mexico. In 1609 Santa Fe was established.

About the beginning of the eighteenth century, the Spaniards began settling Texas in an effort to hold off the French, who were threatening from the east.[2] At about the same time, the Spanish crown felt that California was being threatened by the English, whose ships appeared off the California coast, and by the Hudson's Bay Company, one of whose missions was the "Discovery of a New Passage into the South Sea." In addition, by the mid-eighteenth century reports that the Russians were advancing southward from Alaska were received by the Spanish court, which thereupon began serious attempts to settle California.[3] Missions played an important part, but, in population terms, this meant a handful of Spaniards and as many Indians as they could convert.

---

[1] Matt S. Meier and Feliciano Rivera, *The Chicanos* (New York: Hill and Wang, 1972), p. 19.

[2] *Ibid.*, p. 18.

[3] Irving Berdine Richman, *California under Spain and Mexico* (1911; reprinted., New York: Cooper Square Publishers, 1965), p. 31ff.

In summary, during the seventeenth and eighteenth centuries the Spanish (Hispano) population was located largely in present-day northern New Mexico and southern Colorado along the Rio Grande, with a few settlers in Texas and California. The intervening lands were almost exclusively inhabited by the indigenous Indians and contained very few persons of European origin. As a result, the Hispanos have become identified largely with New Mexico, although by 1970 they had dispersed into neighboring states, especially California.

THE PEOPLE

Much has been written about the colonial population of present-day New Mexico, and since this was the main area of settlement in the seventeenth and eighteenth centuries, let us review this briefly. According to Chavez,[4] Don Juan de Oñate arrived in what is now the state of New Mexico in 1598 with about 130 Spanish soldiers, many with their families, and some Indian servants. Additional soldiers arrived from time to time throughout the seventeenth century, many of whom married the daughters and granddaughters of the first colonists.

In 1680 the northern Pueblos drove out the Spaniards, who retreated into what is now southern New Mexico. In 1693 Don Diego de Vargas recolonized the area with, according to Chavez, the following groups: (a) the native New Mexicans who were the descendants of the Oñate colonization; (b) soldiers from Spain; (c) "Espanoles Mexicanos," 67 Spanish families living in the city and valley of Mexico who had been selected by the viceroy as colonists; (d) the families from Zacatecas,[5] an unknown number of whom had been recruited; and (e) New Mexicans of Guadalupe del Paso, an unknown number of whom chose to move north with Vargas.

Many of the Spaniards came originally from the poor provinces of La Mancha and Estremadura in southern Castile. Apparently they were seeking an opportunity to better themselves, an opportunity they had not had in Spain.

Since men predominated among the Spaniards, there was considerable intermarriage—or interbreeding—with the Indian women, resulting in an increase in the mixed population. There also was some intermarriage of Indian men with Spanish women. Furthermore, many of the *genizaros*, the children of the captives of different Indian nations

---

[4] Fray Angelico Chavez, *Origins of New Mexico Families* (Albuquerque: University of Albuquerque in collaboration with Calvin Horn, Publisher, Inc., 1973), p. ixff.

[5] An area in present-day northwest Mexico.

or tribes who had intermarried and produced aboriginal mixtures, having lost their original Indian tribal affiliation, became "Spaniards." They tended to live in settlements separate from those of the Hispanics. Chavez notes that ultimately these genizaros either amalgamated into the Pueblo Indians or into the lower socioeconomic stratum of Hispanic life.[6]

In addition to these diverse population groups, many non-Spanish European-origin individuals entered New Mexico as traders, soldiers, and adventurers, married local Hispano women, and became part of the Hispano culture. This addition is most clearly seen in the frequency of non-Spanish names among those who classified themselves as "other Spanish" in the 1970 Census (see Chapter 4).

Chavez characterized the Hispano people when he wrote: "Although we were truly Hispanic in blood, language, religion, and customs, we were no longer Spaniards like the clergymen from Spain. . . .Nor were we really Mexicans, as our North European–derived neighbors chose to call us. The differences . . .were all a matter of cultural and linguistic development from a parting of the ways with both Hispanic Europe and Hispanic Middle America down three centuries and a half."[7]

Chavez then compared the Hispanos with those of Mexican origin and distinguished between the two populations as follows:

The Spanish New Mexican has long forgotton the songs brought from Spain by his pioneer forebears. The archaic language brought by them, too, is fast on its way out, sad to say, although replaced in all too rare instances by its modern equivalent through individual effort. Having produced little or no genuine music or poetry of his own, he has for long come to depend on the rich musical lode of Mexico to express his loves and his sorrows. My New Mexican countryman, however, has become so confused as to call it "Spanish music," just as he misnames tacos and enchiladas "Spanish food"—or sees no incongruity when a youth with Amerindian features represents the person of a famous Castilian conquistador.

For this is the bane of a people who have lost sight of their factual "origins and history," even while these were being preserved underneath the surface by "landscape and language." And yet they do not wish to be identified as Mexicans, but correctly as long-time Americans by birth and nationality. Their not being accepted as such in the national picture of the United States has been part of their continuing penance. While being classified as Mexicans, which should bear no stigma at all, they do know, if more with the heart than with the head, that their own ancestry, language, and traditions are distinct from the Mexican, or perhaps that a difference ex-

---

[6] Fray Angelico Chavez, "Genizaros" in Handbook of the North American Indians, ed. Alfonso Ortoz, Smithsonian Institution, vol. 9 (Washington, D.C. 1979) pp. 198–200.
[7] Chavez, My Penitente Land, pp. xi, xii.

ists like the one between a horse and a jackass without their knowing which is which—sometimes afraid that they might be the latter.

The Mexican Nationals and Mexican-Americans, as they are referred to in this part of the country, are just that: children of a large and populous nation called Mexico with a very rich culture and history of her own. As a result, most of them have inherited all kinds of useful knowledges and skills which the Spanish New Mexican is quick to notice. Contrary to a greatly undeserved reputation, the Mexican loves to work, but he does not let the labor of his hands become the master of his heart, and its killer as well. Whether they be considerably Hispanic in descent or practically pure Indian as most of the poorer agricultural immigrants are, the Mexicans belong to one Mexican nation. For "Mexican" is a national term, not a racial one, except for the original Aztecs.

What is most admirable, these Mexican people are justly proud of their vitally intermixed descent and single national identity, while their love for their flag and their observance of patriotic dates are often more intense than those of most of us Americans regarding our own banner and the Fourth of July. Ever considered as aliens in this country, generations of their children born and reared in the big urban centers or agricultural syndicates in other parts of the great Southwest naturally fall back on their parents' and grandparents' national fealties by way of solace or mutual self-defense. The proximity to Mexico and a constant inflow of new immigrants do not help to relieve the problem.

In this regard precisely, the Spanish New Mexicans know that they are not aliens, but natives of their very own landscape for almost four hundred years. Except for the local Indians, all others are but recent immigrants. Unlike the Mexicans, however, they have not known what their original colonial banner was, or what it looked like, save for the nebulous fact that it was a "flag" borne by the only two historical figures that they can remember, Don Juan de Oñate and Don Diego de Vargas. From here they skip to the Stars and Stripes which they deeply love and for which so many have died in several wars with as much devotion as any other Americans.

But all the while they are most conscious of their own Spanish individuality, and yet—like my mother long ago—frustrated by their not being able to explain it. This is not only due to their long isolation from Spain and a developing New Spain more than two centuries long, or because their status as Mexican citizens was so brief, or even because their only education as well as their national allegiance have been exclusively American for almost a century and a half. These are mere externals. The real causes run much deeper in what one calls the native soul.[8]

SOME DEMOGRAPHIC CHARACTERISTICS

TOTAL POPULATION GROWTH

No precise information is available on the numbers of Hispanos, both in the past and at present. This is partly because, with one possi-

---

[8] *Ibid.,* pp. 266–267.

ble exception, no one has ever bothered to count them and because the group as a whole is not easily demarcated, as was indicated in our description of the people. For purposes of obtaining a broad, if not precise, picture, we may begin with the band of under 1000 persons led by Oñate in 1598 into present-day New Mexico. For the sake of statistical convenience, let us assume that there were 1000 Hispano-to-be persons in the year 1600.

The next date and count that seems reasonable is that of Fray Atanasio Dominguez,[9] who made an elaborate survey of the missions in 1776. His population count, obtained by visiting all the missions, came to slightly over 18,000 souls. "Adding the 7,480 souls in Rio Arriba to the 10,781 of Rio Abajo, they amount to (allowing for error) 18,261 souls who now live under the care of twenty priests." This count apparently included the Spanish-origin people plus the converted Indians who lived alongside them. Presumably, additional Spanish-origin people lived elsewhere in the Southwest, but since the large majority lived in the present states of New Mexico and Colorado, we may, for the sake of statistical convenience, set the number as about 20,000 in the year 1800.

For 1940, Zeleny provides an estimate of 260,000 to 270,000 living in New Mexico.[10] No information, apparently, is available for those Hispanos living outside of New Mexico. We conclude then that in 1940 there were between 300,000 and 400,000 Hispanos in the United States.

For 1970 we have our own estimate of about 850,000 living in the entire United States. This is based on the 1970 Census.[11]

The preceding population estimates provide the following average annual rates of growth: (a) 1600–1800, about 1.5% per year; (b) 1800–1940, between 2.0% and 2.5% per year; and (c) 1940–1970, between 2.5% and 3.0% per year. No population estimates are available for post-1970.

---

[9] Fray Francisco Atanasio Dominguez, The Missions of New Mexico, 1776, trans. and ed. Eleanor B. Adams and Fray Angelico Chavez (Albuquerque: University of New Mexico, 1956). The translators added, "Including Santa Fe, the total of the figures given in the manuscript for the Rio Arriba is 7550 persons, and for the Rio Abajo, including Pecos and Galisteo, 10,794, or a population of 18,344 in the interior missions [p. 217]."

[10] Zeleny, Spanish Americans and Anglo Americans, p. 126, and n.3: "Number of Spanish Americans in 1940 based on estimates included in George I. Sanchez, Forgotten People, 30 (for 1930), and Carey McWilliams, Brothers Under the Skin, 128 (for 1940)."

[11] This is the estimated number of persons who checked "Other Spanish" and were native of native parentage.

GEOGRAPHIC DISTRIBUTION IN 1970

The Hispanos had spread over the entire United States by 1970, although precise geographic information is not available. The southwestern states of California, New Mexico, Colorado, and Texas still contain an estimated two-thirds of the population. The remaining third are scattered, with some living in every state, including Alaska and Hawaii.

AGE AND SEX COMPOSITION

In 1970 the median age was estimated to be 19.3 years, as compared with 27.9 years for the total U.S. population (Table 5.1). Women were, on the average, about 1 year older than men. About one in eight was under 5 years of age, a reflection of the high birth rate.

As far as we can estimate, the median age has hovered between 19 and 21 years, at least back to 1850 (Table 5.2). In 1910 and 1850 men apparently were, on the average, 1 or 2 years older than the women. Why the median age seemingly rose between 1850 and 1910 and then had returned to its 1850 level by 1970 is difficult to say. Perhaps there are errors in the basic data, or perhaps changes in mortality, especially that of children, influenced the age composition.

However, the apparent stability over the last century, if not longer, impresses us more than do the possible small variations from one

TABLE 5.1

Estimated Age and Sex Composition of the Hispano Population: U.S. 1970

Age	Total	Percent	Male	Female
Total	826,350	100.0	403,950	422,400
0 to 4 years	105,550	12.8	52,750	52,800
5 to 9 years	116,150	14.1	59,150	57,000
10 to 14 years	108,700	13.1	53,150	55,550
15 to 19 years	95,650	11.6	49,150	46,500
20 to 24 years	77,350	9.4	34,350	43,000
25 to 29 years	55,000	6.7	25,500	29,500
30 to 34 years	47,400	5.7	22,750	24,650
35 to 39 years	40,050	4.8	19,500	20,550
40 to 44 years	40,300	4.9	19,000	21,300
45 to 54 years	62,050	7.5	30,600	31,450
55 to 64 years	41,400	5.0	20,200	21,200
65 and over	36,750	4.4	17,850	18,900
Median age	19.3	–	18.8	19.9

Source: Estimated from PUS data.

TABLE 5.2
Age and Sex Composition of Hispano Population, Estimated: U.S. 1850–1970

	1970[a]			1910[b]			1850[c]		
	Total	Men	Women	Total	Men	Women	Total	Men	Women
Total	100.0	48.9	51.1	100.0	52.4	47.6	100.0	51.2	48.8
Under 5 years	12.8	6.4	6.4	14.0	7.0	7.0	14.7	7.2	7.5
5 to 9 years	14.1	7.2	6.9	12.5	6.3	6.2	13.9	7.4	6.5
10 to 14 years	13.2	6.4	6.7	10.9	5.5	5.4	11.2	5.8	5.5
15 to 19 years	11.6	5.9	5.6	10.6	5.3	5.3	12.8	5.7	7.2
20 to 44 years	31.5	14.7	16.8	36.3	19.3	17.0	35.7	18.7	17.0
45 and over	17.0	8.3	8.7	15.7	9.1	6.6	11.7	6.4	5.2
Median age	19.3	18.8	19.9	21.4	22.7	19.9	19.0	19.6	18.4

[a]Estimated from 1970 Census.
[b]See Appendix D.
[c]From unpublished data for Bernalillo County; apparently transcribed from the 1850 Census by persons unknown. Data supplied by Mr. Larry D. Adcock of the University of New Mexico, Albuquerque.

period to another. By contrast, we note that for the total U.S. population the median age has increased rather consistently, from 18.9 years in 1850, about the same as that of the Hispano population, to 24.1 years in 1910 and to 27.9 in 1970.

The sex composition of the Hispano population has shifted from a majority of men in 1850 and 1910 to a majority of women in 1970. In this respect, this population has paralleled that of the total U.S. population. In 1850 and 1910, men constituted slightly over half of the total U.S. population; in 1970 women constituted a little over half.

SIZE OF FAMILY

In 1970 there were about 4.2 persons per Hispano family, as compared with about 3.1 persons for total U.S. population. In 1910 and 1850, average family size appears to have been almost the same, perhaps 4.3 persons. For total U.S. population, average family size in the nineteenth century was over 4 and may not have been too different from that of the Hispano population. Thus, whereas the total U.S. average decreased significantly, that for the Hispanos appears to have remained almost unchanged.

SUMMARY

So far, little demographic change except for total population growth appears to have occurred during the last century and longer. We believe, however, that in the next generation significant changes will occur that will result in the Hispano population more nearly resembling the U.S. population demographically. These are related to the increased schooling, discussed in the following section.

EDUCATION

YEARS OF SCHOOLING COMPLETED

We now come to a most important demographic factor: the increase in the amount of schooling that the Hispanos received. Since World War I, there has been a vast increase in schooling; how long before World War I this change may have begun we do not know. Of those who were of high-school-completion age around the time of World War I, about 1 in 5 actually completed high school. By 1970 close to 7 in 10 graduated from high school (Table 5.3). The rate of increase in high school graduation appears to have accelerated since World War II and is probably still rising.

Of those who completed high school, over 2 in 5 of the men and some 3 in 10 of the women (aged 20–24) entered college during the 1960s. Of those who entered college, about 1 in 3 completed 4 years.

The educational situation in 1910 appears to have been as follows: Among men age 21 and over, close to 1 in 5 (18%) was reported as illiterate, and among women we estimate some 2 in 5 (40%). However, among persons aged 10–20, only about 1 in 10 (11%) was so reported. This indicates that increased schooling must have begun around the turn of the century or earlier.

Individuals, however, could not have received very much schooling in 1910, judging from the reported school attendance rates: aged 6–9 years, 66% attending; 10–14 years, 91%; 15–17 years, 68%; and 18–20 years, 28%. This pattern suggests late entry into school and remaining only a few years, probably under 8 years.

The possible demographic consequences of increased schooling, however, evince themselves fully only upon the completion of high school. Certainly this is the case in the 1970s, when a "high school dropout" is considered to be a failure. So, increased schooling in the past, insofar as it did not lead to high school graduation, probably con-

TABLE 5.3

Years of Schooling Completed by the Hispano Population,
by Age and Sex: 1970

	Approximate period high school completion	% completed high school	% high school graduates entered college	% college entrants completed college
Men				
20 to 24 years	1965	68	44	17
25 to 29 years	1960	62	37	37
30 to 34 years	1955	56	40	38
35 to 44 years	1947	44	45	51
45 to 54 years	1937	40	39	51
55 and over	WWI	19	46	50
Women				
20 to 24 years	1965	67	32	13
25 to 29 years	1960	57	24	36
30 to 34 years	1955	51	23	33
35 to 44 years	1947	40	26	31
45 to 54 years	1937	33	30	31
55 and over	WWI	23	30	41

tributed but little to changing the demography of the Hispanos; this is
especially so since the Hispanos have always had less schooling than
has the U.S. Anglo society.

It is for this reason that we regard the rapid increase in education
following World War II to be particularly significant. Indeed, the rise in
high school completion between the end of that war and 1970 was
significantly greater for the Hispanos than for the Anglo population. If
the Hispano population should continue its accelerated rate of schooling, it may closely approach that of the latter within a decade or two.

In any event, considerable time is necessary before increased schooling evinces itself in changed demographic behavior. As a rule of
thumb, we should say that demographic consequences appear (in the
available statistics) only about a generation or longer after a population has become significantly more educated. Hence, we are suggesting
that the increased schooling since World War II is only now beginning
to show measurable statistical changes in demographic behavior.

SCHOOL ATTENDANCE, 1970

The extent of school attendance in childhood and the teens is an indication of the extent of final schooling; with rare exceptions, children who drop out of high school will not become college graduates as adults. Hence the rates of school attendance in 1970 are some indication of future levels of education.

Clearly, there was considerable increase in schooling in the two generations between 1910 and 1970. At the youngest ages, 6–9 years, the proportion attending school rose from around two-thirds to over 90%. At ages 10–14 years, there was little increase, with over 90% having attended school in 1910. In the later teens, the high school ages, there were significant increases in attendance by 1970, thereby increasing the probability of college attendance in the later 1970s. Nevertheless, in comparison with the non-Spanish white children, the Hispano children lagged.[12]

FERTILITY

A HISTORICAL NOTE

There may have been little change in the ratio of children under age 5 per 100 women aged 15–44 from the nineteenth century (and perhaps earlier) to the mid-twentieth century. From 1850 to 1960 this ratio, adjusted for child mortality so as to approximate the actual birth rate, was between 80 and 90 children per 100 women.[13] For 1850 and 1910, this is the best estimate we can make, since reliable data on child mortality are not available. For 1950 and 1960, we have more confidence in the available statistics and suspect that the rate may have been closer to 80 than to 90.

By 1970 this rate had plunged considerably to about 65 children (adjusted for child mortality) per 100 women aged 15–44.[14] This rate is still half again higher than that of the U.S. non-Spanish whites, which is about 40.

---

[12] See also Chapter 3 and Appendix Tables G–2 and G–7.

[13] Conceivably the rate might have been even higher if we had added an adjustment for census underenumeration of young children.

[14] A further adjustment for 1970 was made because in the case of outmarriages about 10% of the children born to Hispano women are reported in the 1970 Census as non-Spanish. Hence, the actual number of children under age 5 was increased by 10% and then adjusted for child mortality.

We suspect that this pronounced drop between 1960 and 1970 is a direct result of the increased schooling received by the younger women since World War II. The girls who remained in school and continued their education during the 1950s and early 1960s subsequently became mothers who bore children during the latter half of the 1960s. And they had fewer offspring.

Since the analysis possible on the basis of the ratio of children to women is limited, let us turn to an analysis of the number of children ever born.

CHILDREN EVER BORN ALIVE

The number of children ever born alive to Hispano women aged 15–44 (as of 1970) was 2.0 per woman. Among non-Spanish white women, the average was 1.6; Mexican-origin women averaged 2.2 children. Standardizing these rates so as to take into account the influences of age distribution, schooling, marital status, and employment, the rates become 1.8 for the Hispanos and 2.0 for the Mexican-origin women; the rate for the non-Spanish white women remains unchanged.

The influence of increased schooling leads to a reduction in fertility, holding the other factors constant. Hispano women who had completed high school averaged about 1.7 children, whereas those with less schooling had 2.4 children; this is a 30% reduction. Anglo women living in these five southwestern states averaged slightly under 2 children for those with under 12 years of schooling and something under 1.5 children for those with high school graduation or more. Hence, it is seen that Hispano fertility is greater than that of Anglos by about one-fifth to one-quarter.

The other factors—employment, marital status, and age—also influence fertility, and we can disaggregate[15] them for women aged 35–44 as follows: The combined influences of increased schooling, being employed, and being married and living with spouse lead to a reduction of 54% in the number of children ever born. This total reduction can be apportioned to: having completed high school, 26%; being employed, 20%; not being married and living with spouse, 28%; and the joint influences, 25%. All three factors contribute something, of which high school graduation contributes at least one-third when both its direct and indirect influences are considered.

Ethnicity of husband. Another factor that influences Hispano fertility is the ethnicity of the husband. Women married to non-Hispano

[15] See Appendix E.

husbands had about 20% fewer children than did those married to Hispano husbands. Also, those who had completed high school had about 20% fewer children than did those with less schooling; this holds both for those who married in and those who married out. The average number of children ever born to Hispano women age 35–44 is as follows:

| Wife's schooling | Husbands | |
	Hispano	Non-Hispano
Under 12 years	4.0	3.2
12 or more years	3.2	2.7

The same pattern is found at each age group.

It is significant to note that the combination of completing high school and marrying a non-Hispano leads to almost the same fertility level as that of the non-Spanish white women—the Anglos—in these five southwestern states. Anglo women aged 35–44 who had completed 12 or more years of schooling averaged 2.6 children ever born, and completion of college resulted in an average of 2.3 children.

Childhood language. Whether Spanish or English was spoken at home when the woman was a child also has an influence on her subsequent fertility. Among all women aged 35–44, we find that having been raised in an English-speaking home results in a decrease of 15–20% in the number of children ever born. Further decrease is attributable to increased schooling, and we have as follows:

Homes	Number of children
Spanish speaking	
Under 12 years of schooling	4.8
12 or more years of schooling	3.6
English speaking	
Under 12 years of schooling	3.9
12 or more years of schooling	3.1

Surname. Having a non-Spanish surname also resulted in lower fertility, as is shown for women aged 35–44 who were married and living with their husbands:

Surname	Number of children
Spanish	
Under 12 years of schooling	5.0
12 or more years of schooling	4.1
Non-Spanish	
Under 12 years of schooling	4.1
12 or more years of schooling	3.0

Both more schooling and a non-Spanish surname result in lower fertility. Each contributes around a 20% decrease.

CHARACTERISTICS OF WOMEN IN THE REPRODUCTIVE AGES, 1970

Table 5.4 presents selected characteristics of Hispano and Anglo women in the reproductive ages, by age and years of schooling. With regard to marital status, there is very little difference between the two groups. As for employment, somewhat fewer of the lesser-schooled Hispano women are employed, as compared with the lesser-schooled Anglo women. Among high school graduates, the proportions employed are very similar. The average number of children ever born per woman is higher for the Hispanos, especially for those who had not completed high school. Among high school graduates, the average number of children ever born, although still above that of the Anglo women, more nearly approaches the latter.

SUMMARY

The factors of education, employment, marital status, inmarriage and outmarriage, language spoken in home when a child, and type of surname, are all involved in influencing the level of fertility. As we see it, the extent of schooling permeates all other variables, and for that reason we ascribe considerable importance to schooling as the "engine of change."

Furthermore, all of these factors, with the exception of marital status, seem to indicate a changing society—one whose demographic characteristics at least are becoming similar to those of the general U.S. non-Spanish white society.

TABLE 5.4

Selected Characteristics for Hispano Women in the Reproductive Years, by Years of Schooling Completed: U.S. 1970

Age and characteristics	*Hispano*		*Non-Spanish white 5 Southwestern States*	
	Under 12 years	12 & over years	Under 12 years	12 & over years
15 to 19 years				
% married, spouse present	10.5	21.2	7.2	20.2
% employed	13.4	53.1	16.3	47.1
Av. no. children ever born per woman	.14	.14	.08	.12
20 to 24 years				
% married, spouse present	64.9	58.4	68.4	55.8
% employed	28.4	52.3	31.6	56.2
Av. no. children ever born per woman	1.61	.69	1.40	.50
25 to 29 years				
% married, spouse present	77.6	75.3	77.3	78.2
% employed	28.7	47.5	31.0	47.3
Av. no. children ever born per woman	2.65	1.62	2.45	1.45
30 to 34 years				
% married, spouse present	78.3	80.6	80.3	82.5
% employed	34.5	45.1	37.7	44.4
Av. no. children ever born per woman	3.55	2.51	2.93	2.26
35 to 44 years				
% married, spouse present	76.6	78.3	81.5	82.5
% employed	37.9	53.6	45.0	50.2
Av. no. children ever born per woman	4.19	3.08	3.03	2.59

THE ECONOMIC PICTURE

INTRODUCTION

Hispano society from its very inception was based on subsistence agriculture and livestock raising, especially sheep. There was little if any mining and virtually no manufacturing. Little trade existed during the seventeenth and eighteenth centuries. About the only other economic activity that existed during the seventeenth century was the search for a second Mexico city to be conquered and plundered, as Cortés had done earlier. This "industry" failed, so that only subsistence farming remained.

The Spanish government forbade foreigners to enter the northern provinces, and it was not until the Mexican revolution that the frontier was opened to foreigners. This meant trade with the United States. In 1822 the first successful trade expedition went from Missouri to Santa Fe along the Santa Fe Trail, and commerce became another economic activity. With the United States's acquisition of the Southwest, the volume of trade increased, and finally in 1880 the Atchison, Topeka, and Santa Fe railroad was completed.

Throughout the nineteenth century, there was a gradual increase in nonagricultural activities, but agriculture, subsistence or semisubsistence, apparently remained the major occupation for the large majority. Even commercial agriculture and livestock raising seem not to have been major activities on the part of the Hispanos; the commercial farmers were largely Anglos. The Hispano farmer eked out a living as necessary by working on one of the large ranches or the railroads or at some other job that required little skill. There were many conflicts between the Hispanos and the Anglos over land and water rights after the United States took over, and the Hispanos seemed to have lost out rather consistently. It is definitely not our purpose here to review the entire history of Hispano–Anglo relations. It is sufficient to point out that these relationships, or antagonisms, must have been important in pushing the Hispanos out of agriculture and into nonagriculture jobs, as such jobs arose.[16]

We have briefly reviewed the past in order to emphasize the complete occupational revolution that the Hispanos have undergone. By 1970 the proportion of men engaged in agriculture was between 3 and 4%, probably slightly below the proportion for the total U.S. population. The Hispanos have completed the transformation from subsistence farmers to nonagricultural employees. Let us now concentrate our attentions on the present.

LABOR FORCE PARTICIPATION AND EMPLOYMENT

Men. A little over three-quarters of those aged 16 and over were in the labor force in 1970 (Table 5.5). This rate is only slightly below that found among non-Spanish white men in the total U.S. population. The lower rate for the Hispano men is attributable, in large measure, to

---

[16] For a more complete description of the "agricultural life" led until well into the twentieth century, see, for example, Zeleny, *Spanish Americans and Anglo Americans;* and Robert Coles. *The Old Ones of New Mexico* (Albuquerque: University of New Mexico Press, 1973).

TABLE 5.5
Labor Force Participation and Employment Rates, Hispano Population, by Sex, Age, and Years of Schooling: 1970

	Total			Under 12 years			12 years			13 years & over		
	% in labor force	a/	b/	% in labor force	a/	b/	% in labor force	a/	b/	% in labor force	a/	b/
MEN												
Total	76.6	80.4	6.1	67.3	76.6	7.9	90.8	85.3	5.1	86.6	83.1	2.9
16 to 19	46.9	40.4	12.5	40.9	38.4	14.4	70.7	47.0	9.6	58.1	33.0	0.0
20 to 24	83.5	75.7	6.5	80.0	73.7	10.3	91.8	86.4	5.0	76.8	61.9	4.5
25 to 34	93.5	89.2	4.4	90.0	85.3	6.1	97.1	92.9	3.4	94.0	90.3	3.1
35 to 44	92.7	89.6	4.2	83.0	86.6	5.9	94.4	91.3	3.7	98.0	95.7	0.0
45 to 54	88.0	84.0	6.2	84.4	82.4	6.6	95.1	83.7	6.7	91.3	90.5	3.6
55 and over	53.1	79.6	7.3	47.5	80.5	7.2	77.6	81.4	8.5	74.2	78.7	6.4
WOMEN												
Total	40.9	65.2	8.5	31.8	59.2	10.0	50.5	70.6	8.9	60.8	68.8	3.3
16 to 19	33.9	45.0	13.0	23.0	30.5	16.9	63.2	61.5	10.6	51.6	43.8	0.0
20 to 24	47.7	71.1	9.4	30.9	57.6	15.3	53.9	75.7	10.4	60.7	73.1	2.8
25 to 34	42.0	71.0	6.2	36.6	65.3	6.3	42.6	73.6	7.1	59.7	77.5	3.8
35 to 44	45.6	63.9	8.4	40.1	63.8	9.2	51.2	65.9	8.1	60.5	59.6	5.8
45 to 54	51.4	81.0	8.7	45.0	66.7	10.9	58.7	67.9	7.4	78.3	59.6	0.0
55 and over	25.2	66.2	6.2	19.9	61.0	5.1	39.7	74.0	10.0	50.0	74.1	3.7
20 to 44	44.8	68.9	7.9	36.7	63.2	9.2	48.6	72.6	8.7	60.3	71.7	3.8

a/ Percentage of civilian labor force employed full time.

b/ Percentage of civilian labor force unemployed.

99

their lower level of schooling. Among men aged 20–64, almost all of whom have completed their schooling, we find that about half of the Hispanos have not completed high school; among the non-Spanish white men, however, only a little over one-third are not high school graduates. High school graduates are more likely to be in the labor force than are those with less schooling. Comparison of the two groups aged 20–64, by years of schooling, shows that only slightly fewer Hispanos were in the labor force in 1970 as follows:

Years of Schooling	Hispano (%)	Non-Spanish white (%)
Under 12	84	87
12	94	95
13 and over	89	90
Total population	88	90

Most of the Hispano men in the prime working ages, who were in the civilian labor force, worked full time. Those who had completed high school were slightly more likely to have worked full time as follows:

Years of Schooling	Hispano (%)	Non-Spanish white (%)
Under 12	83	86
12	89	91
13 and over	85	86
Total population	86	88

Unemployment was higher among the Hispano men in 1970, and highest of all among those who had not completed high school. The unemployment rates for men aged 20–64 years were

Years of Schooling	Hispano (%)	Non-Spanish white (%)
Under 12	6.6	4.1
12	4.3	2.7
13 and over	2.7	2.0
Total population	5.1	3.0

In summary, we note that if work is considered to be an advantage, then the Hispano men fare slightly worse in comparison with total U.S.

non-Spanish white men. However, among those who have gone to college, the differences—percentage in labor force, percentage who had worked full time, and percentage unemployed—were minimal. Again, we see the all-pervading influence of schooling.

Chavez's description of the attitude of his people toward work suggests that it is somewhat different from that of the Anglo people.

> Our castizo ['of noble descent'] horror for work is proverbial, as are our sly humor and our hoary idea that nothing debases a man so much as gaining his livelihood by means of a mechanical job. Such is the *castizo* Spanish soul, belligerent and indolent, passing from the violence of passion to complete apathy without bothering to blend the two in order to attain the sustained effort of labor. The poor Indians of El Dorado asked the Spaniards why they neither sowed nor reaped, and in vain did prudent minds in Spain argue that farmers be sent to America.
>
> Now, while recognizing themselves in what has just been said, some of my *paisanos* will not approve of my saying it. *But the fact is that I have made up these last five paragraphs . . .from phrases in Miguel de Unamuno's own assessment of his Castilian countrymen in Spain some decades ago!*[17]

If Chavez is correct, we can infer only that increased modern schooling is changing the traditional attitudes of the Hispanos and is, perhaps, making them more similar to their Anglo neighbors.

Women. Of Hispano women aged 16 and over, two in five were in the labor force in 1970. This rate is exactly the same as that for all non-Spanish white women. The participation rate increases sharply with increased schooling, from 32% among those who had not completed high school to 51% for those who just graduated from high school and 61% among those who had gone to college. This general pattern is found at all ages. From this pattern we deduce that in the future as the amount of schooling received by each age group increases, we can expect increasingly more Hispano women to work for pay or profit.

Among women in the childbearing ages of 20–44, 45% were in the labor force in 1970, only slightly less than the 49% observed among all non-Spanish white women. Again, the differences by amount of schooling are very pronounced: 37% among those who had not finished high school, as compared with 60% for those who had gone to college. These divergences reflect differences in fertility; the less educated have given birth to more children.

Furthermore, of those Hispano women who were in the labor force, very substantial proportions had worked full time. Among women aged 20–44, 63% of the non–high school graduates worked full time during

---

[17] Chavez, *My Penitente Land*, pp. 268–269.

the census week, as compared with over 70% for the high school graduates.

As for the extent of unemployment, this varied inversely with schooling among women, as it had among men. Of the least schooled (aged 20–44), 9.2% reported themselves as seeking work, as compared with 3.8% of those who had gone to college.

During the last two decades, there was a large increase in reported labor force participation. We estimate that in 1950, 2 women in 10 aged 14 and over were in the labor force; in 1960, 3 in 10; and in 1970, 4 in 10. These increases parallel, more or less, those of all women in the United States. Hence just as we are confident that there will be continued increases in labor force participation among all women, so are we confident that in future decades more Hispano women will be in the labor force. This projection, in turn, together with the increased schooling that we see in the future, implies lower fertility in the decades ahead.

CLASS OF WORKER

Among the Hispano men aged 25 and over, about 7 in 10 are private employees; 2 in 10, government workers; and about 1 in 10 is self-employed. In comparison with the non-Spanish white male workers, significantly more of the Hispanos are government employees and significantly fewer are self-employed (Appendix Table G–30). This distribution may reflect the labor market area in which so many Hispanos live. In the western region of the United States, about 17% of the employed non-Spanish white men are government employees, a somewhat smaller proportion than that of the Hispano men.

Among Hispano women aged 25 and over, the distribution by class of worker is about the same as for all non-Spanish white women in the United States, and in the western region about 2 in 10 are government workers, 1 in 20 is self-employed, and the remainder are private employees. Since the Hispanos are all U.S. citizens, there are no citizenship bars to government employment.

FAMILY INCOME

Average (median) income in 1969 of families in which the head was Hispano was $7770, or some $2320 less than that of non-Spanish white families. Income varied greatly in accordance with the number of earners in the family and the sex of the head. The more earners there are, the higher is the income, and families headed by men average higher incomes than do those headed by women, as follows:

	Head	
Number of earners	Men ($)	Women ($)
Total population	8450	3430
None	2440	1560
1	7330	3590
2 or more	9920	7050

The median income for all families depends, in part, on how many are headed by men, how many by women, how many have no earners, and so on. Among Hispano families, 14% were headed by women, as compared with 9% among the Anglo families. The distributions by number of earners are virtually the same for both groups.[18] (See Appendix Table G–31.) If Hispano families had been distributed by sex of head and number of workers in the same manner as were the non-Spanish white families, their median income would have been $7970—about $200 more than was actually observed. Thus, about 10% of the difference in average family income between the two groups can be largely attributed to the fact that more Hispano families are headed by women.

Of the remaining difference in average family income, some of it is probably attributable to regional differences in wage structures and industrial and occupational mixes and some to the lower educational level of the Hispanos. To what extent discrimination per se may be involved, if any, we do not know.

The question may be asked: Why are there relatively more families headed by women among the Hispanos? We do not know how much may be attributed to purely demographic factors, such as higher death rates among men, and how much to cultural factors. A separate study would be required to answer this question.

INDIVIDUAL EARNINGS

Men. Hispano men earned in wages and salaries and from self-employment on the average (median) $5800 in 1969. This is about 20% less than that of non-Spanish whites. As was pointed out in Chapter 3,

[18] Recipients of wages or salaries including the self-employed; excluded are persons who derive their income only from investments, pensions, and so on.

many factors can account for this difference, and we cannot explore this problem within the limits of our study.

Suffice it to say that earnings rise steeply with increased schooling (Table 5.6). Let us look at ages 35–44 and 45–64, for example:

	Median earnings	
Years of schooling	35–44 ($)	45–64 ($)
Under 12	6600	5930
12	7950	8700
13–15	9430	9860
16 or more	11,150	11,990

Men who had completed college earned almost double that of men who had not completed high school.

The earnings pattern of youth aged 14–24 is difficult to interpret. In the early teens many are still going to high school and work only part time, thus lowering the average for those who had completed less than 12 years of schooling. In the later teens and early twenties, many are still attending high school or college and working either part time or at inferior jobs simply to pay their school expenses; these also bring down the average earnings.

At ages 25–34 practically all men, except those who are attending postgraduate college, are available for full-time work. Among the graduate students—those with more than 16 years of schooling—those in their late twenties are the ones least likely to be working in the field for which they studied. It follows, then, that for men under age 35, the median earnings do not indicate the potential earning power of the more schooled. Hence we find that those aged 25–34 who were college graduates had earned only about 50% more than did the high school dropouts.

Among men aged 65 and over, only a select group are still earners. The more schooled often continue to work after this age, if not full time then part time. For the lesser schooled, involuntary retirement generally forces most of them out of employment.[19] As a result, in this age group the college graduates had earned almost three times that of the high school dropouts.

---

[19] By involuntary, we include poor health as well as the recently enacted Federal Age Discrimination in Employment Act which specifies age 70 (with some exceptions) as the minimum permissible mandatory retirement age.

TABLE 5.6
Earnings in 1969, Hispanos by Sex, Age, and Years of Schooling

Years of schooling	MEN						WOMEN					
	14 & over	14-24 years	25-34 years	35-44 years	45-64 years	65+ years	14 & over	14-24 years	25-34 years	35-44 years	45-64 years	65+ years
Total U.S.												
1st quartile	2,690	720	4,900	5,410	4,390	1,020	820	540	1,350	1,300	1,400	830
Median	5,800	1,870	7,010	7,580	7,090	3,170	2,350	1,230	3,010	2,940	3,320	1,900
3rd quartile	8,690	4,370	9,340	10,040	9,800	6,480	4,510	3,070	5,360	5,100	5,380	5,350
Variation*	1.03	1.95	.63	.61	.76	1.72	1.57	2.06	1.33	1.29	1.20	2.38
Under 12 years												
1st quartile	1,780	490	4,250	4,580	3,700	1,010	630	360	630	950	1,160	860
Median	4,940	980	6,010	6,600	5,930	2,620	1,600	730	1,510	2,320	2,720	1,760
3rd quartile	7,430	3,220	7,790	8,800	8,280	5,830	3,460	1,390	2,950	4,000	4,290	4,170
Variation	1.14	2.79	.59	.64	.77	1.84	1.77	1.41	1.54	1.31	1.15	1.88
12 years												
1st quartile	3,830	1,380	5,440	6,020	6,170	990	1,060	760	1,450	1,880	1,630	1,790
Median	6,610	3,190	7,420	7,980	8,700	5,210	2,950	1,980	3,380	3,600	3,790	4,620
3rd quartile	9,190	3,590	9,530	10,130	11,390	6,760	4,770	3,760	4,950	5,890	6,000	7,810
Variation	.81	.69	.55	.51	.60	1.11	1.26	1.51	1.03	1.11	1.15	1.30
13 to 15 years												
1st quartile	3,160	1,110	5,350	7,320	6,400	1,230	1,080	710	1,970	1,750	3,430	460
Median	6,380	2,320	7,950	9,430	9,860	5,410	2,820	1,800	4,310	3,690	5,760	910
3rd quartile	11,140	4,610	10,450	11,850	12,770	9,370	5,270	3,920	5,960	5,650	7,450	3,320
Variation	1.25	1.51	.64	.48	.65	1.50	1.48	1.78	.93	1.06	.70	3.14
16+ years												
1st quartile	5,990	1,730	6,090	7,790	8,200	970	2,450	1,050	3,560	2,340	4,400	760
Median	9,620	3,270	9,030	11,150	11,990	6,730	5,710	2,680	5,880	6,660	7,100	3,210
2rd quartile	13,800	5,850	11,470	16,250	20,110	13,320	7,890	5,980	7,850	8,540	9,620	8,860
Variation	.81	1.26	.60	.76	1.00	1.83	.95	1.84	.73	.93	.73	2.52

*Interquartile range divided by median.

Within each age and level-of-schooling group, there was considerable variation in earnings. Thus, some high school dropouts had earned more than did some college graduates. This is indicated in the line marked "variation" in Table 5.6. Between the ages of 25 and 64 the variation index is smallest, indicating that most men tend to earn around the average amounts. At the younger and older ages, however, the variation is much greater; this probably results from many part-time workers who have lesser earnings, so that the median earnings for the group do not indicate fairly the general level of earnings of all members. We note that among 14–24-year-olds, only 40% of those who worked in 1969 had worked 48 weeks or more; among those aged 65 and over, the proportion is 52%. Among men between ages 25 and 64, however, over 80% had worked 48 weeks or more in 1969.

Women. In comparison with men, Hispano women average half as much earnings or less—some $2400, as compared with $5800. However, direct comparisons are not possible, and we cannot say whether women are paid less for the same work, since (a) many more women work part-time during the year, thus lowering annual average earnings; and (b) men and women tend to work in different occupations and industries. We may express the median earnings of women as a percentage of that of men, with the following results:

Years of schooling	Age		
	25–34 (%)	35–44 (%)	45–64 (%)
Under 12	25	35	46
12	45	45	44
13–15	54	39	58
16 or more	65	60	59

Clearly, among the more schooled, the average earnings of women more nearly approximate those of men.

The index of variation for women is higher than that for men in almost all instances. This reflects the greater prevalence of part-year work for women, as seen in the proportions of all those who worked in 1969 who had worked for 48 weeks or more:

Age	Women (%)	Men (%)
25–34	49	81
35–44	53	83
45–64	65	80

OCCUPATIONS OF MEN

Historical notes. There was significant upgrading in the jobs held by Hispano men between 1950 and 1970 (Table 5.7). The proportion who were professional and related workers increased from about 1 man in 30 in 1950 to 1 man in 10 in 1970. At the other end of the occupational hierarchy, we see that in 1950 almost half the men were in lower-level jobs: laborers, service workers, and farmers or farm laborers. By 1970, however, only about one-fourth of the men were employed in such lower-level jobs.

One way of summarizing the occupational composition is to weight the occupations by the Census Bureau's Socio-Economic Status (SES) scores. These scores are 53 in 1970, 49 in 1960, and 40 in 1950.[20]

The same general pattern holds for each of the three age groups, although comparable data for 1950 are lacking. The SES values are

Age	1970	1960	Increase
14–34	52	42	10
35–44	55	50	5
45 and over	53	48	5

Despite this significant upward movement over the last 20 years, Hispano men were still lower on the occupational ladder in 1970 than were all men in the United States. Among the latter about 17% were in professional and related jobs, and only 15% were in the lower-level jobs of laborer, service worker, or farmer or farm laborer. The higher status of total non-Spanish white men is seen in the SES value of 59, as compared with 53 for Hispano men.

Most important to note is that the SES score for the younger men increased by 10 points between 1960 and 1970, whereas for men aged 35 and over the increase was only 5 points. This pattern is a direct reflection of the increase in schooling, especially at the younger ages, which we shall explore next.

The Significance of Schooling, 1970. Two personal characteristics are instrumental in placing a man on the occupational ladder. One is his age, and the second is the extent of his formal education. Age is important since all youth, however well schooled, have their first jobs at lower levels than they will eventually attain. By around age 35 or 40, most men have risen about as high on the occupational ladder as they

---

[20] Census Bureau, "Methodology and Scores of Socioeconomic Status."

TABLE 5.7

Estimated Occupational Distribution of Employed Hispano Men, by Age: U.S. 1950–1970

	All ages			Age 14 to 34		Age 35 to 44		Age 45+	
	1970	1960	1950	1970	1960	1970	1960	1970	1960
Total	100.0	100.0	100.0	100.0	100.0	100.0	100.0	100.0	100.0
Professional, technical, & kindred workers	9.8	6.4	3.4	9.8	7.1	11.5	6.5	8.4	5.1
Managers & administrators									
except farm	6.7	5.8	5.3	5.8	4.2	8.2	7.2	7.1	7.4
Sales workers	5.3	4.5	NA	5.8	4.9	4.2	3.6	5.1	4.5
Clerical & kindred workers	8.7	9.0	NA	8.9	9.6	8.1	8.3	9.0	8.6
Sub-total, sales & clerical	14.0	13.5	9.3	14.7	14.5	12.3	11.9	14.0	13.1
Craftsmen, foremen, kindred workers	21.9	20.0	16.9	18.4	17.4	25.3	24.8	26.0	21.0
Operatives except transport	16.0	NA	NA	18.6	NA	11.8	NA	14.1	NA
Transport workers	6.0	NA	NA	6.0	NA	8.5	NA	4.2	NA
Sub-total, operatives & transport	22.0	22.5	18.5	24.6	26.1	20.3	20.5	18.3	17.5
Laborers except farm	9.5	14.3	19.0	10.3	14.1	8.7	14.2	8.5	14.7
All service workers	12.2	10.0	7.1	12.8	8.9	9.2	8.6	13.4	13.1
Farmers & farm managers	0.5	1.4	5.7	0.4	1.3	0.8	1.7	0.5	1.3
Farm laborers	3.4	6.1	14.8	3.2	6.4	3.7	4.6	3.7	6.8

Source: 1970 estimated from PUS data. 1960 and 1950 estimated from census data on Spanish surnames for New Mexico and Colorado, adjusted to U.S. totals.

ever will. After that age most men simply hang on.[21] Accordingly, in Table 5.8 we present two age groups: (a) 14–34 years, during which time men are finding their initial step on the ladder; and (b) 35 and over, which represents about the highest rung that this population will ever achieve. Schooling operates within this lifetime cycle.

At each age, the more schooling a man has, the higher on the occupational ladder he is likely to be. This is shown by the SES scores in 1970, as follows:

Years of schooling	Score	Change
Under 12	45	–
12	55	10
13–15 years	65	10
16 or more	82	17

Graduation from college (16 + years) puts the Hispano man on about the same occupational ladder as the non-Spanish white college graduate. Among both groups, three in five were in professional jobs. The main difference between the two populations is that the majority of the Hispano professional men were in classical occupations—lawyers, librarians, religious workers, and so on (See Appendix F)—whereas among the non-Spanish white men, over half were in modern scientific occupations—architects, engineers, physical scientists, and so on. Overall, the SES score for college graduates is exactly the same for the two populations: 82.

The large proportion of Hispano men occupied in the lower level jobs simply reflects their lesser amounts of schooling, as we saw previously. At given levels of schooling, their occupational structure is fairly similar to that of the general population.

More detailed investigation of the state of New Mexico[22] of years of schooling (but not by age) indicates (Tables 5.9 and 5.10)

1. At the lowest schooling levels, the majority of men are employed at lower level jobs.
2. Each increase in number of years of schooling results in some upward mobility.

---

[21] For elaboration of this point, see A. J. Jaffe, "The Middle Years," *Industrial Gerontology*, special issue (September 1971).

[22] The data from New Mexico refer to all Spanish-origin men. For all aged 16 and over, 60% are Hispano; for those with under 8 years of schooling, 56% (44% Mexican origin) are Hispano; and for college graduates, 68% (32% Mexican origin) are Hispano.

TABLE 5.8

Major Occupational Groups, by Years of Schooling, Age, and Sex, Hispano
Male Population: *1970*

			TOTAL		
	Total	−12 years	12 years	13–15 years	16+ years
Total	100.0	100.0	100.0	100.0	100.0
Professionals, total	9.8	1.6*	(6.0)	(19.4)	63.8
Modern science	3.5	0.3†	2.3†	7.3*	(23.3)
Classical	4.5	0.8†	1.7†	5.3†	(37.9)
Semi	(1.8)	0.5†	2.0†	6.8†	2.5†
Managers, non-farm	6.7	(3.7)	(6.7)	(14.6)	14.2*
Employees	4.8	2.1*	4.6*	12.1*	12.1*
Self-employed	1.9	1.6*	2.1†	2.5†	2.1†
Sales	5.3	(3.7)	(6.0)	7.0*	10.4*
Clerical	8.8	(5.1)	13.2	(17.4)	3.3†
Crafts	21.9	23.7	26.1	(16.0)	2.9†
Operatives (except transport)	16.0	20.1	16.9	5.9†	0.8†
Transportation	6.0	7.2	(5.7)	5.3†	0.4†
Laborers non-farm	9.5	13.5	(6.8)	4.2†	0.8†
Farm managers	0.5†	0.6†	0.5†	0.3†	0.4†
Farm laborers	3.4	(5.8)	1.3†	0.6†	0.0
Service total	12.2	15.1	(10.7)	9.3*	2.9†
Household	0.0	0.0	0.0	0.0	0.0
Protective	(1.9)	1.6*	2.4†	2.5†	1.2†
Other	10.3	13.5	(8.3)	6.7†	1.7†
SES score	53	45	55	65	82

() 50–99 cases
*25 to 49 cases
†Fewer than 25 cases

3. With completion of high school there is significant upward movement.
4. Completion of part college provides somewhat more upward
   movement.
5. Graduation from a 4-year college contributes most to the higher
   occupations; at this level of schooling almost all men are
   employed in professional or managerial jobs.
6. Among men who have not graduated from high school, Spanish
   men have somewhat lower-level jobs (as measured by the SES
   scores) than do the Anglo men.
7. High school completion is a more or less equalizing level, and
   among those who have gone on to college, there are no SES differences.

There are some differences between Bernalillo County—a Standard

TABLE 5.8 (cont.)

	Age 14-34					Age 35+			
Total	-12 years	12 years	13-15 years	16+ years	Total	-12 years	12 years	13-15 years	16+ years
100.0	100.0	100.0	100.0	100.0	100.0	100.0	100.0	100.0	100.0
9.8	2.0†	5.7*	20.9*	(61.8)	9.7	1.4†	6.6†	16.7†	(65.2)
(3.3)	0.3†	1.2†	8.3†	24.5*	(3.7)	0.3†	4.2†	5.6†	22.4*
(4.3)	1.1†	2.1†	7.8†	31.4*	(4.6)	0.6†	1.2†	0.8†	(42.8)
2.2*	0.6†	2.4†	4.8†	5.9†	1.4†	0.5†	1.2†	10.3†	0.0
(5.8)	3.0†	5.5*	11.3*	13.7†	7.6	4.3*	8.7*	20.6*	14.5†
(5.3)	2.9†	4.3*	11.3*	13.7†	(4.2)	1.6†	5.1†	13.5†	10.9†
0.5†	0.1†	1.2†	0.0	0.0	(3.4)	2.7†	3.6†	7.1†	3.6†
(5.8)	3.7*	6.9*	6.1†	12.7†	(4.7)	3.6*	4.5†	8.7†	8.7†
8.9	4.1*	(12.5)	16.5*	3.9†	8.6	(5.9)	14.3*	19.0†	2.9†
18.4	18.5	22.0	16.1*	2.9†	25.7	27.8	33.1	15.9†	2.9†
18.7	22.7	22.0	6.5†	0.0	13.1	18.0	8.1*	4.8†	1.4†
(6.0)	6.8*	6.1*	5.2†	1.0†	(6.0)	(7.4)	5.1†	5.6†	0.0
10.2	15.4	7.8†	4.8†	1.0†	8.6	11.9	5.1†	3.2†	0.7†
0.4†	0.6†	0.3†	0.4†	0.0	0.6†	0.6†	0.9†	0.0	0.7†
3.2*	5.7*	1.4†	1.3†	0.0	3.7*	(5.9)	1.2†	0.0	0.0
12.8	17.4	9.7*	10.9*	2.9†	11.6	13.3	12.5*	6.3†	2.9†
0.0	0.0	0.0	0.0	0.0	0.0	0.1†	0.0	0.0	0.0
1.6*	1.1†	1.9†	2.6†	1.0†	2.2*	1.9†	3.3†	2.3†	1.4†
11.2	16.3	7.8*	8.3†	1.9†	9.3	11.3	9.2*	4.0†	1.5†
52	43	54	63	82	54	47	57	68	82

Metropolitan Statistical Area—and the remainder of the state, but this is to be expected, in part because of the urban-rural differences. The main difference, of course, is that there is a significant proportion of farmers and farm laborers outside of Bernalillo County.

As for college graduates, in New Mexico we see that the distinction between scientific and professional jobs previously noted in the total U.S. population is also found in New Mexico. Spanish men are more frequently found in classical occupations, whereas Anglo men are more likely to be in scientific occupations.

In summary, the Hispano who has a 4-year-college degree, and preferably a graduate degree, can compete successfully in the job market. If the situation was barely so in 1970, it will improve in the future, as more of the younger men acquire increasingly more schooling.

TABLE 5.9

Occupational Distribution of Spanish and Anglo Men, by Years of Schooling Completed: Bernalillo County and Remainder of New Mexico, 1970

	Spanish Schooling					Anglo Schooling				
	-8 years	8-11 years	12 years	13-15 years	16+ years	-8 years	8-11 years	12 years	13-15 years	16+ years
Bernalillo County										
Total	100.0	100.0	100.0	100.0	100.0	100.0	100.0	100.0	100.0	100.0
Professional, technical & kindred workers	1.6	2.5	8.0	26.3	65.3	5.0	6.2	14.1	29.1	67.2
Managers, administrators, except farm	3.5	4.9	9.5	11.8	18.6	11.2	12.1	16.9	18.7	16.5
Sales & clerical workers	5.8	9.7	20.6	34.0	12.1	9.1	14.3	21.2	25.7	11.4
Craftsmen	30.7	22.7	22.8	11.0	2.6	28.9	26.1	26.9	12.9	2.2
Operatives, laborers, service workers	56.8	59.5	38.6	16.9	1.4	43.6	40.6	20.5	13.0	2.4
Farmers & farm workers	1.6	0.7	0.5	0.0	0.0	2.2	0.7	0.4	0.6	0.3
Remainder of New Mexico										
Total	100.0	100.0	100.0	100.0	100.0	100.0	100.0	100.0	100.0	100.0
Professional, technical, kindred workers	1.6	2.5	9.8	25.9	67.4	2.2	3.5	9.7	22.3	66.2
Managers, administrators, except farm	3.8	6.0	9.0	14.2	17.6	8.4	9.3	16.1	19.1	17.5
Sales & clerical workers	3.3	8.6	15.8	22.2	7.8	5.4	9.3	12.3	15.2	7.4
Craftsmen	19.9	20.1	21.9	11.6	2.3	28.2	27.6	27.0	17.3	3.3
Operatives, laborers, service workers	54.6	57.5	40.2	21.8	3.6	41.5	41.5	26.8	19.3	3.0
Farmers & farm workers	16.8	5.3	3.3	4.3	1.3	14.3	8.8	8.1	6.9	2.5

Data for special tabulations kindly furnished by L. Adcock.

TABLE 5.10

Socioeconomic Status Scores for Spanish and Anglo Men, by Years of Schooling Completed: New Mexico[a]

Years of schooling	Bernalillo County			Change		Remainder of State			Change	
	Spanish	Anglo	Difference	Spanish	Anglo	Spanish	Anglo	Difference	Spanish	Anglo
Under 8 years	45	53	-8	–	–	39	46	-7	–	–
8-11 years	47	56	-9	2	3	46	50	-4	7	4
12 years	57	65	-8	10	9	55	57	-2	9	7
13-15 years	70	72	-2	13	7	66	64	+2	11	7
16 and over years	84	84	0	14	12	83	82	+1	17	18

[a]Occupational distributions as shown in Table 5.9 weighted by SES scores for major occupation groups as given in U.S. Bureau of the Census, "Methodology and Scores of Socioeconomic Status,"Working Paper no. 15 (1963), p. 13.

OCCUPATIONS OF WOMEN

Of the lesser-schooled Hispano women in the United States—those who had not completed high school—about three in four are found in blue-collar and service jobs (Table 5.11). The more schooling they have had, the more likely they are to be in white-collar jobs. Of those who have completed college, over three-quarters are in professional jobs, exactly the same as in the non-Spanish white female population. Furthermore, in both groups most of the professional women are in classical occupations, largely elementary and secondary school teachers.

Data for New Mexico (Table 5.12) provide direct comparison of the Hispano and Anglo women who are residing in a similar, but not identical, labor market area. The differences between the two groups are

TABLE 5.11

Major Occupational Groups by Years of Schooling, Age, and Sex, Hispano Female Population, 1970

| | | TOTAL | | | |
	Total	-12 years	12 years	13-15 years	16+ years
Total	100.0	100.0	100.0	100.0	100.0
Professionals, total	10.2	3.2*	5.8*	(21.7)	(77.5)
Modern science	(3.8)	0.7†	2.8†	13.0*	14.6†
Classical	5.6	1.9†	2.5†	7.0†	60.7*
Semi	0.8†	0.6†	0.4†	1.7†	2.2†
Managers, nonfarm	(3.4)	3.1*	3.7*	4.3††	3.4†
Employees	(3.0)	2.6†	3.1†	3.9†	2.2†
Self-employed	0.4†	0.5†	0.6†	0.4†	1.1†
Sales	6.1	5.8*	7.1*	6.5†	0.0
Clerical	33.9	14.9	54.7	46.5	13.4†
Crafts	1.6*	2.7†	0.6†	0.4†	2.2†
Operatives	12.3	21.3	6.2*	3.0†	1.1†
Transportation	0.7†	1.1†	0.4†	0.4†	0.0
Laborers, nonfarm	1.4*	2.7†	0.4†	0.4†	0.0
Farm managers	0.0	0.0	0.0	0.0	0.0
Farm laborers	0.2†	0.2†	0.1†	0.4†	0.0
Service total	30.0	44.9	20.7	16.1*	2.2†
Household	(4.3)	(8.6)	1.2†	0.0	1.1†
Protective	0.2†	0.2†	0.1†	0.0	0.0
Other	25.5	36.1	19.4	16.1*	1.1†
SES score	58	48	63	68	84

() 50-99 cases
*25 to 49 cases
†Fewer than 25 cases

TABLE 5.12

Occupational Composition of Spanish and Anglo Women, by Years of Schooling Completed: New Mexico, 1970

| | Spanish Schooling | | | | | Anglos Schooling | | | | |
	-8 years	8-11 years	12 years	13-15 years	16+ years	-8 years	8-11 years	12 years	13-15 years	16+ years
Total	100.0	100.0	100.0	100.0	100.0	100.0	100.0	100.0	100.0	100.0
Professional, technical, & kindred workers	2.3	3.1	8.2	20.7	80.7	4.1	4.4	8.9	24.6	78.8
Managers & administrators except farm	3.5	2.7	3.7	3.8	4.3	4.8	6.3	6.6	5.6	4.7
Sales workers	3.8	9.5	7.4	3.8	2.4	5.8	11.7	9.3	8.7	2.6
Clerical & kindred workers	5.4	17.9	47.1	53.6	9.8	10.2	25.1	50.9	48.4	11.3
Blue-collar workers*	19.2	18.1	10.4	5.5	1.2	21.2	12.7	7.4	3.9	0.9
Service workers except private household	44.8	41.1	21.0	12.1	1.0	40.0	34.9	15.2	7.7	1.4
Private household workers	21.0	7.6	2.1	0.4	0.5	13.9	4.9	1.7	1.1	0.2

Data from special tabulations kindly provided by L. Adcock.

*Including agricultural occupations.

not large, as shown by the SES scores (Table 5.13). Among those who did not complete high school, somewhat more of the Hispano women than of the Anglo are engaged in service jobs, including work in private households. Of women who have completed 4 years of college, on the other hand, there are no differences: 8 in 10 are professional workers, and the other 2 in 10 are found in other white-collar jobs. For both groups of women, as for men, it is clear that completion of high school results in marked upward change in occupational composition. Completion of college results in even more marked upward movement, and at this level of schooling almost all differences between the two groups disappear.

The professional jobs held by the college graduates in New Mexico are the commonly found "women's work," as follows:

Profession	Spanish (%)	Anglo (%)
Teachers	75	63
Registered Nurses	4	5
Other health workers	2	4
All other	19	28

The "all other" group includes a few accountants, physicians, writers and artists, and other miscellaneous workers. Professional women in New Mexico, whatever their ethnicity, have not yet penetrated the male professional occupations.

SUMMARY

The several series of statistics available suggest that the Hispano population is taking on the demographic characteristics of the larger society of which it is part: (a) increased schooling; (b) decreased fertil-

TABLE 5.13

Socioeconomic Status Scores for Spanish and Anglo Women, by Years of Schooling Completed: New Mexico, 1970

Schooling	Spanish	Anglo	Difference	Change	
				Spanish	Anglo
Under 8 years	42	47	−5	−	−
8–11 years	49	54	−5	7	7
12 years	62	65	−3	13	11
13–15 years	69	72	−3	7	7
16 and over years	86	85	+1	17	13

ity; (c) considerable outmarriage; (d) increased use of English at home; (e) increased occupational similarity; and (f) largely urban dwellers.

Where this will lead in another generation we cannot predict; we can only quote Fray Angelico Chavez:

> But when the landscape of New Mexico, already alienated for the most part, has been largely churned up by the bulldozer, and the air filled with English sounds in the accents heard from New England down to Texas, that is, when the old language of Cervantes is no more, it can only mean the end as an entity for an extremely small population. Their long experience of suffering has nothing to hang onto. On the one hand, the true Spanish New Mexican is steadily blending into the general English-speaking milieu, despite all the pride of surname he may keep or any desperate efforts at preserving local bits of folklore, social and religious customs, or native architecture. On the other, the one with *genizaro* antecedents tends to identify himself with what he considers his brown brethren from south of the border.[23]

---

[23] *My Penitente Land,* p. 272.

6

The Mexican Americans[1]

INTRODUCTION

What is now the independent country of Mexico has undergone vast cultural and political changes since the sixteenth century, changes that could have left their imprint on the Mexican-origin population living in twentieth-century United States. Prior to Cortés there were various In-

---

[1] We wish to remind our readers of the excellent study of Grebler, Moore, and Guzman, *The Mexican-American People.* Although the title of the book sounds very similar to the title of our chapter, the materials covered are largely different. By concentrating on only one ethnic population, Grebler *et al.* were able to cover many more aspects than we were able to do. On the other hand, we benefited from the additional statistics first made available in the 1970 Census, which Grebler and his coworkers did not have. In particular, the information for the various educational groups allowed us to investigate many dynamic aspects, something that cannot be done if the only educational data available refer to the entire population.

One point at which we disagree with Grebler *et al.* is their inclusion of the Hispanos with the Mexicans. As we have shown, the histories of the two groups are very different. Furthermore, and what is of the utmost importance, is that when asked in the 1970 Census, over 1 million persons designated themselves as "Other Spanish" rather than as Mexican. Of these, the great majority lived in the five southwestern states and were natives of native parentage. A total of only 155,000 persons of foreign stock gave "Spain" as their original country. Also, at the time of the 1975 Current Population Survey, some 1.4 million designated themselves as "Other Spanish" rather than as Mexican.

Finally, we note that at the time of the 1930 Census, "Mexican" was designated as a separate minority group. Very few persons were so returned in New Mexico and Colorado, since the Spanish "surname" or "language" people in these states were not considered to be Mexican. However, when Spanish "surname" was introduced in subsequent censuses, large numbers were reported in these two states.

dian cultures. The conquistadores imposed Spanish dominance and religion over the Indians and virtually enslaved them. These contacts, together with the interbreeding that occurred, gradually fused the Indian and Spanish cultures into a new one, partly Indian and partly Spanish. By the time of the 1810 revolution, the mestizos were powerful enough to drive out the Spanish army and establish an independent country called Mexico.

Throughout the nineteenth century, other factors influenced Mexican culture including the Austrian archduke Maximilian, a puppet of Napoleon III who became emperor of Mexico. The numbers of French who accompanied Maximilian contributed to the cultural diversity of the country.

Benito Juárez (1806–1872) became president after Maximilian was executed, and Mexico finally emerged as a nation under his leadership. The mestizo class was elevated to positions of power and became the rulers, and Indian blood was recognized. In a sense, the modern-day Mexican—the one who migrated to the United States—finally came into being in the last half of the nineteenth century. He is an acknowledged mixture of Indian, Spanish, and various other European bloods and influences. He differs from the Spaniard living in Spain, the Hispano living in New Mexico, and the natives of other Latin American countries, all of whom have had differing histories and been subject to differing cultural influences since the time of the original Spanish conquest.

SOME DEMOGRAPHIC CHARACTERISTICS

POPULATION GROWTH, 1850–1970[2]

For all practical statistical purposes, the saga of the Mexican Americans begins with the U.S. Census of 1850, which was the first to provide information on the number of Mexican born who were living in the United States. At that time there were 13,300 Mexican-born persons reported as living here. This number had increased to almost 220,000 by 1910, or about a seventeenfold increase.[3] Between 1910 and

---

[2] See also Appendix B, "Observations on the Historical Data about the Mexican-American Population."

[3] It should be noted that the figures for 1850–1900 are for the total Mexico-born population, whereas those for 1910–1970 are for the white Mexico-born population only. The difference is actually very slight, as out of the 221,915 persons listed as being born in Mexico and living in the United States in 1910, 219,802, or 99% were classified as being

1970 the number increased again to almost 750,000, or over a threefold increase (Table 6.1).

The numbers of natives of Mexican parentage grew from about 162,000 in 1910 to over 1.5 million in 1970, or almost a tenfold growth.

In addition, in 1970 there was a total of about 2.25 million persons of Mexican origin who were third and subsequent generations; that is, natives of native parentage.[4]

Thus, in 1970 there were an estimated 4.5 million persons of Mexican descent living in the United States. In the late 1970s, the Census Bureau, on the basis of a sample count, reported 6.8 million persons.[5]

The growth in the number of Mexico-born persons from one decade to another was quite erratic and apparently dependent on conditions in Mexico, as well as on the availability of economic opportunities in the United States.[6] The increase in the numbers of natives of Mexican parentage from one decade to the next, in turn, was dependent on the numbers of those born in Mexico and living in the United States; that is, the size of the parent generation, as well as its age and sex composition.

The large growth of both those born in Mexico and natives of Mexican parentage that took place from 1910 to 1920 and from 1920 to 1930 was apparently related to the combined effects of the Mexican revolution and the increased demand for laborers in agriculture, mining and the maintenance of railroads, particularly in the American Southwest.[7]

The decade of the 1930s appears to be the antithesis of the two that immediately preceded it. The Great Depression and the forced, and semiforced, repatriation of many Mexican Americans to Mexico were apparently of prime importance.[8] It is interesting to note that for the period 1930–1940 there was actually an increase in the number of natives of Mexican parentage, despite the attendant decrease in the

---

white. It was decided to use the white Mexico-born figures because between 1910 and 1950 the U.S. Census Bureau published data on a state basis only for the white population with respect to natives of Mexican parentage.

[4] Number estimated by subtracting the reported total white Mexican stock, as shown in Table 6.1, from the total of 4,532,000 persons who reported themselves as of Mexican origin in the 1970 Census.

[5] See Chapter 10.

[6] For example, it is not known how much of the reported increase between 1850 and 1860 was due to the inclusion of the Gadsden Purchase addition in 1853.

[7] Leo Grebler, *Mexican Immigration to the United States: The Record and Its Implications*, Mexican American Study Project, Advance Report no. 2 (Los Angeles: Division of Research, Graduate School of Business Administration, University of California, Los Angeles, 1966), pp. 20–21.

[8] *Ibid.*, pp. 25–29.

TABLE 6.1
Mexican Stock in Total United States (numbers in thousands)

Year	Mexico born Number	Mexico born Increase No.	Mexico born Increase %	Native White of Mexican parentage Number	Native White of Mexican parentage Increase No.	Native White of Mexican parentage Increase %	Total White Mexican stock Number	Total White Mexican stock Increase No.	Total White Mexican stock Increase %	Native White of Mexican parentage as % of total Mexican stock
1850	13.3									
1860	27.5	14.2	106.8							
1870	42.4	14.9	54.2							
1880	68.4	26.0	61.3							
1890	77.9	9.5	13.9							
1900	103.4	25.5	32.7							
1910	219.8	116.4	112.6	162.2			382.0			42.5
1920	478.4	258.6	117.7	252.0	89.8	55.4	730.4	348.4	91.2	34.5
1930[a]	639.0	160.6	33.6	450.0[a]	198.0	78.6	1089.0	358.6	49.1	41.3
1940	377.4	-261.6	-40.9	699.2	249.2	55.4	1076.6	-12.4	-1.1	64.9
1950	450.6	73.2	19.4	892.0	192.8	27.6	1342.6	266.0	24.7	66.4
1960	572.6	122.0	27.1	1152.3	260.3	29.2	1724.9	382.3	28.5	66.8
1970	746.3	173.7	30.3	1552.3	400.0	34.7	2298.6	573.7	33.3	67.5

Note: Mexico born figures during the 1850 to 1900 period are for the total population, whereas for the 1910 to 1970 period they are for whites only.

[a]Adjusted; see Appendix B.

Sources: The sources for these data were the decennial censuses which were conducted by the U.S. Bureau of the Census and its predecessor organizations:
  1. For Mexico born:
     A. 1940. Vol. II, Characteristics of the Population,Part I, U.S. Summary, p.43
     B. 1950. Special Report, Nativity & Parentage, Part 3, Chapter A, p. 71.
     C. 1960. Detailed Characteristics, U.S.Summary, Final Report PC(1)-1D, p.366
     D. 1970. General Social & Economic Characteristics, U.S. Summary, Final Report PC(1)-D1, p. 382.

  2. For White Natives of Mexican parentage:
     A. 1920. Vol. II, General Report & Analytical Tables, p. 897.
     B. 1940. Nativity and Parentage of the White Population, Country of Origin for the Foreign Stock, pp. 11 and 12. Contains figures for 1930 & 194
     C. 1950. Special Report, Nativity & Parentage, Part 3, Chapter A, p. 75.
     D. 1960. Detailed Characteristics, U.S. Summary, Final Report PC(1)-1D, p. 366
     E. 1970. General Social and Economic Characteristics, U.S. Summary, Final Report PC(1)-C1, p. 382.

number of Mexico-born persons. Still, the latter decrease was enough to offset the increase in natives of Mexican parentage, so that 1930–1940 was the only decade during which the total Mexican stock remained almost unchanged or perhaps decreased slightly.

Up until 1940, over half of the Mexican stock was born in Mexico. The 1940 Census showed that the natives of Mexican parentage outnumbered the foreign born. About two-thirds of the total Mexican stock was classified as native, and this proportion continued almost unchanged to the 1970 Census enumeration (Table 6.2).

The three decades of the 1940s, 1950s, and 1960s witnessed a renewal in the growth of Mexican stock in the United States. In both relative and absolute terms, Mexico-born persons and natives of Mexican parentage increased progressively during each of the decades. Thus, the growth of the total Mexican stock has actually been accelerating since the 1930s.

GEOGRAPHIC DISTRIBUTION, 1970

At this time of all Mexican-origin persons (including natives of native parentage), the great majority lived in California and Texas. Most of the remainder lived in Arizona, Colorado, Illinois, and New Mexico; the others resided throughout the remaining 44 states and the District of Columbia as follows:

Area	Mexican-origin population
Total United States	4,532,000
California	1,857,000
Texas	1,619,000
Arizona	240,000
Illinois	160,000
New Mexico	119,000
Colorado	104,000
All other States	433,000

The five Southwest states contained close to 4 million, or almost 9 in 10 of all those of Mexican descent.

HISTORICAL REDISTRIBUTION, 1870–1970

California and Texas. The Mexican stock (foreign born plus natives of foreign parentage) has been and still was in 1970 largely concentrated in two states: California and Texas. Throughout the period 1850–1970, between 70% and 80% of all Mexico-born persons[9] living

---

[9] The figures for Mexico-born persons that are used in the distribution analysis are for all persons born in Mexico, rather than for whites only, except for 1940 and 1950, when only data for whites were available. This will improve coverage somewhat, although as mentioned in Footnote 3, less than 1% of the Mexican stock was classified as nonwhite.

TABLE 6.2
Percent/Distribution of the Mexican Stock in the Southwest and Other States: 1850–1970

	1850	1860	1870	1880	1890	1900	1910	1920	1930	1940	1950	1960	1970
Mexico born	100.0	100.0	100.0	100.0	100.0	100.0	100.0	100.0	100.0	100.0	100.0	100.0	100.0
Five Southwestern States	92.2	96.2	95.9	97.2	96.8	96.9	91.6	89.1	85.0	88.5	88.4	87.2	85.9
California	48.5	33.3	22.0	12.6	9.2	7.8	15.2	18.2	31.1	35.6	36.0	43.2	54.1
Texas	33.5	45.2	54.2	63.1	66.2	68.7	56.3	51.8	41.5	42.2	43.5	35.1	25.5
Subtotal	82.0	78.6	76.2	75.7	75.4	76.5	71.5	70.0	72.6	77.8	79.5	78.3	79.6
Arizona,Colorado, New Mexico	10.2	17.6	19.7	21.5	21.4	20.4	20.1	19.1	12.4	10.7	8.9	8.9	6.3
Illinois	.2	.1	.2	.1	.2	.2	.3	.8	3.4	2.7	2.8	4.4	6.6
Remaining 42 contiguous states	7.6	3.7	3.9	2.7	3.0	2.0	8.1	10.1	11.6	8.8	8.8	8.4	7.5
Population (in 000)	13.3	27.5	42.4	68.4	77.9	103.4	221.9	486.4	641.5	377.4	450.6	575.7	759.4
Natives of Mexican parentage	--	--	--	--	--	--	100.0	100.0	100.0	100.0	100.0	100.0	100.0
Five Southwestern States	--	--	--	--	--	--	97.9	95.5	92.7	90.8	88.6	87.0	85.3
California	--	--	--	--	--	--	10.8	16.2	22.2	31.5	35.7	38.6	44.4
Texas	--	--	--	--	--	--	67.0	59.5	51.5	46.5	42.4	39.1	32.8
Subtotal	--	--	--	--	--	--	77.8	75.7	73.7	78.0	78.1	77.7	77.2
Arizona, Colorado, New Mexico	--	--	--	--	--	--	20.1	19.8	19.0	12.8	10.5	9.3	8.1
Illinois	--	--	--	--	--	--	.1	.3	1.2	1.9	2.5	3.2	4.3
Remaining 42 contiguous states	--	--	--	--	--	--	2.0	4.2	6.1	7.3	8.9	9.8	10.4
Population (in 000)	--	--	--	--	--	--	162.2	252.0	847.8	699.2	892.8	1159.0	1577.8

Note: Mexico-born figures for 1940 and 1950 are for whites only, whereas for the other dates they are for total Mexico-born. Natives of Mexican parentage figures are for whites only, except for 1960 and 1970, when the total population is considered. The 1930 figures are those listed in the 1930 Census and are thus uncorrected.

in the United States resided in these two states. Of the natives of Mexican parentage, between 7 and 8 in 10 resided in these two states during the decades from 1910 to 1970 (Table 6.2). Presumably, in earlier decades these natives had also been largely concentrated, as were their parents, in California and Texas.

Apparently the distribution of the Mexican stock between these two states has fluctuated from time to time in accordance with economic opportunities. In 1850 California contained almost half of the Mexico-born population, and Texas, only about one-third. This probably reflected the influence of the California gold rush.

From 1860 to 1900 the proportion in California declined drastically to less than 1 in 10, whereas in Texas it had increased to over two-thirds by 1900. This shift reflects the rise of the cattle industry and perhaps the expansion of agricultural crops, such as cotton. In any event, during this 40-year period there was only a moderate increase, as compared with later decades (see Table 6.1), in the total number of Mexico-born persons in the United States. Accordingly, even relatively small increases in economic opportunities in Texas as compared with California were sufficient to redistribute the population from California to Texas.

Beginning around the turn of the century, agriculture began to grow in California, and the proportion of Mexico-born persons in this state also began to grow rapidly. By 1910 the proportion of this group in California had increased to 15% and in Texas had decreased to 56%. With the continued growth of job opportunities in California as compared with Texas, the population of the former state grew rapidly, in terms of both Mexican stock and others.

The distribution of the natives of Mexican parentage followed suit. In 1910 only 11% were in California, and two-thirds were in Texas. In subsequent decades, the proportion in California rose rapidly, whereas in Texas it declined.

By 1970 about half of the Mexican stock lived in California, and about 30% in Texas. (See Figures 6.1 through 6.4.) There were about 1,100,000 persons in the former state and about 700,000 in the latter.

Arizona, Colorado, and New Mexico. These states, when added to California and Texas, constitute the Census Bureau's "Five Southwestern States." However, none of the three, either separately or together, ever contained a large proportion of the Mexican stock. In 1850 they held only 1 in 10 of the Mexico-born population. By 1870 this proportion had increased to 2 in 10 (or one-fifth) and remained around

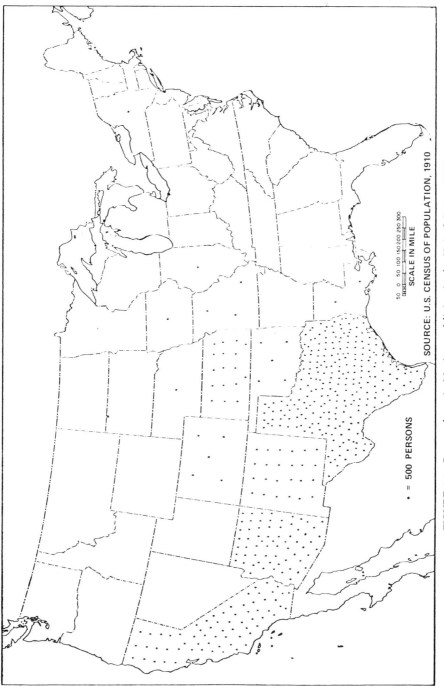

= 500 PERSONS

SCALE IN MILE
50 0 50 100 150 200 250 300

SOURCE: U.S. CENSUS OF POPULATION, 1910

FIGURE 6.1. *Persons born in Mexico and living in the United States, 1910.*

126

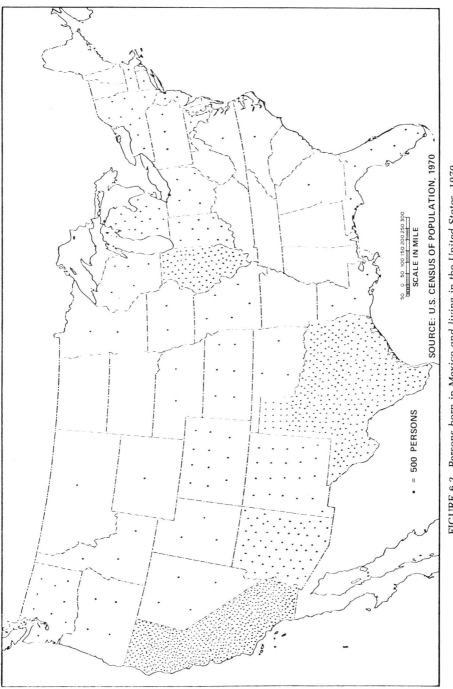

• = 500 PERSONS

50 0 50 100 150 200 250 300

SCALE IN MILE

SOURCE: U.S. CENSUS OF POPULATION, 1970

FIGURE 6.2. *Persons born in Mexico and living in the United States, 1970.*

127

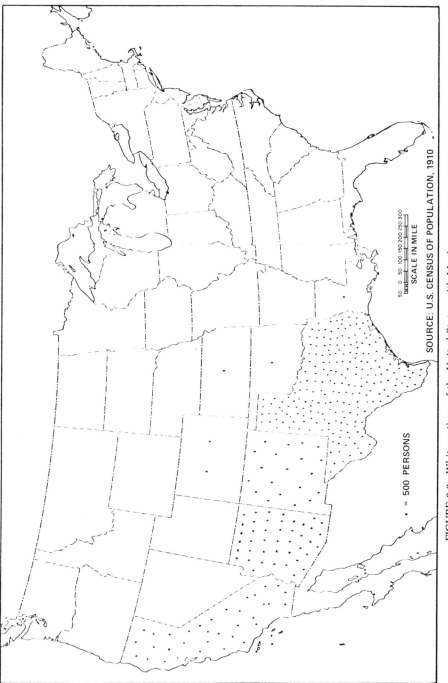

• = 500 PERSONS

SOURCE: U.S. CENSUS OF POPULATION, 1910

SCALE IN MILE

50 0   50 100 150 200 250 300

FIGURE 6.3. *White natives of the United States with Mexican parentage, 1910.*

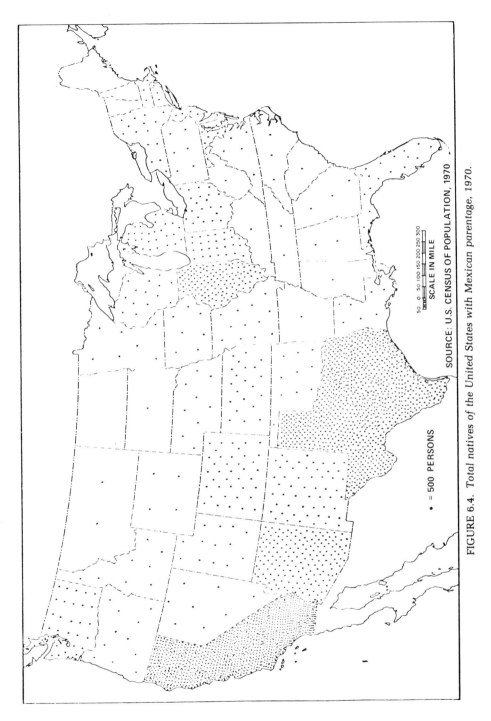

• = 500 PERSONS

50 0 50 100 150 200 250 300

SCALE IN MILE

SOURCE: U.S. CENSUS OF POPULATION, 1970

FIGURE 6.4. *Total natives of the United States with Mexican parentage, 1970.*

this figure until 1920. One-fifth of the natives of Mexican parentage also resided in these three states in 1910 and 1920.

Since 1920 the proportions of Mexico-born persons and natives of Mexican parentage declined significantly in Arizona, Colorado, and New Mexico. By 1970 only about 7% of the Mexican stock was living here.

There were considerable numbers of persons: (a) who were natives of native parentage; (b) who considered themselves to be of Mexican descent; and (c) who lived in these states in 1970. If we add in these third and subsequent generations, we find that about 10% of all persons of Mexican descent lived in these three states.

Remaining States. Of the remaining 43 contiguous states, only Illinois contained a significant number of persons of Mexican stock. Indeed, in 1970 Illinois contained more such persons than did Arizona, Colorado, or New Mexico. Illinois's rise to fame by 1970 (it contained about 5% of the total Mexican stock by this date) is of recent origin. In 1910 and earlier, there were almost none; and even in 1950 this state contained only some 2.5% of the total Mexican stock. The remaining 42 contiguous states altogether included less than 1 in 10 of the Mexican stock in 1970. This percentage has been fairly constant since 1910.

Summary. Figures 6.1 through 6.4 clearly illustrate the major redistributions that occurred between 1910 and 1970. Several of the more important characteristics are as follows:

1. California's ascendency over Texas for both Mexico-born persons and the natives of Mexican parentage is clearly visible.
2. The rather large growth in Illinois stands out.
3. The scattering of persons, particularly the natives of Mexican parentage, into the Northeast, Florida, southern Great Plains, southern Mountain states, and the Northwest is also evident. The Southeast, except for Florida, and northern tier of states, except for Washington, are largely empty of Mexican stock.

This redistribution of population in large measure reflects the redistribution of economic opportunity for persons of Mexican stock. The availability of black labor in the Southeast and the large scale migration of southern blacks, Puerto Ricans, Cubans, and other Spanish Americans into the Northeast probably largely curtailed economic opportunities for Mexican labor in those two areas. In the

Southwest and California, however, there were ample job opportunities for Mexican- and Asian-origin workers.

URBAN–RURAL DISTRIBUTION

More of the Mexicans were urban dwellers in 1970 than was the case among the general U.S. population. Among the former, 85% lived in urban areas, as compared with a little less than three-quarters of the latter (Table 6.3). Conversely, many fewer lived on farms or in rural nonfarm areas.

The situation in 1970 was quite different from that in earlier decades. In 1910 the Mexican population was only about one-third urban, considerably below that of the total U.S. population. Although there was a considerable increase in the proportion of Mexican Americans living in urban areas between 1910 and 1930, even at the latter date somewhat fewer of them lived in urban areas, as compared to the total population. Since 1930 there was a rapid increase in the extent of urbanization of the Mexican population, so that by 1970 a proportion larger than that of the the total U.S. population was living in urban areas.

About one in four Mexican Americans lived in cities of 1 million or more population in 1970, the large majority—over 800,000—in Los Angeles; Chicago and Houston had over 100,000 each. In contrast, of the total U.S. population, less than 1 in 5 lived in these very large cities.

AGE AND SEX COMPOSITION

There has been little change in the median age of the Mexican-origin population in the United States since 1910 (Table 6.4). Estimates for 1910, 1930, 1970, and the latter 1970s indicate the median has fluctuated only slightly between 19 and 21 years over the close to 70-year period. This is considerably younger at each time period than is the median age of the total population of the United States, which was 24 years in 1910, 26.4 in 1930, and 28.1 years in 1970. This younger age composition is to be expected, considering that Mexican Americans have had significantly higher fertility than has the total U.S. non-Spanish white population.

In both 1910 and 1930, Mexican-American men appear to have been somewhat older than were the women, insofar as more of them were aged 20 and over. Men also had somewhat larger proportions in the young adult and middle years of life. By 1970, however, Mexican-American women had slightly higher proportions in these age groups

TABLE 6.3
Urban–Rural Composition of the Mexican-Descent Population by Nativity, and Total U.S. Population: 1910, 1930, 1970

| | MEXICAN DESCENT | | | | | | | TOTAL U.S. | | |
| | 1910 | 1930 | | | 1970 | | | 1910 | 1930 | 1970 |
	Total	Total	Native	Foreign born	Total	Native	Foreign born			
Total	100.0	100.0	100.0	100.0	100.0	100.0	100.0	100.0	100.0	100.0
Urban	32.4	50.9	46.4	56.8	85.5	85.0	87.9	45.7	56.2	73.5
Rural	67.6	49.1	53.6	43.2	14.5	15.0	12.1	54.3	43.8	26.5
Nonfarm	NA	25.1	25.6	24.5	12.9	13.4	10.5	NA	19.3	22.4
Farm	NA	24.0	28.0	18.7	1.6	1.6	1.6	NA	24.5	4.1

TABLE 6.4

Age and Sex Composition of the Population of Mexican Descent: 1910, 1930, 1970

Age	1910			1930			Numbers (000) 1970			Percent 1970		
	Total	Male	Female	Total	Male	Female	Total	Male	Female	Total	Male	Female
Total	100.0	52.5	47.5	100.0	53.2	46.7	4532.4	2245.3	2287.1	100.0	49.5	50.5
Under 5 years	13.7	6.9	6.8	15.1	7.5	7.6	583.7	289.9	293.8	12.9	6.4	6.5
5 to 9 years	12.7	6.4	6.2	14.5	7.3	7.2	635.0	318.9	316.2	14.0	7.0	7.0
10 to 14 years	11.2	5.7	5.6	10.4	5.3	5.1	597.1	301.3	295.8	13.2	6.7	6.5
Under 15 years	37.6	19.0	18.6	40.0	20.1	19.9	1815.8	910.0	905.8	40.1	20.1	20.0
15 to 19 years	10.4	5.2	5.2	9.7	4.8	4.8	509.4	255.4	254.0	11.2	5.6	5.6
20 to 44 years	40.8	21.8	19.0	38.4	21.7	16.7	1469.6	717.0	752.6	32.4	15.8	16.6
20 to 24 years	–	–	–	10.3	5.7	4.6	382.5	184.8	197.7	8.4	4.1	4.3
25 to 29 years	–	–	–	9.5	5.4	4.1	308.1	150.3	157.8	6.8	3.3	3.5
30 to 34 years	–	–	–	7.1	4.1	3.0	274.1	132.6	141.5	6.1	2.9	3.1
35 to 44 years	–	–	–	11.5	6.6	4.9	505.0	249.3	255.6	11.1	5.5	5.6
15 to 44	51.2	27.0	24.2	48.1	26.5	21.5	1979.0	972.3	1006.6	43.7	21.5	22.2
45 to 54 years	–	–	–	6.7	3.8	2.9	336.8	168.3	168.6	7.4	3.7	3.7
55 to 64 years	–	–	–	3.2	1.8	1.4	212.2	103.0	109.2	4.7	2.3	2.4
65 to 74 years	–	–	–	1.4	0.8	0.6	127.3	62.7	64.6	2.8	1.4	1.4
75+ years	–	–	–	0.6	0.3	0.3	61.2	28.9	32.3	1.4	0.6	0.7
45+ years	11.2	6.5	4.7	11.9	6.6	5.3	737.5	362.9	374.7	16.3	8.0	8.3
Median	21.3	22.4	20.0	20.1	21.5	18.5	–	–	–	19.3	19.0	19.6

Sources: See Appendix B fof derivation of estimated age-sex composition of Mexican Americans in 1910. 1930 data from U.S. Bureau of the Census, Fifteenth Census of the United States: 1930. Population. Vol. II, "General Report, Statistics by Subjects," Chapter 10. 1970 data from PC(2)16. Table 3.

than did men. The percentages in the age range of 15–44 years are as
follows:

Year	Total (%)	Men (%)	Women (%)
1910	51.2	51.7	50.8
1930	48.1	49.8	46.1
1970	43.7	43.3	44.0

A major factor explaining the predominance of men in these ages in the
early decades of the twentieth century was the sizable immigration of
Mexican workers during this period.

The sex composition has also shifted from a preponderance of males
to females during this period. Again, this reflects the increased proportions of natives in the Mexican population. About 53 % of the Mexican-
American population was male in both 1910 and 1930; the sex ratios
were 113 and 114, respectively. By 1970, 49.5 % of the Mexican population was male; the sex ratio was 98.

As we noted earlier in this chapter, there was considerable
geographic redistribution of the Mexican population between 1910 and
1930 and between 1930 and 1970, primarily from Texas to California.
In the 2 decades between 1910 and 1930, men clearly predominated in
this movement. Texas, in 1910, had been settled by Mexican
Americans for a long time and held about 60% of the total foreign
stock of that population who were living in the United States. By 1930
the sex ratio in Texas was only 106. In California, on the other hand,
where the Mexican stock grew very rapidly during these 2 decades, the
sex ratio was 118. In Illinois, where there also was considerable growth
between 1910 and 1930, the sex ratio was 170 in 1930. The sex ratios in
other areas as well clearly indicate that men took the lead in the
geographic redistribution. Either Mexico-born males went directly to
California and states outside of the Southwest or men already residing
in the Southwest moved to other states.

Although the sex ratio has declined considerably since 1930, in 1970
Mexican-descent men in states outside the five southwestern states still
outnumber women. In Texas and California, for example, the sex ratios
are 99 and 95, respectively. By contrast, the sex ratio in Illinois was
109, and it was 105 in all other outlying states. It appears, then, that
whereas the contribution of immigration to high sex ratios among Mexican Americans has declined considerably, the continued redistribution of Mexicans outside areas of traditional residence appears to be

led by men. As we noted previously, this redistribution is undoubtedly linked to economic opportunities.

SIZE OF FAMILY

In 1970 there were about 4.6 persons per Mexican family, as compared with 3.1 for the total United States. Mexican families were larger than Hispano, Puerto Rican, and Cuban families, which averaged 4.2, 4.0, and 3.7 persons, respectively.

EDUCATION

YEARS OF SCHOOLING COMPLETED

Perhaps the single most important change in the sociodemographic characteristics of Mexican Americans in the last several decades has been the increase in educational attainment. Although still lagging about a generation behind the total population as of 1970, overall levels of schooling have improved considerably since the early decades of the twentieth century.

Since detailed educational attainment data are not available in published form, historical trends have been estimated on the basis of age. Knowing the age of the person, we know in about what time period he or she would have been of elementary school age, of secondary school age, and of college age. Hence, we can estimate the amount of schooling received in the several historical time periods.

In addition to age, another important indicator of educational attainment is nativity. Native persons generally have received more formal schooling than have their foreign-born parents or grandparents. This is most clearly evident in the younger age groups. Over time, the U.S.-born Mexicans have become an increasingly larger proportion of the total population of Mexican descent, and we can expect this proportion to continue to increase over the next several decades. Thus, the educational level of the younger native Mexican-American population is an indicator of their socioeconomic status in future decades.

The decades since World War I witnessed a vast increase in schooling; for the period prior to that time, we have little information. Based on educational data for 1970, about 1 in every 10 Mexican Americans who were of high-school-completion age about the time of World War I had actually completed high school (Table 6.5). By about the end of World War II, 1 in 5 was a high school graduate. By comparison, ap-

TABLE 6.5

Years of Schooling Completed by the Mexican–Origin Population, by Age, Sex, and Nativity: 1970

Age	Approximate period high school completion	% completed high school Native	% completed high school Foreign born	% high school graduates entered college Native	% high school graduates entered college Foreign born	% college entrants completed college Native	% college entrants completed college Foreign born
MEN							
20 to 24 years	1965	56	38	34	38	9	14
25 to 29 years	1960	50	28	35	39	25	27
30 to 34 years	1955	41	22	35	42	37	40
35 to 44 years	1947	30	15	39	45	35	56
45 to 54 years	1937	20	17	33	42	38	38
55 and over	WWI	9	9	36	44	31	40
WOMEN							
20 to 24 years	1965	53	32	26	25	9	15
25 to 29 years	1960	45	26	20	29	34	30
30 to 34 years	1955	38	19	22	29	35	39
35 to 44 years	1947	25	17	20	31	30	39
45 to 54 years	1937	16	16	18	31	31	27
55 and over	WWI	9	9	26	36	33	39

proximately half of both men and women aged 20–24 in 1970 had graduated from high school. It appears, then, that the rate of increase in high school completion has actually accelerated since the end of World War II and is still rising.[10]

On the basis of data on illiteracy in 1910 and 1930 censuses, the situation at that time appears to have been that (a) about 3 in 10 in the Mexican-American population aged 10 and over were reported as illiterate in both 1910 and 1930;[11] and (b) the foreign born had higher illiteracy rates than did the natives: 32% versus 22% in 1930.[12]

---

[10] See Chapter 10.

[11] In 1930 the census figures for illiteracy were total aged 10 and over, 27.5%; men, 24.5%; and women, 31.1%. For 1910 the proportions illiterate are not as precisely known. However, we believe that they were about the same magnitude for both dates. Illiteracy is defined by the U.S. Census Bureau as the inability to read and write in *any* language. Thus, if the Mexican Americans had been literate in Spanish only, they would have been recorded as being literate.

[12] In Mexico in 1930 the illiteracy rate was about double that reported for the Mexican Americans. This difference may have been due to any one or a combination of the following: (a) differences in census procedures, although on the surface they appear to have been similar; (b) selective migration; and (c) the possibility that some of the younger immigrants attended school in the United States and became literate.

These illiteracy rates were far higher than were those of the general population. In 1910 the general rate was 7.7%; it decreased to 4.3% in 1930. In a way, perhaps it is not surprising that the Mexican-American rate did not decrease, since this population was continuously augmented by numbers of illiterate immigrants.[13]

Although school attendance rates increased significantly between 1910 and 1930, it is safe to say that the majority of Mexican Americans in 1930 were not well schooled. The attendance rates in 1910 and 1930 are as follows:

Mexican Americans				U.S. population		
1910		1930				
Age	Percentage	Age	Percentage	Age	1910 (%)	1930 (%)
6–14	54	7–13	79	7–13	63	95
15–17	36	14–17	52	14–17	59	73
18–20	8	18–20	8	18–20	15	21

What school attendance may signify in terms of intellectual achievement, however, is difficult to say. Children can go to school for many years without advancing beyond the third or fourth grade. Indeed, this was the general picture in Texas, as presented by Kibbe,[14] for the pre–World War II period and the war years.

We can view the end results of school attendance by noting the average (median) number of years of schooling completed. Those who were of school attendance age in 1910 managed to complete an average of about 5 years of schooling. Those who were of school attendance age in 1930 reported about 7 years of schooling completed.[15]

Even 7 years of completed schooling, however, is unimportant relative to the total U.S. population. The 1910 school-age population

---

[13] About two-thirds of the population aged 10 and over and living in Mexico was illiterate in 1910. That this prevalence of illiteracy continued past 1930 is clear, for as recently as 1970 almost 4 in 10 of the population aged 40 and over and living in Mexico were reported in the Mexican census as illiterate.

[14] Pauline R. Kibbe, *Latin Americans in Texas* (Albuquerque: University of New Mexico Press, 1946), chap. 7, 8.

[15] The figures are for Mexican-stock persons of Spanish surname in 1960, as reported by the U.S. Census Bureau, in the states of Arizona, California, Colorado, New Mexico, and Texas. Persons aged 45–64 in 1960 were taken as being representative of those who were of school age in 1910; whereas those aged 35–44 were considered as representative of the 1930 school-age cohort.

had completed an average of 8 or 9 years of schooling, and the 1930 school-age cohort, about 11 years. Thus, close to half of the U.S. population that had gone to school around 1930 had completed high school or more. Among comparable Mexican Americans, on the other hand, over half had not completed elementary school. A difference of this magnitude clearly indicates that the increased rates of school attendance of the Mexican Americans could have little meaning relative to that of the schooling of the general U.S. population.

As noted above, both age and nativity are important indicators of educational attainment. Levels of schooling are higher for the youngest age groups, both natives and foreign born alike. Differences persist, however, between natives and foreign born even when controlling for age. In the years between World Wars I and II, slightly under 30% of native males, compared with approximately 17% of foreign-born males, completed high school. Comparable figures for women were about 22% and 16%, respectively.

The years following World War II represent the first point in time at which at least 50% of the school-age population first achieved completion of high school. This was limited to native Mexican Americans; the foreign born had still to achieve this goal as of 1970. The effect of the foreign born on overall levels of educational attainment has diminished over time, however, as their proportions of the total Mexican population have declined.

The proportion of women completing high school is almost, but not quite, as high as that of men. Among natives aged 20–24 in 1970, 56% of the men and 53% of the women had done so (Table 6.5). Among the foreign born, we see the same difference by sex, although the proportions finishing high school are lower.

When it comes to entering college, however, many more men than women do so. This difference has persisted over the years and still shows no signs of decreasing. Once they have entered college, the proportions completing 4 years are about the same for both men and women. Perhaps this indicates a greater motivation to receive a college education on the part of many women.

Area of residence also appears to be significant in terms of levels of schooling. Of the five southwestern states, Texas lags far behind: Only 44% of the men aged 20–24 had completed high school, compared with 55% in California and even higher proportions in Arizona, Colorado, and New Mexico. Outside the five states, Illinois had only 42% of Mexican men and 46% of women completing high school, whereas the remaining states had 59% of the men and 56% of the women graduating from high school. In 1970 both Illinois and Texas also had fairly sizable proportions of foreign born. By contrast, California, despite a large foreign-born population, had levels of schooling significantly higher. Clearly, those Mexicans who live outside the traditional areas of residence have higher levels of educational attainment (see Table 6.19).

We have suggested elsewhere[16] that completion of high school seems to be the critical point in terms of changes in demographic behavior. The increased proportions of Mexican Americans who have completed high school since the end of World War II appear to be particularly significant. Should the accelerated rate of schooling continue, in another 20 or 30 years we may expect levels of educational attainment of Mexican Americans to approach significantly more closely those of their Anglo neighbors.

SCHOOL ATTENDANCE, 1970

Of critical importance in estimating future levels of schooling is the extent of school attendance of the present school-age cohort. Those who drop out of school at an early age are not likely to become college graduates at a later date. Conversely, the higher the proportions of those who remain in school, the more likely will be increases in the proportions of those who go to college.

We have already reviewed the increased levels of education among Mexican adults over the last 60 years. What changes in school attendance have occurred? At the elementary school level (between the ages of approximately 6 and 14), the proportion attending school rose from slightly more than half in 1910 to about 8 in 10 by 1930. In 1970 more than 9 out of 10 children of Mexican descent were attending school and there were further increases during the 1970s. The change is much more dramatic among the high school aged. Only 52% of those aged 14–17 years in 1930 were attending school. Well over three-fourths of high-school-aged Mexican Americans were attending school in 1970. Despite these gains, however, Mexican Americans lagged behind the non-Spanish white population, among whom more than 9 in 10 were attending school. Thus, whereas we can anticipate that Mexican Americans in the future will be more schooled, it may well be another generation before they attain levels comparable to the non-Spanish white population.

For ages 7–19, 84% of the Mexican-origin youth were attending school in 1970, in comparison with 90% for non-Spanish white youth. However, among the former, 1 in 5 was below the modal grade for his

---

[16] See Chapter 3.

age, as compared with 1 in 15 among the latter. About the same proportion of each group, 2%, was above the modal grade. Although many Mexican youth are attending school, too many fail to make sufficient progress.

FERTILITY

A HISTORICAL NOTE

Ratio of Children to Women. Little change in the fertility of the Mexican-American population occurred between the mid-nineteenth century (and perhaps earlier) to the mid-twentieth. From 1850 to 1960 the ratio of children under age 5 to women aged 15–44 ranged between 80 and 90, as we saw in Chapter 3.[17] In the earlier decades perhaps this rate was closer to 90 and by the mid-twentieth century perhaps closer to 80; the data are not accurate enough to depict such a change if it did occur. By 1970 the rate fell to about 60 and may have fallen further to about 56 by the late 1970s.

It is thought that the decrease in 1970 reflects the increased schooling of the post–World War II years. The larger proportion of girls who remained in school and continued their education during the 1950s and early 1960s subsequently entered the childbearing period and by the latter half of the 1960s and first half of the 1970s were having fewer children.

The child–woman ratio of Mexican-origin women in 1970, however, is still significantly above that of the non-Spanish white women who had a ratio of about 40. Nevertheless, the large decline noted for the Mexican-origin women must indicate a changing socioeconomic–demographic environment that is conducive to lower fertility. Some of the socioeconomic changes that occurred between 1930 and 1970 were

1. Among the adult population—persons aged 20 and over—the proportion born in Mexico decreased from 71% in 1930 to 29% in 1970.
2. The sex ratio shifted from a preponderance of men at the earlier date to a small preponderance of women at the later date among persons aged 15–44. In 1930 about 45% were women, and in 1970, 51% were women.
3. In 1970 the population was more urban, 86% as compared with

---

[17] The number of children under age 5 was adjusted to allow for child mortality, but no adjustment was made for the census undercount of babies.

51% in 1930. Indeed, by 1970 there was almost no rural farm population left; this segment constituted only 2% of the total Mexican-origin population. The rural nonfarm population thus constituted 12% of the total. Indeed, this group is less rural than is the total white population, among whom about 73% were urban, 23% rural nonfarm, and 4% rural farm.

4. Educational levels increased significantly between 1930 and 1970, as we noted previously.

The Mexican-born Women, 1910–1970. Since the foreign-born women in earlier years were little schooled, we can compare those with less than 8 years of completed schooling in 1970 and 1960 with the total foreign born in 1940 and 1910 (Table 6.6).

At ages 15–34 there was little change in reported average numbers of children ever born. The middle or late 30s seem to be the turning point; fertility among women aged 35 and over declined from 1910 to 1970.

Reconstruction of the history of these women at about the end of the childbearing period, age 40–44, suggests that there was a decline around the turn of the century—perhaps associated with the prior disturbances leading to the Mexican revolution of 1910—and another decline at the time of World War II. The estimated average number of children ever born per 100 women aged 40–44 is as follows:

1880—640	1910—560	1950—470
1890—620	1920—560	1960—410[18]
1900—620	1930—520	1970—480
	1940—530	

AVERAGE NUMBER OF CHILDREN EVER BORN

The Picture in 1970. The number of children ever born alive to Mexican-origin women as of 1970 was 2.2 per woman, compared to 1.6 among non-Spanish white women. When these rates are standardized to control for the influences of age distribution, schooling, marital status, and employment, the rate becomes 2.0 for the women of Mexican origin; the rate for the non-Spanish white women remains unchanged.

---

[18] This average is based on 142 women who reported 576 children in the 1960 Public Use Sample (PUS). If we assume a possible 10% sampling variation for each figure, then the true figure could be a value approaching 500. The 1960 average seems to be so out of line with the averages for 1950 and 1970 that we are inclined to believe that it results from sampling variation.

TABLE 6.6
Children per 100 Women* Born in Mexico, by Age: 1910–1970

Age	1910	1940	1960	1970	% change 1910 to 1970
15 to 19 years	28	NA	20	30	7.1
20 to 24 years	136	NA	148	141	3.7
25 to 29 years	257	NA	255	263	2.3
30 to 34 years	371	NA	384	382	3.0
35 to 39 years	510	NA	421	462	−9.4
40 to 44 years	554	NA	406	482	−13.0
45 to 54 years	623	512	456	481	−22.8
55 to 64 years	615	562	552	478	−22.3
65 to 74 years	638	576	531	510	−20.1
15 to 24 years	84	NA	91	94	11.9
25 to 34 years	307	NA	324	328	6.8
15 to 34 years	192	207	218	240	25.0
35 to 44 years	530	450	413	471	−11.1
45 and over	623	538	511	492	−21.0

a
Women having under 8 years of schooling.

Source: 1910 and 1940, from U.S. Bureau of the Census, 1940, Differential Fertility 1940 and 1910, Tables 40 and 43. 1960 and 1970 from Public Use Sample (PUS) files.

There appears to be little or no difference in fertility by nativity or place of residence after standardizing; nor does there appear to be urban–rural differences. For example, among women aged 35–44, the average number of children ever born was 3.7 for all of these several groups. Whatever slight variation there may be in this number could be due to defects in the data.[19] To a large extent, this lack of differences is due to the similarity in other social, economic, and demographic characteristics, which apparently outweighs the possible effects of nativity and residence. In addition, by 1970 the Mexican-origin popula-

---

[19] This average of 3.7 children is the standardized number; the standard is comprised of the numbers of non-Spanish white women in each marital status, employment, and schooling level, as shown in Appendix C.

tion, whether residing within the five southwestern states or in other areas of the United States, was predominantly urban; indeed, some 80% of the Mexican-origin population resided in Standard Metropolitan Statistical Areas (SMSAs) in 1970. Clearly, then, we must look to other factors to explain the decrease in Mexican fertility during the 1960s.

Increased schooling plays a major role in reducing fertility. Of those Mexican-origin women who had completed high school, the standardized rate was about 1.8, compared to 2.6 for those who had less schooling. This results in a decrease in fertility of about 38%, compared with only 19% among non-Spanish whites. For those who have gone on to college, the reduction is 47 percentage points for Mexican women compared with 37 for the non-Spanish white women. Nevertheless, Mexican fertility remains about 20% higher than that of non-Spanish white women.

In addition to schooling, other factors such as employment, marital status, and age also influence fertility. For women aged 35–44, we estimate that the combined influences of increased schooling, being employed, and being other than married and living with spouse lead to a reduction of 69% in the number of children ever born. The reduction from having completed high school is 25%; from being employed, 20%; from other marital status, 23%; and the joint influence accounts for 32% of the reduction. When both the direct and indirect influences of increased schooling are considered, education accounts for at least one-third of the total reduction in fertility (see Table 6.7).

Ethnicity of Husband. Another important influence on fertility is the ethnicity of the husband. Women married to non-Mexican husbands had about 20–25% fewer children than did those married to Mexican husbands. Outmarriage appears to be as important as education in reducing fertility, and higher levels of schooling, together with marriage to non-Mexican husbands, resulted in further reduction in the fertility of these women. The average number of children ever born to Mexican women aged 35–44 are

	Husbands	
Wife's schooling	Mexican	Non-Mexican
Under 12 years	5.0	3.4
12 or more years	3.7	3.0

TABLE 6.7

Selected Characteristics for Native and Foreign–Born Mexican Women in the Reproductive Years, by Years of Schooling Completed: U.S. 1970

Age and characteristics	Native						Foreign born	
	0-7 years	8-11 years	12 years	13+ years	-12 years	12+ years	-12 years	12+ years
15 to 19 years								
% married, spouse present	15.8	9.8	17.0	10.7	10.7	16.1	12.5	16.9
% employed	15.5	14.3	51.4	54.9	14.5	51.9	20.3	52.9
Av. no. children ever born per woman	.26	.12	.14	.11	.14	.13	.15	.16
20 to 24 years								
% married, spouse present	57.5	65.1	52.8	40.8	62.7	49.8	65.9	50.6
% employed	28.2	30.1	55.4	62.3	29.5	57.1	31.4	52.0
Av. no. children ever born per woman	1.71	1.54	.69	.35	1.59	.61	1.30	.59
25 to 29 years								
% married, spouse present	72.0	77.2	76.3	68.8	75.4	74.6	81.5	78.1
% employed	28.0	30.5	47.7	62.6	29.6	51.1	27.0	40.9
Av. no. children ever born per woman	3.14	2.72	1.81	1.21	2.87	1.68	2.55	1.55
30 to 34 years								
% married, spouse present	76.2	80.1	79.6	76.5	78.5	78.9	83.4	84.3
% employed	26.8	35.8	47.9	56.3	31.9	49.8	28.2	37.1
Av. no. children ever born per woman	4.27	3.67	2.78	2.18	3.67	2.64	3.67	2.54
35 to 44 years								
% married, spouse present	76.3	79.6	79.8	75.4	77.9	79.0	80.9	82.3
% employed	29.0	39.9	50.5	63.7	34.1	53.0	31.3	41.1
Av. no. children ever born per woman	5.09	4.22	3.27	2.74	4.68	3.17	4.62	3.15

Although the average number of children ever born varies by age of woman, these patterns are the same for every age group.

Influence of Language and/or Surname. Two other factors of some importance in reducing fertility among Mexican-origin women in the United States are language and surname. Mexican-origin women aged 35–44 years who had spoken English as children at home had more schooling and fewer children than did those who had spoken Spanish; 59% of English-speaking women had completed high school, compared with only 23% among those who spoke Spanish. The average numbers of children per woman were

Language spoken at home as child	Under 12 years of schooling	12 or more years of schooling
Spanish	4.5	3.1
English[a]	3.8	2.9

[a] Almost all women who reported a language other than Spanish reported English.

Among lesser-schooled women, those who had spoken English as children had about 12% fewer children than did those who spoke Spanish. Differences in the average numbers of children ever born were less among the high school graduates: Spanish-speaking women in this group had an average of only about 7% more children than did the English-speaking women. Thus, it appears that the influence of language is somewhat greater among the lesser schooled.

The reverse holds true when comparing differences among women with Spanish surnames and those with non-Spanish surnames. Spanish-surnamed women had higher levels of fertility at each level of education than did those with non-Spanish surnames. However, among the more-schooled women, non-Spanish surname resulted in a 17% reduction in fertility, whereas among the lesser schooled, non-Spanish surname accounted for a decrease of only 10%. The average numbers of children ever born per woman aged 35–44 were

Surname	Under 12 years of schooling	12 or more years of schooling
Spanish	4.6	3.3
Non-Spanish	4.1	2.7

CONTINUOUS EMPLOYMENT AND FERTILITY

That women who were employed at the time of the 1970 Census enumeration had, on the average, a smaller number of children ever born than did women not employed has been shown. We now will see that Mexican women who have been employed "continuously" have significantly lower fertility than do women who reported that they had never worked; women who reported "intermittent" work had an intermediate number of children.

From the 1970 Census we have information for women who reported that they had been employed in 1965 and 1969 and were employed at the time of the 1970 Census; these women are designated as "continuously" employed. Information is also given for women who said that they had never worked. The remaining women reported having been employed at various dates in the past; these are designated as "intermittently" employed.[20]

The influence of continuous employment on numbers of children born (Table 6.8) can be illustrated for women aged 35–44 who were married only once and were living with their husbands at the time of the census.

Women	Under 12 years of schooling	12 or more years of schooling
Continuously employed	3.9	2.9
Intermittently employed	4.8	3.7
Never employed	5.5	4.3

As is seen from these rates, increased schooling also reduces fertility, as does being married more than once, widowed, divorced, separated, or never married (Table 6.8). We estimate that for this age group each of these three factors reduces fertility by about 1–1.5 children. All three in combination reduce fertility about 4 children.

Increased schooling clearly lowers fertility directly and indirectly, insofar as Mexican-origin women who have completed high school are more likely to have been employed continuously (Table 6.8). On the other hand, there is little difference in the proportions who were married only once and living with their husbands between the lesser and

---

[20] See Jaffe and Ridley, "Lifetime Employment of Women."

TABLE 6.8

Mexican–Origin Women, Average Number of Children Ever Born per Woman, by Extent of Employment, Marital Status, Age, and Years of Schooling Completed: 1970

	Under 12 years schooling			12+ years schooling		
	25 to 29	30 to 34	35 to 44	25 to 29	30 to 34	35 to 44
Married once, spouse present						
Employed "continuously"	2.15	3.36	3.93	1.22	2.30	2.94
Employed "intermittently"	2.89	4.00	4.83	2.04	3.04	3.66
Never employed	3.39	4.43	5.49	2.77	3.28	4.26
% employed "continuously"	9	12	17	25	26	30
All other marital status						
Employed "continuously"	1.51	2.15	2.84	.79	1.12	1.39
Employed "intermittently"	2.29	3.61	4.26	1.48	2.45	3.23
Never employed	2.16	3.45	4.23	*	*	*
% employed "continuously"	23	27	31	46	49	53
Percent of all women married once and spouse present	68	69	66	67	71	70

*Fewer than 50 women in sample.

Data from special tabulation of PUS file.

the more schooled or for the several age groups; increased schooling has no indirect influence via marital status upon employment.

CHARACTERISTICS OF WOMEN IN THE REPRODUCTIVE AGES, 1970

Table 6.9 presents selected characteristics of Mexican-origin women by nativity, age, and years of schooling;[21] comparable data for the Hispano and Anglo women in the five southwestern states are shown in Table 5.4.

Let us examine the characteristics of women aged 20–44, the prime childbearing years. The standardized[22] rates are as follows:

---

[21] Additional information is presented in Appendix Tables G–18 to G–20.

[22] Standardized on the basis of the age distribution of all non-Spanish white women in the United States, as shown in Appendix C.

Years of schooling	Standardized percentage married			
	Mexican origin			
	Native	Foreign born	Hispano	Anglo
Under 12	74	78	74	77
12 or more	71	74	73	75
	Standardized percentage employed			
Under 12	32	30	33	37
12 or more	53	43	51	50

We see with regard to marital status:

1. Somewhat fewer of the more schooled are married.
2. Many more of the more schooled are employed.
3. More of the Mexican born than of the natives are married.
4. About the same proportions of the Mexican-born and Anglo women are married.
5. The native Mexican-origin and Hispano women have about the same proportions married, which are below those of the Mexican-born and Anglo women.

As regards employment we find

1. Many more of those with 12 years or more of schooling are employed.
2. The smallest proportions employed are found among the Mexican-born women, and the highest proportions, among the Anglos.
3. The native Mexican-origin and Hispano women are intermediate and have close to the same employment rates.

On the basis of these findings, we might conclude that the Mexican-born women might have fertility higher than that of the native women, for more of the former are married and fewer are employed. Yet, as we saw, they both have about the same fertility after allowing for amount of schooling, employment, and marital status. This suggests that other factors—perhaps cultural ones—are operating to produce the observed fertility rates.

THE REPUBLIC OF MEXICO

This country continues to have high fertility in the 1970s, as it had in the past. Those Mexican-born persons who migrated north to the United States have more or less the same fertility levels as do their com-

TABLE 6.9
Selected Characteristics for Women of Mexican Origin by Age, Years of Schooling, and Area of Residence: 1970

Age and characteristics	5 Southwestern States		Other States	
	-12	12+	-12	12+
15 to 19 years				
% married, spouse present	10.8	15.1	11.6	20.9
% employed	14.7	51.0	20.2	54.7
Av. no. children per woman	.14	.14	.13	.18
20 to 24 years				
% married, spouse present	62.1	49.3	70.7	53.4
% employed	30.0	56.2	28.1	57.0
Av. no. children per woman	1.50	.60	1.60	.61
25 to 29 years				
% married, spouse present	77.2	73.9	78.4	80.5
% employed	28.9	50.4	30.8	44.7
Av. no. children per woman	2.76	1.65	2.66	1.72
30 to 34 years				
% married, spouse present	80.0	79.9	83.5	80.0
% employed	30.4	47.8	35.5	47.4
Av. no. children per woman	3.84	2.65	3.79	2.57
35 to 44 years				
% married, spouse present	78.1	79.7	82.7	80.3
% employed	33.2	50.9	38.1	53.7
Av. no. children per woman	4.64	3.21	4.77	3.00

patriots who remained south of the border, after taking into consideration levels of schooling and employment and marital status. As long as migration from the Republic of Mexico to the United States continues, the fertility of the Mexican born who are living north of the border will continue to be high.

Historical Note. In Mexico there seems to have been little change over the years in the child–woman ratio. We estimated that this ratio, adjusted for child mortality, was about 80 in 1910 and 1930 and the same or perhaps higher—possibly 85 or so—in 1970.[23] The reported numbers of children under age 5 per 100 women aged 15–44 were as follows:

---

[23] A. J. Jaffe and R. J. Rios, "Demographic and Related Developments in Latin America during the 1960s" (Paper presented at the Annual Meeting of the Latin American Studies Association, Madison, Wisconsin. 1973), Table 3.

Women	1970	1960
Total Mexico	82	79
Urban	75	73
Rural	94	85
Urban as percentage of rural	80%	86%

Whether there was a true increase in rural fertility we cannot say; perhaps decreases in child mortality largely account of the increased ratios. Although we hesitate to say that the fertility rate increased in Mexico between 1960 and 1979, we do feel confident that there was no significant decrease during this period. We do not think that child mortality decreased sufficiently so that the child–woman ratio could increase while the numbers of births and the birth rates actually decreased.

One possible explanation for this apparent stability is that Mexico is still predominantly rural. In 1970 of all women in the reproductive ages of 15–44, almost two-thirds were rural.[24] Another explanation may be that despite recent increases in school attendance, the large majority of women of childbearing age still have little schooling,[25] in 1970 only two in eight had completed 6 years of schooling and another one in eight had gone to post– primary schooling (7 years or more). As we shall see, fertility decreases only with the completion of primary school (6 years); few women have had enough schooling so that it had any appreciable effect on fertility.

Children Ever Born as of 1970.[26] Women aged 40–44, about the end of the childbearing years, averaged 6.2 children. This number is close to what was reported by older cohorts, indicating that there has been no significant change over the last generation, if not longer.

---

[24] This figure excludes the population classified by the Mexican census as Indian, virtually all of whom are rural dwellers.

[25] See Appendix Table G–8.

[26] These data were obtained from a special tabulation of a 1% sample of the 1970 Mexican Census. The sample was kindly furnished by CELADE, and we made the tabulation. Women classified as Indian and those who reported religion other than Roman Catholic were excluded from the tabulation. The specific items compare with those for the United States, as follows:

1. *Children ever born* should be more or less similar.
2. *Married:* In Mexico we do not know whether the woman is or is not living with her husband. In the United States we used married *and* living with husband.
3. *Schooling:* We attempted to make the two countries as comparable as possible by converting "primary" and "secondary" school designations into years completed.

Furthermore, and what is so important for purposes of our analysis, the fertility differentials found south of the border parallel those found to the north—in the United States.

1. Fertility decreases with increased years of schooling.
2. Employed women have fewer children than do those not employed.
3. Married women have more children than do unmarried women.
4. Rural women have more children than do urban women.

These differentials can be illustrated with data for women ages 35–44 (Table 6.10). Rural married women who were not employed and had never attended school averaged 7.1 children ever born. Urban married women who had completed 7 or more years of schooling and were employed averaged 3.7 children. Urban women who were not married, (widowed, divorced, and never married), had 7 or more years of schooling, and were employed averaged about 1.1 children ever born.

Schooling apparently lowers fertility only if the woman has completed primary school, that is, 6 grades. Comparison of the averages for those reporting no schooling versus those reporting some, but not completion of primary education, shows the averages to be virtually identical. Those women who completed primary school but went no further averaged close to one child fewer than did those having less schooling. Continuing on into secondary school resulted in about one-half child less, on the average (Table 6.10).

Being *married* at the time of the Mexican census resulted in an average number of children ever born, on the order of two or three times that of women who were not married. As we shall see, however, we suspect that there may have been underreporting of children by women who were not married.

Being *employed* resulted in an average decrease of between one-half and three-quarters of a child.

Living in an *urban* rather than a *rural* area resulted in a decrease of perhaps one-third of a child.

These estimates of the possible influence of each of the variables are only approximations. We feel that the quality of the census data do not permit more refined and exact estimates. Nevertheless, they do indicate that all of these factors play a role in reducing fertility.

---

4. *Employment*: Employed women in Mexico were those who reported that they had worked 7 months or more in 1969 and were other than unpaid family workers or domestic servants. In the United States employment means having any type of job during the census week.
5. *Urban–rural* should be more or less similar.

TABLE 6.10

Average Number of Children Ever Born, by Age, Marital Status, Schooling, and Urban–Rural Residence: Mexico, 1970

		NOT EMPLOYED (Schooling)				*EMPLOYED* (Schooling)			
	Total	None	Under 6 grades	6 grades	7+ grades	Total	None	Under 6 grades	6 grades	7+ grades

	Total	None	Under 6 grades	6 grades	7+ grades	Total	None	Under 6 grades	6 grades	7+ grades
URBAN										
Married										
15 to 19 years	1.06	1.22	1.12	1.03	.56	.75	*	1.16	.41	*
20 to 24 years	2.16	2.33	2.46	1.91	1.69	1.10	*	1.27	1.20	.85
25 to 29 years	3.30	3.79	3.80	3.13	1.74	2.18	*	2.25	2.18	1.88
30 to 34 years	4.87	5.29	5.35	4.36	3.79	3.32	4.30	3.98	2.87	2.84
35 to 44 years	6.12	6.53	6.63	5.41	4.62	4.75	5.74	5.41	4.41	3.66
Other marital										
15 to 19 years	.08	.10	.06	.12	.05	.03	.42	.06	.00	.00
20 to 24 years	.21	.38	.32	.16	.09	.10	.25	.24	.08	.03
25 to 29 years	.75	.92	1.01	.66	.33	.49	1.86	1.10	.30	.22
30 to 34 years	1.18	1.27	1.37	1.04	.74	1.22	2.65	1.66	.91	.74
35 to 44 years	2.73	3.26	3.08	1.81	2.04	2.29	3.55	3.28	1.72	1.15
RURAL										
Married										
15 to 19 years	1.01	1.08	1.02	.86	.80	.68	.84	.65	*	*
20 to 24 years	2.35	2.48	2.41	1.94	2.16	1.51	1.82	2.00	1.02	.74
25 to 29 years	3.95	4.12	4.11	3.20	3.38	2.54	3.11	3.22	1.93	1.54
30 to 34 years	5.36	5.50	5.62	4.40	3.97	4.07	4.80	4.68	3.50	2.87
35 to 44 years	6.91	7.08	7.10	5.80	5.03	5.41	5.87	5.88	5.02	3.65
Other marital										
15 to 19 years	.07	.09	.04	.05	.03	.02	.05	.03	.01	.00
20 to 24 years	.32	.42	.35	.22	.21	.17	.45	.27	.09	.06
25 to 29 years	.87	1.05	.83	.64	.68	.57	1.34	1.21	.33	.12
30 to 34 years	1.62	1.63	1.76	1.30	1.15	1.50	2.89	1.76	.78	.53
35 to 44 years	3.17	3.62	3.00	2.04	*	3.00	4.25	3.60	1.85	.96

*Rate not shown where there are fewer than 25 women in sample.

Source: Special tabulation of the 1% sample of the 1970 Mexican Census of Population.

Comparison with the Mexican-Born Living in the United States. Precise comparisons are not possible, since, as we noted previously, the three social factors are only approximately comparable. Furthermore, it is not clear precisely which Mexican-born women living in the United States should be compared with which Mexican women living south of the border. Hence in Table 6.11 we show the specific rates for four

TABLE 6.11

Comparison of Average Number of Children Ever Born, by Age, Marital Status, Employ-ment, and Schooling: U.S. Mexican Population and Mexico: 1970

	UNITED STATES		MEXICO	
	Born in Mexico -12 yrs school	All Mexican origin -8 years school	Urban	Rural
15 to 19 years				
Married, spouse present				
Employed	.69	1.19	.75	.68
Not employed	.90	1.00	1.06	1.01
Other marital status				
Employed	.05	.15	.03	.02
Not employed	.05	.12	.08	.07
20 to 24 years				
Married, spouse present				
Employed	1.40	1.74	1.10	1.51
Not employed	1.78	2.19	2.16	2.35
Other marital status				
Employed	.35	.48	.10	.17
Not employed	.71	.91	.21	.32
25 to 29 years				
Married,spouse present				
Employed	2.37	2.87	2.18	2.54
Not employed	2.91	3.36	3.30	3.95
Other marital status				
Employed	.99	1.18	.49	.57
Not employed	2.02	2.18	.75	.87
30 to 34 years				
Married, spouse present				
Employed	3.64	3.91	3.32	4.07
Not employed	3.99	4.52	4.87	5.36
Other marital status				
Employed	1.90	2.00	1.22	1.50
Not employed	3.12	3.10	1.18	1.62
35 to 44 years				
Married, spouse present				
Employed	4.31	4.63	4.75	5.41
Not employed	5.16	5.55	6.12	6.91
Other marital status				
Employed	2.49	2.94	2.29	3.00
Not employed	4.28	4.54	2.73	3.17

groups: (a) all women born in Mexico and living north of the border who had not completed high school; (b) all Mexican-origin women in the United States who had not completed 8 years of schooling (Mexican born predominate in this group; (c) urban women living south of the border; and (d) rural women living south of the border.

For summary purposes, we standardized each group on the distribution of all women living in Mexico by age, marital status, and employment. The standardized rates are, respectively:

Women	Number of Children
U.S. residents	
Group *a*	2.4
Group *b*	2.7
Mexico residents	
Group *c*	2.6
Group *d*	3.0
Total of *c* and *d*	2.9

If the most comparable groups are *b* and *c*, then there is little difference in fertility between women north and south of the border. From the viewpoint of schooling, presumably those U.S. residents who had not completed elementary school are, educationally, most similar to the women living in Mexico, since very few of the latter went beyond six grades.

But which women living south of the border should the women living in the United States be compared with, the urban or the rural? It is not known from whence the migrants came, urban or rural Mexico, or both.

Marital status is of special interest. Among women who were reported as *not* married, the fertility rates in Mexico are significantly below those of women living in the United States. We suspect that this resulted from underreporting in the Mexican census of children ever born to women who reported themselves as not married at the time of the census. We can think of no other explanation since (a) the census procedures for counting the number of children ever born alive appear to be reasonably comparable in the two countries; and (b) we know of no cultural transformation that occurs at the border and leads to higher fertility among those women who are other than married and spouse present.

If there was less reporting of children south of the border, then the standardized fertility rates previously noted should be greater than those we calculated. If so, then we conclude that there was some small but unmeasurable decrease in fertility among the migrants to the

United States, unless the migrants are a selected group and are not strictly comparable to a cross section of all women living in Mexico.

Another complicating factor is that some of the Mexican-born women who were living in the United States in 1970 arrived here when they were children, that is, under age 15. As nearly as can be estimated,[27] between 20 and 25% did so. Many of these women must have attended school in the United States and probably received more schooling than they would have received if they had remained in Mexico. In addition, they may have been subjected to more Anglo cultural influence than were those who arrived in the United States as adults.

In summary, then, we conclude that little happens to fertility when the migrants cross the border from south to north. As long as fertility continues to be high in Mexico, and as long as migrants continue to arrive in the United States, the high fertility pattern observed in the United States will continue to be reinforced. With sufficient schooling—high school graduation or more—fertility does fall, as was noted previously. In the absence of such increased schooling, fertility will remain high.

THE ECONOMIC PICTURE

LABOR FORCE PARTICIPATION AND EMPLOYMENT

Men. About the same proportion of Mexican men aged 16 and over as of non-Spanish white men were in the labor force in 1970: 78% versus 75%, respectively (Table 6.12). Men who had completed high school were more likely to be in the labor force than were those with less schooling. Of those who had not completed high school, 74% were in the labor force, as compared with 80% of the college graduates. If the analysis is limited to ages 20–64—the prime working years—we find that the variation is narrowed, but the pattern remains; 88% of those with under 12 years of school were in the labor force, as compared with 92% of the college graduates.

Most of the Mexican men in the prime working ages who were in the civilian labor force had worked full time. There was little difference by level of schooling completed.

The unemployment rate was significantly higher for the Mexican-origin men aged 20–64 than for the non-Spanish white men. Those with

---

[27] Estimated from U.S., Bureau of the Census, Census of Population, 1970, *Subject Reports*, Final Report PC (2)–1A, *National Origin and Language* (Washington, D.C.: Government Printing Office, 1973), table 17. Because so many women did not report year of immigration and because of the obvious errors in this table, it is not possible to make a closer estimate.

TABLE 6.12

Labor-Force Participation and Employment Rates, Mexican–Origin Population by Sex, Age, and Years of Schooling: 1970

Age	*Total*			*Under 12 years*		
	% in labor force	a/	b/	% in labor force	a/	b/
MEN						
Total	78.2	81.9	5.8	74.3	80.5	6.4
16 to 19 years	45.3	44.7	13.8	41.3	42.9	14.3
20 to 24 years	84.4	76.7	8.5	85.7	78.4	9.3
25 to 34 years	92.1	86.9	5.0	90.8	85.1	5.9
35 to 44 years	93.3	88.2	4.0	92.6	87.0	4.6
45 to 54 years	90.4	87.0	4.2	89.5	85.9	4.5
55 and over	52.1	78.7	5.8	49.9	77.5	6.2
20 to 64 years	89.2	85.5	5.0	88.3	84.8	5.5
WOMEN						
Total	36.5	67.1	8.8	30.2	63.3	10.1
16 to 19 years	30.8	46.8	14.5	24.0	38.7	15.9
20 to 24 years	47.9	70.7	9.3	34.5	66.2	11.5
25 to 34 years	40.3	71.1	7.5	34.2	67.2	9.2
35 to 44 years	41.5	68.6	8.0	37.6	66.4	9.1
45 to 54 years	40.3	70.0	7.7	36.7	68.0	8.6
55 and over	17.7	64.4	8.4	16.4	62.5	9.4
20 to 44	42.5	70.1	8.2	35.7	66.6	9.6

a/ Percentage of civilian labor force employed full time.

b/ Percentage of civilian labor force unemployed.

* Under 50 cases in sample.

more schooling had lower unemployment rates, and among college graduates, the rates for the two groups of men were virtually identical:

Years of schooling	Mexican origin (%)	Non-Spanish white (%)
Under 12	5.5	4.1
12	4.2	2.7
13–15	4.8	2.8
16 or more	1.6	1.4
Total population	5.0	3.0

Women. About one-third of the Mexican-origin women were in the labor force; this is less than the rate for the non-Spanish white women.

TABLE 6.12 (cont.)

12 years			13 to 15 years			16+ years		
% in labor force	a/	b/	% in labor force	a/	b/	% in labor force	a/	b/
89.4	86.7	4.8	85.5	80.0	5.0	90.0	87.1	1.7
67.6	54.1	12.0	63.9	37.1	10.0	0.0	0.0	0.0
88.0	82.3	7.4	74.2	58.6	8.4	74.8	63.6	6.1
95.3	91.0	3.7	92.3	87.9	4.2	92.0	86.7	1.6
94.7	92.4	2.3	96.0	91.2	2.5	96.5	90.0	0.9
93.0	91.9	3.4	94.7	89.6	4.0	97.6	91.3	1.9
75.7	85.6	3.8	73.3	87.2	3.4	65.2	86.7	2.7
92.6	89.3	4.2	87.3	81.5	4.8	92.4	87.5	1.6
53.5	73.9	7.1	56.4	69.5	6.2	62.9	73.8	4.7
61.0	63.1	12.2	61.9	45.8	10.8	0.0	0.0	0.0
61.2	76.3	8.2	63.7	64.7	7.5	76.5	73.8	4.9
48.5	76.2	5.9	54.0	74.7	4.9	65.7	74.2	4.7
52.8	73.0	5.6	55.0	75.4	5.7	63.0	73.5	4.9
56.1	74.3	5.5	61.4	81.0	4.0	67.1	80.9	2.1
31.9	77.0	3.3	23.7	*	*	34.6	*	*
53.7	75.4	6.7	58.3	70.2	6.2	66.5	73.9	4.8

These figures for the total populations aged 16 and over, however, obscure significant differences by level of schooling. Among women who had not completed high school, 3 in 10 of each population were in the labor force. However, among the more schooled, larger proportions of the Mexican-origin women were in the labor force:

Years of schooling	Mexican origin (%)	Non-Spanish white (%)
Under 12	30	30
12	54	48
13–15	56	47
16 or more	63	58
Total population	37	41

The rate for all Mexican-origin women aged 16 and over is reduced below that of the non-Spanish white women simply because there are so many more little-schooled women among the Mexican-origin group.

Of the Mexican-origin women in the labor force, about two in three had worked full time during the census week. Of all women who had worked in 1969, about two in five had been employed 48 weeks or more.

Unemployment in 1970 was significantly higher among Mexican-origin women aged 16 and over than among the non-Spanish white women: 8.8%, as compared with 4.9%. The less schooled had higher unemployment rates; the rate was 10.1% for those who had not finished high school, as compared with 4.7% for college graduates (Table 6.12).

CLASS OF WORKER

Most Mexican-origin men and women are employees of private companies. Close to 9 in 10 of the foreign born and 8 in 10 of the natives are such employees. Among the foreign born, about 6% are government employees and 7% are self-employed. There are many more government employees among the natives, about 17%, and the same proportion, 7%, who are self-employed (see Appendix Table G–30).

FAMILY INCOME

Average (median) income in 1969 of families headed by Mexican Americans was $6960, or about $4500 below that of non-Spanish white families (Appendix Table G–36). Income varied greatly in accordance with the number of earners in the family and the sex of the head. The more earners, the higher the family income was, and families headed by men had higher average incomes than did those headed by women:

Number of earners	Head	
	Men ($)	Women ($)
None	2400	1000
1	6170	3540
2 or more	9270	6370

For Mexican-American families, 1 in 7 was headed by a woman, as compared with 1 in 11 of the non-Spanish white families. This factor provides a partial explanation for the lower median income for all

Mexican families. There is very little difference between the two populations in the number of earners in the families; about half of all the families in each population has two or more earners. If the Mexican families had had the same distribution by sex of head as did the non-Spanish white families, the former's median income would have been raised slightly: from $6960 to perhaps $7200.

Even $7200 is significantly below that of the non-Spanish white families. This indicates that other factors must play an important role in depressing income, and one such factor undoubtedly is the lower educational level, especially of the foreign-born Mexicans. As was noted previously, the native Mexican-origin persons had completed more years of schooling, and as we shall see, more of them have better-paying jobs. The influence of schooling is reflected in a comparison of the average (median) income of families headed by native with that of families headed by the foreign born:

	Head	
Family	Native ($)	Foreign born ($)
Total population	7310	6460
Male head	7830	6860
Female head	3570	3910

Clearly, families headed by native men have significantly higher income than do those headed by foreign-born men. Among families headed by women, however, the foreign born have higher incomes.

What does this analysis suggest about family income in the future, say a generation hence? By that time many more of the families will be headed by native persons who probably will be more schooled; hence, they will have higher earnings, and family income will be greater than it is in 1970 and will approach that of the non-Spanish white families. An indication that this may be occurring is furnished by family income data for the period 1976–1978;[28] we may compare data for this year with that of 1969 (data collected in 1970), as follows:

1. In 1969 Mexican families with male heads averaged about 65% of the income of non-Spanish white male-headed families.

[28] Data from Census Bureau, *Persons of Spanish Origin, 1969,* and from Census Bureau, P–60, # 118, Table 20. The estimated median incomes for the Mexican-origin families for the average of 1976–1978 were male heads, $12,600; female heads, $6200.

2. In 1976–1978 the Mexican families averaged about 70% of the latter.
3. In 1969 Mexican families with women heads averaged about 50% of that of non-Spanish white female-headed families.
4. In 1976–1978 the Mexican families averaged about 70% of the latter.

Apparently the gap is closing. Whether it will continue to do so and when the median income of Mexican-American families may—or will—more closely approximate that of Anglo families, we do not know.

INDIVIDUAL EARNINGS

Men. Mexican men earned an average (median) of $4960 in 1969; this is the amount received from wages and salaries and self-employment income (Tables 6.13–6.15). These Mexican-origin men had earned slightly over two-thirds as much as did the average non-Spanish white men.

Average, or median, earnings tend to increase with (a) increased schooling; (b) increased age of worker; and (c) being born in the United States rather than in Mexico. For example, let us look at the medians for men ages 25–34 and 35–44:

	Age 25–34		Age 35–44	
Years of schooling	Native ($)	Foreign born ($)	Native ($)	Foreign born ($)
Under 12	5510	5060	6270	5520
12	7100	6580	8030	7370
13–15	7590	6920	9220	8000
16 or more	8360	7370	11,040	11,400

Men who had completed college earned some two-thirds or more above that of men who had not completed high school. Native men at each schooling level earned some 10–15% more than did those men born in Mexico. Increasing age seems to add as much or perhaps somewhat more, as does being born in the United States.

With each age and level of schooling group, there was considerable variation in earnings. Thus, some high school dropouts had earned more than did college graduates. This is indicated in the line marked "variation" (Tables 6.13–6.15). Between the ages of 25 and 64, the variation index is smallest, indicating that most men tend to earn around the average amount. At the younger and older ages, however, the variation is much greater; this is probably a result of many working

TABLE 6.13

Earnings in 1969, Mexican Descent, Total United States, by Sex, Age, and Years of Schooling

Years of schooling	MEN						WOMEN					
	14 & over	14-24 years	25-34 years	35-44 years	45-64 years	65+ years	14 & over	14-24 years	25-34 years	35-44 years	45-64 years	65+ years
Total U.S.												
1st quartile	$2,390	740	3,990	4,340	3,450	1,040	$ 790	550	1,050	1,080	1,060	730
Median	4,960	1,960	6,100	6,650	5,720	2,260	2,100	1,240	2,630	2,730	2,550	1,700
3rd quartile	7,620	4,170	8,340	9,100	8,180	5,030	5,920	2,950	4,400	4,460	4,240	3,640
Variation*	1.05	1.75	.71	.72	.83	1.77	2.44	1.94	1.27	1.24	1.25	1.71
Under 12 years												
1st quartile	2,070	600	3,470	3,870	3,220	1,000	670	450	770	920	960	690
Median	4,470	1,430	5,340	5,990	5,260	2,130	1,670	850	1,890	2,290	2,280	1,540
3rd quartile	6,960	3,580	7,450	8,150	7,580	4,900	3,320	1,920	3,440	3,820	3,770	3,270
Variation	1.09	2.08	.75	.71	.83	1.83	1.59	1.73	1.41	1.27	1.23	1.68
12 years												
1st quartile	3,250	1,410	5,140	6,070	5,550	1,520	1,160	860	1,550	1,940	1,900	920
Median	6,050	3,020	7,030	7,950	7,790	3,260	2,930	2,170	3,330	3,720	3,870	2,740
3rd quartile	8,490	5,390	9,050	10,070	10,130	6,810	4,650	3,740	5,060	5,630	5,760	5,290
Variation	.87	1.32	.56	.50	.59	1.62	1.19	1.35	1.06	1.00	1.00	1.59
13 to 15 years												
1st quartile	2,640	1,180	5,030	7,060	6,090	1,860	1,170	810	2,200	2,490	2,130	+
Median	6,310	2,450	7,480	9,090	8,560	3,440	2,940	1,860	4,110	4,480	4,610	
3rd quartile	9,300	4,540	9,760	11,540	11,390	5,990	4,920	3,650	5,720	6,590	6,950	
Variation	1.06	1.37	.63	.49	.62	1.20	1.28	1.53	.85	.91	1.04	
16+ years												
1st quartile	5,570	1,410	5,330	7,710	8,210	+	3,050	1,440	3,340	3,920	3,700	+
Median	8,900	2,890	8,180	11,030	11,500		5,590	3,200	5,630	6,530	6,520	
3rd quartile	12,830	5,300	11,130	15,460	17,820		7,630	5,290	7,390	8,960	9,500	
Variation	.82	1.35	.71	.70	.84		.89	1.20	.72	.77	.89	

*Interquartile range divided by median.

+ Too few cases in sample, under 500 inflated population.

Source: Special Census tabulation.

TABLE 6.14

Earnings in 1969, Mexican Descent, U.S. Born, Total United States, by Sex, Age, and Years of Schooling

Years of schooling	MEN						WOMEN					
	14 & over years	14-24 years	25-34 years	35-44 years	45-64 years	65+ years	14 & over years	14-24 years	25-34 years	35-44 years	45-64 years	65+ years
Total U.S.												
1st quartile	$2,250	700	4,190	4,570	3,530	1,050	760	540	1,200	1,090	1,040	790
Median	5,040	1,870	6,370	6,970	5,990	2,210	2,080	1,200	2,730	2,810	2,610	1,830
3rd quartile	7,790	4,030	8,660	9,400	8,520	5,170	3,940	2,910	4,810	4,640	4,430	3,900
Variation*	1.10	1.78	.70	.69	.83	1.86	1.53	1.98	1.32	1.26	1.30	1.70
Under 12 years												
1st quartile	1,820	530	3,570	3,980	3,260	990	620	400	760	890	930	750
Median	4,410	1,210	5,510	6,270	5,480	2,010	1,550	790	1,880	2,280	2,310	1,620
3rd quartile	7,080	3,290	7,640	8,980	7,780	4,820	3,250	1,760	3,430	3,870	3,840	3,420
Variation	1.19	2.28	.74	.80	.82	1.91	1.70	1.72	1.42	1.31	1.26	1.65
12 years												
1st quartile	3,220	1,400	5,220	6,170	5,790	1,910	1,150	840	1,610	2,010	1,810	840
Median	6,100	2,980	7,100	8,030	7,960	3,550	2,940	2,150	3,400	3,790	3,910	2,870
3rd quartile	8,570	5,410	8,190	10,210	10,350	7,790	4,650	3,120	5,240	5,720	5,790	5,580
Variation	.88	1.36	.42	.50	.57	1.66	1.19	1.06	1.07	.98	1.02	1.65
13 to 15 years												
1st quartile	2,620	1,220	5,140	7,240	6,200	1,390	1,160	810	2,370	2,780	2,090	1,660
Median	6,300	2,490	7,590	9,220	8,750	3,030	2,910	1,350	4,190	4,650	4,740	3,200
3rd quartile	8,680	4,500	9,900	11,660	11,540	5,980	4,140	3,600	5,820	6,730	7,060	5,850
Variation	.96	1.32	.63	.48	.61	1.51	1.02	1.51	.82	.85	1.05	1.31
16+ years												
1st quartile	5,690	1,400	5,580	7,790	8,300	1,820	3,160	1,560	3,540	4,510	4,550	890
Median	9,000	2,960	8,360	11,040	11,410	7,400	5,700	3,360	5,760	6,770	6,820	2,670
3rd quartile	12,780	5,500	11,250	14,760	17,000	10,780	7,670	5,320	7,470	9,140	9,950	6,180
Variation	.79	1.39	.68	.63	.76	1.21	.79	1.12	.68	.68	.79	1.98

*Interquartile range divided by median.

Source: Special Census tabulation.

TABLE 6.15
Earnings in 1969, Mexican Descent, Foreign Born, Total United States, by Sex, Age, and Years of Schooling

Years of schooling	MEN						WOMEN					
	14 & over years	14-24 years	25-34 years	35-44 years	45-64 years	65+ years	14 & over years	14-24 years	25-34 years	35-44 years	45-64 years	65+ years
Total U.S.												
1st quartile	$2,670	980	3,530	3,840	3,210	1,040	890	630	1,010	1,050	1,110	700
Median	4,830	2,640	5,440	5,840	5,310	2,190	2,210	1,560	2,430	2,480	2,490	1,540
3rd quartile	7,200	4,650	7,520	8,030	7,660	4,970	3,790	3,240	3,930	3,920	3,980	3,160
Variation*	.94	1.39	.74	.72	.84	1.80	1.31	1.67	1.20	1.16	1.15	1.60
Under 12 years												
1st quartile	2,530	880	3,300	3,640	3,040	1,010	810	540	910	960	1,000	670
Median	4,560	2,480	5,060	5,520	4,980	2,050	1,980	1,230	2,140	2,290	2,260	1,450
3rd quartile	6,780	4,440	7,030	7,590	7,190	4,740	3,490	2,800	3,580	3,700	3,700	2,860
Variation	.93	1.44	.74	.72	.83	1.82	1.36	1.84	1.25	1.20	1.19	1.51
12 years												
1st quartile	3,420	1,560	4,690	5,280	5,000	1,410	1,300	910	1,390	1,600	2,140	970
Median	5,940	3,260	6,580	7,370	7,310	3,700	3,030	2,310	3,290	3,270	3,760	1,900
3rd quartile	8,290	5,450	8,460	9,500	9,670	6,590	4,690	4,090	4,120	4,900	5,690	4,650
Variation	.82	1.19	.57	.57	.64	1.40	1.12	1.38	.83	1.01	.95	1.94
13 to 15 years												
1st quartile	3,090	1,150	4,520	5,730	5,850	2,570	1,340	840	1,700	1,700	2,200	1,720
Median	6,370	2,480	6,920	8,000	8,200	5,000	3,200	1,960	3,580	3,690	4,300	4,600
3rd quartile	9,060	4,750	9,050	10,680	10,940	7,800	5,230	3,990	5,330	5,580	6,760	6,700
Variation	.94	1.45	.65	.62	.62	1.05	1.22	1.51	1.01	1.05	1.06	1.08
16+ years												
1st quartile	5,320	1,660	4,770	7,410	6,970	1,780	2,010	1,270	2,240	2,510	1,920	1,030
Median	8,930	2,800	7,370	11,400	11,760	5,110	4,340	3,190	4,290	5,060	4,760	3,190
3rd quartile	14,320	4,980	10,490	21,080	19,120	11,130	7,040	5,220	6,710	7,570	8,160	6,250
Variation	1.01	1.19	.78	1.20	1.03	1.83	1.16	1.24	1.04	1.00	1.31	1.64

*Interquartile range divided by median.

Source: Special Census tabulation.

163

part time and receiving lesser earnings, so that the median earnings for the group do not indicate fairly the general level of earnings of most members. We note that among 14–24-year-olds, only 40% of those who had worked in 1969 had worked 48 weeks or more; among those aged 65 and over, the proportion was 46%. Among men between ages 25 and 64, however, almost 80% had worked 48 weeks or more in 1969.

Women. Mexican-origin women averaged only about 42% as much earnings as did Mexican-origin men: $2100 as compared with $4960 (Tables 6.13–6.15). However, direct comparisons are not possible, as more women work part time during the year and women are more likely to be in occupations and industries different from those of men.

Native women had higher earnings generally than did those who were foreign born, after taking into account age and years of schooling. We illustrate this below.

	Age 25–34		Age 35–44	
Years of schooling	Native ($)	Foreign born ($)	Native ($)	Foreign born ($)
Under 12	1880	2140	2280	2290
12	3400	3290	3790	3270
13–15	4190	3580	4650	3690
16 or more	5760	4290	6770	5060

For only those who had not completed high school do the two nativity groups earn, on the average, more or less the same amounts. Number of years of schooling is obviously very important; college graduates earned between two and three times as much as did high school dropouts. Having been born, and presumably raised, in the United States rather than in Mexico adds something on the order of one-fifth more to earnings.

The native women had worked a little more in 1969 than had the foreign born, which may account for a small part of their higher average earnings. The proportions who had worked 48 weeks or more in 1969 were as follows:

Age	Native (%)	Foreign born (%)
25–34	44	42
35–44	50	44
45–54	51	50
55–64	55	51

In most instances the index of variation for women is higher than that for men. This reflects the greater prevalence of part-time work for women.

OCCUPATIONS OF MEN

A Historical Note. Overall, Mexican-American men in 1970 were on the intermediate rungs of the occupational ladder, lower than were non-Spanish white men in the United States. Indeed, their movement up the occupational ladder lags about a generation behind that of the total U.S. male population. Nevertheless, their present position is a marked improvement over the 1930 situation, both absolutely and in comparison with the non-Spanish white men. We think that their lower position is associated with the higher fertility previously observed. Furthermore, we think that the improved occupational situation since 1930 is associated with declines in fertility during these 40 years.

In 1970, only 1 in 10 of the men was employed in agriculture; in 1930, 4 in 10 were so employed. At both dates the proportion of all men in the United States so employed was about half that of the Mexican-origin men (Table 6. 16).

There was only 1 craftsman in every 5 workers in 1970, a figure virtually identical to that of total U.S. However, only 1 Mexican American in 15 in 1930 was so employed. Almost 1 in 5 was a white-collar worker in 1970, whereas in 1930 only 1 in 15 was employed in this category. Out of 20 workers, in 1970 only 1 was a professional worker, as compared with 1 in 100 in 1930.

In 1930, 1 in 3 was a nonfarm laborer and 1 in 3 was a farm laborer. In short, 2 in 3 were on the bottom rung of the occupational ladder. By 1970, only 1 in 7 was a nonfarm laborer, and 1 in 11 was a farm laborer. Less than one-quarter were employed in these two bottom categories in 1970, as compared with two-thirds in 1930.

One way of noting the great change over these four decades—a change greater than that which occurred among all men in the United States—is to weight the proportions in each occupation by the Socio-Economic Status (SES) scores presented in the 1960 U.S. Census, thus deriving an overall occupational scale. When this is done, we find that in 1970 the score for the Mexican-origin men was 46,[29] as compared with 33 in 1950 and 24 in 1930. Among all men in the United States,

---

[29] By the late 1970s, there may have been a further increase in SES scores; see Chapter 10.

TABLE 6.16

Occupational Distribution of Mexican–Origin Men Aged 14 and Over:
1930–1970

	1970	1960	1950	1930
Total	100.0	100.0	100.0	100.0
Professional	5.4	3.1	1.7	1.0
Managers, nonfarm	4.2	3.5	3.5	2.5
Sales	3.3	3.0	NA	1.9
Clerical	5.7	4.1	NA	1.0
Sales and clerical	9.0	7.1	5.4	2.9
Craftsmen	20.5	16.4	13.1	6.5
Operatives total	27.2	23.4	18.4	8.6
Laborers, nonfarm	13.3	17.6	20.7	33.6
Farmers	0.6	1.7	3.0	8.5
Farm laborers	9.6	19.2	27.5	32.8
Service except private				
household	10.2	7.9	6.6	2.2
Private household	0.1	0.1	0.2	1.5
SES	46	39	33	24

1970 = Mexican origin or descent

1960 = 5 States, Spanish surname, Mexican born or parentage

1950 = Spanish surname, Arizona, California, Texas

1930 = Mexican

Notes:

The data for 1960 were further adjusted by taking into
consideration the relationship of the Mexican stock in these
five states in 1970, to the total Mexican origin population
in the United States in 1970.

The data for 1950 were further adjusted by taking into consideration
the relationship between total Spanish surname in these three states
in 1970, to the total Mexican origin population in the United States
in 1970.

however, the score increased only from 43 in 1930 to 50 in 1950 and to 58 in 1970.

The abysmal state of Mexican workers in 1930 can be further emphasized by closer inspection of the 1% of the men who received a census classification of "professional and technical." This classification included 3935 men, who are apportioned as follows:

Occupation	Number of persons
Musicians and music teachers	1033
Actors, dancers, athletes, and so on	435
Artists and art teachers	152
Clergymen	365
Authors, editors, and reporters	104
Semiprofessional and recreational workers (approximate)	1200
Subtotal	3289

There were only 93 lawyers and judges, 159 physicians and surgeons, 28 dentists, and 57 chemists, assayers, and metallurgists reported. Clearly, the statement that 1% were professional workers is an exaggeration in realistic terms.

The Situation in 1970. Of the Mexican-origin men, 1 in 10 was a professional or manager, in comparison with over 1 in 4 of the non-Spanish white men. Another 1 in 10 of the former were other white-collar workers; 2 in 10 were craftsmen; 1 in 10 was in agriculture, mostly as farm laborers; and close to half were in the lower manual occupations of operatives, laborers, and service workers (Table 6.17). Among the non-Spanish whites, on the other hand, only some 3 in 10 were in these lower manual occupations, and 1 in 20 was engaged in agriculture mostly as farmers and farm managers rather than as laborers.

Increased schooling is of overriding importance for the Mexican-origin men in climbing the occupational ladder. At each level of schooling, these men differ little from the comparably schooled non-Spanish white men. The comparative SES scores are

Years of schooling	Mexican origin	Non-Spanish white	Difference
Total population	46	59	13
Under 12	41	49	8
12	53	58	5
13–15	63	67	4
16 or more	81	82	1

With increasing schooling, the Mexican-origin men rapidly approach the Anglos, and among college graduates there are few differences. Among the latter, over 6 in 10 Mexican-origin men are professional

TABLE 6.17

Major Occupational Group, by Years of Schooling, Age, and Sex, Mexican Descent: 1970

	TOTAL Years of schooling				
	Total	−12 years	12 years	13–15 years	16+ years
Total	100.0	100.0	100.0	100.0	100.0
Professional, total	5.4	1.2	5.5	19.2	62.6
Modern science	1.8	0.3	1.3	6.4	27.6
Classical	2.4	0.6	2.2	5.9	32.5
Semiprofessional	1.2	0.3	2.0	6.9	2.5
Manager, nonfarm, total	4.2	2.5	6.1	9.9	15.7
Employee	3.0	1.5	4.6	7.8	13.4
Self-employed	1.2	1.0	1.5	2.1	2.3
Sales	3.3	2.2	5.3	8.8	4.5
Clerical	5.7	3.2	11.1	15.1	5.6
Craftsmen	20.5	20.5	24.3	17.5	4.3
Operatives (excl. transp.)	20.6	22.4	21.0	11.1	1.8
Transportation	6.6	7.3	6.4	3.2	0.9
Laborer, nonfarm	13.3	16.0	8.9	4.9	0.8
Farm manager	0.6	0.7	0.3	0.2	0.2
Farm laborer	9.6	13.2	1.8	0.6	0.7
Service, total	10.2	10.9	9.4	9.2	2.9
Household	0.1	0.1	0.0	0.0	0.0
Protective	0.8	0.5	1.7	2.3	0.8
Other	9.3	10.3	7.7	6.8	2.2
SES	46	41	53	63	81

workers, a figure almost identical to that of the non-Spanish whites. Furthermore, within the professional category the two groups are distributed between modern science and classical occupations in close to the same manner; very few of either group are technicians or semiprofessional workers.

In summary, it is clear that the low occupational position of the Mexican-origin men, as a totality, is due to their low level of schooling. If they had had the same amount of schooling as the non-Spanish whites, the Mexican-origin men would have been much higher on the occupational ladder.

OCCUPATIONS OF WOMEN

About 2 in 5 Mexican-origin women were employed in white-collar jobs; the majority were clerical workers. This compares with about 2 in 3 of the non-Spanish white women. Only 1 in 4 Mexican women was occupied as an operative, and 1 in 4 was a service worker (Table 6.18).

With increased schooling, more women are found in professional and managerial jobs. We may compare those who had not completed high school with college graduates, as follows:

TABLE 6.17 (cont.)

	14-34 Years of schooling					35-44 Years of schooling					45+ Years of schooling			
Total	-12 years	12 years	13-15 years	16+ years	Total	-12 years	12 years	13-15 years	16+ years	Total	-12 years	12 years	13-15 years	16+ years
100.0	100.0	100.0	100.0	100.0	100.0	100.0	100.0	100.0	100.0	100.0	100.0	100.0	100.0	100.0
5.9	1.2	4.8	19.5	63.8	6.3	1.2	7.0	19.1	66.1	3.9	1.2	6.1	18.1	55.0
1.7	0.2	1.0	5.4	24.4	2.4	0.4	1.1	8.4	31.3	1.6	0.3	2.5	7.4	28.1
2.6	0.7	1.7	5.9	35.8	2.8	0.6	3.3	5.6	32.8	1.7	0.6	2.6	5.9	26.0
1.7	0.3	2.1	8.2	3.6	1.0	0.3	2.6	5.0	2.0	0.5	0.2	1.0	4.8	0.9
3.0	1.5	3.9	6.8	11.6	5.3	3.0	9.4	13.9	17.5	5.1	3.3	10.7	16.4	20.8
2.5	1.1	3.4	5.8	10.7	3.9	1.9	6.8	10.8	15.8	2.9	1.6	6.5	11.3	14.7
0.5	0.4	0.5	1.0	0.9	1.4	1.0	2.6	3.0	1.7	2.3	1.8	4.2	5.1	6.1
3.9	2.5	5.2	8.9	3.9	2.6	1.5	5.8	7.2	3.2	3.1	2.3	5.1	10.8	7.6
7.1	3.6	11.8	16.4	7.0	4.7	2.7	9.6	15.3	4.6	4.2	3.2	9.9	9.9	4.3
17.8	17.1	22.0	15.2	4.6	23.7	24.3	28.2	21.1	3.7	21.9	21.6	28.2	21.8	4.8
23.1	25.7	23.4	12.5	3.0	20.3	22.9	18.0	9.6	0.9	16.8	18.0	15.2	7.9	0.9
6.1	6.7	6.5	3.6	0.9	7.6	8.8	6.2	2.2	0.9	6.5	6.8	6.4	3.4	0.9
13.4	16.5	10.6	5.6	1.1	11.6	14.2	5.8	4.0	0.3	14.7	16.8	6.4	3.4	0.9
0.3	0.3	0.1	0.1	0.0	0.5	0.5	0.5	0.2	0.3	1.2	1.3	0.4	0.6	0.4
9.0	13.8	2.0	0.8	0.5	8.9	11.8	1.5	0.4	0.6	11.3	13.4	1.6	0.3	1.3
10.5	11.2	9.7	10.5	3.6	8.4	9.0	8.1	7.0	2.0	11.3	12.0	9.8	7.4	3.0
0.1	0.1	0.0	0.1	0.0	0.1	0.1	0.0	0.0	0.0	0.1	0.2	0.0	0.0	0.0
0.9	0.4	1.5	2.3	0.7	0.8	0.4	2.1	2.4	0.6	0.8	0.6	1.8	2.3	1.3
9.5	10.7	8.2	8.1	3.0	7.5	8.5	5.9	4.6	1.4	10.4	11.3	8.0	5.1	1.7
46	40	51	62	78	48	42	56	65	83	44	40	56	65	80

Occupation	Under 12 years (%)	16 or more years (%)
Professional and managerial	8.5	79.9
Clerical and sales	31.1	13.0
Blue-collar and services	60.4	7.1

There is comparatively little difference between the occupational composition of Mexican-descent and non-Spanish white women at each schooling level. The SES scores are as follows:

Years of schooling	Mexican origin	Non-Spanish white	Difference
Total population	52	63	11
Under 12	45	49	4
12	61	64	3
13-15	69	71	2
16 or more	84	85	1

TABLE 6.18

Major Occupational Group, by Years of Schooling, Age, and Sex, Mexican Descent: 1970

	TOTAL Years of schooling					14-34 Years of schooling					35+ Years of schooling				
	Total years	-12 years	12 years	13-15 years	16+ years	Total years	-12 years	12 years	13-15 years	16+ years	Total years	-12 years	12 years	13-15 years	16+ years
Total	100.0	100.0	100.0	100.0	100.0	100.0	100.0	100.0	100.0	100.0	100.0	100.0	100.0	100.0	100.0
Professional, total	6.4	2.2	5.3	19.2	76.2	6.5	2.0	4.4	15.7	75.8	6.2	2.4	7.1	28.3	76.8
Modern science	1.9	0.7	2.0	8.7	9.1	1.8	0.4	1.6	7.2	9.6	2.0	0.9	2.8	12.6	8.3
Classical	4.0	1.3	2.5	9.6	65.4	4.2	1.4	2.0	8.1	64.5	3.7	1.1	3.5	13.3	66.7
Semiprofessional	0.5	0.2	0.8	1.0	1.7	0.5	0.2	0.8	0.4	1.7	0.5	0.3	0.8	2.4	1.8
Manager, nonfarm, total	2.1	1.6	2.6	3.1	3.7	1.2	0.6	1.6	2.4	2.9	3.1	2.4	4.7	4.8	4.8
Employee	1.4	0.9	2.0	2.5	3.2	1.0	0.6	1.4	2.0	2.5	1.8	1.2	3.3	3.8	4.2
Self employed	0.7	0.7	0.6	0.6	0.5	0.2	0.1	0.2	0.4	0.4	1.2	1.2	1.4	1.0	0.6
Sales	5.7	5.0	7.3	7.2	1.2	5.6	5.1	6.4	7.3	0.8	5.8	4.9	9.0	6.8	1.8
Clerical	25.4	11.3	49.9	51.8	11.8	33.1	14.8	53.6	56.0	13.3	16.9	8.6	42.3	41.0	9.5
Craftsmen	2.4	2.9	1.9	1.1	1.0	1.9	2.4	1.6	1.2	0.8	3.0	3.3	2.4	1.0	1.2
Operatives (excl. transp.)	26.5	36.0	14.3	4.3	2.5	23.1	34.9	13.7	4.0	2.1	30.3	36.8	15.6	5.1	3.0
Transportation	0.4	0.4	0.4	0.1	0.0	0.3	0.4	0.3	0.0	0.0	0.4	0.4	0.6	0.3	0.0
Laborer, nonfarm	1.9	2.6	0.9	0.6	0.0	2.0	3.1	1.0	0.5	0.0	1.7	2.2	0.6	0.7	0.0
Farm manager	0.1	0.1	0.1	0.1	0.0	0.1	0.2	0.1	0.0	0.0	0.1	0.1	0.0	0.3	0.0
Farm laborer	4.2	6.5	0.7	0.4	0.0	4.4	8.1	0.8	0.4	0.0	4.0	5.2	0.6	0.3	0.0
Service, total	24.9	31.4	16.6	12.2	3.7	21.7	28.4	16.4	12.5	4.2	28.6	33.7	17.1	11.3	3.0
Household	5.4	7.9	1.6	1.0	1.0	3.4	5.7	1.3	0.7	0.8	7.5	9.5	2.2	1.7	1.2
Protective	0.1	0.1	0.1	0.3	0.0	0.1	0.1	0.0	0.1	0.0	0.2	0.2	0.3	0.7	0.0
Other	19.4	23.4	14.9	10.9	2.7	18.2	22.6	15.1	11.7	3.3	20.9	24.0	14.6	8.9	1.8
SES	52	45	61	69	84	54	45	61	68	83	50	45	61	70	84

Clearly, with increased schooling the occupational composition of the Mexican-origin women rapidly approaches that of the non-Spanish white women until among college graduates there is virtually no difference. This pattern is the same as that previously observed for men.

Since 1950 there was significant movement up the occupational ladder, as we saw for men. In 1970 the SES score was 52, as compared with 48 2 decades earlier. The occupational distribution at the two dates compares as follows:

Occupation	1970 (%)	1950 (%)[a]	Difference (%)
Professional, technical, and kindred workers	6.4	3.7	2.7
Farmers and farm managers	.1	.2	− .1
Managers, officials, and proprietors, except farm	2.1	3.3	− 1.2
Clerical and kindred workers	25.4	12.1	13.3
Sales workers	5.7	9.2	− 3.5
Craftsmen, foremen, and kindred workers	2.4	1.5	.9
Operatives and kindred workers	26.9	35.0	− 8.1
Private household workers	5.4	12.3	− 6.9
Service workers (except private household)	19.5	13.6	5.9
Farm laborers and foremen	4.2	7.3	− 3.1
Laborers, nonfarm	1.9	1.8	.1

[a] Data for 1950 are from E. P. Hutchinson, *Immigrants and Their Children, 1850–1950* (New York: John Wiley & Sons, 1956), p. 340ff.

Clearly, there was movement into white-collar jobs and service work excluding private household workers. Movement was out of operative, private household, and agriculture occupations. This movement undoubtedly was influenced by the increased schooling observed between the end of World War II and 1970.[30]

THE VARIOUS MEXICAN POPULATIONS IN THE UNITED STATES

For present analytical purposes, we are considering as the two main populations: (a) those living in the five southwestern states; and (b) those living elsewhere. Within the southwestern states, however, the residents of Texas and of California appear to be quite different.

[30] By the late 1970s, there may have been a further increase in SES scores; see Chapter 10.

Hence we may subdivide these five states into: California, Texas, and the remainder (Arizona, New Mexico, and Colorado). Of those residing outside the Southwest, the residents of Illinois may differ from the others. Therefore, insofar as data permit, we shall describe the characteristics of these five populations; in some cases, however, comparisons are limited to the southwestern states versus the remainder of the United States.

In anticipation of the data to be presented in following sections, we summarize that we are more impressed with the homogeneity of the groups than with their relatively small differences.

DEMOGRAPHIC CHARACTERISTICS

Nativity. In California and the states outside of the Southwest, there are larger proportions of foreign born (Table 6.19). Whether this indicates direct movement from Mexico or migration out of Texas and the remaining three southwestern states cannot be determined with any certainty.

Age. There is very little difference in the age compositions of the several areas. Close to 60% of each population is aged 15 and over.

Sex Composition. Texas has the smallest percentage of men, and the states outside of the Southwest have the highest percentage. For the population aged 15 and over, these figures are, respectively, 48% and 52%. This suggests that men may have migrated out of Texas to other areas, particularly to the northern and eastern states.

Marital Status of Women. Among women aged 20–44, the smallest proportion reported as married and living with spouse was in Texas, 69%; the largest proportion, 73%, was observed outside the Southwest. It appears that as more men become available, more women become married.

However, in the states outside the Southwest, we find the largest proportions of women whose husbands are not Mexican. In the southwestern states, between 10 and 20% of the Mexican women had husbands who were not of Mexican origin; in the other states, about 40% had non-Mexican husbands.

Family Heads. The smallest proportion of family heads who were women was observed outside the Southwest. This corresponds with the previous observation that in these outlying states is found the largest

TABLE 6.19
Selected Demographic Characteristics of the Mexican–Origin Population, by Area of Residence: 1970

	Total United States	Cali- fornia	Texas	Arizona, Colorado New Mexico	All other
% foreign born	18.0	23.4	13.4	11.2	19.3
% distribution by age					
Total	100.0	100.0	100.0	100.0	100.0
Under 15 years	40.0	39.6	39.4	40.3	39.4
15 to 44 years	43.7	45.0	41.8	42.2	46.0
45 to 64 years	12.1	11.8	13.4	12.7	10.7
65 and over	4.2	3.6	5.4	4.7	3.9
15 and over	59.9	60.4	59.2	59.7	60.6
% men					
Age 15 and over	49.2	49.4	47.7	48.9	52.6
Age 15 to 44	49.1	49.4	47.6	49.0	52.1
Marital status of women, age 20 to 44					
% married, spouse present	70.9	71.5	68.8	72.4	73.3
% husband non-Mexican	18.0	20.0	9.0	16.0	39.0
% family heads women	13.4	14.1	13.7	13.7	10.2
Schooling					
Men age 20 to 24					
% completed elementary school	82.5	84.8	76.1	90.0	84.6
% completed high school	51.9	54.7	44.1	59.1	55.4
% high school graduates who entered college	35.2	36.1	35.9	34.6	32.5
% college entrants who completed college	10.9	8.5	10.8	13.5	16.4
% college graduates	2.0	1.7	1.7	2.8	3.0
Women, age 20 to 24					
% completed elementary school	80.4	83.6	73.3	86.6	85.1
% completed high school	49.6	52.9	43.0	53.1	54.2
% high school graduates who entered college	26.0	26.0	26.9	24.3	25.5
% college entrants who completed college	11.8	10.0	14.6	8.0	13.2
% college graduates	1.5	1.4	1.7	1.0	1.8

proportion of women who were married and living with their husbands. Within the three subareas of the Southwest, there were virtually no differences in the proportions of families headed by women.

Schooling. The smallest proportions of high school graduates are found in Texas, for both men and women and for all age groups. The other four areas had significantly larger proportions of high school graduates, although the differences among them were minimal. Why Texas is so unusual, we do not know.

Summary. Overall demographic differences among the populations residing in the several areas appear to be minimal.

WOMEN IN THE REPRODUCTIVE AGES AND FERTILITY

Comparisons are possible between the five southwestern states as a group and the rest of the United States separately for those who did and those who did not complete high school.

Fertility. There is little difference in the average number of children ever born alive per woman between these two groups. The standardized[31] rates are as follows:

		Years of schooling	
Women	Total	Under 12	12 or more
Mexican origin			
5 southwestern states	2.0	2.6	1.7
All other	1.9	2.7	1.6
Non-Spanish white			
5 southwestern states	1.5	2.0	1.4
All other	1.6	2.0	1.4

Mexican-American women have higher fertility than do the non-Spanish white women, even after controlling for schooling, age, marital status, and employment.

Nevertheless, if the former have completed high school and resided outside of the five southwestern states, their fertility tended to approach that of the non-Spanish white women. This tendency is in agreement with our previous observations that more Mexican-origin women residing outside the Southwest had married non-Mexican husbands, that increased schooling is related to increased outmarriage, and that outmarriage resulted in lower fertility.

Some Characteristics of the Women. Mexican-origin women who lived outside the Southwest were somewhat more likely to be married

---

[31] Standardized for age, marital status, and employment. See Appendix C.

and living with their husbands than were the women residing in the Southwest. This is observed for each age group and for the two levels of schooling (Table 6.20).

The former are also more likely to be employed. Whether this resulted from more employment opportunities elsewhere in the United States or from other reasons is not readily determinable.

ECONOMIC CHARACTERISTICS

Labor Force. The proportion of men aged 20–64, the prime working years, who are in the civilian labor force was about 86%, with little variation from one state to another (Table 6.20). Illinois was exceptional with 93% in the labor force, and the other states outside the Southwest had the lowest proportion, 79%.

Illinois also had the lowest unemployment rate at the time of the 1970 Census, 3.1%, and California had the highest, 6.3%. The other areas had between 4 and 5% unemployed.

Women in Illinois aged 20–44, the reproductive years, had the highest proportion in the labor force, 60%, the other outlying states had 48%, and the five southwestern states had around 40%.

Unemployment of women was higher than that of men. In Texas 6.1% of the Mexican-origin women were unemployed, and in Illinois 6.4% were unemployed. California had the highest rate, 9.8%.

Occupations of Men. There are few differences in the occupational composition of the Mexican-origin men who reside in the various parts of the United States (Table 6.21). A few more in the five southwestern states and almost none in Illinois are engaged in agriculture. On the other hand, more men in Illinois are operatives. This uniformity undoubtedly reflects the relatively uniform schooling levels throughout the country that lead to the men being largely in manual jobs. Precisely which jobs they fill, however, reflects job opportunities in the areas in which they live.

The SES scores reflect this uniformity, and are for the total United States, for California, and for Texas, 46; for Arizona, for Colorado, and for New Mexico, 45; for all other states and for Illinois (included in all other states), 47.

Occupations of Women. As for men, the occupational composition is quite uniform throughout the country. Very few are engaged in agriculture in any area. More are operatives in Illinois, and in the

TABLE 6.20
Selected Economic Characteristics for the Mexican–Origin Population by Area of Residence: 1970

	United States	California	Texas	Arizona Colorado New Mexico	All other Total	All other Illinois	Other
Labor force							
Men age 20 to 64							
% in civilian labor force	85.9	86.8	86.4	84.6	83.1	93.2	79.0
% unemployed	5.2	6.3	4.1	5.0	4.4	3.1	5.0
Women age 20 to 44							
% in civilian labor force	42.5	43.4	39.3	38.4	51.5	60.2	47.9
% unemployed	7.9	9.8	6.1	6.8	7.3	6.4	7.7
Mean family income, 1969	$7690	8640	6200	7000	9200	10000	8870
Personal income, 1969 population aged 16+							
Men	$5170	5750	4190	4880	5620	6490	5450
Women	$2430	2690	2000	2140	2800	3280	2630

TABLE 6.21

Occupational Distribution, Mexican–Origin Employed Population Aged 16, by Sex and Area of Residence: 1970

| | MEN | | | | | |
	U.S.	Calif.	Texas	Ariz., Colo. New Mex.	All other	Illinois*
Total	100.0	100.0	100.0	100.0	100.0	100.0
Professional, Technical & Kindred Workers	5.3	5.1	4.6	6.2	7.0	3.8
Managers, Officials & Proprietors, ex. Farm	4.0	3.5	4.8	4.1	3.2	2.1
Sales Workers	3.2	2.8	4.0	3.4	2.5	2.0
Clerical & Kindred Workers	5.8	6.0	5.6	4.9	5.9	6.9
Craftsmen, Foremen & Kindred Workers	21.0	21.0	22.8	19.3	19.1	18.1
Operatives & Kindred Workers	27.0	28.2	24.6	24.3	32.1	40.9
Laborers, nonfarm	13.4	12.5	13.7	16.3	13.1	15.3
Farmers & Farm Managers	0.6	0.4	0.1	0.8	0.4	0.1
Farm Laborers & Foremen	9.2	10.1	9.2	9.0	6.5	0.7
Private Household Workers	0.1	0.1	0.1	0.1	0.0	0.0
Service Workers ex. Private Household	10.4	10.3	10.5	11.5	10.2	10.1
SES score	46	46	46	45	46	47

*Included in "all other."

Southwest more are service workers. The proportions in white-collar jobs, as well as the SES scores, barely vary from one area to another. These are as follows:

Area	White-collar (%)	SES score
United States	40	52
California	39	54
Texas	40	52
Arizona, Colo- rado, New Mexico	41	52
All other	41	54
Illinois	37	54

TABLE 6.21 (*cont.*)

	WOMEN					
	U.S.	Calif.	Texas	Ariz., Colo. New Mex.	All other	Illinois*
Total	100.0	100.0	100.0	100.0	100.0	100.0
Professional, Technical & Kindred Workers	6.4	5.5	6.8	6.7	8.1	4.4
Managers, Officials & Proprietors, ex. Farm	1.9	1.6	2.2	2.0	2.0	0.6
Sales Workers	5.7	4.9	7.3	5.7	4.4	4.8
Clerical & Kindred Workers	25.9	27.0	24.0	26.1	26.8	26.8
Craftsmen, Foremen & Kindred Workers	2.3	2.2	2.6	1.5	2.3	2.7
Operatives & Kindred Workers	25.9	31.5	20.3	18.2	28.3	43.8
Laborers, nonfarm	1.8	1.7	1.8	1.5	2.0	2.0
Farmers & Farm Managers	0.1	0.1	0.1	0.0	0.2	0.0
Farm Laborers & Foremen	3.9	5.3	2.9	2.5	2.8	0.2
Private Household Workers	5.5	4.0	8.2	6.7	2.6	1.0
Service Workers ex. Private Household	20.6	16.2	23.8	29.1	20.5	13.7
SES score	52	54	52	52	54	54

*Included in "all other."

Family Income. Mean family income was $10,000 in Illinois, the highest of any area. The lowest was Texas with $6200, and the other three southwestern states averaged only $7000. California and the outlying states (excluding Illinois) averaged slightly under $9000 (Table 6.20).

Undoubtedly, several factors produce these differing average incomes. Probably the higher proportion of women in the labor force in Illinois and the other outlying states is one factor that helps to account for the larger average income in these areas. A second factor is the larger proportion of men in the labor force in Illinois. Another factor is the higher per capita income of men and women (as we shall see) in Illinois, followed by California and the other outlying states. Finally,

Social Security and public assistance or welfare programs may add a little more in Illinois, California, and other outlying areas.[32]

Personal Income. Men who resided in Illinois had the highest average (mean) income in 1969, $6490, and residents of Texas had the lowest, $4190 (Tables 6.22 and 6.23). The pattern of personal income is similar to that of family income. California was in second place, followed by the other outlying states (excluding Illinois), and then the three southwestern states of Arizona, Colorado, and New Mexico.

The same pattern is seen for the income of women. The mean income was highest in Illinois, $3280, and lowest in Texas, $2000. Regional differences persist even after taking educational levels into account (Table 6.22). For example, let us illustrate with age 35–44, for which median earnings in 1969 were as follows:

Years of schooling	Men		Women	
	5 southwestern states ($)	All other ($)	5 southwestern states ($)	All other ($)
Under 12	5730	7220	2200	3030
12	7870	8510	3660	4050
13–15	9040	9490	4180	4970
16 or more	10,600	12,550	6770	NA

Previously, we noted that there were very few differences among the several areas with respect to occupational composition. This suggests that the wage structures in these various states were sufficiently different to account for a significant part of the variation in average in-

---

[32] Average incomes per family recipient in 1969 were as follows:

Area	From Social Security ($)	From assistance or welfare ($)
United States	1380	1410
California	1440	1700
Texas	1210	920
Arizona, Colorado, and New Mexico	1470	1280
Outlying		
Total	1640	1300
Illinois	1740	1580
Other	1620	1240

TABLE 6.22

Earnings in 1969, Mexican Descent, Five Southwestern States, by Sex, Age, and Years of Schooling

Years of schooling	MEN						WOMEN					
	14 & over	14-24 years	25-34 years	35-44 years	45-64 years	65+ years	14 & over	14-24 years	25-34 years	35-44 years	45-64 years	65+ years
Total U.S.												
1st quartile	$2,330	710	3,900	4,170	3,340	1,020	$ 770	540	980	1,020	1,000	680
Median	4,810	1,890	5,970	6,440	5,490	2,190	2,050	1,220	2,600	2,620	2,440	1,610
3rd quartile	7,460	4,040	8,220	8,890	7,940	4,830	3,810	2,900	4,300	4,330	4,080	3,490
Variation*	1.07	1.76	.72	.73	.84	1.74	1.48	1.93	1.28	1.26	1.26	1.75
Under 12 years												
1st quartile	2,020	560	3,390	3,740	3,150	990	650	420	770	880	920	640
Median	4,320	1,370	5,170	5,730	5,150	2,070	1,640	830	1,980	2,200	2,190	1,470
3rd quartile	6,770	3,460	7,240	7,880	7,520	4,730	3,250	1,950	3,500	3,730	3,690	3,160
Variation	1.10	2.12	.74	.72	.85	1.81	1.58	1.84	1.38	1.30	1.26	.44
12 years												
1st quartile	3,240	1,350	5,080	5,940	5,310	1,650	1,120	820	1,590	1,900	1,780	860
Median	5,990	2,980	6,980	7,870	7,590	3,300	2,890	2,100	3,380	3,660	3,780	2,490
3rd quartile	8,440	5,330	9,020	9,920	9,960	6,610	4,580	3,720	4,960	5,580	5,820	4,850
Variation	.87	1.34	.56	.51	.61	1.50	1.20	1.38	1.00	1.01	1.07	1.60
13 to 15 years												
1st quartile	2,670	1,160	4,990	7,060	6,000	1,660	1,170	810	2,270	2,240	2,150	1,640
Median	6,330	2,440	7,480	9,040	8,430	3,530	2,910	1,850	4,090	4,180	4,660	3,100
3rd quartile	9,260	4,590	9,760	11,400	11,180	5,530	4,850	3,580	5,690	6,410	7,350	5,630
Variation	1.04	1.41	.64	.48	.61	1.10	1.26	1.50	.84	1.00	1.12	1.30
16+ years												
1st quartile	5,590	1,410	5,540	7,480	7,870	740	3,150	1,570	3,600	4,560	3,810	710
Median	8,900	2,820	8,320	10,600	11,060	2,440	5,630	3,310	5,770	6,770	6,630	2,710
3rd quartile	12,630	5,330	11,200	14,470	17,160	7,090	7,550	5,260	7,280	9,360	9,620	5,670
Variation	.79	1.39	.68	.66	.84	2.60	.78	1.11	.64	.71	.88	1.83

*Interquartile range divided by median.

Source: Special Census tabulations.

TABLE 6.23
Earnings in 1969, Mexican Descent, All Other States by Sex, Age, and Years of Schooling

Years of schooling	MEN						WOMEN					
	14 & over years	14-24 years	25-34 years	35-44 years	45-64 years	65+ years	14 & over years	14-24 years	25-34 years	35-44 years	45-64 years	65+ years
Total U.S.												
1st quartile	$2,800	900	4,640	4,170	4,960	1,180	880	580	1,470	1,600	1,580	1,070
Median	5,940	2,410	6,880	6,450	7,120	2,570	2,460	1,370	3,200	3,400	3,290	2,410
3rd quartile	8,500	4,890	8,940	8,390	9,440	6,320	4,420	3,280	5,100	5,140	4,980	4,560
Variation*	.96	1.66	.63	.73	.63	2.00	1.44	1.97	1.13	1.04	1.03	1.45
Under 12 years												
1st quartile	2,530	670	4,170	5,170	3,660	1,110	720	410	650	1,310	1,420	1,070
Median	5,629	1,820	6,420	7,220	6,000	2,430	1,890	820	1,430	3,030	3,040	1,940
3rd quartile	8,030	4,460	8,450	9,500	7,910	5,950	3,760	1,800	3,100	4,490	4,470	3,820
Variation	.98	2.08	.67	.60	.71	1.99	1.61	1.70	1.71	1.05	1.00	1.42
12 years												
1st quartile	3,370	1,680	5,450	6,970	6,450	+	1,400	970	1,630	2,310	1,800	+
Median	6,400	3,210	7,270	8,510	8,200	·	3,140	2,530	3,360	4,050	3,980	
3rd quartile	8,780	5,700	9,150	10,830	10,540		5,060	4,290	5,250	5,970	5,580	
Variation	.85	1.25	.51	.45	.50		1.17	1.31	1.08	.90	.95	
13 to 15 years												
1st quartile	2,490	1,290	4,660	7,390	7,280	+	1,160	850	1,580	2,780	2,500	+
Median	6,160	2,510	7,220	9,490	9,380		3,180	1,910	3,940	4,970	5,550	
3rd quartile	8,260	4,160	9,520	12,500	11,930		5,410	4,070	5,550	7,380	6,620	
Variation	.94	1.14	.67	.54	.50		1.34	1.69	1.01	.93	.74	
16+ years												
1st quartile	5,490	1,410	5,520	7,890	8,590	+	2,250	+	2,580	+	+	+
Median	8,930	3,070	8,080	12,550	11,400		5,440		5,380			
3rd quartile	13,420	5,140	11,110	21,260	14,750		8,170		8,130			
Variation	.89	1.21	.69	1.07	.54		1.09		1.03			

*Interquartile range divided by median.
+Too few cases in sample, under 500 inflated population.

Source: Special Census tabulation.

comes, since wage and salary income accounts for the major part of all family income. Comparison of the five southwestern states with the others complicates the analysis somewhat, insofar as more men in the Southwest are engaged in agriculture, a notoriously low paying industry. Nevertheless, area differences in wage structures must be important in explaining both personal and family income differences among the Mexican-origin workers.

Summary. Texas is the "land of least opportunity" to the Mexican American. To become more schooled and to better himself or herself financially, residence in Illinois or California is recommended. The other states tend to be in between.

SUMMARY

The Mexican-origin people may be changing their demographic characteristics least rapidly of the several groups we are studying. Change is occurring, however, especially in California and the states outside of the Southwest. When two in five of the Mexican-origin married women in these outlying states, and one in five in California, have non-Mexican husbands, demographic and cultural change must be occurring there. Furthermore, the younger people are becoming more schooled. Increased schooling is both an indicator of and a force for change. By itself, increased schooling does not solve all social and economic problems, but it does provide a glimpse into the future. For, as we have seen, the more schooled have demographic characteristics more nearly similar to those of the non-Spanish whites than do the lesser schooled.

We suspect that an important reason for the relatively low rate of change for this group is the continuous influx of Mexican born from south to north of the border. These immigrants bring with them their traditional demographic and cultural traits and thus reinforce the traditional traits north of the border. Of considerable significance is that most of these immigrants have little schooling, a factor that operates against their acquiring the North American's demographic characteristics.

In addition to the immigrants, large numbers of U.S. Mexicans visit the country of Mexico and are thus exposed to the life and culture south of the border. To what extent such visits and exposures influence them on their return to the United States, we have no way of knowing.

We only suspect that such visits to the southland can reinforce the original culture in the northland.

Furthermore, demographic change and increases in schooling in Mexico are taking place at such a slow rate that it will be at least another two or three decades before a "new" Mexican immigrant is likely to cross the border in any significant numbers. Hence the old Mexican culture as it is found north of the border will continue to be reinforced for some time to come.

Over the next several generations, we believe, larger numbers of the Mexican Americans will be high school and college graduates, and many of these people will merge demographically and perhaps otherwise into Anglo society, especially if they leave the Southwest. The little schooled, however, will continue in their accustomed demographic manner and will be reinforced continuously by little-schooled immigrants. Since in the country of Mexico population and labor force growth is continuing at high rates, and the growing economy cannot provide enough jobs for the increasing labor force, both legal and illegal migration northward across the border will continue indefinitely into the future.

7

The Puerto Rican–Origin Population

INTRODUCTION[1]

Columbus on his second voyage to the New World reached the present island of Puerto Rico in November 1493.[2] From this time on, the Spanish colonial history of the island was interwoven with that of Cuba, many of the other Caribbean islands, and Florida and the southeastern portion of present United States.

Before the Spanish conquest, the island had been occupied by the Arawaks, who had come from South America.[3] By 1493 the Caribs, who also had come from South America, were taking over the Caribbean islands; they held the Lesser Antilles but apparently had not yet reached Puerto Rico, although they had reached the Virgin Islands.

The Puerto Ricans of today are the descendants of these Indians and the past waves of Spanish and other migrants to the island. The original Indian population as a separate entity was wiped out within a few decades after the arrival of the Spaniards; the only Indian blood in the population today has been transmitted through interbreeding in the

---

[1] See also A. J. Jaffe, *People, Jobs and Economic Development* (Glencoe, Ill.: Free Press, 1959), chap. 2–4. Enrique R. Bravo, ed. and comp., *An Annotated Selected Puerto Rican Bibliography*, trans. Marcial Cuevas (New York: The Urban Center, Columbia University, 1972), is a comprehensive bibliography covering various aspects.

[2] Samuel Eliot Morison, *The European Discovery of America, The Southern Voyages, 1492–1616* (New York: Oxford University Press, 1974) for information about Columbus and other explorers.

[3] Julian H. Steward, "The Circum-Caribbean Tribes," in *Handbook of South American Indians*, ed. Julian H. Steward, Smithsonian Institution, Bureau of American Ethnology, vol. 4 (Washington, D.C. 1945), p. 23ff.

past. Spaniards continued to arrive throughout the sixteenth and subsequent centuries.

By 1591 there were 300 Spanish settlers on the island; by the end of the sixteenth century, about 1000. From the early seventeenth century, blacks were imported, primarily to build military fortifications. Throughout this century, Spanish artisans, soldiers, and convicts continued to come to Puerto Rico, for much labor was needed for the great fortifications being erected. These sources of labor were insufficient, and during the eighteenth century, convicts from other areas of Spanish America were also brought in. Once the military fortifications were substantially completed, however, there was no need for additional labor, and immigration stopped. The bulk of the people who had been imported to build the great fortifications remained on the island as subsistence farmers.

Since Puerto Rico was a Spanish colony for over 4 centuries, until 1898, when it became a possession of the United States, the island people retain many Spanish elements in their culture. Spanish is the language used in the public schools, although English is also taught and the trend is toward bilingualism. Compared with other Latin America countries, the Puerto Ricans are very "American," but continental Americans find them quite "Spanish." In short, Puerto Rico is an area in transition, midway between the Spanish and the English—American cultures, in the habits, attitudes, and the outlook of its people.

Politically and economically, the island is part of the United States. It was administered as a territory until 1952, when it was granted commonwealth status. This new status has not provided any substantial change in the insular government's powers or in its relations with the federal government. As a commonwealth, Puerto Rico is self-governing in virtually all domestic matters but does not participate in the formulation of federal law and policy. The federal Constitution, however, applies to Puerto Rico as it applies to any state in the union. The commonwealth constitution, adopted in 1952, must and does conform to the federal Constitution. This means, among other things, that private property is as fully recognized and protected on the island as in any part of the mainland United States. In addition, Puerto Rico's relations with foreign countries are the same as are those of any state in the union, and Puerto Rican residents are subject to service in the United States armed forces in the same manner and under the same conditions as are residents of the U.S. mainland.

On the other hand, the U.S. Congress has exempted Puerto Rico from federal taxes; neither the federal income tax nor federal excise taxes are collected on the island. Furthermore, all federal excise taxes collected on Puerto Rican products (e.g. rum and tobacco) that are sold on the mainland are turned back to the commonwealth treasury, as are the import duties collected in the federal customs house in San Juan. Puerto Rico is, however, an integral part of the U.S. economy. It shares the American currency and its tariffs. There are no barriers to the movement of either goods or people between the mainland and the island.

Geographically, Puerto Rico is a densely settled Caribbean island about 161 km long and 56 km wide with a population of 3,300,000 in 1977. The advantages of a benign tropical climate are offset by a mountainous terrain. Despite the luxuriant foliage everywhere, most of the island is not suited to agriculture and possesses few natural resources basic to economic development.

From 1493 to 1898 Puerto Rican economy was primarily agricultural, or, to be more precise, a combination of agriculture and defense. The people were mostly subsistence or semisubsistence farmers; only small amounts of produce were exported. The military establishment maintained by the Spaniards was the other major industry of the island. There was little else. From the time of U.S. annexation to about the World War II period, agriculture continued to be the leading activity, and sugar cane, the main cash crop. Poverty was the rule, and unemployment was common. Birth and death rates were high. Tuberculosis and other diseases of malnutrition and overcrowding were widespread, and public-health facilities were inadequate. Schools were few in the rural areas, and the population was generally uneducated. In short, the island was a typical underdeveloped area. Since World War II, economic growth has proceeded at a rapid pace until at present the economic and social situation of the islanders compares favorably with many parts of Europe. Instead of an underdeveloped country, Puerto Rico must now be considered to be at least semideveloped.

When World War II ended, surplus airplanes were available for civilian use, and very inexpensive air transportation between Puerto Rico and New York City was established. Jobs on the mainland were available at that time, and the stage was set for large-scale migration away from the island. The poor, the unemployed, the little schooled—all sought jobs in New York City, the "land of promise and hope." And there were no legal barriers to movement from Puerto Rico. Since the end of World War II, great economic improvements have occurred in the island, and the concomitant social, cultural, and demographic developments have produced a "new" Puerto Rican. Description of these changes and their effects on migration from the island, together with implications for future migration, will be discussed in the last section of this chapter.

SOME DEMOGRAPHIC CHARACTERISTICS

POPULATION GROWTH

Prior to World War II, there were relatively few island-born persons living on the U.S. mainland (Table 7.1). Of these, an unknown number were the children of non-Spanish Americans who had resided on the island as either businessmen or government officials and who happened to have been born there.[4] In part, this lack of large-scale migration was attributable to the relatively high cost of transportation. Another factor may have been the large-scale immigration of Europeans to the U.S. labor markets, together with the movement of southern blacks to northern cities in response to the job opportunities created by World War I. With the cessation of European immigration in the 1920s, following the immigration laws of the earlier part of that decade, there could have been increased migration from the island of Puerto Rico. That there was some increase is clear, as the island-born population increased from about 12,000 in 1920 to 53,000 in 1930. The Great Depression of the 1930s, however, hindered any further large-scale migration.

Following the end of World War II and concomitant decreases in transportation costs, large-scale migration from Puerto Rico ensued. Such migration was assured, insofar as jobs also became available, especially in the New York City area. These jobs included both those in nonagricultural occupations and a number as farm laborers in the northeast U.S. mainland. The number of migrants—that is, island-born persons residing on the mainland—increased greatly, reaching over 800,000 by 1970. In the meantime, the number of their children born on the mainland also increased greatly, from about 75,000 in 1950 (the first date for which information is available) to some 580,000 in 1970. Together there were slightly under 1.5 million persons of Puerto Rican origin living on the mainland.

In 1970, the population of the island was 2,700,000. Add this to the 1,400,000 persons of Puerto Rican origin reported on the mainland at

---

[4] The U.S. Census classifies persons simply by place of birth without reference to ethnic identity, except for data in the 1970 Census. The data in Table 7.1, except for the line "3rd and subsequent generations," are strictly by place of birth of the person or of his or her parent or parents.

TABLE 7.1

Puerto Ricans in the U.S. Mainland and in New York City by Place of Birth: 1910–1970

| | Numbers (in thousands) | | | | | | |
	1970	1960	1950	1940	1930	1920	1910
Total U.S.	1429.4	NA	NA	NA	NA	NA	NA
1st and 2nd generations	1391.5	892.5	301.4	NA	NA	NA	NA
Born in Puerto Rico	810.1	617.0	226.1	70.0	52.8	11.8	1.5
Born in Mainland	581.4	275.5	75.3	NA	NA	NA	NA
3rd and subsequent generations							
Born in Mainland of Mainland-							
born parents	37.9	NA	NA	NA	NA	NA	NA
New York City	846.7	NA	NA	NA	NA	NA	NA
1st and 2nd generations	817.7	612.6	245.9	NA	NA	NA	NA
Born in Puerto Rico	473.3	429.7	187.4	63.3	46.0	7.7	0.6
Born in Mainland	344.4	182.9	58.5	NA	NA	NA	NA
3rd and subsequent generations	29.0	NA	NA	NA	NA	NA	NA
Percent resident in							
New York City	59.2	NA	NA	NA	NA	NA	NA
1st and 2nd generations	58.8	68.6	81.6	NA	NA	NA	NA
Born in Puerto Rico	58.4	69.6	82.9	90.4	87.1	65.3	40.0
Born in Mainland	59.2	66.4	77.7	NA	NA	NA	NA
3rd and subsequent generations	76.5	NA	NA	NA	NA	NA	NA

Sources of data: 1950 to 1970, 1st and 2nd generations from 1970 Census,
Puerto Ricans in the United States, PC(2)-1E, p. XI.

1910 to 1940, 1st and 2nd generations from 1950 Census,
Puerto Ricans in Continental United States, P-E, No. 3, Table A.

Estimates of 3rd and subsequent generations obtained by
subtracting the reported numbers in the 1st and 2nd
generations from the total Puerto Rican origin population
as reported in 1970 Census, Persons of Spanish Origin.

that time, and we see that of the over 4,000,000 total Puerto Ricans,
about one-third were living on the mainland. By the late 1970s, the
island population had increased to 3.3 million, and the mainland
population, to about 1.8 million.[5]

---

[5] For the island population, see *Statistical Abstract of the United States, 1979* (Washington, D.C.: Government Printing Office, 1979), p. 874. For the mainland population, see Chapter 10.

Actually, the volume of migration fluctuated greatly from one period to another, and in some years more people returned to the island than left it. The peak period of movement to the mainland was in the first half of the 1950s, when there was a net outflow of over 250,000 persons. The second half of the 1950s was not far behind. On the other hand, between 1970 and 1977 there was a net movement to the island of about 200,000 persons; this includes refugee Cubans and other foreign born.

It is clear that much of the impetus for this movement away from Puerto Rico comes from the job opportunities on the mainland. The peak migration to the mainland coincided with the lowest levels of unemployment there—the early 1950s. Small amounts of migration from, or return migration to, the island, on the other hand, coincided with periods of high unemployment on the mainland. We can only infer that these movements reflect different employment opportunities.

GEOGRAPHIC DISTRIBUTION IN 1970

More than 6 in 10 Puerto Ricans lived in the state of New York, almost all in New York City, in 1970, and 2 in 10 lived just across the Hudson River in New Jersey. Six more states together accounted for another 2 in 10: Massachusetts, Connecticut, Pennsylvania, Illinois, California, and Florida. Fewer than 1 in 10 lived in the remaining 42 states plus the District of Columbia. Clearly, the Puerto Rican population is far more concentrated than is the general population (Figure 7.1 and Table 7.2).

Since 1950, the population has dispersed a bit more throughout the U.S. mainland. Less than 2 in 10 had lived outside New York City in 1950; a little more than 3 in 10, in 1960; and 4 in 10, in 1970 (Figure 7.2). This dispersal was mainly to areas adjacent to New York City, especially New Jersey.

The Puerto Ricans are central-city folk. Some 8 in 10 live in the large central cities, 1 in 10 lives in the surrounding suburbs, and 1 in 10 lives in the nonmetropolitan areas. This is in great contrast to the total U.S. population, of which only about 3 in 10 live in central cities.

Outside of New York State, the Puerto Rican population is somewhat more dispersed into the suburbs and the nonmetropolitan areas than is the case in New York. Nevertheless, this dispersal is significantly less than it is for the general population of the United States.

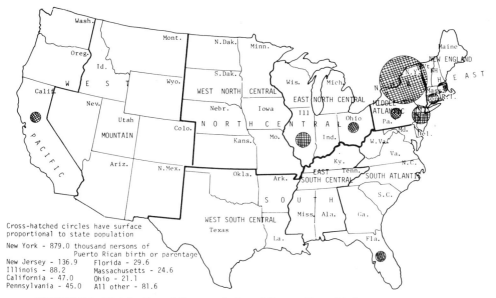

Cross-hatched circles have surface
proportional to state population

New York - 879.0 thousand persons of
Puerto Rican birth or parentage
New Jersey - 136.9   Florida - 29.6
Illinois - 88.2   Massachusetts - 24.6
California - 47.0   Ohio - 21.1
Pennsylvania - 45.0   All other - 81.6

FIGURE 7.1. *Distribution of the population of Puerto Rican birth or parentage, 1970.*

PERCENTAGE CHANGE IN THE POPULATION
OF PUERTO RICAN BIRTH OR PARENTAGE
1960-1970

Blank - less than 100% change*
Hatched - 100 - 120% change
Cross hatched - more than 120%

*Actually the average for this group was below 50%

FIGURE 7.2. *Percentage change in the population of Puerto Rican birth or parentage, 1960–1970.*

191

TABLE 7.2

Geographical Distribution of the Puerto Rican–Born Population Living in the Mainland, 1940–1970, and of Puerto Rican Parentage, 1970

| | Island born | | | | | | Mainland born Puerto Rican parentage 1970 | |
| | Numbers (000) | | | Percent distribution | | | | |
	1970	1950	1940	1970	1950	1940	No.	%
Total	810.1	226.1	70.0	100.0	100.0	100.0	581.4	100.0
Northeast	657.8	200.6	65.0	81.2	88.7	93.0	468.6	80.6
New York State	505.9	191.3	63.3	62.5	84.6	90.6	373.1	64.2
New York City	473.3	187.4	61.5	58.4	82.9	88.0	344.4	59.2
Remainder of State	32.6	3.9	1.8	4.0	1.7	2.6	28.7	4.9
Remainder of region	151.9	9.3	1.8	18.7	4.1	2.6	95.5	16.4
North Central	79.3	8.6	0.9	9.8	3.8	1.3	56.5	9.7
South	43.3	9.7	1.8	5.4	4.3	2.6	26.4	4.5
West	29.6	7.2	2.2	3.6	3.2	3.1	29.9	5.1

Sources of data: 1970 from Puerto Ricans in the United States PC(2)1E, Tables 1 and 13.

1950 from Puerto Ricans in Continental United States P-E, No. 30,Table 1.

PLACE OF BIRTH

About 4 in 10 persons had been born on the U.S. mainland, according to the 1970 Census. In 1950, only 3 in 10 had been born here. The remaining population—well over half at both dates—had migrated from the island (Figure 7.3). By 1990 it is expected that the majority will have been born on the mainland and may constitute some 6 in 10 of the total Puerto Rican population.

Of those born on the Mainland (as of 1970), practically all were the children of migrants. As nearly as we can estimate, there are very few persons who were born here of mainland-born parents. In another couple of decades, of course, this third generation will be much larger.

AGE AND SEX COMPOSITION

The Puerto Rican population averaged about 20 years of age (median age) in 1970, as compared with about 28 years for the general population (Table 7.3). This 20-year average fails to tell the entire story, however. Those born on the island averaged about 30 years, whereas

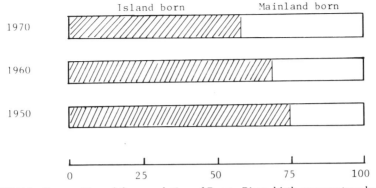

FIGURE 7.3. *Composition of the population of Puerto Rican birth or parentage by place of birth.*

those who had been born on the mainland averaged only slightly under 10 years. The latter, clearly, are as yet predominantly small children. In several decades, however, the average age of these mainland born will approach that of the general population.

The preponderance of youngsters, especially among the mainland born, makes itself evident in the school situation. Of all the mainland born in 1970, over half were of school age, namely, age 5–19. Among the island born, however, only one in five was of school age. With such large proportions of school-age children, especially among the mainland born, the school situation is affected insofar as the Puerto Ricans are "overrepresented." On the other hand, the schools have the opportunity to educate these children to live on the mainland.

Among the total Puerto Rican population, there were 97 males for every 100 females in 1970. This figure is slightly higher than that for the general U.S. population, among whom there were only 95 males per 100 females.

Since there are almost equal numbers of males and females under the age of about 20, let us consider the adult population—those aged 20 and over. Among the Puerto Ricans on the mainland (in 1970), there were about 90 men per 100 women. Among the general U.S. population, there were also about 90 men per 100 women. The Puerto Ricans are no different.

SIZE OF FAMILY

In 1970, there were about 4 persons per Puerto Rican family, as compared with about 3.1 per family for the total U.S. population. In 1950, the average was about the same for the Puerto Rican families. Mexican

TABLE 7.3

Persons of Puerto Rican Origin, by Age, Sex, and Place of Birth: Mainland U.S. 1970 (numbers in thousands)

Age	Total				Mainland born				Born outside Mainland			
	Total No.	%	Men	Women	Total No.	%	Men	Women	Total No.	%	Men	Women
Total	1429.4	100.0	704.9	724.5	646.0	100.0	330.2	315.8	783.4	100.0	374.8	408.6
Under 5 years	204.8	14.3	105.4	99.3	183.1	28.4	95.1	88.0	21.6	2.8	10.3	11.3
5 to 13 years	341.6	23.9	173.9	167.7	265.6	41.1	135.8	129.8	76.0	9.7	38.1	37.9
14 to 19 years	174.0	12.2	88.6	85.3	92.2	14.3	48.0	44.3	81.7	10.4	40.7	41.1
20 to 24 years	135.8	9.5	64.8	71.0	32.4	5.0	15.5	16.9	103.3	13.2	49.2	54.1
25 to 34 years	230.9	16.2	109.6	121.3	34.1	5.3	16.6	17.5	196.8	25.1	93.0	103.8
35 to 44 years	163.4	11.4	78.9	84.5	22.1	3.4	11.0	11.2	141.3	18.0	68.0	73.3
45 to 54 years	93.4	6.5	45.1	48.3	8.5	1.3	4.4	4.1	84.9	10.8	40.7	44.2
55 to 64 years	51.3	3.6	24.0	27.3	4.7	0.7	2.2	2.4	46.6	6.0	21.8	24.8
65 years and over	34.2	2.4	14.5	19.7	3.2	0.5	1.5	1.7	31.0	4.0	13.0	18.0
Median age	19.8		19.0	20.7	9.7		9.6	9.8	30.5		30.3	30.8

Source: Census Bureau, PC(2)-1C, Persons of Spanish Origin, Table 5.

194

and Hispano families are larger than are Puerto Rican families—4.6 and 4.2 persons, respectively—and Cuban families are smaller—3.7 persons. These varying family sizes reflect varying levels of fertility, as well as other social and economic factors.

EDUCATION

YEARS OF SCHOOLING COMPLETED

By 1970, the mainland born had completed more years of schooling than had the island born. Furthermore, there have been large increases in the amount of schooling received over the last several decades among both the mainland and island born. Nevertheless, the Puerto Rican–origin group had completed fewer years of schooling than had the Cuban or Central and South American-origin groups or the Hispanos. Only the Mexican-origin group was as little schooled as were the Puerto Ricans in 1970.

By age 20–24, almost everyone who will complete high school has done so. Among the mainland-born Puerto Ricans, about 6 in 10 of this age group had completed 12 years of school. For the non-Spanish whites, Cubans, and Central and South Americans, 8 or more in 10 of this age group were high school graduates (Table 7.4 and Appendix Table G–3). Among the island born, only some 4 in 10 had finished high school.

The older people had fewer years of schooling than had the younger ones. In 1970, half of all mainland born between the ages of 25 and 44 were high school graduates. However, in 1950 only one-third of the people in this age group had finished high school.

Among the island born (ages 25–44), one in four was a high school graduate in 1970, as compared with one in eight in 1950. Clearly, there has been marked improvement over the last several decades. Nevertheless, this progress is insufficient, since high school completion is a requisite for better jobs and higher pay in mainland society. Too, many Puerto Rican–origin people have insufficient schooling to compete successfully in the economic sphere.

Of the mainland-born Puerto Rican high school graduates, relatively few go to college; about one-third of the men and somewhat fewer of the women do so. Of the Island born, even fewer continue into college. Among the non-Spanish white population, close to half of the men and women who graduate from high school have gone to college.

In 1950, more of the Puerto Rican high school graduates had entered

TABLE 7.4
Years of School Completed by the Puerto Rican–Origin Population, by Age, Sex, and Place of Birth: Mainland, 1970

	Approx. period high school completion	% completed high school		% high school graduates entered college		% college entrants completed college	
		Mainland born	Island born	Mainland born	Island born	Mainland born	Island born
Men							
20 to 24 years	1965	59	37	35	24	14	16
25 to 29 years	1960	54	29	31	24	44	41
30 to 34 years	1955	55	23	34	18	30	29
35 to 44 years	1947	46	22	41	27	42	39
45 to 54 years	1937	35	19	37	30	52	40
55 and over	WWI	12	12	37	37	16	53
Women							
20 to 24 years	1965	64	37	28	19	16	19
25 to 29 years	1960	54	29	26	20	41	33
30 to 34 years	1955	52	23	14	22	39	34
35 to 44 years	1947	47	19	23	24	44	34
45 to 54 years	1937	36	15	35	31	35	44
55 and over	WWI	16	10	27	33	31	34
Age 25 to 44							
1970							
Men		51	24	36	24	40	37
Women		50	23	22	22	42	34
1950							
Men		33	14	42	38	43	46
Women		35	13	31	34	45	44

college than in 1970 (Table 7.4). From this we can infer only that in earlier periods the relatively small number who did graduate from high school were a select group, more ambitious, perhaps, and so had entered college.

Of those who had entered college, somewhat fewer completed college than those among the non-Spanish white students. The net result is that a far smaller proportion of the Puerto Ricans are college graduates than are the non-Spanish whites. Of mainland-born Puerto Ricans aged 25–29, some 8% of the men and 6% of the women had completed college; among the non-Spanish whites in this age group, the respective proportions were 22% and 15%.

SCHOOL ATTENDANCE ON THE MAINLAND

1970. Fewer of the Puerto Rican youth aged 7–19 attend school than is observed for other groups (Appendix Table G–7). The overall (standardized) attendance rate is 76% for these youth, as compared with over 80% for all the other Spanish-American groups and 90% for the non-Spanish group. Furthermore, among the Puerto Rican youth, more of them are below the modal grade for their age, 18.6%, as compared with 6.8% for the non-Spanish whites. On the other hand, more of the former are above the modal grade, 5.9%, as compared with 2.2% of the latter.

The mainland-born young people have significantly higher school attendance rates than do the island born (Table 7.5 and Figure 7.4). Indeed, the rates of the former nearly approach those of the U.S. non-Spanish white youth. The largest differences appear in the high school and college ages, 14–24. It appears that many of the island born drop out, either after completing elementary school or in the early part of the high school period. The differences persist into the age 25–34, when many more of the mainland than of the island born are still attending school. Presumably many of these older people are attending college either on a full-time or part-time basis. Why the island born are less likely to continue in school, we do not know, unless lack of English-language competency leads to early dropouts.

At the college-attendance age of 20–24, only 7% of the Puerto Ricans were attending school, as compared with 23% of the non-Spanish whites (Appendix Table G–7). Such relatively low school-attendance rates in 1970 indicate that there are not likely to be any great advances in years of schooling completed in the next decade or two. Only when the mainland born comprise the large majority of the Puerto Rican population will there be significantly large increases in schooling.

TABLE 7.5

School Attendance Rates of the Puerto Rican Population by Age, Sex, and Place of Birth: Mainland 1970 and 1960, and Urban Residents in Commonwealth, 1970

| | Mainland | | | | | | Common-wealth 1970 |
| | 1970 | | | 1960 | | | |
Age and sex	Total	Main-land born	Island born	Total	Main-land born	Island born	
Total	46.8	67.4	27.7	NA	NA	NA	50.5
3 and 4 years old	10.6	10.4	11.4	NA	NA	NA	6.4
5 and 6 years old	72.4	73.7	67.5	66.4	67.0	64.7	60.2
7 to 13 years old	94.9	95.6	93.2	94.9	95.7	94.2	93.1
14 to 17 years old							
Male	85.5	90.7	78.5	75.8	83.5	73.7	82.8
Female	83.7	90.0	75.8	72.5	84.9	69.5	84.2
18 to 24 years old							
Male	18.4	32.6	13.3	10.9	21.4	9.5	33.6
Female	14.3	26.3	10.3	8.4	13.6	7.6	31.6
25 to 34 years old	2.5	6.8	1.9	3.3	5.5	3.1	7.4

Data for Puerto Rican population 1970 from U.S. Census, Puerto Ricans in the U.S., PC(2)1E, Table 4. For 1960 from Puerto Ricans in the U.S., PC(2)1D, Table 3.

Data for the Commonwealth, 1970, from U.S. Census, PC(1)D53, Table 115.

1960 versus 1970. There were significant increases in school attendance over this decade. At both dates almost all of the 7–13-year-olds were reported as attending school, both for the mainland and island born (Table 7.5).

For youth between the ages of 14 and 17 years, there were significant increases in school attendance for both boys and girls and for both mainland and island born. The latter, the island born, nevertheless, continued to lag considerably behind the mainland born; there is no indication that the island born were catching up with the latter.

At the high-school-graduation and college-going ages of 18–24 years, there were also increases in school attendance for all groups. The mainland born, however, forged rapidly ahead of the island born; the distance between the two groups widened considerably.

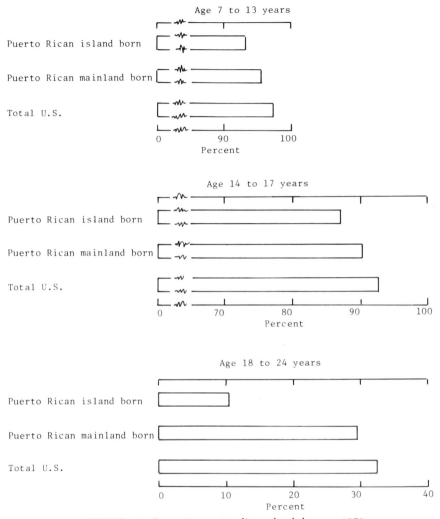

FIGURE 7.4. *Percentages attending school, by age, 1970.*

SCHOOL ATTENDANCE IN THE COMMONWEALTH, 1970

Since the Puerto Rican population resident on the mainland is concentrated largely in the large cities, especially New York, we may compare school attendance on the mainland with that in the urban areas of the Commonwealth of Puerto Rico (Table 7.5). We find that:

1. Under age 7 more mainlanders attend school.
2. Between ages 7 and 13, a few more mainland born attend school

as compared with the commonwealth; but among the island born who have migrated to the mainland, the same proportion attend school as in the commonwealth.

3. Between ages 14 and 17, the prime high-school-dropout age, the attendance rate of the mainland born surpasses that of the commonwealth residents, but the migrants from the island lag behind.
4. At age 18 and over, the mainland born and those residing in the commonwealth have more or less the same school attendance rates; the migrants from the commonwealth to the mainland, however, lag considerably.

In summary, there appears to be a big increase in school attendance between the migrants from the commonwealth and the generation born on the mainland. Why the migrants lag behind their contemporaries who remained in the commonwealth, we do not know.

FERTILITY

INTRODUCTION

It has been commonly assumed that Puerto Rican women, on the U.S. mainland as well as on the island, have high fertility. It is true, if one looks only at the birth rate, that is, the average number of children born per 100 women aged 15–44 years, that Puerto Rican women have a large number of children. However, the apparent higher fertility of Puerto Rican women is due to their age structure as well as to their socioeconomic status. Furthermore, on the island of Puerto Rico, the standardized number of children ever born is also close to that of the mainland non-Spanish white women, although the crude fertility rate is significantly higher. Once we have taken into account (standardized for) the influences of age composition, schooling, marital status, and employment, we find little difference between the Puerto Rican and non-Spanish white women.

The crude and standardized numbers of children ever born per 100 women aged 15–44 compare as shown in the table on the following page.

THE RESIDENTS ON THE MAINLAND

Place of Birth. Women born on the island of Puerto Rico had only slightly higher fertility than had those born on the mainland, on the average about one-tenth child more.

Women who were born on the island had considerably more children than did those born on the mainland, but this was largely because

Women	Crude rate	Standardized rate	
		Amount	Ratio to non-Spanish white
Non-Spanish White	158	158	–
Island of Puerto Rico			
Total	198	175	111
Urban	170	163	103
Rural	230	183	116
Puerto Rican origin living on mainland			
Total	206	165	104
Born in Puerto Rico	234	169	107
Born on mainland	119	156	99

the former had less schooling, more of the women were married and living with their husbands, and fewer of these island-born women were employed. Furthermore, their age distribution was far more favorable to higher fertility. Consequently, once we standardize for these variables, we find that the island-born women have only slightly higher fertility: 169 children ever born per 100 island-born women versus 156 per 100 mainland born. Furthermore, both groups have almost the same fertility as the total U.S. non-Spanish white population: 158 children per 100 women.

The effects of the differences in age distribution are particularly noticeable. Among those born on the mainland, two in five were aged 15–19, and at this age the birth rate is very low. Indeed, these women averaged only a bit more than 20 years in age (median age), whereas the island-born women averaged (median) a little under 30 years. Thus, most of the younger mainland born were still unmarried.

Furthermore, having been raised on the mainland, they all had gone to school there and many had completed high school. Among women aged 20–24 in 1970, of those born on the mainland about two-thirds had completed high school, whereas of the island born only slightly more than one-third had this much schooling. In addition, the mainland born were more likely to be employed and to be employed in white-collar jobs.

Island-born women who had migrated to the mainland since 1965 had substantially the same basic fertility as had the earlier migrants (i.e., prior to 1965). The standardized number of children ever born per 100 women was 166 for the former, as compared with 170 for the latter.

Recent migrants were considerably younger than were the earlier migrants. About half of the former were under age 25 in 1970, whereas half of the latter were age 30 or over. Otherwise, there was very little difference between the two groups; the proportions who were married with spouse present, those who had completed 12 years or more of schooling, and the proportions employed were all quite similar.

Years of Schooling. Completion of high school is tantamount to taking on the demographic characteristics of the non-Spanish white population. In regard to the several demographic factors that we have considered, the Puerto Rican–origin high school graduates tend to resemble the general U.S. non-Spanish white women who have completed high school (Table 7.6). There are few differences, age group by age group, as regards employment. As for marital status, significantly more of the non-Spanish white women are married and living with their husbands than are the Puerto Rican–origin women (Table 7.7). There is comparatively little difference between the island-born and mainland-born high school graduates. There are vast differences, however, between these women and those who have not completed high school. As a result of having fairly similar demographic characteristics, the Puerto Rican–origin women who have completed high school have about the same level of fertility as do the non-Spanish white high school graduates.

The influence of schooling persists even after controlling for age, marital status, employment, and place of residence. Indeed, completing high school leads to a reduction of 25–30% in the number of children. Completion of college could possibly lead to an even larger decrease in fertility, but, unfortunately, we do not have the necessary data to calculate reliable rates for college graduates.

The crude influence of years of schooling, that is, without controlling for employment and marital status, seems to be somewhat greater for the mainland-born Puerto Rican–origin women than for the non-Spanish white. The rates per 100 women aged 15–44 (standardized only for age) are as follows:

| | Rate | | Index (under 12 yrs. = 100) | |
Years of schooling	Puerto Rican origin	Non-Spanish white	Puerto Rican origin	Non-Spanish white
Under 12	197	198	100	100
12	145	160	74	81
13 and over	108	124	55	63
16 and over	NA	111	NA	56

TABLE 7.6

Children Ever Born per 100 Women Aged 35–44, by Years of School Completed, Employment, and Marital Status

| | Residence, 1970 | | | | | |
| | New York City[a] | | | Remainder of U.S. | | |
	Under 12 years	12+ years	b/	Under 12 years	12+ years	b/
Non-Spanish white						
Married, spouse present						
Employed	241	246	102	302	270	89
Not employed	304	294	97	350	313	89
Other marital status						
Employed	136	99	73	226	159	70
Not employed	200	186	93	265	238	90
Puerto Rican origin						
Island born						
Married, spouse present						
Employed	267	233	87	353	268	76
Not employed	370	310	84	450	305	68
Other marital status						
Employed	221	167	76	297	206	69
Not employed	393	319	81	446	370	83
Mainland born						
Married, spouse present						
Employed	281	216	77	328	275	84
Not employed	314	236	75	352	302	86
Other marital status						
Employed	205	142	74	234	126	54
Not employed	338	189	56	324	136	42

[a]For non-Spanish white population, area is the New York-New Jersey SMSA.

[b]Twelve or more years of schooling as percentage of under 12 years.

Puerto Rican–origin women who have gone on to college have a rate only about 55 % of that of those who have not finished high school; fertility decreased 45 %. Among the non-Spanish white women, entry into college results in a decrease in fertility of some 37 %; only if they have completed college does their fertility rate fall as much as that of the mainland-born Puerto Rican–origin women.

Whether this apparent influence of increased years of schooling is directly the result of schooling, or whether employment and marital status act as intermediaries, cannot be determined with certainty. We are of the opinion that some college education has as much influence on the Puerto Rican women as does college completion on the non-Spanish white women.

TABLE 7.7
Selected Characteristics by Years of Schooling Completed for Puerto Rican-Origin and Non-Spanish White Women: Mainland 1970 and Island 1970

Age and characteristics	Non-Spanish White		Puerto Rican Origin				Island	
			Mainland born		Island born			
	Under 12 years	12+ years	Under 12 years	12+ years	Under 12 years	12+ years	Under 12 years	12+ years
15 to 19 years								
% married, spouse present	6.9	16.0	6.5	21.5	23.3	23.4	11.5	7.4
% employed	19.4	49.1	14.3	44.8	15.5	50.6	5.5	20.6
Av. no. children ever born per woman	.08	.10	.11	.17	.35	.19	.16	.04
20 to 24 years								
% married, spouse present	68.0	53.9	56.1	48.2	62.3	57.5	55.3	33.4
% employed	33.6	57.6	25.2	57.6	21.3	51.9	15.8	47.5
Av. no. children ever born per woman	1.38	.50	1.54	.57	1.72	.71	1.50	.41
25 to 29 years								
% married, spouse present	79.2	80.7	56.7	66.3	64.5	73.9	70.4	65.7
% employed	32.3	44.8	21.1	44.0	18.1	40.2	19.4	57.1
Av. no. children ever born per woman	2.39	1.51	2.31	1.58	2.68	1.60	2.87	1.34
30 to 34 years								
% married, spouse present	81.2	84.6	66.2	79.7	66.4	76.9	74.9	74.5
% employed	37.3	41.9	25.6	48.5	21.1	38.2	22.4	55.1
Av. no. children ever born per woman	3.01	2.36	2.84	2.29	3.31	2.36	3.72	2.07
35 to 44 years								
% married, spouse present	81.7	84.8	67.2	74.2	67.5	75.1	71.1	74.3
% employed	44.0	49.1	35.1	53.6	29.5	46.7	21.4	55.5
Av. no. children ever born per woman	3.09	2.73	3.09	2.35	3.65	2.74	4.53	2.52

Comparison with the Island. Each of these two variables has a depressive effect upon fertility after holding constant all the other factors (age, place of birth, place of residence, education, and either marital status or employment). We are attempting to answer the question: does marital status or employment have the more depressive effect?

We hypothesize as follows:
1. The pattern on the island of Puerto Rico is the broad cultural environment from which the migrants have come.
2. The pattern on the mainland, among the non-Spanish whites, is the broad cultural environment among which the migrants and their children are residing, and which presumably influences them.

We now try to determine where the Puerto Rican–origin population fits between these two patterns. Our conclusions are as follows:

1. The normal pattern on the island of Puerto Rico, at least in 1970, was for marital status to be more important than employment. Of two groups of employed women (after holding other factors constant), those who were married and living with spouse had higher fertility. Similarly, of two groups of women who were not employed, those who were married and living with spouse had higher fertility. On the other hand, of two groups of women who were married, spouse present, those who were employed had only somewhat lower fertility than did those not employed. We conclude that marital status is more important than employment status. Of course, this is employment status as of 1970. What the story would be if we had complete lifetime work histories we do not know for certain, but we believe that the pattern would be largely unchanged. Data from the Commonwealth of Puerto Rico indicate that women who are employed at any given moment of time are likely to have been in the labor force much of their adult lives. On the other hand, those not employed at any given time are likely not to have been in the labor force most of the time.[6]
2. The same pattern holds for the non-Spanish white population of the mainland.
3. The Puerto Rican migrants to New York City, as well as to the remainder of the U.S. mainland, show the opposite pattern. Employment is far more important than marital status in influencing fertility. Why this is so, the statistics do not tell us. We can only speculate that the

---

[6] Jaffe and Ridley, "Lifetime Employment of Women."

migrants are a population especially concerned with economic advancement—or employment problems. This may be what distinguishes them from those who remain on the island. Accordingly, employment per se may be a more influential factor in their lives than it is in the lives of nonmigrants. In addition, perhaps the mere fact of leaving the island may have led to discarding certain restraints on behavior, restraints that are part and parcel of life on the island. Puerto Rican women speak of having more freedom on the mainland, especially in New York City, and being less under the domination of men than is the situation on the island. Exactly how much truth there is in such statements, we do not know.

4. The daughters of the migrants, those born on the mainland, have a mixed pattern. In New York City among those having under 12 years of schooling, employment is still the major factor. On the other hand, among mainland-born New York residents who are high school graduates and among those living outside the city, in some cases employment appears to be more influential and in other cases marital status appears so. Hence, we can only assume that the women born here are beginning to acquire the demographic behavior patterns of the general U.S. white non-Spanish population among whom they live.

5. We predict, then, that the second and subsequent generations born on the mainland will be demographically indistinguishable from the general population.

Combined Influences of Education, Marital Status, and Employment. Of the total decrease in fertility among all Puerto Rican–origin women aged 35–44, completion of high school and being employed are equally important.

Among all Puerto Rican–origin women aged 35–44, the number of children ever born was reduced between 50 and 60% as a result of completing high school, being employed, and being other than married with husband present. Of this total decrease, about 30% was due to the higher education, and 30%, due to employment. One-fifth of the decrease was attributable to not being married with husband present, and one-fifth, to the joint operation of all three factors.

This pattern is substantially different from that of the non-Spanish white women in the United States. The total reduction in fertility was about the same as for the Puerto Rican–origin women—between 50 and 60%. However, being other than married with husband present accounted for over 40% of the decrease; being employed, over 20%; the joint influence, 20%; and completion of high school accounted for the least, hardly 15% of the total decrease (Table 7.8).[7] The index of difference between the two populations, using the non-Spanish whites as the standard, is 25 (Table 7.8).

The mainland-born Puerto Rican women, whether living in New York City or outside of it, are somewhat more similar to the non-Spanish white than are the island-born women. Indeed, the mainland born who live outside of New York City most nearly resemble the non-Spanish white women who live outside of the states of New York and New Jersey. The index of difference is only 9. The island-born women living outside of New York City, however, are substantially different, having an index of 38. Thus, it appears that these mainland-born Puerto Rican–origin women who live outside New York demographically approach the general population among whom they live.

1960 versus 1970. As with the Mexican-origin women, for the Puerto Rican women the general patterns of fertility by age, education, and nativity remained unchanged between 1960 and 1970. However, overall fertility was higher in 1970; the standardized rates for women aged 15–44 (Table 7.9) are as follows:

	Island born		Mainland born	
Years of schooling	1960	1970	1960	1970
Under 12	202	233	154	177
12 and over	136	160	—[a]	130

[a] Too few cases to permit calculation of rate.

Did fertility decrease during the 1960s as compared with the 1950s among young women aged 15–24? Among those born on the U.S. mainland and who had under 12 years of schooling, the number of children ever born decreased from 48 to 35; among those with more schooling (high school graduates), it may have decreased from 46 to 38. (Because of the small number of cases in 1960 we are not confident of that rate.) Among the women born in Puerto Rico, however, there were increases

---

[7] It can be argued that we have not really measured the influence of marital status per se for the non-Spanish white women. This is because some 85% of these women were married and living with their husbands. This is a significantly higher proportion than is observed among any Puerto Rican–origin group. Whenever a characteristic begins to encompass 100% of the universe, customary ways of measuring its influence (such as we used here) are deficient.

TABLE 7.8

Relative Influence of Selected Factors in Reducing Fertility: Puerto Rican–Origin Women and Non-Spanish White Women Age 35-44, 1970

	Puerto Rican Origin Residence 1970						Non-Spanish White		
			Mainland						
			New York City		Remainder				
	Island	Total	Island born	Main-land born	Island born	Main-land born	Total	Remainder	NY-NJ SMSA
Total reduction in children ever born	70	56	55	52	54	64	57	55	67
% of reduction due to:									
Education	23	30	22	31	41	27	14	20	9
Employment	14	32	47	21	43	23	23	26	27
Marital status	20	18	13	17	7	30	42	36	40
Joint (all 3)	43	20	18	31	9	20	21	18	24
Total	100	100	100	100	100	100	100	100	100
Index of difference[a] with non-Spanish white, total	19	25	32	27	47	13	0	9	7
with non-Spanish white remainder					38	9		0	11

[a]The index of difference is interpreted as follows: If the two groups are identical, the index equals 0. If they are completely different, the index equals 100.

TABLE 7.9

Children Ever Born Born per 100 Women of Puerto Rican–Origin by Age, Years of
Schooling Completed, and Nativity, and Standardized Rates: U.S. 1960 and 1970

Age and years of schooling	Born in Puerto Rico		Born in Mainland Puerto Rican parentage	
	1960	1970	1960	1970[a]
Under 8 years schooling				
15 to 24 years	117	139	†	(56)
25 to 34 years	285	312	†	(204)
35 to 44 years	337	395	†	†
45 and over	377	406	†	(227)
8 to 11 years schooling				
15 to 24 years	68	93	49	31
25 to 34 years	225	274	206	253
35 to 44 years	269	313	†	(338)
45 and over	267	278	†	236*
Under 12 years schooling				
15 to 24 years	89	106	48	35
25 to 34 years	259	292	202	238
35 to 44 years	311	360	259	322
45 and over	347	369	411	229
12 years and over schooling				
15 to 24 years	63	61	46*	38
25 to 34 years	163	188	158*	166
35 to 44 years	(215)	278	†	227
45 and over	(180)	241	†	236*

Data from the 1960 and 1970 Public Use Samples.

() 50–99 women
* 25–49 women
† less than 25 women

[a]Includes a small number of 3rd and subsequent generations.

in fertility for women at levels of schooling under 8 years and 8–11 years; among high school graduates, there was no apparent change. We cannot reconcile these apparently differing movements.

WOMEN ON THE ISLAND [8]

The Puerto Rican–born women living on the mainland apparently differ from those living on the island. For the age group 35–44 years, the less-schooled women living on the island in 1970 had higher fertility. The more-schooled women living on the island had lower fertility. The rates for Puerto Rican–born women per 100 women compare as follows:

	Residence	
Years of schooling	Mainland	Island
Under 8	395	654
8–11	313	359
12 and over	278	203

These sets of rates suggest that the migrants from the island were a select group and not a cross section of all island residents. Furthermore, the socioeconomic conditions under which the island and mainland populations live are quite different in many respects. In particular, there are many rural residents on the island, especially among the lesser schooled, and rural women have higher fertility than do urban ones.

THE ECONOMIC PICTURE

LABOR FORCE PARTICIPATION AND EMPLOYMENT

Men. About the same proportion of Puerto Rican–origin men as of non-Spanish white men in the United States in 1970 was in the labor force: 76% versus 77%. The more schooling a man has, the more likely he is to be in the labor force (Table 7.10). Of those who had not completed high school, 72% were in the labor force, as compared with 85% of the college graduates. If we limit our analysis to ages 20–64—the

---

[8] U.S., Bureau of the Census, Census of Population: 1970, *Detailed Characteristics: Puerto Rico*, PC(1)–D53 (Washington, D.C.: Government Printing Office,); rates calculated from data on numbers of women as given in Table 117 and numbers of children as given in Table 129.

prime working years—we find that the variation is narrowed but the pattern remains; 82% of those with less than 12 years of school were in the labor force, as compared with 86% of the college graduates.

Most of the Puerto Rican men in the prime working ages, 20–64 years, who were in the civilian labor force had worked full time. There was little difference by level of schooling completed.

The unemployment rate was significantly higher for the Puerto Rican–origin men aged 20–64 than for the non-Spanish whites. Those with more schooling had lower unemployment rates, and among college graduates the rate for the Puerto Rican men was virtually identical to that of the non-Spanish whites.

Years of schooling	Puerto Rican origin (%)	Non-Spanish white (%)
Under 12	5.8	4.1
12	4.0	2.7
13–15 years	5.0	2.8
16 and over	1.6	1.4
Total population	.5.3	3.0

Women. About one-third of the Puerto Rican–origin women were in the labor force in 1970; this is less than the rate for the non-Spanish white women. However, at each level of schooling, the two groups had substantially the same participation rates. Among college graduates, for example, 60% of the former and 58% of the latter were in the labor force. The rate for all Puerto Rican women is substantially reduced below that of the non-Spanish white women simply because there are so many more little-schooled women among the Puerto Ricans. The participation rate increases sharply with increased schooling (Table 7.10), from 26% among those who had not completed high school to 60% of the college graduates.

Among women in the childbearing ages of 20–44, both the level of labor-force-participation rates and the pattern by years of schooling are almost identical to that of all women aged 16 and over.

Of those Puerto Rican–origin women in the labor force, about three in four had worked full time during the census week, as compared with two in three of the non-Spanish white women. As regards weeks worked in 1969, about half of the Puerto Rican women had been employed 48 weeks or more; this is the same for non-Spanish white women. Altogether, about one Puerto Rican woman in four had worked full time at the time of the 1970 Census enumeration *and* 48 weeks or more in 1969.

TABLE 7.10

Labor-Force-Participation and Employment Rates, Puerto Rican–Origin Population by Sex, Age, and Years of Schooling: 1970

	Total			Under 12 years		
	% in labor			% in labor		
Age	force	a/	b/	force	a/	b/
MEN						
Total	75.7	84.2	6.2	72.1	83.6	6.8
16 to 19 years	41.0	55.0	17.7	37.2	54.0	18.0
20 to 24 years	81.5	80.9	7.7	80.0	81.3	8.9
25 to 34 years	87.6	87.1	5.4	85.9	86.2	6.3
35 to 44 years	87.7	88.8	4.4	85.9	88.7	4.5
45 to 54 years	83.5	87.9	4.1	81.4	87.6	4.8
55 and over	50.0	83.9	5.1	47.6	83.1	4.8
20 to 64 years	84.3	86.5	5.3	82.4	86.8	5.8
WOMEN						
Total	32.4	72.5	8.5	25.8	70.8	10.0
16 to 19 years	26.8	55.7	14.0	21.8	49.7	16.6
20 to 24 years	40.4	76.9	8.2	25.2	72.5	13.4
25 to 34 years	29.5	73.1	8.7	23.3	73.3	10.3
35 to 44 years	37.4	75.6	6.6	32.8	75.3	7.5
45 to 54 years	39.5	75.0	6.9	34.7	74.9	6.9
55 and over	19.1	68.0	9.7	16.7	68.9	8.2
20 to 44 years	34.7	75.1	7.9	26.9	74.0	9.8

a/Percentage of civilian labor force employed full time.

b/Percentage of civilian labor force unemployed.

* Under 50 cases in sample.

Unemployment in 1970 was significantly higher among Puerto Rican women aged 16 and over than among the non-Spanish white women: 8.5% as compared with 4.9%. The less schooled had higher unemployment rates; the rate was 10% for those who had not finished high school, as compared with 5.5% for the college graduates (Table 7.10).

CLASS OF WORKER

Most Puerto Rican–origin men and women were employees of private concerns. Between 8 and 9 in every 10 of the island born and 8 in every 10 of the mainland born were such employees. The others were mostly government employees; very few were self-employed (Appendix Table G–30). Since the Puerto Rican–born are all U.S. citizens, there are no citizenship barriers to their employment by the federal, state, or local governments. Consequently, almost as large a proportion

TABLE 7.10 (cont.)

12 years			13 to 15 years			16+ years		
% in labor force	a/	b/	% in labor force	a/	b/	% in labor force	a/	b/
88.0	87.0	4.8	79.5	79.2	5.2	85.1	87.1	1.6
66.8	60.3	16.7	44.2	*	*	0.0	0.0	0.0
88.3	85.1	5.7	72.1	61.8	7.4	68.4	*	*
93.4	89.6	3.5	87.4	87.1	2.9	84.8	88.3	2.6
93.5	90.1	3.7	94.2	86.8	6.6	95.3	88.3	1.3
90.3	91.4	1.4	92.6	83.9	4.8	94.2	*	*
62.1	84.3	10.0	*	*	*	*	*	*
91.1	88.7	4.0	83.1	80.0	5.0	86.0	87.4	1.6
50.4	77.0	6.6	56.2	70.7	5.5	60.3	66.9	5.5
52.3	68.2	9.2	*	*	*	0.0	0.0	0.0
60.7	84.2	5.4	57.6	64.0	5.1	67.2	*	*
42.2	73.9	6.9	51.0	71.6	5.9	59.3	66.7	7.4
49.1	76.7	5.6	66.7	78.9	2.6	60.6	*	*
58.9	73.8	7.4	72.7	*	*	*	*	*
38.4	66.7	11.8	*	*	*	*	*	*
50.3	78.9	6.0	57.1	70.1	4.8	61.9	66.4	4.5

are government employees as is the proportion among the non-Spanish white population. More mainland born are such employees, but this probably reflects their greater amount of schooling as compared with the island born.

Of the population aged 25 and over, the classes of worker are as follows:

	Men		Women	
Class of worker	Mainland born (%)	Island born (%)	Mainland born (%)	Island born (%)
Private employees	79	84	78	80
Self-employed (including unpaid family workers)	4	5	2	2
Government employees	17	11	20	18

FAMILY INCOME

Average (median) income in 1969 of families headed by Puerto Ricans was $6230, the least of any Spanish-American group and close to $4000 below that of non-Spanish white families (Appendix Table G–36). Income varied greatly in accordance with the number of earners in the family and the sex of the head. The more earners, the higher the family income; families headed by men average higher incomes than do those headed by women, as follows:

Number of earners	Head	
	Men ($)	Women ($)
Total population	7240	3220
None	2460	2420
1	6090	4560
2 or more	10, 060	8430

Women headed one in 4 Puerto Rican families, as compared with 1 in 11 non-Spanish white families. This factor helps to explain the low median income for all Puerto Rican families. Another factor is the relatively small proportion of families having two or more earners; only about one-third of Puerto Rican families had this number, as compared with half of the non-Spanish white families. If the Puerto Rican families had had the same distribution by sex of head and by number of earners in family as among the non-Spanish whites, the former's median income would have been close to $7700, or about $1500 higher than the observed median of $6230.

Even $7700 is significantly below that of non-Spanish white families; this means that other factors play an important part in depressing family income. One factor undoubtedly is the lower educational level of the Puerto Ricans, especially of the island born. We saw previously that the mainland born had completed more years of schooling, and, as we shall see, more of them have better-paying jobs. The influence of schooling can be seen by comparing the average (median) income of families headed by island born and mainland born. These median incomes are as follows:

Head of family	Mainland born ($)	Island born ($)
Total population	7520	6000
Male	8850	6900
Female	3180	3230

It is clear that families headed by male mainland-born persons have significantly higher incomes than do those headed by island born. Increased income reflects increased schooling, at least in part. Average income of the mainland-born-male-headed families is about 85% of that of non-Spanish-white-male-headed families, as compared with about 60% for the families with lesser-schooled island-born male heads. Among families headed by women, family incomes are about 55% of those of non-Spanish-white-female-headed families for both the mainland born and island born.

We may estimate the amount of family income if Puerto Rican families had had the same distribution of men and women heads and numbers of earners as among the non-Spanish whites. For families headed by mainland born, median income would have been close to $9000, or almost 90% of that of non-Spanish white families.

Puerto Rican families headed by island born would have had an estimated $7500 income, or perhaps some three-quarters of that of non-Spanish Whites.

What does this analysis suggest about the possible future family income? To begin, in the next generation far more of the families will be headed by mainland born who will be more schooled and hence will have higher earnings and family income. Also, future migrants from the island will be more schooled and hence can be expected to have higher earnings than do the largely unschooled migrants of the post–World War II years.

At present, all we can say (based on 1970 information) is that the low median family income of $6230 will likely increase in the future and will more closely approach that of the non-Spanish white families.

INDIVIDUAL EARNINGS

Men. Puerto Rican men earned an average of $5340 in 1969; this is the median amount received from wages, salaries, and self-employment income (Table 7.11). These men had earned about three-quarters that of the average non-Spanish white man.

Average (median) earnings tend to increase with (a) increased schooling; (b) increased age of worker; and (c) being born on the mainland. For example, let us look at the averages for men aged 25–34 and 35–44 as shown in the table on top of the following page. Men who had completed college had earned some three-quarters more than had men who were high school dropouts. Mainland born, at each schooling level, earned between 15 and 20% more than did the island born. Increasing age seems to be of least importance, adding perhaps 10% to average earning (Tables 7.12 and 7.13).

Years of schooling	Age 25–34		Age 35–44	
	Mainland born ($)	Island born ($)	Mainland born ($)	Island born ($)
Under 12	6090	5360	6110	5640
12	7420	6470	7720	6630
13–15	8630	7300	9440	7610
16 or more	10, 650	8440	12, 980	11, 210

The low median earnings of all Puerto Rican men relative to those of the non-Spanish white men are accounted for, to a large extent, by lack of schooling and having been born on the island. Mainland-born Puerto Rican–origin men who have gone to college earned virtually the same as did non-Spanish white men who had gone to college (see Appendix Table G–32). On the other hand, Puerto Rican high school dropouts had earned significantly less than did non-Spanish white dropouts.

One difference between the two groups in the earning patterns of the more schooled is that there are fewer big earners among Puerto Rican men. Let us examine the third quartile for college graduates (the earnings three-quarters of the way up from the least to the most) as follows:

Age	Puerto Rican		Non-Spanish white ($)
	Mainland born ($)	Island born ($)	
25–34	14,530	11,490	13,430
35–44	18,820	16,580	21,220

Although the average earnings are about the same for the mainland born and for the non-Spanish whites, the latter have many more big earners. This probably reflects the greater prevalence of highly paid professional and managerial workers. It also suggests that many of the non-Spanish whites have completed graduate college work, whereas, perhaps, the Puerto Rican men stop with the bachelor's degree.

Within each age and level-of-schooling group, there was considerable variation in earnings. Thus, some high school dropouts had earned more than had some college graduates. This is indicated in the line marked "variation" in Table 7.11. Between the ages of 25 and 64, the variation index is smallest, indicating that most men tend to earn around the average amounts. At the younger and older ages, however, the variation is much greater; this probably occurs because many

TABLE 7.11
Earnings in 1969, Total Puerto Rican Descent, by Sex, Age, and Years of Schooling

Years of schooling	MEN						WOMEN					
	14 & over	14-24 years	25-34 years	35-44 years	45-64 years	65+ years	14 & over	14-24 years	25-34 years	35-44 years	45-64 years	65+ years
Total U.S.												
1st quartile	$3,440	1,230	4,310	4,570	4,280	2,030	$1,650	900	1,910	2,440	2,550	1,220
Median	5,340	3,170	5,790	6,150	5,810	4,310	3,420	2,520	3,620	3,820	3,810	2,840
3rd quartile	7,220	5,230	7,620	8,020	7,670	6,340	4,930	4,330	5,280	5,220	5,240	4,490
Variation*	.71	1.27	.57	.56	.58	1.00	.96	1.36	.93	.73	.71	1.15
Under 12 years												
1st quartile	3,330	940	4,050	4,330	4,090	1,760	1,460	660	1,790	2,370	2,480	870
Median	5,080	3,000	5,410	5,780	5,530	3,810	3,170	1,700	3,340	3,610	3,660	2,190
3rd quartile	6,770	4,910	6,920	7,540	7,090	5,390	4,450	3,430	4,640	4,730	4,800	3,950
Variation	.68	1.32	.53	.56	.54	.95	.94	1.63	.85	.65	.63	1.41
12 years												
1st quartile	3,960	1,790	5,050	5,500	5,280	3,020	2,030	1,740	2,020	2,550	2,680	2,000
Median	5,960	3,860	6,500	7,170	6,940	5,910	3,880	3,570	4,020	4,330	4,250	3,080
3rd quartile	7,920	6,030	8,580	9,200	9,210	9,650	5,450	4,970	5,770	5,810	6,200	4,870
Variation	.66	1.10	.54	.52	.57	1.12	.88	.90	.93	.75	.83	.93
13 to 15 years												
1st quartile	2,680	1,280	5,390	5,760	6,470	4,510	1,580	910	2,770	3,100	3,690	3,300
Median	5,920	2,420	7,600	8,060	8,220	5,600	4,060	2,490	4,840	5,180	6,180	3,790
3rd quartile	8,810	4,370	9,830	10,680	11,270	7,950	6,310	4,710	6,690	7,650	7,770	8,750
Variation	1.04	1.28	.58	.61	.58	.61	1.17	1.53	.81	.88	.66	1.44
16+ years												
1st quartile	5,730	1,680	6,600	8,000	8,780	5,650	2,760	2,000	2,320	4,550	3,300	3,710
Median	9,820	3,650	9,810	12,710	13,240	9,640	6,090	4,220	5,780	7,860	6,550	7,910
3rd quartile	14,590	6,170	12,630	19,330	22,080	11,000	8,470	6,270	7,830	10,180	9,530	9,000
Variation	.90	1.23	.61	.89	1.00	.56	.94	1.01	.95	.72	.95	.67

*Interquartile range divided by median.

Source: Special Census tabulation.

TABLE 7.12
Earnings in 1969, Puerto Rican Descent, by Place of Birth, Sex, Age, and Years of Schooling Born on Island

Years of schooling	14 & over years	14-24 years	25-34 years	35-44 years	45-64 years	65+ years	12 & over years	14-24 years	25-34 years	35-44 years	45-64 years	65+ years
Total U.S.												
1st quartile	$3,660	1,690	4,220	4,420	4,250	1,900	$1,930	1,070	2,090	2,520	2,570	1,350
Median	5,350	3,600	5,660	5,890	5,730	4,200	3,490	2,780	3,540	3,790	3,760	3,000
3rd quartile	7,060	5,350	7,360	7,610	7,530	6,490	4,850	4,330	5,020	5,010	5,050	4,900
Variation*	.64	1.02	.55	.54	.57	1.09	.84	1.17	.83	.66	.66	1.18
Under 12 years												
1st quartile	3,570	1,620	4,050	4,250	4,070	1,820	1,780	820	1,950	2,430	2,470	1,260
Median	5,150	3,580	5,360	5,640	5,470	3,930	3,300	2,210	3,280	3,630	3,620	2,820
3rd quartile	6,720	5,150	6,170	7,210	6,990	5,950	4,780	3,720	4,470	4,730	4,710	4,670
Variation	.61	.99	.40	.52	.53	1.05	.91	1.31	.77	.63	.62	1.21
12 years												
1st quartile	4,110	2,060	4,960	5,170	5,300	†	2,190	1,800	2,280	2,770	3,040	†
Median	5,940	4,000	6,470	6,630	6,800		3,910	3,540	3,960	4,300	4,480	
3rd quartile	7,800	5,920	8,400	8,370	8,420		5,370	4,910	5,550	5,680	6,060	
Variation	.62	.96	.53	.48	.46		.81	.88	.83	.68	.67	
13 to 15 years												
1st quartile	2,030	1,050	5,150	5,710	6,170	†	1,770	940	2,360	3,000	2,860	†
Median	6,270	2,250	7,300	7,610	8,170		3,940	2,540	4,700	4,560	5,120	
3rd quartile	8,030	4,650	8,440	9,990	10,980		6,180	4,680	6,820	6,520	7,340	
Variation	.96	1.60	.45	.56	.59		1.12	1.47	.95	.77	.88	
16+ years												
1st quartile	5,730	1,890	5,450	8,030	8,170	†	3,270	1,630	3,110	4,390	5,010	†
Median	9,530	3,570	8,440	11,210	12,740		6,410	4,000	6,040	7,690	7,590	
3rd quartile	13,830	5,680	11,490	16,580	21,120		8,490	6,980	8,220	10,060	10,550	
Variation	.85	1.06	.72	.76	1.02		.81	1.34	.85	.74	.73	

*Interquartile range divided by median.
†Too few cases in sample, under 500 inflated population.

Source: Special Census tabulation.

TABLE 7.13
Earnings in 1969, Puerto Rican Descent, by Place of Birth, Sex, Age, and Years of Schooling Born on Mainland

Years of schooling	MEN						WOMEN					
	14 & over	14–24 years	25–34 years	35–44 years	45–64 years	65+ years	14 & over	14–24 years	25–34 years	35–44 years	45–64 years	65+ years
Total U.S.												
1st quartile	$2,050	740	5,000	5,570	5,170	2,550	$1,140	720	2,210	2,570	2,280	1,080
Median	5,340	2,140	6,870	7,640	7,250	5,160	3,240	2,130	4,350	4,290	3,800	2,510
3rd quartile	7,950	4,770	8,680	10,030	9,550	8,560	5,250	4,470	6,080	6,180	5,770	5,980
Variation*	1.10	1.88	.54	.58	.60	1.16	1.27	1.76	.89	.84	.92	1.79
Under 12 years												
1st quartile	1,250	560	4,160	4,260	4,470	2,070	740	480	2,100	2,490	2,300	1,080
Median	4,400	1,350	6,090	6,110	6,400	3,650	2,220	950	3,760	3,820	3,620	1,940
3rd quartile	6,950	3,840	7,730	7,780	8,330	6,210	4,260	2,670	5,080	5,180	5,200	2,760
Variation	1.30	2.43	.59	.58	.60	1.13	1.59	2.30	.79	.70	.80	.87
12 years												
1st quartile	3,600	1,570	5,670	6,130	6,000	+	1,980	1,700	2,150	2,430	2,220	+
Median	6,260	3,670	7,420	7,720	8,250		4,000	3,630	4,520	4,420	3,750	
3rd quartile	8,270	5,170	8,870	9,900	10,350		5,570	5,180	6,060	6,140	5,890	
Variation	.75	.98	.43	.49	.53		.90	.96	.87	.84	.98	
13 to 15 years												
1st quartile	2,070	1,170	6,130	7,350	+	+	1,300	880	2,730	+	+	+
Median	5,530	2,330	8,630	9,440			3,940	2,380	5,150			
3rd quartile	9,470	4,080	11,010	12,410			6,366	4,710	7,070			
Variation	1.34	1.25	.57	.54			1.28	1.61	.84			
16+ years												
1st quartile	6,540	1,890	8,000	8,240	+	+	2,670	2,090	3,610	+	+	+
Median	10,340	4,220	10,650	12,980			6,360	5,070	7,080			
3rd quartile	15,480	6,770	14,530	18,820			8,600	6,820	7,960			
Variation	.86	1.16	.61	.81			.93	.93	.61			

*Interquartile range divided by median.

+Too few cases in sample, under 500 inflated population.

Source: Special Census tabulation.

work part time and receive lesser earnings, so that the median earnings for the group do not indicate fairly the general level of earnings of all members. We note that among 14–24-year-olds, only 50% of those who had worked in 1969 had worked 48 weeks or more; among those aged 65 and over, the proportion was 69%. Among men between ages 25 and 64, however, about 80% had worked 48 weeks or more in 1969.

Women. Puerto Rican–origin women averaged about two-thirds the earnings of Puerto Rican men: $3420 as compared with $5340. However, direct comparisons are not possible, as many more women work part time during the year, and women are more likely to be in occupations and industries different from those of men.

The mainland-born women had higher average earnings than did the island born; this probably reflects more schooling of the former. We see this clearly for ages 25–34 as follows:

Years of schooling	Mainland born ($)	Island born ($)
Under 12	3760	3280
12	4520	3960
13–15 years	5150	4700
16 and over	7080	6040

From this information we see that schooling is most important; college graduates earned about twice as much as high school dropouts. Being mainland born added 10–15% to the average earnings.

We may ask: Did the higher earnings of the mainland born result from having worked more weeks in 1969? The answer is no. Of all mainland-born women between the ages of 25 and 54 who had worked in 1969, 6 in 10 had worked 48 weeks or more. The proportion for the island born is identical.

In almost all instances, the index of variation for women is higher than that for men. This reflects the greater prevalence of part-time work for women (Table 7.11).

OCCUPATIONS OF MEN

The Situation in 1970. Puerto Rican–origin men were slightly higher on the occupational ladder than were Mexican-origin men but were below those of Cuban or Central and South American origin. Also, they were below that of all non-Spanish white men in the country. The greatest deficit for Puerto Rican–origin men in comparison with the total U.S. population was in the professional and managerial (nonfarm) occupations. Of the former, about 1 in 11 was in these highest occupations, whereas among all men 3 in 10 were high on the ladder (Table 7.14).

Half of all Puerto Rican–origin men were employed as operatives or as service workers (virtually none were private household workers, i.e., servants). Fewer of the Mexican origin were in these two occupations; instead, more of them than of the Puerto Rican–origin men were laborers, both farm and nonfarm (Tables 7.14 and 7.15).

The average Socio-Economic Status Score (SES) score for the Puerto Rican–origin men in 1970 was 50. This is lower on the ladder than is the score for all non-Spanish white men, 59. On the other hand, it is slightly above that of the Mexican-origin men who had an SES score of 46.

Place of Birth. Puerto Rican–origin men born on the mainland have much higher-paying jobs than do men born on the island (Table 7.14). This undoubtedly reflects the increased schooling of the former and, occupationally at least, their improved integration into the mainland economy and society.

Let us first look at ages 20–24, when young men are beginning (or have recently begun) their occupational careers. Among men in this age group born in Puerto Rico, 6% were in professional and managerial jobs, and 17% more, in lower-level white-collar jobs. Among those born on the mainland, 14% were in professional and managerial jobs, and 32%, in lower-level white-collar occupations. Altogether, about half of the mainland born had white-collar jobs, as compared with one-quarter of the island born.

On the lower rungs of the occupational ladder, we find that half of the island born took jobs as operatives and laborers, as compared with only one-quarter of the mainland born.

The SES scores were, respectively, 49 for the island born and 58 for the mainland born, or virtually the same as for all U.S. males. Clearly and unequivocally, the average mainland-born youth entered the occupational ladder at a significantly higher rung than did his island-born counterpart. This is turn indicates that the former will, most likely, end his occupational career higher on the ladder than if he had entered at a lower rung.[9]

Men in the age group 35–44, or perhaps up to age 50, have, by and large, climbed as high on the occupational hierarchy as they will

[9] See A. J. Jaffe and R. O. Carleton, *Occupational Mobility in the United States, 1930–1960* (New York: King's Crown Press, 1954), chap. 7.

TABLE 7.14

Occupational Distribution of Employed Puerto Rican–Origin Men, by Place of Birth and Age: 1950 and 1970

			Total Mainland			
	Total		*Age 20 to 24 in 1970*		*Age 35 to 44 in 1970*	
	Age 14 & over 1970	1950	Born in Puerto Rico	Puerto Rican parentage	Born in Puerto Rico	Puerto Rican parentage
Total	100.0	100.0	100.0	100.0	100.0	100.0
Professional	4.7	5.0	3.4	10.3	3.6	13.6
Managers, nonfarm	4.2	5.6	2.5	3.6	4.6	8.6
Sales	3.9	NA	3.8	8.3	3.3	7.0
Clerical	10.4	NA	13.4	23.2	8.0	11.8
Sales & clerical	14.3	9.4	17.2	31.5	11.3	18.8
Craftsmen	16.5	11.3	12.9	15.8	17.0	19.3
Operatives	33.6	31.1	41.0	18.8	35.2	20.5
Laborers, nonfarm	8.0	7.7	8.7	7.2	7.6	5.9
Farmers	0.1	0.3	0.0	0.1	0.0	0.1
Farm laborers	1.4	2.7	1.9	0.4	1.4	0.4
Service	17.2	26.9	12.3	12.3	19.3	12.9
SES score	50	47	49	58	49	59

Occupational classification for 1950 adjusted to 1970 classification.

Sources of data: Mainland 1970 from Persons of Spanish Origin (PC(2)–1C) Table 8; for New York City, Table 16.

Data by age for 1970 from Puerto Ricans in the United States (PC(2)–1E), Table 7.

Data for 1950 from Puerto Ricans in Continental United States (PE, No. 30), Tables 4 and 5.

ever achieve.[10] Among mainland-born men in this age group, almost 1 in 4 is employed as a professional or manager (nonfarm). This is a significant increase over the proportion of youth—men aged 20–24—in these better jobs. Of the island-born men, however, only about 1 in 12 was employed in these better jobs. The SES score for the island born is 49, as compared with 59 for the mainland born.

As of 1970, of course, the great majority of all Puerto Rican–origin men of labor-force age were island born, about 9 in 10; only 1 in 10 was born on the mainland. And the island born have far less formal schooling, as we saw previously. Hence as of 1970, the occupational composition of the total Puerto Rican–origin men reflects largely the lower educational level of the numerous island born. It will probably require

---

[10] Jaffe, "Middle Years." See especially chap. 6.

another several decades—depending in part on the future volume of migration[11] from the island and the characteristics of the future migrants—before the more-schooled mainland born will be numerous enough to affect the occupational composition of the total population.

SCHOOLING

As indicated by the place-of-birth analysis, the amount of schooling is of overriding importance in determining occupational position (Table 7.15). High school dropouts tend to be operatives and service workers; college graduates are professionals and managers. Indeed, the occupational distribution of Puerto Rican college graduates closely parallels that of non-Spanish white men (see Appendix Table G–38). The SES score for the former is 80, and for the latter, 82; the slight difference has no significance. In this respect, the role of schooling is the same for the Puerto Ricans and all other Spanish-origin groups. The "road to success," even though it is full of potholes, is the educational system.

Comparison with 1950. At this earlier date, an even larger proportion of men of labor-force age were island born and had comparatively little schooling. By and large, the occupational composition was similar to that in 1970 but perhaps slightly lower; the SES score in 1950 was 47, as compared with 50 in 1970 (Table 7.14). This small improvement probably reflects the entry of mainland-born and more-schooled men into the labor force during these two decades.

By 1950, men born on the mainland were considerably further up the occupational ladder than were their island-born fathers. Carl Raushenbush commented: "The second generation Puerto Ricans stand midway between the first generation and the general population."[12] We suspect that considerable upward movement, particularly among the second generation, occurred in the intervening two decades.

---

[11] Schooling is increasing on the island as well, so that future migrants may be significantly better schooled than were migrants prior to 1970. However, their ability to handle the English language will also be important; more years of schooling in the Spanish language alone will hardly suffice to obtain a managerial job, for example, on the mainland.

[12] Carl Raushenbush, "A Comparison of the Occupations of the First and Second Generation Puerto Ricans in the Mainland Labor Market," in *Puerto Rican Population of New York City*, ed. A. J. Jaffe (New York: Bureau of Applied Social Research, Columbia University, 1954), p. 57.

TABLE 7.15

Major Occupational Groups by Years of Schooling, Age, and Sex, Puerto Rican Descents: 1970

	TOTAL					14-34				
	Years of schooling					Years of Schooling				
		-12	12	13-15	16+		-12	12	13-15	16+
	Total	years	years	years	years	Total	years	years	years	years
Total	100.0	100.0	100.0	100.0	100.0	100.0	100.0	100.0	100.0	100.0
Professional, total	4.6	1.4	6.4	20.5	57.4	4.7	1.5	6.0	21.4	63.4
Modern science	1.6	0.3	1.8	7.6	31.5	1.6	0.2	2.0	7.2	33.7
Classical	2.0	0.8	2.5	6.3	25.1	2.1	0.9	2.2	7.2	28.7
Semiprofessional	1.0	0.4	2.1	6.5	0.8	1.0	0.3	1.8	6.9	1.0
Manager, nonfarm,total	4.2	3.0	5.5	10.1	17.5	3.4	2.3	4.9	8.2	10.9
Employee	3.2	2.0	4.6	8.7	15.5	2.8	1.8	4.2	7.6	10.9
Self-employed	1.0	1.0	0.9	1.5	2.0	0.6	0.6	0.8	0.7	0.0
Sales	4.1	3.5	5.0	8.9	6.0	4.3	3.7	4.3	10.2	5.9
Clerical	10.3	7.5	18.4	20.5	6.8	12.0	8.3	20.0	23.7	6.9
Craftsmen	15.5	14.9	19.5	13.7	2.8	15.4	14.6	19.6	11.8	3.0
Operatives (excl transp)	26.8	31.1	18.2	8.9	2.4	28.2	33.7	19.1	7.2	3.0
Transportation	6.8	7.1	7.2	2.9	0.4	7.3	7.7	7.6	2.6	0.0
Laborers, nonfarm	7.9	8.9	6.2	2.9	0.0	8.1	9.3	6.3	3.3	0.0
Farm manager	0.1	0.1	0.1	0.2	0.0	0.1	0.1	0.7	0.0	0.0
Farm laborer	1.5	1.8	0.6	0.2	0.4	1.6	2.1	0.7	0.0	1.0
Service total	18.3	20.7	12.9	11.2	6.4	14.9	16.7	11.0	11.5	5.9
Household	0.1	0.1	0.0	0.0	0.0	0.0	0.1	0.0	0.0	0.0
Protective	1.5	0.9	3.1	3.6	3.2	1.4	0.7	3.3	3.0	2.0
Other	16.8	19.7	9.8	7.6	3.2	13.4	16.0	7.8	8.6	4.0
SES	49.8	46.3	55.3	65.2	80.0	50.3	46.6	55.3	65.8	80.2

OCCUPATIONS OF WOMEN

About two in five Puerto Rican–origin women are employed in white-collar jobs, a proportion not much different from that of all non-Spanish white women. With increased schooling, increasingly more Puerto Rican–descent women are found in professional and managerial jobs (Table 7.16). We may compare those who had not completed high school with college graduates as follows:

Class of worker	Less than 12 years (%)	16 and over years (%)
Professional and managerial	2.6	77.8
Clerical and sales	20.6	18.1
Blue collar and services	76.8	4.1

There is little difference between the occupational composition of the Puerto Rican and non-Spanish white women at each schooling level. The SES scores are as follows:

TABLE 7.15 (cont.)

| | 35–44 Years of schooling | | | | | 45+ Years of schooling | | | |
Total	-12 years	12 years	13–15 years	16+ years	Total	-12 years	12 years	13–15 years	16+ years
100.0	100.0	100.0	100.0	100.0	100.0	100.0	100.0	100.0	100.0
4.8	1.3	7.2	22.4	61.8	4.3	1.5	7.1	15.3	44.6
1.8	2.1	1.2	10.6	36.8	1.6	0.4	1.8	5.9	23.0
2.0	0.7	3.6	4.7	25.0	1.8	0.7	2.5	4.7	20.3
1.0	0.4	2.4	7.1	0.0	0.9	0.4	2.8	4.7	1.4
4.5	3.4	5.5	11.8	19.7	6.0	4.3	8.5	15.3	24.3
3.4	2.3	4.8	10.6	15.8	3.9	2.3	6.7	10.6	21.6
1.1	1.0	0.7	1.2	3.9	2.1	2.0	1.8	4.7	2.7
3.8	3.0	7.0	5.9	2.6	4.0	3.3	5.7	7.1	9.5
8.5	7.4	13.4	10.6	5.2	7.9	5.7	17.4	18.8	8.1
17.1	16.8	22.3	18.8	1.3	13.3	13.3	14.9	15.3	4.1
26.0	30.4	15.3	11.8	0.0	23.4	26.0	17.0	11.8	4.1
7.3	7.5	8.2	3.5	1.3	4.8	5.2	3.9	3.5	0.0
7.0	7.8	5.3	1.2	0.0	8.4	9.3	6.7	3.5	0.0
0.8	0.1	0.0	0.0	0.0	0.3	0.2	0.4	1.2	0.0
1.4	1.7	0.5	1.2	0.0	1.2	1.5	0.4	0.0	0.0
19.0	20.6	15.3	12.9	7.9	26.5	29.8	18.1	8.2	5.4
0.2	0.2	0.2	0.0	0.0	0.0	0.1	0.0	0.0	0.0
1.7	0.9	3.8	7.1	5.3	1.3	1.3	0.7	2.4	2.7
17.2	19.6	11.3	5.9	2.6	25.2	28.4	17.4	5.9	2.7
50.0	46.9	55.2	64.0	81.1	48.4	45.1	55.3	63.9	78.4

Years of schooling	Puerto Rican	Non-Spanish white
Total population	56	63
Under 12	50	52
12	62	64
13–15	70	71
16 and over	84	85

More of the Puerto Rican–origin women born on the mainland have jobs higher on the occupational ladder than do the island-born women (Table 7.17). We may compare the two groups in 1970 as follows:

Occupations	Mainland born (%)	Island born (%)
Professional and managerial	12.3	8.0
Clerical and sales	57.0	28.5
Blue-collar and service	30.7	63.5

TABLE 7.16

Major Occupational Groups by Years of Schooling, Age, and Sex, Puerto Rican Descent: 1970

WOMEN

	TOTAL Years of schooling					14-34 Years of schooling					35+ Years of schooling				
	Total	-12 years	12 years	13-15 years	16+ years	Total	-12 years	12 years	13-15 years	16+ years	Total	-12 years	12 years	13-15 years	16+ years
TOTAL	100.0	100.0	100.0	100.0	100.0	100.0	100.0	100.0	100.0	100.0	100.0	100.0	100.0	100.0	100.0
Professional, total	7.2	1.6	6.4	25.2	73.7	7.3	1.9	5.5	23.5	73.0	7.2	1.5	8.6	28.5	74.4
Modern science	2.3	0.5	2.7	9.7	14.6	2.2	0.5	2.3	8.0	12.4	2.4	0.5	3.7	13.0	17.1
Classical	4.4	1.1	3.1	12.2	58.5	4.7	1.4	2.8	13.0	59.6	4.1	0.8	3.7	10.6	57.3
Semiprofessional	0.5	0.1	0.7	3.3	0.6	0.4	0.0	0.5	2.5	1.1	0.6	0.2	1.2	4.9	0.0
Manager, nonfarm, total	1.7	1.0	2.3	3.3	4.1	1.5	1.0	1.6	2.9	3.4	1.9	1.0	4.2	4.1	4.9
Employee	1.5	0.7	2.3	3.0	4.1	1.4	0.8	1.6	2.9	3.4	1.5	0.5	4.0	3.3	4.9
Self-employed	0.2	0.3	0.1	0.3	0.0	0.1	0.1	0.0	0.0	0.0	0.4	0.5	0.2	0.8	0.0
Sales	4.1	4.8	3.1	3.3	2.9	4.0	5.5	2.1	5.0	1.1	4.2	4.1	5.6	0.0	4.9
Clerical	29.9	15.8	54.5	47.6	15.2	39.0	21.9	60.1	50.4	18.0	17.9	10.1	40.1	42.3	12.2
Craftsmen	2.4	3.0	1.9	1.1	0.0	2.4	3.4	1.8	0.8	0.0	2.4	2.7	2.7	1.6	0.0
Operatives, excl. trans.	39.6	56.2	18.8	9.4	1.2	32.2	50.4	16.7	7.6	1.1	49.3	61.6	24.5	13.0	1.2
Transportation	0.3	0.5	0.1	0.0	0.0	0.2	0.4	0.1	0.0	0.0	0.5	0.6	0.2	0.0	0.0
Labor, nonfarm	0.7	0.9	0.5	0.0	0.0	0.8	1.2	0.5	0.0	0.0	0.6	0.7	0.2	0.0	0.0
Farm manager	0.0	0.0	0.1	0.0	0.0	0.0	0.0	0.0	0.0	0.0	0.0	0.0	0.0	0.0	0.0
Farm laborer	0.2	0.3	0.1	0.0	0.0	0.2	0.4	0.1	0.0	0.0	0.2	0.3	0.0	0.0	0.0
Service, total	13.9	15.8	12.3	10.0	2.9	12.3	14.0	11.5	9.7	3.4	15.9	17.5	14.2	10.6	2.4
Household	0.9	1.3	0.4	0.0	0.0	0.7	1.2	0.4	0.0	0.0	1.1	1.4	0.5	0.5	0.0
Protective	0.3	0.3	0.2	0.3	0.0	0.2	0.1	0.2	0.4	0.0	0.4	0.5	0.2	0.0	0.0
Other	12.7	14.2	11.7	9.7	2.9	11.4	12.7	11.0	9.2	3.4	14.4	15.5	13.5	10.6	2.4
SES	56.2	49.7	62.4	69.8	84.0	58.6	51.8	63.0	70.0	83.7	53.1	47.9	53.1	69.4	84.4

TABLE 7.17

Major Occupational Groups for Employed Women of Puerto Rican Descent, by Place and Birth, 1950 and 1970

| | 1950, age 14 and over | | | 1970, age 16 and over | | |
| | | Mainland | Island | | Mainland | Island |
	Total	born	born	Total	born	born
Total	100.0	100.0	100.0	100.0	100.0	100.0
Professional, technical & kindred	3.4	6.1	3.1	7.3	10.4	6.5
Managers & officials except farm	1.2	1.8	1.1	1.6	1.9	1.5
Clerical, sales, kindred	11.0	39.4	7.8	34.1	57.0	28.5
Craftsmen, foremen, kindred	1.7	1.9	1.7	2.4	1.3	2.7
Operatives	72.5	37.1	76.5	39.8	13.3	46.3
Private household workers	2.3	2.2	2.3	1.0	1.1	0.9
Other service workers	6.5	9.9	6.1	12.4	14.2	11.9
Laborers, except farm and mine	1.0	0.8	1.0	1.1	0.5	1.2
Farmers & farm managers	0.1	0.8	0.0	0.0	0.2	0.0
Farm laborers	0.3	0.0	0.3	0.3	0.1	0.4
SES score	49	57	48	56	63	54

Source: U. S. Census 1950, <u>Puerto Ricans in Continental U.S.</u>, P-E, No. 30, Table 4.

U.S. Census 1970, <u>Puerto Ricans in the U.S.</u>, PC(2)1E, Table 7.

Between 1950 and 1970 there was considerable upward movement for both groups, undoubtedly reflecting increased schooling (Table 7.17). The SES scores are as follows:

Puerto Ricans	1970	1950	Difference
Total population	56	49	7
Mainland born	63	57	6
Island born	54	48	6

THE VARIOUS PUERTO RICAN POPULATIONS

As noted previously, some 6 in 10 of the Puerto Rican–origin people live in New York City—the state and the city are virtually synonymous, since very few live elsewhere in New York State—and 4 in 10 live in other states. We shall show in this section that these two groups differ significantly from each other and that those who reside outside New York City—especially the mainland born—more nearly resemble demographically the non-Spanish white population than do the city's residents.

We also present brief data on selected geographic groups within New York City: (a) the South Bronx and East Harlem; (b) the rest of the Bronx, Manhattan, and Brooklyn; and (c) Queens and Richmond.

NEW YORK CITY VERSUS ALL OTHERS

Demographic Characteristics. With regard to *age* and *nativity*, there are significant differences between those residing in New York versus those in the rest of the country. The New Yorkers who had been born on the island averaged (median age) close to 32 years, whereas those living in other states averaged a little over 27 years of age. Very likely the New York residents represent the earlier streams of migration from the island. Those who reside in other states, on the other hand, possibly are from more recent streams of migration, together with migration out of New York, of some of the younger island born.

Of those born on the mainland, the average age (median) of the New York residents was between 9 and 10 years, whereas those living in other states averaged under 9 years. This may reflect the more recent settlement in these states, as we indicated previously.

There is practically no difference between New York State and the remainder of the mainland in the proportion of the population who are mainland born. This follows in large measure from the simple fact that so many of the mainland born are young children and as a matter of course accompany their parents to whatever state the parents choose as residence.

New York State—which means New York City—may feel the impact of this age factor more than do other states. Close to 6 in 10 of all mainland born in New York were of school age in 1970. The total Puerto Rican population constituted about one-tenth of New York City's total population, but the Puerto Ricans of school age constituted about 1 in 6 of all school-age youngsters in the city. Clearly, the age composition has implications for the operations of the school system.

As for sex composition, among the population aged 20 and over, women predominated in New York State, and men were in the majority in other states. About 55% of the adult Puerto Rican population in New York State were women, and 45%, men, whereas outside this state 48% were women, and 52%, men. This pattern implies either an out-movement of men from New York prior to 1970 or direct migration from the commonwealth to states other than New York.

The shortage of men in New York has implications for a wide variety of social and economic conditions. Fewer men means fewer families containing both husband and wife, for example. This, in turn, can contribute to the increase of families headed by women and to more families on welfare, especially those receiving Aid to Dependent Children. What additional complications there may be for children raised in fatherless homes, we leave to others to describe.

Fewer men also means that more Puerto Rican women remain un-married and childless, or that they marry non-Puerto Ricans. As we shall see, both results seem to have occurred in New York.

The excess of adult men in other states implies a set of social and economic conditions for the Puerto Rican population quite different from that in New York. As we shall see, for example, New York families averaged lower income than did Puerto Rican families living elsewhere, and more of the former had incomes below the poverty level in 1970.

Why there is a deficit of men in New York and an excess in other states will be discussed subsequently.

The school attendance rates among Puerto Ricans living outside New York are somewhat higher than they are for New York residents. Why this is so, we do not know. We know only that for mainland-born children living outside New York the school-attendance rates are but slightly below those for the total U.S. population. The school atten-dance rates compare as shown in the table on top of the following page.[13] We may note in passing that the Puerto Rican residents of New Jersey resemble the New York City residents with regard to school at-tendance.

More persons living outside of New York had completed high school (Table 7.18). For example, among the mainland born aged 20–24, less than 6 in 10 living in New York were high school graduates, as com-pared with close to 7 in 10 of those who resided in other states. This lat-

---

[13] U.S., Bureau of the Census, Census of Population: 1970. *Subject Reports*, Final Report PC(2)–1E, *Puerto Ricans in the United States* (Washington, D.C.: Government Printing Office, 1973), Table 4.

Age	New York State	North Central	South	West
7–13 years				
Mainland born	95.2	96.2	97.6	97.3
Island born	92.6	94.5	96.8	96.4
14–17 years, males				
Mainland born	90.1	93.0	90.6	92.2
Island born	78.8	80.0	84.7	85.0
14–17 years, females				
Mainland born	89.8	92.0	92.8	92.4
Island born	74.3	78.7	86.9	90.7

ter figure approaches that of the U.S. non-Spanish white population. Relatively fewer of the island born than of the Mainland born had completed high school. Nevertheless, among these people as well, fewer of those living in New York had completed high school.

The failure to complete high school, especially in New York, is a direct reflection of the large high-school-dropout rate that occurred during the 1960s. In New York about 3.5 in 10 of all mainland-born youth who had entered high school in this period dropped out. The dropout rates for boys was significantly higher than for girls throughout the United States. Why there were such high dropout rates, especially among boys, is a question we cannot answer.

As for family and marital status, many more women aged 20–44 who live outside of New York are married and living with their spouses, as compared with New York residents (Figure 7.5). Significantly more island-born women are married with spouse present than are mainland-born women. Some two in three of those born on the island are thus married, as compared with less than three in five of those born here. The above pattern was true in 1960 also, but at that date a significantly larger proportion of all women (aged 20–44) were married and living with their spouses. The proportions in 1970 are as follows:

Residence	Mainland born (%)	Island born (%)
New York	54	62
Other States	66	75

This pattern, and decreases since 1960, reflect, in part at least, the ratio of men to women that we mentioned previously. For persons in this age

TABLE 7.18

Percentages High School Graduates, by Age, Sex, and Place of Birth of the Puerto Rican Population, by Place of Residence in 1970

	Residence	
Sex and age	New York State	Other States
MEN		
20 to 24 years		
Mainland born	55	66
Island born	33	41
25 to 34 years		
Mainland born	53	59
Island born	26	27
35 to 44 years		
Mainland born	44	49
Island born	20	23
WOMEN		
20 to 24 years		
Mainland born	62	70
Island born	36	38
25 to 34 years		
Mainland born	49	61
Island born	25	28
35 to 44		
Mainland born	45	49
Island born	17	25

Source: Census Bureau, PC(2)-1E, Puerto Ricans in the United States, Table 5.

range, there were 84 men for every 100 women in New York State, as contrasted with 109 men per 100 women in the other states (in 1970). As a rule, the larger the proportion of men, the larger is the proportion of women who are married. In 1960 there had been almost equal numbers of men and women in New York State and a large excess of men in other states. As a result, the proportion of women who were married and living with their husbands in 1960 was significantly higher than in 1970.

The comparatively lesser proportion of women who were married with spouse present in New York, in turn, has implications for family life. The number of families with women heads, the numbers on welfare, and so on, especially for a not-well-schooled population, tends to increase in the absence of a male earner in the family. Among the Puerto Rican population the non-married-spouse-present woman is not

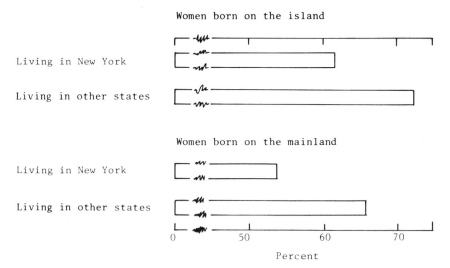

FIGURE 7.5. *Percentages of women aged 20–44 who are married and living with spouse,* 1970.

likely to be a well-paid professional career woman; she is more likely to be a widow, divorcée, or one whose husband is elsewhere—in another state or perhaps living on the island. In any event, the family that she heads suffers both economically and socially from the absence of a marriage partner.

As we expect, a smaller proportion of the families in New York consist of husband and wife (with or without children under age 18) than is the situation in other states (Figure 7.6). Conversely, the proportion of families headed by women is significantly higher in New York.

A little over half of all Puerto Rican families consist of husband, wife, and children under age 18; another 2 in 10 consist of husband and wife without young children; and 1 in 4 has a female head, almost always with young children. In 1960 a larger proportion of the families consisted of husband, wife, and children, and a smaller proportion were headed by women. These changes fit the changes in marital status previously described.

Marriage to non–Puerto Ricans is prevalent. Over two in three of those born on the mainland (married persons aged 20–44) and who were living outside of New York were reported as married to non–Puerto Ricans. In New York, one in three was married to a non–Puerto Rican.

Far fewer of the island-born people had married out: 1 in 10 of those living in New York and about 2 in 10 of those residing elsewhere. This

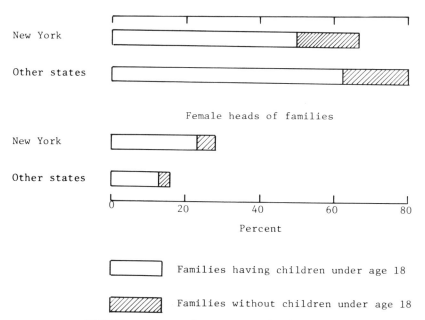

FIGURE 7.6. *Types of Puerto Rican families, 1970.*

is to be expected, since many of them were already married when they migrated and hence, almost by definition, had Puerto Rican spouses.

Presumably, the outmarriage rate is lower in New York City because the number of Puerto Ricans is so large that individuals generally can find partners within the community. In other states that have far fewer Puerto Ricans, the situation facilitates outmarriages. Presumably, in the future married couples will continue to migrate from the island, but if so many of their children marry non–Puerto Ricans, we must ask what will happen to their Puerto Rican identity. The identification problem will be even more difficult for the children of parents who themselves are only part Puerto Rican. Exactly what will happen, we cannot predict.

FERTILITY

Women living in New York City had lower fertility than did those living elsewhere on the U.S. mainland (Table 7.19).

After standardizing (for age, marital status, employment, years of schooling completed), it appears that the New York City Puerto

TABLE 7.19

Children Ever Born per 100 Puerto Rican–Origin Women, Mainland Born and Living on Mainland, 1970

| | | | | Residence 1970 | | | | | |
| | Total | | | New York City | | | Elsewhere | | |
Age and characteristics	Total	Under 12 Years	12+ Years	Total	Under 12 years	12+ years	Total	Under 12 years	12+ years
15-19 total	12	11	17	12	11	13	13	11	26
Married spouse present	73	85	51	73	86	47	73	83	57
Employed	54	61	43	48	65	18	59	57	63
Not employed	80	93	54	79	92	55	80	97	54
Other marital status	6	6	7	6	6	6	6	6	11
Employed	4	5	2	4	5	2	5	6	0
Not employed	7	6	13	7	7	9	7	6	25
20-24 total	94	154	57	97	158	57	88	146	58
Married spouse present	126	180	89	130	177	94	121	188	79
Employed	70	117	57	72	109	60	67	138	53
Not employed	154	194	113	156	192	118	151	197	104
Other marital status	60	121	29	65	136	26	47	75	35
Employed	26	60	18	27	66	19	25	52	15
Not employed	107	154	54	112	161	43	90	113	78
25-29 total	195	231	158	208	240	168	171	209	145
Married spouse present	210	244	182	214	235	192	205	266	169
Employed	149	194	128	137	159	123	164	250	131
Not employed	234	257	210	239	251	223	225	272	192
Other marital status	169	215	112	198	248	126	108	129	89
Employed	79	96	71	82	89	79	74	105	58
Not employed	231	249	181	262	282	198	144	141	148
30-34 total	259	284	229	247	260	224	282	342	234
Married spouse present	272	303	240	251	267	228	304	374	254
Employed	232	257	217	203	213	198	263	304	238
Not employed	292	317	257	269	279	250	330	411	265
Other marital status	226	246	183	239	248	214	189	241	125
Employed	171	189	155	173	172	173	167	228	129
Not employed	269	270	261	277	274	296	227	251	103
35-44 total	278	309	235	261	296	205	300	330	267
Married spouse present	294	322	260	273	304	227	317	344	288
Employed	273	302	250	249	281	216	295	328	275
Not employed	308	331	269	286	314	236	332	352	302
Other marital status	239	283	163	241	284	163	236	282	164
Employed	180	214	144	179	205	152	183	234	126
Not employed	304	334	206	229	338	189	298	324	236

Rican–origin women have about 10% lower fertility than do those residing elsewhere. The standardized rates (for women aged 15–44) are as follows:

Residence	Puerto Rican		Non-Spanish white
	Island born	Mainland born	
New York City	162	148	139 [a]
Remainder of U.S.	178	164	161

[a] New York–New Jersey Standard Metropolitan Statistical Area.

Clearly, the Puerto Rican–origin women, especially those born on the mainland, are rapidly approaching the reproductive-behavior patterns of the general population.

That life in New York City had a lowering influence on fertility is clear, as even the recent migrants (those who arrived since 1965) who live in this city have lower fertility than do those who reside elsewhere on the U.S. mainland, as follows:

Residence in 1970	Island-born women	
	Living on the island in 1965	Living on the mainland in 1965
New York City	150	164
Remainder of U.S.	179	177

Why New York City has this influence, we cannot say. Perhaps there is some selective factor operating so that women with potentially lower fertility remain in, or move to, the city. We are inclined to think, rather, that there is something in the life in the city that has this lowering effect. Residence in New York City (after controlling for these several factors) leads to a decrease on the order of about one-half child by the end of the childbearing period. We make the following comparisons for women aged 35–44 (rates per 100 women), standardized for marital and employment status, as follows:

	Island born		Mainland born	
Residence	Under 12 years schooling	12 and over years schooling	Under 12 years schooling	12 and over years schooling
New York City	322	267	291	206
Remainder of U.S.[a]	398	291	319	250
Difference	76	24	28	44
New York City, percentage of remainder	81	92	91	82

[a] The higher fertility in the areas outside of New York cannot be explained in terms of rural versus urban residence, since all the Puerto Rican–origin population is highly urbanized.

Economic Characteristics. Outside of New York, larger proportions of men and women are in the labor force. This is true both for the mainland born and island born. For men in the prime working ages of 20–64 we have as follows:

Men	New York (%)	Other States (%)
Total population	81	88
Mainland born	79	88
Island born	82	89

For women in the childbearing ages of 20–44 we find as follows:

Women	New York (%)	Other states (%)
Total population	30	41
Mainland born	42	48
Island born	28	39

These differences are clearly significant, but why New York differs so greatly—why fewer were in the labor force in 1970—we do not know.

Average (mean) family income for New York families whose heads were born on the island was $6300 in 1969. The average family outside of New York whose head was born on the mainland reported having received $9600. The latter is still below the national average, but not much so. Families headed by island born and living outside of New

York, as well as New York families headed by mainland born, averaged about $7600.

Clearly the several factors reviewed—distribution of men, educational level, place of birth, place of residence, work opportunities for women, occupation, job earnings—have all come together in the overall figure of average family income. The mainland born living outside of New York are better educated, have better jobs, and earn more. In turn, more men live outside the state, and fewer families are headed by women. There are more husband and wife families, and the combination produces a higher family income.

The major part of the family income comes from wages and salaries; among families living outside New York and headed by mainland born, 9 in 10 have such income, a proportion comparable to that of the non-Spanish white U.S. population. The smallest proportions are found in New York State, where about three-quarters have wage and salary income.

Conversely, the largest proportion of families whose heads were born on the island and who receive public assistance are found in New York State: 30%.

The amount of personal income that a person receives depends, among other factors, on occupation, education, age and sex, and where the person lives. Mainland-born men aged 25–64 who lived outside New York reported the highest of all, $8000 average (mean), as compared with $5500 for island-born men living in New York. The superior education and occupations of the mainland born likely explain their larger incomes.

For women aged 25–64 who had received income in 1969, there were virtually no differences between New York State and the other states. Mainland-born women averaged about $4100, and island born, about $3300, regardless of where they lived. Presumably there is little economic motivation for Puerto Rican women to move outside of New York State.

The occupational composition of men in New York in 1970 did not differ greatly from that of men living in other states. The lesser schooling of New York men resulted in somewhat fewer being in professional jobs. On the other hand, the kind of job opportunities available in New York resulted in far more clerical workers, fewer operatives, and more service workers (Table 7.20). The major difference is between the mainland born and island born. The former are significantly higher on the occupational ladder regardless of state of residence.

Substantially the same observations can be made about the occupa-

TABLE 7.20

Occupational Composition by Sex, Place of Birth, and State of Residence for the Puerto Rican–Origin Population, 1970

	MEN				WOMEN			
	Mainland born		Island born		Mainland born		Island born	
	N.Y.	Other States	N.Y.	Other States	N.Y.	Other States	N.Y.	Other States
Professional, technical, and kindred	8.4	12.6	3.3	4.6	9.2	12.6	6.0	7.3
Managers, officials except farm	5.8	6.2	4.4	3.2	1.9	1.9	1.6	1.5
Sales workers	7.3	6.0	4.4	2.7	6.1	7.9	3.8	4.0
Clerical workers	21.2	9.1	12.0	5.8	57.5	38.1	27.8	20.0
Craftsmen & foremen	15.5	18.7	15.5	15.7	1.0	1.8	2.8	2.6
Operatives including transportation	19.3	24.5	32.0	41.5	11.1	17.4	43.9	49.9
Laborers except farm	7.6	10.2	6.0	10.9	0.4	0.6	1.2	1.3
Service workers	14.7	11.9	22.1	12.1	12.8	19.8	12.9	12.8
Farmers	0.0	0.0	0.0	0.0	0.0	0.0	0.0	0.0
Farm laborers	0.3	0.9	0.3	3.5	0.0	0.0	0.0	0.8
Total	100.0	100.0	100.0	100.0	100.0	100.0	100.0	100.0

tional composition of women. More of the women outside of New York are in professional occupations; on the other hand, many more of the New Yorkers are clerical workers. As with men, the differences between the mainland born and island born are much greater than between New Yorkers and others.

THE NEW YORK AREA

The New York metropolitan area, including adjacent portions of New Jersey and Connecticut, in 1970 contained more Puerto Ricans than did the San Juan metropolitan area—about 965,000 versus 851,000. The city of New York contained double the number of persons who resided in the city of San Juan—818,000 versus 453,000.

The population is concentrated in three boroughs: Bronx, Manhattan, and Brooklyn (Figure 7.7). Only 1 in 20 lived in Queens or Richmond in 1970. The South Bronx and East Harlem are often thought of as the areas "where Puerto Ricans live." Actually, these two areas together contain only 3 in 10 of all New York Puerto Ricans, and six in 10 are scattered elsewhere in the Bronx, Brooklyn, and Manhattan. The South Bronx and East Harlem are the most densely Puerto Rican in-

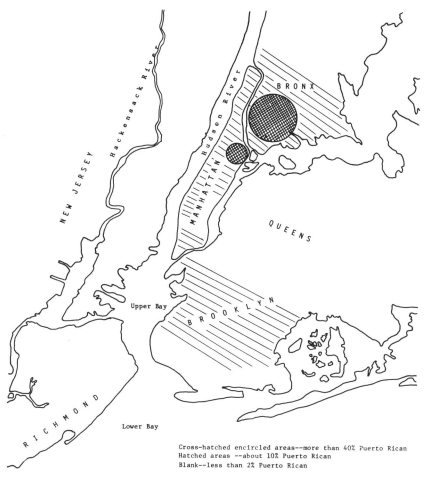

Cross-hatched encircled areas--more than 40% Puerto Rican
Hatched areas --about 10% Puerto Rican
Blank--less than 2% Puerto Rican

FIGURE 7.7. *Density of Puerto Ricans in New York City.*

sofar as close to half the people who live there are Puerto Rican. In other parts of the Bronx, Manhattan, and Brooklyn, the Puerto Ricans may constitute only 1 or 2 in 10 of the total population. Queens and Richmond, for all practical purposes, are "suburbs" and contain very small Puerto Rican populations.

This observed geographic distribution reflects what appears to be a fundamental socioeconomic pattern. In the three boroughs—Bronx, Manhattan and Brooklyn—fertility as measured by the number of children under 5 per 100 women aged 15–44 equals 51 children per 100 women. The rates for the South Bronx and East Harlem are about the same: 51. In Queens and Richmond, there are only 46 children; this is the identical fertility rate as for the entire metropolitan area. But the Puerto Ricans who live in Brooklyn and Queens are better off economically and have had more years of schooling (Figure 7.8) compared to those who live in the other three boroughs. Clearly, the time-honored relationship—more education and fewer children—still exists within New York City.

THE RESIDENTS OF THE ISLAND

INTRODUCTION

We are interested in the residents of the Commonwealth of Puerto Rico because: (a) there will continue to be considerable migration to the U.S. mainland over the next several decades at least; and (b) the migrants bring with them their fertility and demographic characteristics. Hence in attempting to assess the future fertility levels of the Puerto Rican–origin population that will be residing on the mainland, we should know something about present (1970) and likely future developments on the island. As the characteristics of the people on the island change, so will the characteristics of the migrants to the mainland.

Vast socioeconomic changes have taken place on the island since the end of World War II, and we shall review them briefly. We do know, as shown previously in this chapter, that the number of children ever born to women living on the island was only slightly higher than that of the non-Spanish white U.S. mainland women (in 1970) after controlling for age, education, marital status, and employment. During the 1940s and 1950s, however, fertility had been considerably higher.[14] What is the outlook for the future and how may it influence the mainland-resident women? This is clearly seen as follows: women aged 35–44 in 1970 averaged 4 children ever born; in 1960 women in this age group had averaged 4.8 children. These are the averages for the entire commonwealth without standardizing for employment status, education, or other variables.

Hence we ask: What is the outlook for the future? How may a changing birth rate on the island influence fertility on the mainland via the migrants?

---

[14] Jaffe, *People, Jobs, and Economic Development.*

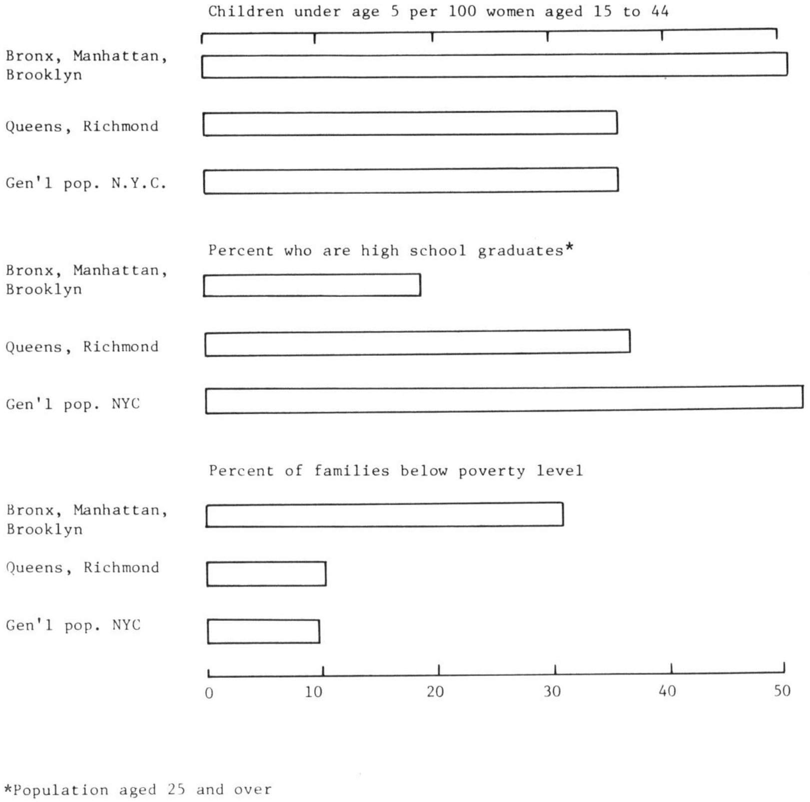

Children under age 5 per 100 women aged 15 to 44

Bronx, Manhattan, Brooklyn

Queens, Richmond

Gen'l pop. N.Y.C.

Percent who are high school graduates*

Bronx, Manhattan, Brooklyn

Queens, Richmond

Gen'l pop. NYC

Percent of families below poverty level

Bronx, Manhattan, Brooklyn

Queens, Richmond

Gen'l pop. NYC

0   10   20   30   40   50

*Population aged 25 and over

FIGURE 7.8. *Fertility, education, and poverty in New York City, 1970.*

THE VOLUME AND FUTURE OF MIGRATION

Between 1940 and 1974 it is estimated that there was a net migration of close to three-quarters of a million islanders to the mainland. The actual number of people who moved must have been significantly larger, since there was a return movement. However, we do not know exactly how many returned.

It is clear that much of the impetus for this movement away from the island comes from the job opportunities on the mainland.[15] It might be argued, however, that the great economic growth on the island since

———————

[15] *Ibid.* See also Rita M. Maldanado, "Why Puerto Ricans Migrated to the United States in 1947–73," *Monthly Labor Review* 99 (September 1976), p. 7ff. The author suggests that after 1967 noneconomic variables began to play a more important role in migration, although the economic still remained as the most important.

World War II should have provided employment there. Gross commonwealth product increased over three times between 1960 and 1972—somewhat less if inflation is taken into account, but still considerably. Indeed, by 1972 gross domestic product (in 1954 dollars) per person was about $1200, as compared with some $700 in 1960. Yet unemployment on the island remained consistently high over the years, about 12%.

With economic growth, employment increased almost 3% per year, as did unemployment, since the numbers of persons of working age increased at the same 3% per year. Economic growth and its attendant increases in population have been unable to outstrip population growth. Clearly, many Puerto Rican workers had no choice but to seek employment elsewhere.

In summary, we expect employment conditions on the island to continue to be insufficient for an indefinite time into the future. And we expect further movement to the mainland whenever there are jobs available there.

We cannot predict exactly for how many decades migration to the mainland will continue but will hazard a guess that it will continue into the twenty-first century, unless there are no jobs on the mainland. Although we realize fully that employment opportunities are variable from year to year, we believe that over the course of a generation there will be enough job openings on the mainland to attract substantial numbers of migrants.

A look at the island reveals that the birth rate began to decrease significantly only in the early 1960s. Population increase—the excess of births over deaths modified by migration—is averaging about 50,000 per year in the 1970s. Only in the last decade has there been any substantial decrease—a decrease from 60,000 persons—in the annual amount of natural increase. Hence, it will require at least another decade before the increases in the numbers of persons of working age begin to slow down enough for employment to begin to catch up. After that, it will take at least several decades for the decreased rate of population growth to have its full effect. Conceivably, in another 30 years increases in employment and population growth will become synchronized to the point that migration could diminish considerably.

THE CHANGING SOCIOECONOMIC SCENE

Education. Since World War II, the number of years of schooling completed by island residents has risen considerably. The women migrants to the mainland of two decades ago came from a population in which only 20–25% had completed 4 years of high school. On the other hand, the young island adult women, from among whom so many of the migrants of the 1970s and 1980s will come, have much more schooling; half or more will have completed high school (Table 7.5). If and when they reach the mainland, they are likely to have lower fertility corresponding to their increased amount of schooling.

Labor Force Participation. With the growth of the commonwealth economy, many more women are reporting as having entered the labor force. This suggests that it they migrate to the mainland, more of them will be accustomed to work for pay or profit and will be likely to do so. It is thus possible that in the future there will be an increase over 1970 in the proportions of mainland women who will be employed, and hence a corresponding decrease in fertility.

Marital Status. This also appears to be changing in the direction of lower fertility. There was a decrease between 1960 and 1970 in the proportion who were married and living with their husbands (from 69% in 1960 to 64% in 1970, for women aged 20–44). Although the decrease was small, it is likely to have some influence on fertility.

Summary. Socioeconomic conditions on the island are changing in such a manner that lower fertility in the future appears to be assured. This, in turn, leads to the probability that future migrants—in the 1970s, 1980s, and later—will have significantly lower fertility than did the migrants in decades immediately following World War II.

SOME IMPLICATIONS FOR THE MAINLAND

We have seen already that the mainland-born women who have completed high school—and the majority have done so—already have fertility at about the level of the U.S. non-Spanish white women. Add to this that there is considerable marriage of Puerto Rican women to non-Spanish men and that such unions have lower fertility. Hence, we can envisage with confidence significantly lower fertility for the Puerto Rican–origin women living on the mainland in future years.

8

The Cuban Americans

INTRODUCTION

The history of Spanish exploration, settlement, and attempted settlement in what is now the southeastern United States antedates that of the southwestern United States. Geographically, the present state of Florida is close enough to the several Spanish Caribbean islands so that the very earliest explorers visited or at least had heard about the mainland. The Spaniards referred to all of the mainland, or at least the Southeast, as Florida, and believed that gold and riches were to be obtained there. Whether any of these people should be called the original Cuban Americans, we leave to the reader to decide; we note here simply that the Cuban immigration to the United States in the latter half of the twentieth century has roots in the distant past.[1]

Ponce de León was one of the first, if not the first, Spaniard to disembark in present-day Florida. He arrived in 1513 from modern Puerto Rico. Possibly other Spanish ships had momentarily stopped on the Florida coast prior to this date, but apparently no attempts at exploration or settlement had been made. In 1521 Ponce de Leon attempted a settlement in Florida, was wounded by the Indians, and returned to Cuba, where he died. We may say he was a "Cuban" by death, if not by birth.

---

[1] For interesting accounts of some of these early explorations, see, for example, John Upton Terrell's account of Cabeza de Vaca's journeys, *Journey into Darkness* (New York: William Morrow & Co., 1962); Garcilasco de la Vega, *The Florida of the Inca*, trans. John and Jeannette Varner (Austin: University of Texas Press, 1951); Morison, *European Discovery*.

Next, in 1526 Lucas Vázquez de Ayllon arrived from Santo Domingo in an effort to explore and possibly settle, but he did not last long. Then, in 1528 Panfilo de Narváez arrived with a large expedition. This too was almost completely wiped out by the indigenous Indians and the physical difficulties encountered. Cabeza de Vaca was one of the four survivors who walked from the eastern United States across the continent and into Mexico City.

Hernando do Soto arrived in 1539 as governor and captain general of Florida and the island of Santiago de Cuba. Possibly, this makes him the first "Cuban." His explorations were numerous, and they carried him to the Mississippi River. He also was killed by the Indians and was buried in the river.

Others continued to arrive in Florida, and in September 1565 Pedro Menéndez de Avilés founded the present-day city of Saint Augustine, Florida, near the place where Ponce de León had landed in 1513. Spaniards, including people from the various Caribbean islands, continued to arrive in Florida. Finally, the United States took possession in 1821, and Florida was admitted as a state in 1845.

SOME DEMOGRAPHIC CHARACTERISTICS

POPULATION GROWTH

Following the acquisition of Florida from Spain by the United States, there were two waves of immigrants. The first extended to about 1950 and was in effect a more or less constant trickle, interrupted only by the Great Depression of the 1930s. Following Fidel Castro's assumption of power, there was a huge migration to the United States, so that by the 1970s the bulk of the Cuban-origin population of the United States was the result of immigration since the late 1950s. The general pattern of immigration and population growth is shown by the data on Cuban-born persons living in the United States from 1870 to 1970 (Table 8.1).

It is unlikely that prior to 1870 there were many Cuban-origin persons living in the United States. In 1869 Vincente Martinez Ybor moved his cigar manufacturing business to Key West,[2] after which there was a continuous, if not large, flow of Cubans. Some were cigar makers and others represented a wide variety of service occupations for the Cuban

---

[2] M. Estelle Smith, "The Spanish Speaking Population of Florida," in *Spanish Speaking People in the United States*, ed. June Helm (Seattle: University of Washington Press, 1968).

TABLE 8.1

Estimated Growth of the Cuban Stock: 1870–1975 (numbers in thousands)

	Foreign born	Native foreign parentage	Total
1870	5.3	NA	NA
1880	6.9	NA	NA
1890	NA	NA	NA
1900	11.1	NA	NA
1910	15.1	NA	NA
1920	14.9	NA	NA
1930	18.5	17.0	35.5
1940	18.0	NA	NA
1950	33.7	NA	NA
1960	79.2	45.3	124.5
1970[a]	439.0	122.0	561.0

[a]Number of foreign born plus natives of foreign parentage as reported in the 1970 Census, PC(1)-D1, Table 192. Note that in volume PC(2)-1C, Table 1, of the same census, the total number of Cubans including third and subsequent generations is given as 545,000.

population. In 1886 the cigar manufactory was moved to Tampa, and the Cuban section became known as "Free Havana."

Thus, there was a steady increase from about 5300 Cuban-born persons living in the United States in 1870 to some 15,000 at the time of World War I and to between 18,000 and 19,000 in 1930. Between that date and 1940, there apparently was no increase. To some extent, the flow of Cuban immigrants reflects the movements of the cigar industry. Up to the time of World War I, there was a steady increase in cigar production. Then, as cigarette smoking became popular, the production and consumption of cigars in the United States started to decrease. At the same time, the first cigar-making machines were introduced. Hence, there was little need for additional cigar makers. Since the 1950s, both production and consumption have increased, but by this time almost all cigars are machine made; the machines are attended by women operators rather than by the earlier male hand-rollers.

Since Cuban immigrants had been living in the United States for some time, it is only logical that there would be many children born here. By 1930 (the first time for which we apparently have information on native persons of Cuban parentage), there were about as many first generation U.S. born as Cuban-born persons. How many of second and subsequent generations of U.S. born there were, we do not know.

Following World War II, there was substantial immigration; the numbers of Cuban born living in the United States increased from some 18,000 in 1940 to 79,000 in 1960. We suspect that many of these immigrants came for the same reasons as did the Puerto Ricans—for jobs. By 1960 the number of first generation U.S.-born persons also had increased to about 45,000. If past immigration and fertility trends had continued, we can assume that the Cuban-origin population in the United States in the 1970s would have constituted an insignificant minority of the total U.S. population.

In 1959, however, with the advent of Castro, the number of Cuban born living in the United States increased to 439,000 by 1970. By this time also, the number of native persons of Cuban origin had increased to over 120,000. Included in this figure is an unknown number of second and subsequent generations born in the United States. Altogether there were about 560,000 in 1970. In the late 1970s, there were about 700,000 living in the United States.[3] In 1970, in addition to those living on the mainland, some 33,000 were recorded as residing in Puerto Rico.

GEOGRAPHIC DISTRIBUTION IN 1970

Close to half of the Cuban-origin population lived in Florida in 1970—one-quarter of a million persons. Another 90,000 lived in New York; 70,000, in New Jersey; close to 50,000, in California; and 20,000 in Illinois. The remaining 70,000 were scattered among the other states, except that none were reported in Vermont and Montana and eight other states each counted under 100 Cuban-origin persons.

NATIVITY COMPOSITION

In 1970 almost 8 in 10 were persons who were born in Cuba, and the remaining 2 in 10 were those born in the United States of Cuban-born parents. This follows from the recency of the migration. The shorter the

---

[3] See Chapter 10.

time that a population has lived in the United States, the fewer children will have been born here.

On the other hand, in 1960, almost 4 in 10 of the Cuban stock were persons born in the United States. This indicates that many of their parents must have been here for two decades or longer prior to 1960.

AGE AND SEX COMPOSITION

In 1970 the median (average) age was 31.3 years, as compared with 28 years for the total U.S. population (Table 8.2). Among those born in Cuba, the median age was 36 years, and among those born here, the median was only 9.3 years. In the future, as more children are born in the United States, we can expect the median age for the total population to decline. If there should be only little immigration in future years, it is probable that in another generation the median age will be about the same as that for the total U.S. population.

Women predominate among the Cuban born; of every 100 some 53 are women, and 47, men. Of those born in the United States, however, there are almost equal numbers of males and females.

SIZE OF FAMILY

There was an average of 3.7 persons per family having a Cuban head in 1970. This is significantly smaller than the average family size of 4.6 for Mexican, 4.2 for Hispano, and 4.0 for Puerto Rican families. However, Cuban families are still larger than those in total U.S.; there were 3.1 persons per family in the total population.

EDUCATION

YEARS OF SCHOOLING COMPLETED

As is found among other Spanish-origin groups, younger Cuban persons have much more schooling than do older ones. Of persons aged 55 and over who were of high-school-completion age around the time of World War I, about 1 in 5 had completed high school. By 1970, among 20–24-year-olds, of those born in the United States over 8 in 10, and of the foreign born close to 7 in 10, had graduated from high school (Table 8.3). In future years we can expect 9 in 10, or more, to have completed high school.

Of those who completed high school, some three in five of the men

TABLE 8.2
Persons of Cuban Origin, By Age, Sex, and Nativity: U.S. 1970 (numbers in thousands)

	Total				Foreign born			U.S. born		
	Total	Percent	Men	Women	Total	Men	Women	Total	Men	Women
Total	544.6	100.0	258.1	286.5	444.4	207.3	237.1	100.2	50.8	49.4
Under 5 years	40.6	7.5	20.5	20.1	7.8	3.7	4.1	32.8	16.8	16.0
5 to 13 years	98.6	18.0	50.1	48.5	62.2	31.6	30.6	36.4	18.6	17.8
14 to 19 years	53.9	9.9	26.9	27.0	45.9	23.0	22.9	8.1	3.9	4.1
20 to 24 years	31.1	5.7	13.8	17.3	27.4	12.0	15.4	3.7	1.8	1.9
25 to 34 years	76.1	14.0	34.3	41.8	70.4	31.4	38.9	5.8	2.9	2.9
35 to 44 years	92.4	17.0	44.3	48.0	88.2	42.1	46.2	4.1	2.2	1.9
45 to 54 years	70.6	13.0	34.3	36.3	66.7	32.5	34.2	3.9	1.8	2.1
55 to 64 years	46.1	8.5	20.0	26.1	43.1	18.4	24.7	3.0	1.6	1.4
65 and over	35.1	6.4	13.6	21.4	32.6	12.5	20.1	2.4	1.1	1.3
Median age	31.1		30.2	32.7	36.0	35.5	36.4	9.3	9.2	9.4
20 and over	351.5		160.6	190.9						

Source: 1970 Population Census, Persons of Spanish Origin (PC(2)-1C), Table 5.

TABLE 8.3
Years of Schooling Completed by the Cuban–Origin Population, by Age, Sex, and Nativity: U.S. 1970

	Approx. period high school completion	% completed high school		% high school graduates entered college		% college entrants completed college	
		U.S. born	Foreign born	U.S. born	Foreign born	U.S. born	Foreign born
MEN							
20 to 24	1965	82	70	61	57	23	22
25 to 29	1960	77	66	51	60	40	38
30 to 34	1955	68	48	41	59	44	45
35 to 44	1947	67	45	61	57	49	52
45 to 54	1937	44	47	52	58	41	63
55 and over	WWI	15	41	29	51	17	70
WOMEN							
20 to 24	1965	81	66	50	39	15	19
25 to 29	1960	75	58	47	39	48	35
30 to 34	1955	66	43	26	49	43	35
35 to 44	1947	60	46	39	43	47	53
45 to 54	1937	40	42	41	38	33	67
55 and over	WWI	20	25	43	33	50	57

Source: Public Use Sample.

and about half of the women (age 20–24) entered college during the 1960s. Of these, between one-third and one-half completed 4 years.

The Cuban population has more schooling than do the U.S.-born, Mexican-origin, Puerto Rican–origin, and the Hispano populations, and the same as that of the Central and South American origin and of all non-Spanish whites in the United States.

SCHOOL ATTENDANCE, 1970

Somewhat fewer of the youngsters—ages 7–19—attend school than is observed in the U.S. non-Spanish white population (Appendix Table G–7). The overall (standardized) attendance rate for those of Cuban origin is 83.4%, as compared with 90.5% for the non-Spanish white population. Furthermore, more of the Cuban youngsters are below the modal grade for their age, 13.6% as compared with 6.8% for the non-Spanish white. On the other hand, perhaps slightly more Cubans are above mode, 4.0% versus 2.2%.

At ages 20–24, the college ages, somewhat more Cuban-origin people are attending school, 26.8% versus 22.7%. At ages 25–34 the picture is reversed: 4.4% of the Cubans attend school, as compared with 6.2% of the U.S. population.

Up to about age 17, the latter high school years, about the same proportion of boys and girls attend school. Fewer young women go to college, however, so that in the college ages the school attendance rate for women is below that of the men.

FERTILITY

The number of children ever born alive to Cuban women aged 15–44 (as of 1970) was 1.3 per woman. Among non-Spanish white women, the average was 1.6; Puerto Rican–origin women averaged 2.1, and Mexican-origin women averaged 2.2 children. Standardizing these rates to take into account the influences of age distribution, schooling, marital status, and employment decreases the average number of children ever born alive to Cuban women to 1.2, to Puerto Rican women to 1.7, and to Mexican-origin women to 2.0 children. The average for the non-Spanish white women remains unchanged—1.6. Clearly, the women of Cuban descent have low fertility.

Increased schooling leads to a small reduction in fertility, holding other factors constant. Cuban women who had completed high school averaged about 1 child, whereas those with less schooling averaged close to 1.3 children (holding constant employment status and marital status).

Employment of the women is also related to lower fertility. Employed women (holding constant years of schooling and marital status) in 1970 averaged about 1 child, whereas those not working averaged 1.3 children.

Marital status obviously is related to fertility, given the nature of our society. Married women living with their husbands averaged close to 1.5 births, whereas other women (widowed, divorced, separated, never married) averaged about .75 child (holding schooling and employment constant).

The relative influence of these three factors upon fertility of women aged 35–44 is estimated to be as follows:

1. Completing high school results in about a 14% decrease.
2. Being employed decreases fertility about 26%.
3. Not being married and living with spouse is the most important and decreases fertility some 40%.
4. The joint contribution of all three factors adds another 20%. Altogether, fertility is cut in half by the combined operation of all three factors.

There is no doubt that the fertility of Cuban women is close to, if not below, the replacement level. Among women aged 35–44 in 1970, it was only about 70% of that of the non-Spanish white women in the United States. By this age, women have almost all the children they ever will have; their fertility is nearly ended. We compare the fertility—average number of children ever born alive per woman—of Cuban with the non-Spanish white women as follows:

Years of schooling	Cuban	Non-Spanish white
Total population	2.0	2.9
Under 12	2.1	3.1
12 and over	1.9	2.7

Cuban women average close to one child less as compared with the non-Spanish white women.

Whether this difference will persist in the next generation—that is, women aged 35–44 in 1990 or the year 2000—we cannot say. Perhaps the low fertility of present-day Cuban women is because they are migrants—one might say forced migrants. If this is the case, we can expect fertility among women born in the United States to rise in the future and approach that of the non-Spanish white. On the other hand, if the low Cuban fertility is due to other factors, cultural ones perhaps, then the lower fertility may persist well into the future.

At this time (1976) it appears that the fertility of the non-Spanish whites will decrease significantly by the year 2000, that is, women aged 20–24 in 1970 will have significantly fewer children by the year 1990 than did women aged 35–44 in 1970. This is indicated by the analysis of Anderson,[4] on the basis of which we can expect an average of perhaps 2 to 2.2 children per woman at the end of the century.

As for the Cuban-origin women, we estimate that they will continue to average at least two children per woman. Hence in another generation the two populations will have more or less similar fertility.

CHARACTERISTICS OF WOMEN IN THE REPRODUCTIVE AGES, 1970

Table 8.4 presents selected characteristics of Cuban and non-Spanish white women in the reproductive ages by age and years of schooling. At virtually every age and school level, significantly lower proportions of Cuban women are married and living with their husbands. Conversely, the Cuban women have greater proportions employed than do non-Spanish white women. This is observed for all ages and for both the lesser and more schooled. These two characteristics help to explain the lesser number of children ever born to the Cuban women.

THE ECONOMIC PICTURE

LABOR FORCE PARTICIPATION AND EMPLOYMENT

Men. A somewhat larger proportion of the Cuban-origin men aged 16 and over than of all non-Spanish white men in the United States are in the labor force, 83% versus 77%, respectively. The Cubans, as recent newcomers to the United States, presumably are impelled to devote their energies in an attempt to become economically established here. Since average earnings (see pp. 259–262) are lower for the

---

[4] Jeanne L. Anderson, "Trends in Expected Family Size in the United States," *New York Statistician* 26 (March–April 1975.) p. 1ff.

TABLE 8.4

Selected Characteristics for Women of Cuban Origin in the Reproductive Years, by Years of Schooling Completed: U.S. 1970

Age and characteristics	Cuban descent		Non-Spanish white Total U.S.	
	Under 12 years	12 & over years	Under 12 years	12 & over years
15 to 19 years				
% married, spouse present	5.5	16.0	6.9	16.0
% employed	21.7	70.6	19.3	49.1
Av. no. children ever born per woman	.06	.09	.08	.10
20 to 24 years				
% married, spouse present	49.5	45.5	68.0	53.9
% employed	51.1	67.1	33.6	57.6
Av. no. children ever born per woman	.81	.37	1.38	.50
25 to 29 years				
% married, spouse present	74.7	71.5	79.2	80.7
% employed	42.9	58.1	32.3	44.8
Av. no. children ever born per woman	1.64	1.28	2.39	1.51
30 to 34 years				
% married, spouse present	79.1	78.9	81.2	84.6
% employed	47.4	54.3	37.3	41.9
Av. no. children ever born per woman	1.91	1.73	3.01	2.36
35 to 44 years				
% married, spouse present	81.9	78.4	81.7	84.8
% employed	53.0	66.5	44.0	49.1
Av. no. children ever born per woman	2.01	1.92	3.09	2.73

Cubans, this factor may propel additional men—and women, as we shall see—into the labor force.

The more schooling a man has, the more likely he is to be in the labor force (Table 8.5). Of those who did not complete high school, 77% were in the labor force, as compared with 92% of the college graduates. If we limit our analysis to ages 20–64—the prime working years—we see that the variation is narrowed but that more of those with more years of schooling are in the labor force; 91% of those who did not complete high school were in the labor force, as compared with 96% of the college graduates. For all schooling—the total male popula-

TABLE 8.5

Labor-Force-Participation and Employment Rates, Cuban-Origin Population, Age, and Years of Schooling: 1970 by Sex,

Age	*Total*			*Under 12 years*		
	% in labor force	a/	b/	% in labor force	a/	b/
MEN						
Total	82.8	86.8	3.7	77.4	85.0	4.2
16 to 19 years	41.4	44.6	8.8	37.4	44.4	10.6
20 to 24 years	79.7	75.1	6.6	84.9	82.1	7.7
25 to 34 years	95.1	91.2	2.5	93.4	89.7	3.6
35 to 44 years	95.3	91.4	3.1	94.1	88.8	3.7
45 to 54	94.7	90.4	2.9	92.3	89.2	2.7
55 and over	63.9	84.1	4.7	58.3	83.1	4.8
20 to 64	92.0	89.3	3.3	90.7	88.5	3.7
WOMEN						
Total	50.2	76.1	7.1	43.3	73.8	9.0
16 to 19 years	37.9	43.5	7.4	29.9	31.0	9.9
20 to 24 years	64.7	76.1	4.7	58.9	74.3	5.9
25 to 34 years	57.0	78.6	7.5	53.5	78.8	8.8
35 to 44 years	62.6	79.3	6.3	58.4	78.0	8.2
45 to 54	60.4	80.6	7.3	57.6	80.8	8.5
55 and over	23.9	73.0	10.2	20.6	69.8	12.6
20 to 44 years	60.8	78.5	6.5	56.6	77.9	8.1

a/Percentage of civilian labor force employed full time.

b/Percentage of civilian labor force unemployed.

tion—92% of the Cuban men aged 20–64 were in the labor force, as compared with 90% of the non-Spanish white men in the total U.S. population.

Most of the Cuban men in the prime working ages, 20–64 years, who were in the civilian labor force had worked full time. There was not much difference by level of schooling, although slightly fewer of those who had not completed high school, in comparison with high school graduates, had worked full time (Table 8.5).

The unemployment rate was slightly higher for the Cuban-origin men aged 20–64 than for the non-Spanish whites, although the differences are hardly significant. Those with more schooling had lower unemployment rates as follows:

TABLE 8.5 (cont.)

12 years % in labor force	a/	b/	13 to 15 years % in labor force	a/	b/	16+ years % in labor force	a/	b/
87.1	88.2	4.1	87.8	86.9	2.3	92.3	90.7	2.4
60.9	43.8	4.7	33.3	57.1	0.0	0.0	0.0	0.0
86.3	82.1	8.3	69.0	63.0	3.7	83.1	71.1	6.7
95.8	92.2	2.4	96.5	92.0	1.1	96.6	92.4	1.8
95.4	93.8	3.2	96.7	94.6	1.5	98.5	95.0	1.5
97.5	90.9	4.0	96.5	91.2	3.7	97.3	92.8	2.0
66.9	86.0	5.5	81.6	85.9	4.2	76.8	84.0	3.8
93.6	90.9	4.0	89.8	87.4	2.4	96.0	91.5	2.1
56.3	80.1	5.9	61.9	70.7	4.0	68.4	81.7	4.9
66.2	69.1	4.3	54.5	27.8	0.0	0.0	0.0	0.0
65.7	83.0	5.3	71.6	66.1	3.3	62.2	82.6	0.0
59.0	80.1	7.7	58.8	73.5	3.7	66.0	79.8	7.1
64.1	84.0	3.7	63.9	74.1	3.2	78.6	78.7	6.5
60.7	80.3	5.8	63.9	76.8	8.7	73.3	82.7	3.6
26.8	72.5	9.8	42.2	74.0	3.7	47.3	92.3	0.0
62.3	82.2	5.6	64.1	71.4	3.4	72.4	79.4	6.2

Years of schooling	Cuban origin (%)	Non-Spanish white (%)
Under 12	3.7	4.1
12	4.0	2.7
13–15	2.4	2.8
16 and over	2.1	1.4
Total population	3.3	3.0

In summary, as far as labor force participation and employment are concerned, Cuban-origin men are at least as well off—or were in 1970—as is the general U.S. non-Spanish white male population.

Women. Half of the Cuban-origin women aged 16 and over were in the labor force, a rate substantially above that of two in five for all U.S. non-Spanish white women. The participation rate increases sharply with increased schooling, from 43% for those who had not finished high school to 68% for college graduates. This pattern is found at all ages, although it is clearest in the ages above the childbearing years. From this pattern we deduce that as more Cuban-origin women receive more schooling in the future, we can expect more of them to be in the labor force.

Among women in the childbearing ages of 20–44, 6 in 10 were in the labor force in 1970, as compared with 5 in 10 for the non-Spanish white women. Again, the differences by years of schooling are pronounced, ranging from 57% among those who had less than 12 years of schooling to 72% for college graduates.

Of those Cuban women in the labor force, three in four had worked full time during the census week, as compared with two in three of the non-Spanish white women. As regards weeks worked in 1969, a few more Cuban than U.S. non-Spanish white women had been employed 48 weeks or more. At ages 25–54 more Cuban-origin women had worked 48 weeks or more, and at ages 55 and over more Anglo women had worked a full year. Only about half of all Cuban-origin women who were in the labor force in 1970 had worked continuously. About one in four of these women had worked full time at the time of the 1970 Census enumeration *and* 48 weeks or more in 1969. About another one in four women had worked intermittently, either part time or in and out of the labor force, or had periods of unemployment in 1969.

Unemployment in 1970 was higher among Cuban women aged 16 and over than among the non-Spanish white, 7.1% versus 4.9%. The less schooled had higher unemployment rates (Table 8.5).

We noted previously that Cuban-origin women had lower fertility than did U.S. non-Spanish white women. We suspect that the higher labor-force-participation rates among the former account for part of this lower fertility. Over the next generation, we think, labor force participation among the two groups of women will approach each other; the differences, if any, will be smaller. Hence, in the future labor force participation per se will probably play a lesser part in explaining any fertility differences that there may be between the two groups of women.

CLASS OF WORKER

Most Cuban men and women are employees of private concerns. One in 10 of the men and 1 in 33 of the women are self-employed, and the remainder, about 1 in 15, are government employees. Of the non-Spanish white population, significantly more are self-employed and government workers. However, among the Cubans there are great differences between those born in Cuba and those born in the United States; many more of the natives work for the government. Of the population aged 25 and over, workers are classed as follows:

	Men		Women	
Class of worker	Foreign born (%)	Native (%)	Foreign born (%)	Native (%)
Private employees	86	65	91	81
Self-employed (including unpaid family workers)	9	11	3	5
Government employees	5	24	6	14

Presumably, the small percentage of government employees among the Cuban born reflects that so many are not yet citizens and are thus barred from such employment. Among the natives, the large percentage of government workers—larger than among the total U.S. non-Spanish white population—probably reflects the types of jobs available in the areas where the Cuban-origin population lives.

FAMILY INCOME

Average (median) income in 1969 of families in which the head was of Cuban origin was $8690, or about $1400 less than that of non-Spanish white families. Income varied greatly in accordance with the number of earners in the family and the sex of the head. The more earners, the higher the family income, and families headed by men average higher incomes than do those headed by women as follows:

	Head	
Number of earners	Men ($)	Women ($)
Total population	9200	4900
None	1640	1310
1	9060	4570
2 or more	10,670	8740

The median income for all families depends on how many are headed by men, how many by women, and how many earners there are. Among Cuban families, 12% were headed by women, as compared with 9% among non-Spanish white families. However, significantly more Cuban families had two or more earners (Appendix Table G–37). If Cuban families had the same distribution by number of earners as did the non-Spanish whites, and the same distribution by sex of head, then average (median) family income would have been between $8200 and $8300, $400–500 less than they actually had. Clearly, Cuban family income was as high as it was observed to be only because so many members were employed. It was noted previously that many more Cuban women were in the labor force, and they contributed substantially to raising family income.

Why Cuban family income was lower than that of non-Spanish white families, we do not know. Certainly regional differences in wage structure—wages are lower in Florida than in other parts of the United States—and in occupational and industrial mix contribute to the lower Cuban family income. To what extent discrimination per se may be playing a part, if any, we do not know.

It was noted earlier in this chapter that somewhat more Cuban families were headed by women. This may reflect in part the sex distribution; among all Cuban-origin persons aged 20 and over, 54% were women, whereas among the non-Spanish whites about 52% were women. What other factors may be contributing to the larger proportion of Cuban families headed by women, we do not know.

INDIVIDUAL EARNINGS

Men. On the average, Cuban men earned slightly over $5700; this is the median amount received from wages, salaries, and self-employment income (Table 8.6). These men earned between one-fifth and one-quarter less than did non-Spanish white men. Many factors account for this difference, as was discussed in Chapter 3.

Earnings rise sharply with increased years of schooling. For example, let us look at ages 35–44 and 45–64 as follows:

	Median earnings	
Years of schooling	35–44 ($)	45–64 ($)
Under 12	5660	5020
12	6630	5960
13–15	7690	6870
16 and over	9230	8440

TABLE 8.6
Earnings in 1969, Cuban Descent, by Sex, Age, and Years of Schooling

Years of schooling	MEN						WOMEN					
	14 & over	14-24 years	25-34 years	35-44 years	45-64 years	65+ years	14 & over	14-24 years	25-34 years	35-44 years	45-64 years	65+ years
Total U.S.												
1st quartile	$3,440	780	4,730	4,500	3,950	1,810	$1,680	770	1,880	2,280	2,140	840
Median	5,710	2,020	6,790	6,490	5,740	3,760	3,260	1,890	3,410	3,580	3,400	1,920
3rd quartile	8,110	4,560	9,240	9,030	7,890	6,450	4,580	3,800	4,850	4,820	4,530	3,450
Variation*	.82	1.87	.66	.70	.69	1.23	.89	1.60	.87	.71	.70	1.36
Under 12 years												
1st quartile	2,960	600	4,000	3,840	3,440	1,530	1,360	550	1,460	1,920	1,890	700
Median	4,980	1,350	5,930	5,660	5,020	3,310	2,920	1,200	2,930	3,250	3,170	1,690
3rd quartile	6,960	3,700	7,850	7,660	6,790	5,670	3,950	2,790	4,160	4,220	3,980	2,960
Variation	.80	2.30	.65	.67	.67	1.25	.89	1.87	.92	.71	.66	1.34
12 years												
1st quartile	3,720	1,220	5,000	5,010	4,350	1,790	2,000	1,240	2,100	2,540	2,340	+
Median	5,810	2,790	6,600	6,630	5,960	3,590	3,470	2,760	3,510	3,730	3,620	
3rd quartile	7,970	5,320	8,850	9,100	7,830	5,800	4,770	4,480	4,870	4,850	4,870	
Variation	.73	1.47	.58	.62	.58	1.12	.80	1.17	.79	.62	.70	
13 to 15 years												
1st quartile	4,030	1,000	5,440	5,720	4,750	+	1,630	810	2,400	2,530	2,370	+
Median	6,640	2,520	7,620	7,690	6,870		3,570	1,910	4,170	4,130	3,930	
3rd quartile	9,180	4,870	9,840	9,960	9,430		5,170	3,900	5,910	5,600	5,720	
Variation	.78	1.54	.58	.55	.68		1.00	1.62	.84	.74	.85	
16+ years												
1st quartile	5,700	1,880	6,400	6,520	5,770	3,390	3,080	1,970	3,080	3,220	3,220	+
Median	8,590	3,950	10,060	9,230	8,440	5,860	4,550	3,180	4,770	4,810	4,420	
3rd quartile	12,810	6,800	13,480	14,300	12,560	9,650	7,220	5,400	7,350	7,300	7,270	
Variation	.83	1.25	.70	.84	.80	1.07	.91	1.08	.90	.85	.92	

*Interquartile range divided by median.

†Too few cases in sample, under 500 inflated population.

Source: Special Census tabulation.

Men who had completed college earned about two-thirds more than did men who had been high school dropouts.

The earnings pattern of youth aged 14–24 is difficult to interpret. In the early teens, many are still going to high school and work only part time, thus bringing down the average for those who had completed less than 12 years of schooling. In the later teens and early twenties, many are attending college and either working part time or working at inferior jobs simply to pay their college expenses. Hence average annual earnings are at a minimum under age 25.

Among men aged 65 and over, only a select group are still earners. The more schooled often can continue to work after this age, if not full time then part time. For the lesser schooled, mandatory retirement generally forces most of them out of employment. As a result, in this age group average annual earnings were also well below those of men in the prime working ages of 20–64.

Within each age and level of schooling group, there was considerable variation in earnings. Thus, some high school dropouts had earned more than some college graduates. This is indicated in the line marked "variation" in Table 8.6. Between the ages of 25 and 64, the variation index is smallest, indicating that most men tend to earn around the average amounts. At the younger and older ages, however, the variation is much greater; this probably results from the fact that many work part time and have lesser earnings, so that the median earnings for the group do not indicate fairly the general level of earnings of all members. We note that among 14–24-year-olds, only 40% of those who worked in 1969 had worked 48 weeks or more; among those aged 65 and over, the proportion is 65%. Among men between ages 25 and 64, however, about 80% had worked 48 weeks or more in 1969.

Women. The earnings of Cuban-descent women average less than 60% of men's earnings—$3260 as compared with $5710. However, direct comparisons are not possible, since many more women work part time during the year, and women are more likely to be in occupations and industries different from those of men. We may express the median earnings of women as a percentage of that of men as follows:

Years of schooling	Age		
	25–34 (%)	35–44 (%)	45–64 (%)
Under 12	49	57	63
12	53	56	61
13–15	55	54	57
16 and over	47	52	52

In most instances, women average between 50% and 60% of men's earnings. Among the Cubans, neither age nor years of schooling appears to be a major factor in differentiating the earnings of men and women.

In almost all instances, the index of variation for women is higher than that for men. This reflects the greater prevalence of part-time work for women, as shown in the following proportions of all those who had worked in 1969, who had worked for 48 weeks or more:

Age	Women (%)	Men (%)
25–34	52%	81%
35–44	58	79
45–64	59	78

OCCUPATIONS

Men. Despite the recency of their migration into the United States, Cuban-descent men are almost as high on the occupational ladder as are the non-Spanish white men (Appendix Table G–38). The Socio-Economic Status (SES) score in 1970 was 57 for the Cubans and 59 for the latter. About 13% of the Cuban men were in professional occupations, as compared with 15% of the latter. On the other hand, one-quarter of the former were operatives (including transportation), whereas under one-fifth of the non-Spanish whites were in this occupational category. Almost no Cuban men—one-half of 1%—were occupied in agriculture; of the non-Spanish white men, close to 5% were in this category.

Ordinarily, youth enter the world of occupations at the lower levels and work their way up as they become older and more experienced. Among the Cuban men, this pattern is reversed; the SES score for those aged 14–34 was 60, as compared with 56 for men aged 35 and over. It is thought that this reversal may reflect more schooling and competence in the English language on the part of the younger men (Table 8.7). Furthermore, many of the younger men had attended school in the United States and thus acquired a better command of the English language. For the better white-collar jobs, a good command of English is virtually a necessity; for the lower white-collar jobs, it is not so important. As we go down the occupational ladder, the need to speak, read, and write English well decreases rapidly.

Schooling obviously is important in determining one's position on the occupational ladder. Among Cuban college graduates—16 or more years of schooling completed—55% were in professional occupations,

TABLE 8.7

Major Occupational Group, by Years of Schooling, Age, and Sex, Men of Cuban Descent: 1970

	Total					14–34				
		Years of schooling					Years of schooling			
		-12	12	13-15	16+		-12	12	13-15	16+
	Total	years	years	years	years	Total	years	years	years	years
Total	100.0	100.0	100.0	100.0	100.0	100.0	100.0	100.0	100.0	100.0
Professional, total	12.8	1.9	6.7	16.7	55.5	13.9	2.4	8.7	18.1	65.1
Modern Science	7.1	0.5	2.3	6.9	36.9	7.4	0.5	2.7	7.1	47.4
Classical	3.6	1.1	2.3	3.2	14.7	3.0	1.3	2.3	2.5	12.9
Semiprofessional	2.1	0.3	2.2	6.6	3.8	3.5	0.6	3.7	8.6	4.8
Manager, nonfarm, total	7.8	5.0	8.2	13.5	10.9	8.0	4.4	7.7	15.2	9.6
Employee	5.1	2.7	5.4	10.3	8.0	6.3	2.8	6.0	12.5	8.6
Self-Employed	2.6	2.3	2.8	3.2	2.9	1.8	1.5	1.7	2.7	1.0
Sales	6.0	4.2	8.4	10.3	4.5	7.8	5.9	10.8	10.0	3.3
Clerical	10.8	6.2	14.7	20.4	11.0	14.6	8.3	21.0	22.3	9.1
Craftsmen	18.0	20.3	23.0	14.2	5.8	16.5	18.8	19.8	13.2	5.3
Operatives (excl. transp.)	19.9	28.5	17.4	9.9	4.5	16.9	27.3	12.1	8.3	2.9
Transportation	4.4	5.7	4.5	3.3	0.8	5.4	7.1	6.2	2.7	1.9
Laborers, nonfarm	5.5	8.0	4.3	2.8	1.6	5.6	8.9	4.6	2.5	0.5
Farm manager	0.1	0.1	0.1	0.2	0.2	0.0	0.0	0.0	0.0	0.0
Farm laborers	0.4	0.6	0.1	0.2	0.5	0.5	0.9	0.0	0.0	0.5
Services, total	14.2	19.5	12.6	8.3	4.6	11.0	16.0	9.1	7.6	1.9
Household	0.1	0.2	0.0	0.0	0.1	0.1	0.1	0.0	0.0	0.0
Protective	0.6	0.7	0.8	0.6	0.1	0.5	0.5	0.4	0.7	0.0
Other	13.5	18.5	11.8	7.7	4.4	10.4	15.4	8.7	6.9	1.9
SES	57.2	48.6	57.5	65.5	78.0	60.3	49.5	60.5	69.9	81.9

and another 11 % were managers. Among the non-Spanish white college graduates, somewhat more men were in these higher occupations: 59 % in professional occupations and 20 % in managerial posts. Among those who had not completed high school, however, very few of either group were in such higher occupations.

All in all, there is a consistent resemblance between the two groups of men by educational level. The SES scores are as follows:

Years of schooling	Cuban	Non-Spanish white
Total population	57	59
Under 12	49	49
12	58	58
13–15	66	67
16 and over	78	82

TABLE 8.7 (cont.)

	35-44 Years of schooling					45+ Years of schooling			
Total	-12 years	12 years	13-15 years	16+ years	Total	-12 years	12 years	13-15 years	16+ years
100.0	100.0	100.0	100.0	100.0	100.0	100.0	100.0	100.0	100.0
11.7	1.6	5.3	17.4	51.4	12.8	1.8	5.5	13.1	53.0
6.5	0.6	2.0	6.5	33.9	7.3	0.4	2.0	7.0	33.3
3.4	0.7	1.7	4.5	14.8	4.3	1.2	2.7	3.5	15.7
1.7	0.3	1.7	6.5	2.7	1.2	0.2	0.9	2.5	4.0
7.2	4.6	8.7	11.9	10.9	8.0	5.9	8.4	11.6	11.6
4.4	2.4	5.6	8.5	6.2	4.7	2.8	4.6	7.5	8.8
2.9	2.1	3.1	3.5	4.7	3.3	3.1	3.8	4.0	2.8
5.7	4.1	6.7	11.9	5.1	4.7	3.0	7.1	9.0	4.8
8.3	4.8	10.1	15.4	12.8	9.3	5.8	11.3	21.6	10.9
20.9	23.0	27.9	17.9	5.8	17.0	19.3	22.6	12.6	6.1
23.0	32.3	20.4	8.5	5.4	20.3	26.4	21.0	14.6	4.8
4.8	6.6	3.9	4.0	0.8	3.1	4.0	3.1	4.0	0.3
5.6	7.7	4.5	3.5	1.6	5.5	7.6	3.8	3.0	2.3
0.1	0.0	0.3	0.0	0.4	0.2	0.2	0.0	1.0	0.3
0.?	0.2	0.0	0.5	0.8	0.5	0.6	0.2	0.5	0.3
12.4	15.2	12.3	9.0	5.1	18.6	25.3	17.0	9.0	5.8
0.0	0.0	0.0	0.0	0.0	0.3	0.4	0.0	0.0	0.3
0.4	0.1	1.7	0.0	0.0	1.0	1.4	0.7	1.0	0.3
12.0	15.1	10.6	9.0	5.1	17.4	23.5	16.4	8.0	5.3
56.4	49.1	56.0	64.7	76.6	56.0	47.7	55.4	62.5	77.1

Women. About two in five Cuban women are employed in white-collar jobs, a proportion not much different from that of all non-Spanish white women (Table 8.8). With increased schooling, increasingly more Cuban-descent women are found in professional and managerial jobs. We may compare those who had not completed high school with college graduates as follows:

Class of worker	Under 12 years (%)	16 and over years (%)
Professional and managerial	3	49
Clerical and sales	17	25
Blue-collar and service	80	26

TABLE 8.8

Major Occupational Group, by Years of Schooling, Age, and Sex, Women of Cuban Descent: 1970

	TOTAL					14-34					35+				
	Years of schooling					Years of schooling					Years of schooling				
	Total	-12 years	12 years	13-15 years	16+ years	Total	-12 years	12 years	13-15 years	16+ years	Total	-12 years	12 years	13-15 years	16+ years
Total	100.0	100.0	100.0	100.0	100.0	100.0	100.0	100.0	100.0	100.0	100.0	100.0	100.0	100.0	100.0
Professional, total	9.5	2.1	6.2	14.7	46.9	8.6	2.7	5.3	13.2	50.4	10.1	1.8	7.0	16.7	45.6
Modern science	2.8	0.9	2.4	4.6	11.1	2.3	0.9	1.9	3.0	11.3	3.2	0.9	2.8	6.7	11.1
Classical	5.3	0.8	2.9	6.5	31.1	4.5	1.6	2.1	6.4	29.6	5.8	0.6	3.6	6.7	31.6
Semiprofessional	1.4	0.4	0.9	3.6	4.6	1.8	0.3	1.2	3.8	9.6	1.1	0.5	0.7	3.3	2.8
Manager, nonfarm, total	1.4	0.8	1.9	2.5	1.6	1.3	0.6	1.8	0.8	4.3	1.5	0.9	2.1	4.8	0.6
Employee	1.1	0.4	1.4	2.5	1.6	1.0	0.3	1.4	0.8	4.3	1.1	0.5	1.5	4.8	0.6
Self-employed	0.3	0.4	0.5	0.0	0.0	0.2	0.3	0.4	0.0	0.0	0.4	0.5	0.7	0.0	0.0
Sales	5.2	5.0	6.5	5.5	2.1	7.2	8.5	6.9	6.8	1.7	3.9	3.2	6.2	3.8	2.2
Clerical	25.4	11.9	39.4	49.3	23.0	39.0	20.6	54.1	59.8	27.8	16.2	7.3	25.9	35.9	21.2
Craftsmen	2.6	3.0	2.9	1.9	0.5	2.4	3.0	2.5	1.1	0.9	2.7	3.1	3.3	2.9	0.3
Operatives, excl. transp.	41.9	58.9	31.3	16.0	20.2	29.8	48.9	19.2	10.2	12.2	50.0	64.3	42.4	23.4	23.1
Transportation	0.2	0.2	0.2	0.2	0.7	0.2	0.1	0.4	0.0	0.0	0.2	0.0	0.0	0.0	0.0
Labor, nonfarm	1.0	1.3	0.8	0.4	0.0	1.0	1.3	0.9	0.4	0.9	1.0	1.3	0.8	0.5	0.6
Farm manager	0.0	0.0	0.0	0.0	0.0	0.0	0.0	0.0	0.0	0.0	0.0	0.0	0.0	0.0	0.0
Farm laborer	0.2	0.3	0.2	0.2	0.0	0.2	0.4	0.2	0.0	0.0	0.2	0.2	0.2	0.0	0.0
Service, total	12.7	16.3	10.6	9.3	5.1	10.3	13.8	9.0	7.9	1.7	14.2	17.6	12.2	11.0	6.3
Household	1.3	2.3	0.5	0.0	0.5	0.7	1.2	0.4	0.0	0.9	1.8	3.0	0.7	0.0	0.3
Protective	0.0	0.1	0.0	0.2	0.0	0.0	0.0	0.0	0.0	0.0	0.1	0.1	0.0	0.5	0.0
Other	11.3	13.9	10.1	9.1	4.6	9.7	12.7	8.6	7.9	0.9	12.3	14.5	11.5	10.5	6.0
SES	56.4	47.4	59.3	65.8	72.6	60.2	52.4	63.1	68.5	76.6	53.8	46.9	56.1	63.4	71.0

In comparison with the non-Spanish white women, the Cuban-origin women are not as high on the occupational ladder. The SES scores are as follows:

Years of schooling	Cuban	Non-Spanish white
Total population	56	63
Under 12	47	52
12	59	64
13–15	66	71
16 and over	73	85

It is evident that:

1. The Cubans are below the non-Spanish white at every schooling level. Probably English-language ability plays an important part; even some of the Cuban college graduates may be at a disadvantage.
2. With increased schooling, the rise up the occupational ladder is sharp for both groups.
3. With increased schooling, the Cuban women do not climb as rapidly as do the non-Spanish white women. The difference in SES scores between college graduates and high school dropouts is 25 points for the former and 33 points for the latter.
4. As among the men, at each schooling level the younger women have somewhat higher SES scores, probably reflecting a greater English-language facility.

The professional jobs held by Cuban-origin college women tend to be those commonly held by women. About 4 in 10 are teachers, mainly in elementary and secondary schools. Another 16% hold various positions in the field of health, and under 50% are found in the variety of other professional and technical jobs. This distribution approximately parallels that of all college women in the United States in professional occupations, of whom slightly under half are teachers and another quarter or so are working in the field of health.

THE SEVERAL CUBAN POPULATIONS

INTRODUCTION

We noted previously that close to one-half of the Cuban-descent population lived in Florida, almost all in the Miami metropolitan area, with a little over one-quarter in New York and New Jersey and the remainder of nearly one-quarter dispersed among the 47 other states. In this section we shall see that there are significant demographic and economic differences among these three populations. What they have in common is that they reported being of Cuban origin and were urban dwellers, metropolitan-area dwellers, in fact. In other respects, they often differ significantly.

In summary of the information to be presented following:

1. Selective migration of Cuban immigrants and their children—that is, selective with respect to the states in which they were residing in 1970—was one element in differentiating the geographic groups to be discussed.
2. Intrinsic differences among the various states in which they resided must have influenced the Cuban population; the Cubans who live in metropolitan New York and those in metropolitan Miami are subject to different local influences.
3. The smaller the concentration of Cubans in any one geographic area, the more likely they are to resemble demographically the non-Spanish population among whom they live.

These three factors are not completely independent of each other, of course. There must be strong interrelationships—joint influences—that, unfortunately, we cannot untangle. Only the end result of the influences of all the factors can be discerned. For example, the dispersed Cubans have more schooling than do those living in large Cuban concentrations; how much was due to the dispersal of the more schooled and how much to the school facilities in the areas of residence cannot be determined.

The geographic areas studied are, therefore, the Miami standard metropolitan statistical area, the New York–northern New Jersey standard metropolitan statistical area, and the rest of the country, which consists of many small concentrations, that is, small in comparison with these two metropolitan areas.

DEMOGRAPHIC CHARACTERISTICS

Nativity. The smallest proportion of native, or U.S.-born, Cubans is found in Florida and New Jersey, and the largest, in the "all other states" category and New York (Table 8.9). This pattern suggests either that there was selective migration of natives to New York and these other states or that there had been relatively large numbers of natives living in these places before 1970.

With respect to the possibility of selective migration, it is seen that

TABLE 8.9

Selected Demographic Characteristics of the Cuban-Origin Population by States of Residence: 1970

| Characteristics | U.S. | States of residence | | | | All other States |
| | | Florida | New Jersey & New York | | | |
			Total	N.J.	N.Y.	
Nativity						
% native	19	16	19	14	23	23
% natives born in different state	20	17	12	20	9	30
Age						
Median age, years	32	33	32	31	33	29
% total under age 15	27	25	28	30	26	30
% total 55 and over	15	18	13	11	17	12
% total 15 to 54	58	57	59	59	57	58
% all women aged 15 to 44	45	45	47	49	45	45
Sex						
Men as % of total	47	46	48	48	48	49
Men 15 and over as % of total 15 and over	46	44	47	47	47	48
Marriage & family						
% women 16+ married, spouse present	58	57	58	62	55	62
% women 20 to 44 married, spouse present	72	71	70	73	68	75
% women married, spouse present, husband non-Cuban	17	13	19	10	26	23
% families with female head	12	12	14	12	15	11
Fertility						
Children under 5 per 100 women aged 15 to 44	31	27	33	34	33	38
Schooling						
% population aged 3 to 34 attending school	50	52	45	46	44	54
Men aged 25 to 34						
% completed high school	58	54	57	52	60	64
% high school graduates entered college	58	53	54	48	58	68
% college graduates	14	9	14	11	17	20
Women aged 25 to 34						
% completed high school	52	52	46	42	50	58
% high school graduates who entered college	43	41	37	36	37	54
% college graduates	8	8	4	3	5	12
Males, age 16 to 21						
% high school dropouts	19	19	23	26	21	15

Source: 1970 U.S. Census, Persons of Spanish Origin, PC(2)1-C, various Tables.

some 30% of the native Cubans in the "all other states" had been born in states other than the ones in which they were living in 1970. This percentage is very close to that of the total non-Spanish native population of the United States. As for New York State, which has a high proportion of native Cubans, few of whom had been born in other states, we may infer that a substantial number of natives prior to 1970 had lived in New York and that many of the New York–born Cubans had moved elsewhere, either across the Hudson River to New Jersey or to California or other states around the country.[5]

In summary, if we assume that Florida was the home state for most of the Cuban-origin population, then substantial numbers of those born there dispersed around the country. Also, presumably most of those born in Cuba had entered the United States via Florida, and some subsequently migrated to other states.

Age. There is not much difference in median age among the several regional groups. The median age in "all other states" is about 29 years, or some 3 years below that of all Cubans in the United States. This probably reflects the migration of younger people, as well as the higher birth rate (to be discussed later in this chapter); the more young children there are, the lower the median age is. The median age in "all other states" is close to that of the total U.S. white population, about 28 years.

The older population, those aged 55 and over, constitute about 18% of those living in Florida, close to the proportion in the U.S. white population. New York State also has a relatively large proportion of older persons. In the remaining states, there are comparatively few older Cuban-origin persons.

Sex Composition. Florida has a significantly larger proportion of women, 54% female and 46% male. Elsewhere in the United States, the Cuban-origin populations have sex ratios close to those of the total white population of the United States, just over 50% female. Among the population aged 15 and over, the same pattern is found; in Florida 56% are women, as compared with 52% in "all other states."

Marriage and Family. New York State and the group of "all other states" are at opposite ends. New York State—the New York metropolitan area—has the smallest proportion of women who are married and living with their husbands, whereas the "all other" group has the

---

[5] No information is available that permits checking directly these several inferences.

largest proportion. This is true for all women aged 16 and over and for those in the childbearing years of 20–44. Florida is in between, and New Jersey tends to resemble the "all other" group.

There is no ready explanation of why New York is low in the proportion of women who are married and living with their husbands. As we saw, the proportions of men and women are very similar in New York as compared with the "all other" group. Indeed, Florida, which has a smaller proportion of Cuban men than has New York, had somewhat higher proportions of women who were married and living with their husbands.

New York also has the highest proportion of Cuban-origin women who were married to non-Cubans, 26%. In one respect this is surprising, since the large majority of the Cuban population was born in Cuba, and many arrived in the United States already married to Cubans. Outmarriage (as was discussed in Chapter 4) is most common among those born in the United States and among those foreign born who arrived in the United States as small children and grew up here. These latter two groups constitute only a small proportion of the total Cuban population. Hence, we infer that far more than 26% of the married native Cuban women living in New York are married to non-Cubans.

In the "all other" category, 23% of the women were married to non-Cubans. We infer that here also, as in New York, far more than one-quarter of the native women are married to non-Cubans. Unfortunately, we do not have direct information for these several states on the extent of outmarriage among U.S.-born Cuban women.

A small amount of outmarriage, 13%, is reported for Florida—the Miami metropolitan area. This is understandable in light of both the large proportion of Cuban born and the large Cuban population (which constitutes about one-fifth of the area's white population). Presumably, in a population of close to one-quarter million persons marriageable persons would have little difficulty in finding marriage partners of their own ethnicity, if they so desired.

In New Jersey, only 10% of the married women reportedly were married to non-Cubans. There is no ready explanation for this, especially in light of the large proportion of outmarriages in New York, just across the Hudson River.

We summarize by noting that outmarriage is most prevalent where there are relatively few of the ethnic group. Geographic dispersal is conducive to outmarriage.

As for families, 12% of all Cuban families in the United States are headed by women, a figure some 3% above that of the U.S. non-Spanish white population. New York State has the largest proportion,

15%, as would be expected from the previous observation that this state had the smallest proportion of women who were married and living with their husbands. "All other states" had the smallest proportion of Cuban families headed by women and, as we noted, the largest proportion of married, spouse present. Also, this group had a relatively small proportion of older persons, aged 55 and over, among whom women predominate and where we can expect to find more female heads.[6]

Fertility. The only available measure for the several geographic regions is the number of children under age 5 per 100 women aged 15–44. This ratio is 31 for the total Cuban population, 27 in Florida, and 38 in the "all other states." The last rate is close to that of the total U.S. non-Spanish white population. New York State is in between, with a rate of 33.

Possible explanations for the higher rate in the "all other" group lie in the larger proportion of women between the ages of 20 and 44 who are married and living with their husbands and the smaller proportion who are in the labor force (as we shall see). On the other hand, the women in this group of states have the most schooling.

Extent of Schooling. Just half of the Cuban-origin population in the United States between the ages of 3 and 34 were attending school in 1970. The lowest proportion, 44%, was observed in New York. The highest was found in the "all other" group, 54%, which is very close to that of the U.S. non-Spanish white population. In Florida, 52% were attending school. Why school attendance is so low in New York and New Jersey, we cannot say.

In the "all other" group of states, both men and women of Cuban origin between the ages of 25 and 34 have the highest rate of high school completion—64% of the men and 58% of the women. These are significantly below figures for the U.S. non-Spanish white population but are higher than those for Cubans living elsewhere. Conversely, the smallest proportion of high school dropouts was in "all other states." Among male youth aged 16–21, only 15% were dropouts, as compared with 19% in Florida and 21% in New York.

Of those who did complete high school, the largest proportions who entered college were also in the "all other states" category, for both men and women. Finally, we note that in age 25–34, 20% of the men and 12% of the Cuban women were college graduates, proportions very close to those of the total non-Spanish white population.

---

[6] In the total U.S. Cuban population aged 55 and over, close to 14% of the families are headed by women.

Summary. The Cuban-origin population residing in "all other states"—that is, those living in relatively small Cuban communities scattered over the entire country, more nearly resembles the U.S. non-Spanish white population. This group is characterized by more natives than are found among Cubans living in Florida, or in the New York–northern New Jersey metropolitan area, a somewhat younger population, a somewhat larger proportion of men, more women who are married and living with their husbands, more outmarriage with non-Cubans, a higher fertility rate, and more schooling.

We suspect that this combination of characteristics resulted from selective migration away from the main centers of Cuban population—probably the more schooled were more inclined to move—together with residing in a cultural milieu that is less Cuban and more American.

ECONOMIC CHARACTERISTICS

Labor force participation. Somewhat more of the Cuban men aged 20–64 living in Florida and in New York–northern New Jersey than of those living in "all other states" were in the labor force. Nevertheless, the latter group had about the same rate as that of all non-Spanish white men in this age group (Table 8.10).

Among women aged 20–44, the childbearing period, the smallest labor-force-participation rate was observed in New York, and the highest, in Florida. The "all other" group was in between. Nevertheless, significantly more women in the several regional Cuban groups than in the U.S. non-Spanish white population were in the labor force.

Family Income. Average (mean) family income in 1969 was highest in the group "all other"; these families averaged over $10,500, or close to $2000 more than did the Florida families (Table 8.10). Indeed, the $10,500 is just slightly short of the average for all non-Spanish white families. This higher income in "all other states" is explainable in large part in terms of the larger personal income of the individual family members (described in the following section), which in turn is attributable, in part at least, to their increased schooling. As well, somewhat more of these families are headed by men, in comparison with the Florida and New Jersey–New York Cuban families. On the other hand, more of the Florida families had two or more earners; this, in theory, could have resulted in a higher family income. Among the families in "all other states," 60% had two or more earners, the exact proportion for all Cuban families in the United States.

TABLE 8.10
Selected Economic Characteristics of the Cuban-Origin Population by States of Residence: 1970

Characteristics	U.S.	Florida	States of residence			All other States
			New Jersey & New York			
			Total	N.J.	N.Y.	
% in labor force						
Men, aged 20 to 64	92	92	94	95	92	89
Women, aged 20 to 44	61	64	59	69	51	58
Number earners in family						
Total	100%	100%	100%	100%	100%	100%
None	7	6	7	5	8	7
One	33	31	36	30	41	33
Two or more	60	63	57	65	51	60
Average (mean) family income, 1969	$9480	8800	9620	9450	9750	10,560
Average (mean) personal income population aged 16+ 1969						
Men	$6100	5420	6440	6160	6650	6970
Women	3050	2680	3360	3160	3490	3460

Personal Income. This was highest, for both men and women, in "all other states." Men averaged close to $7000, as compared with $5400 in Florida. Women averaged over $3400, as compared with under $2700 in Florida. Such higher individual incomes help to explain the higher family income in the "all other" group. This is easily seen by calculating what family income would be in hypothetical families in which both husband and wife received the average incomes for each sex, as follows:

Area	Income ($)
United States	9150
Florida	8100
New Jersey	9320
New York	10,140
New Jersey–New York	9800
All other states	10,430

These differences among the several states are not easily explainable. Some of the factors involved are (a) differences in occupational structure, as we shall see; (b) variations in regional wage and salary structures (e.g., average earnings of production workers in manufacturing in Florida [1969] were $2.89 per hour, whereas the average for the total U.S. population was $3.36); and (c) possible differences in pay for the same work to Cubans as compared with non-Cubans; (d) differences in the amount of time worked in 1969; and (e) differences in the amount of schooling, as was noted previously.

Occupations of Men. The occupational composition of those living in Florida is somewhat different from that of those residing in New Jersey and New York or elsewhere in the United States (Table 8.11). The former includes a few more craftsmen and laborers, somewhat fewer operatives, fewer professional workers, and whatever few Cuban farm workers there are. We may summarize the three areas by means of the SES scale and find that men in Florida and in New Jersey–New York have scores of 56, whereas men in "all other states" have a score of 60.[7] The area differences are clearly significant. Indeed, the men in the "all other" group have an SES score that is about the same, or slightly above that, of all U.S. non-Spanish white men, 60 as compared to 59 (see Appendix Table G–38).

These regional differences may reflect variations in the demand for types of labor in the several areas and, undoubtedly, some differences in the educational levels of Cuban-origin men who live in Florida as compared with New York and New Jersey and the combined group of "all other states." As we saw previously, those living outside of Florida, New Jersey, and New York have significantly more schooling, and more schooling is related to having better jobs.

Occupations of Women. Those residing outside of Florida, New Jersey, and New York have somewhat higher-level jobs but still below those of all women in the United States (Table 8.11). The respective SES scores are Florida, 55; New York–New Jersey, 56; "all other states," 59; and all non-Spanish white women in the United States, 63.

One possible explanation for the lower proportion of white-collar workers may be English-language problems. Most of the Cuban women were born in Cuba and despite their having more schooling, many may not have sufficient command of the English language to hold white-collar jobs. Yet, white-collar jobs are the mainstay of the female labor

---

[7] Census Bureau, "Methodology and Scores of Socioeconomic Status," p. 13.

TABLE 8.11

Occupational Distribution of Employed Cuban-Origin Persons by Sex and Area of Residence: U.S. 1970 (population aged 16 years and over)

	MEN				WOMEN			
	Total	Florida	New York & New Jersey	All other States	Total	Florida	New York & New Jersey	All other States
Total	100.0	100.0	100.0	100.0	100.0	100.0	100.0	100.0
Professional, technical & kindred workers	12.9	10.0	11.5	20.2	8.5	5.9	8.8	13.9
Managers & administrators exc. farm	7.4	8.2	7.3	6.2	1.3	1.5	1.1	1.2
Sales workers	5.5	7.1	4.4	4.1	5.0	6.4	3.7	3.8
Clerical & kindred workers	10.7	10.3	11.5	10.5	26.2	25.0	26.5	28.2
Craftsmen, foremen, & kindred workers	18.1	20.8	15.1	16.5	2.6	2.4	2.8	2.8
Operatives incl. transport workers	24.2	21.4	27.9	24.9	42.8	43.7	45.8	37.0
Laborers exc. farm	6.1	7.7	5.3	4.3	0.9	0.9	0.6	1.2
All service workers	14.4	13.7	16.9	12.8	12.4	13.8	10.6	11.8
Farmers & farm managers	0.2	0.3	0.0	0.2	0.0	0.0	0.0	0.0
Farm laborers	0.4	0.6	0.1	0.3	0.3	0.5	0.1	0.2

Source: 1970 U.S. Census, Persons of Spanish Origin, PC(2)-1C.

force; of jobs held by all U.S. women, 6 in 10 are in this category. If this explanation is correct, then it may help to explain the higher SES score in the "all other" category. Not only does the population have more years of schooling but also more were born in the United States and hence can be assumed to have an adequate command of the English language.

SUMMARY

Most of the Cuban-origin population living in the United States in 1970 had been here no longer than one decade; hence most of the 1970 U.S. resident population had been born in Cuba. And they must have brought with them their Cuban heritage. Apparently, also, the immigrants were a selective segment of the total population living in Cuba, so that those who are living in the United States in the 1970s are not necessarily representative of the general population living on the island of Cuba.

Demographically, we can characterize the U.S. resident Cuban-origin population as reasonably similar to that of the non-Spanish white population of the country. As of 1970, they are more similar to the non-Spanish whites than are the Mexican-American or Hispano populations and are at least as similar, demographically, as are those of Puerto Rican origin. The Cuban-origin population that resides outside of the Miami and the New York–northern New Jersey metropolitan areas are even more nearly similar demographically to the non-Spanish White population. Dispersion facilitates convergence.

Furthermore, the rate of outmarriage among those born in the United States is very high (Chapter 4). Accordingly, in the future as increasingly larger proportions of the Cuban-origin population are U.S.-born, and as there are so many outmarriages and, as a consequence, children who are only part Cuban, the Cubans will be indistinguishable demographically from the general non-Spanish white population of the United States. To what extent persons will retain their Cuban self-identity is another matter, about which we have no information. Amaro and Portes[8] are of the opinion that: "As time passes the Cuban immigrants will become assimilated into the North American culture and society. . . ." They add that the large Cuban population in Miami acts to slow down the "process of assimilation" but not to stop it.

---

[8] Nelson Amaro and Alejandro Portes, "Una sociologia del exilio; Situacion de los grupos Cubanos en Estados Unidos," *Aportes*, no. 23 (January 1972), p. 23–24.

Finally, we should note that the Cuban-origin population is no different from the Hispano- or Puerto Rican–origin populations living in the United States as far as trends in demographic characteristics are concerned. Both of the latter groups are also becoming similar demographically to the non-Spanish white population; in another generation or two they also will be indistinguishable demographically. Both will have high rates of outmarriage as well, so that their original cultures are becoming "diluted."

In general, these Spanish-American groups are recapitulating the history of earlier immigrants to the United States, especially those from Europe. Each group has its own timetable for becoming similar demographically to the general U.S. population, but sooner or later they do merge. The Cuban-origin population simply appears to be speeding along to demographic similarity.

9

The Central and South American–Origin Population

INTRODUCTION

In recent years substantial numbers of immigrants from Central and South America have come to the United States.[1] These persons are from such diverse Latin American countries as Guatemala on the north and Chile and Argentina on the south, excluding Portuguese Brazil (Table 9.1). Their cultural heritages are as diverse as are the countries from which they come. Guatemalans, for example, tend to resemble Mexicans in their demographic characteristics, whereas many of the migrants from such South American countries as Chile are descended from non-Spanish European stock. They are treated here as a single population, since the Census Bureau publishes few separate statistics for each country.[2] Thus, while we confine ourselves to analysis of Central and South Americans from Spanish-speaking nations, it is well to keep in mind that this is far from a homogeneous population, culturally or demographically.

---

[1] During the 1960s a sizable number of these persons were Cubans, who are described separately in Chapter 8. However, since the mid-1960s, there has been a substantial increase in immigration from other Caribbean nations as well. See Charles B. Keely, "Effects of the Immigration Act of 1965 on Selected Population Characteristics of Immigrants to the United States," *Demography*, 8 (May 1971), p. 157–169.

[2] Little other than totals by country of origin is available. There are too few cases for analysis by country of origin in the Public Use Sample (PUS) files to permit separate analysis.

TABLE 9.1

Country of Origin of the Central and South American Stock, by Nativity: U.S. 1970 (numbers in thousands)

	Total foreign stock	Foreign born	Native of foreign or mixed parentage
Total	527	342	185
Central America	187	114	73
Guatemala	27	17	10
British Honduras	14	9	5
Honduras	31	19	12
Nicaragua	28	16	12
El Salvador	23	16	7
Costa Rica	26	17	9
Panama	38	20	18
South America	340	228	112
Colombia	84	63	21
Venezuela	17	11	6
Ecuador	49	37	12
Peru	35	22	13
Bolivia	10	7	3
Uruguay	7	5	2
Chile	25	15	10
Argentina	67	45	22
Other South America	46	23	23

SOME DEMOGRAPHIC CHARACTERISTICS

TOTAL POPULATION

In 1950 the Census Bureau reported some 57,000 foreign-born white persons from Spanish-speaking nations in Central and South America living in the United States.[3] This number excludes persons from Cuba, Mexico, the Dominican Republic, and Portuguese Brazil, as well as the English-speaking Caribbean islands. The Central American countries of Nicaragua, Panama and El Salvador and the South American countries of Colombia, Venezuela, Chile, and Argentina accounted for more than half of these persons.

By 1970 this figure had increased to slightly more than a half million persons of Central and South American stock (foreign born and natives

---

[3] U.S., Bureau of the Census, Census of Population: 1950. *Special Reports.* P–E no. 31, *Nativity and Parentage* (Washington, D.C.: Government Printing Office, 1952), Table 12. Note that these figures are only for foreign-born whites. We have no information on the number of Spanish-speaking nonwhites from these countries.

of foreign or mixed parentage) living in the United States.[4] Of these, almost two out of three were foreign born. As an indication of the recency of this migration, 44% of the foreign born immigrated between 1965 and 1970, and an additional 25%, between 1960 and 1964. In 1970 persons from Panama and Honduras constituted the largest groups from the Caribbean and Central America, whereas Colombians and Argentinians contributed the greatest numbers from South America. In the late 1970s there were an estimated 800,000 (see Chapter 10).

GEOGRAPHIC DISTRIBUTION IN 1970

More than two-thirds of the Central and South Americans live in large urban areas. The New York Standard Metropolitan Statistical Area (SMSA) had the greatest concentration, some 150,000 persons. An additional 30,000 were living in New Jersey SMSAs within commuting distance to New York City—approximately a third of the total population of Central and South Americans in the United States. Further south along the East Coast, Washington, D.C., had 23,000, followed by Miami with 19,000. Smaller concentrations lived in Philadelphia, Boston, and Providence. Thus, two out of every five persons of Central and South American stock were located in the large urban areas along the East Coast.

On the West Coast, some 86,000 Central and South Americans lived in the Los Angeles–Long Beach SMSA, 42,000 in San Francisco–Oakland, with some 10,000 in San Diego and San Jose, roughly one-fourth of the total population.

The remaining 200,000 were scattered throughout the United States, with Chicago having the largest number, some 22,000. Small numbers were living in Cleveland, Detroit, and Milwaukee. Thus, only about one in every four Central and South Americans was living outside the nation's largest metropolitan areas in 1970.

NATIVITY COMPOSITION

In 1970 almost two out of three persons of Central and South American stock were foreign born.[5] The remaining one-third were the

---

[4] Census Bureau, PC(2)–1A, *National Origin and Language,* Table 10, and U.S. Summary, Table 192.

[5] Discussion of the characteristics of Central and South Americans is limited to foreign stock. Apparent misinterpretation by respondents in central and southern United States of the category "Central and South American" in the 1970 Census led to a substan-

children of these parents. Given the recency of the migrants, it is not surprising that the foreign born should outnumber their children. However, if immigration continues even at current levels,[6] the next generation should see natives outnumbering the foreign born.

AGE AND SEX COMPOSITION

The median age of persons of Central and South American stock in 1970 was 24.9, somewhat younger than the non-Spanish white population, which had a median age of 28 years (Table 9.2). Those born in Central and South America, however, had a median age of close to 31 years, compared with only about 11 years among those born in the United States. Compared with other Spanish-origin groups, foreign-born Central and South Americans are considerably younger than Cubans (36 years) and Mexicans (38 years) and are about the same as persons of Puerto Rican birth (30 years). Again, this is indicative of the recency of these migrations. Since more than two-thirds of Central and South Americans came to the United States only during the decade preceding the 1970 Census, and most of these were young people in the prime working ages, their U.S.-born children would be concentrated in the youngest age groups; indeed, their median age is only slightly above that of the U.S.-born Cuban-origin persons.

As is true of the non-Spanish white population, Central and South American women outnumber men. Of every 100 persons of all ages of Central and South American origin, there were 53 women and 47 men, due to the preponderance of females among the foreign born. Among the U.S. born, however, males outnumber females slightly. Among persons aged 15 and over, there was somewhat greater preponderance of women; of every 100, 54 were women and 46 men.

EDUCATION

YEARS OF SCHOOLING COMPLETED

Educational attainment is of major importance in understanding the socioeconomic status of a people. It is perhaps of even greater impor-

---

tial overstatement of natives of native parentage. See U.S., Bureau of the Census, Census of Population: 1970, *Subject Reports,* Final Report PC(2)–1C, *Persons of Spanish Origin* (Washington, D.C.: Government Printing Office, 1973), p. ix.

[6] See Keely, "Effects of the Immigration Act of 1965." Cf., also, Charles B. Keely, "Effects of U.S. Immigration Law on Manpower Characteristics of Immigrants," *Demography,* 12 (May 1975), p. 179–191.

TABLE 9.2

Persons of Central and South American Origin, by Age, Sex, and Nativity: U.S. 1970 (numbers in thousands)

	Total				Foreign born			U. S. born		
	Total	Percent	Men	Women	Total	Men	Women	Total	Men	Women
Total	577.9	100.0	274.3	303.6	369.2	169.0	200.2	208.7	105.3	103.4
Under 5 years	69.0	11.9	35.5	33.5	9.3	4.7	4.7	59.6	30.8	28.8
5 to 9 years	63.3	11.0	32.4	30.9	22.1	11.3	10.8	41.2	21.1	20.1
10 to 14 years	54.2	9.4	27.7	26.4	27.3	13.7	13.5	26.9	14.0	12.9
15 to 19 years	50.7	8.8	25.3	25.4	31.1	15.3	15.8	19.6	10.0	9.6
20 to 24 years	52.4	9.1	23.6	28.7	38.8	17.0	21.7	13.6	6.6	7.0
25 to 29 years	58.1	10.0	27.1	31.0	49.3	22.7	26.6	8.8	4.4	4.4
30 to 34 years	53.7	9.3	25.0	28.7	46.4	21.5	24.9	7.3	3.5	3.8
35 to 44 years	83.6	14.5	38.6	45.0	67.6	30.8	36.8	16.0	7.8	8.2
45 to 54 years	45.4	7.8	19.2	26.2	36.2	15.0	21.2	9.2	4.2	5.0
55 to 64 years	25.2	4.3	10.3	14.9	21.5	8.5	13.0	3.7	1.8	1.9
65 and over	22.4	3.9	9.5	12.9	19.6	8.4	11.2	2.8	1.1	1.7
Median	24.9	–	23.4	25.6	30.7	29.9	31.4	10.7	10.3	11.1

Source: 1970 Population Census, Persons of Spanish Origin, PC(2)-1C, Table 5.

tance in facilitating the adjustment of recent migrants to the social, cultural, and economic milieu of the host country.

Levels of schooling achieved by Central and South Americans compare favorably with those of all U.S. non-Spanish whites (Table 9.3). In general, younger persons have completed more years of school than have older ones. Among men aged 55 years and over, almost 6 out of 10 U.S.-born Central and South Americans completed high school, more than the 4 in 10 among foreign-born men. By comparison, only 1 out of every 3 Anglo men 55 years and over had completed high school.

Of the high-school-completion-age group just prior to World War II, 2 out of 3 U.S. born were high school graduates, compares with somewhat over half of the foreign born and U.S. non-Spanish whites. The same pattern holds for those completing high school in the late 1940s and 1950s. By 1970 among both U.S.-born and non-Spanish white men aged 20–24, more than 8 in 10 had graduated from high school, compared with just under 7 in 10 of the foreign born.[7]

The proportion of U.S.-born Central and South American women who graduated from high school is roughly the same as that of non-Spanish white women at all ages except those 55 years and older. Among the younger women, approximately the same proportions completed high school as did men. Foreign-born women, on the other hand, had significantly lower proportions of high school graduates than did either the U.S.-born Cuban women or non-Spanish white women, particularly among the 20–24-year-olds. Again, this may reflect a larger proportion of lesser-schooled women among more recent migrants,[8] many of whom are attracted to the United States by the labor market for domestic servants.

Among those who completed high school during the 1960s, more

---

[7] This fairly low proportion of high school graduates among the foreign born may be indicative of a more diverse migrant stream since 1960. Recent Immigration and Naturalization Service statistics indicate a shift in the numbers of immigrants toward the Caribbean area countries where levels of schooling among migrants are lower than those for migrants from Latin American countries such as Argentina and Chile. See Keely, "Effects of the Immigration Act of 1965"; Keely notes a proportionate decline in professional occupations and an increase in blue-collar-level workers from nations in the Western Hemisphere, particularly since the mid-1960s. This provides indirect support for belief in a decline in overall levels of schooling.

[8] A recent analysis of the Colombian population in New York City, for example, indicated that whereas the median number of years of schooling of Colombian women was fairly close to that for the city as a whole, some 22% of these women, particularly those in the younger age groups, had less than an elementary school level of education. See Mary G. Powers and John J. Macisco, Jr., "Colombians in New York: 1970" (MS, Fordham University: 1976).

TABLE 9.3
Years of Schooling Completed by the Central and South American–Origin Population, by Age, Sex and Nativity: U.S. 1970

	Approx. period high school completion	% completed high school		% high school graduates entered college		% college entrants completed college	
		U.S. born	Foreign born	U.S. born	Foreign born	U.S. born	Foreign born
MEN							
20 to 24 years	1965	83.1	65.7	54.4	56.0	32.6	20.7
25 to 34 years	1957	76.3	69.5	58.5	60.2	61.6	47.5
35 to 44 years	1947	72.0	64.1	61.2	59.6	49.0	59.6
45 to 54 years	1937	65.6	56.9	45.0	54.7	61.1	61.2
55 and over	WWI	57.8	42.5	56.7	56.9	49.1	57.5
WOMEN							
20 to 24 years	1965	83.9	40.9	57.7	39.0	17.9	20.5
25 to 34 years	1957	77.4	60.5	48.6	42.2	50.3	38.1
35 to 44 years	1947	76.0	55.0	37.0	39.1	39.9	43.3
45 to 54 years	1937	53.4	49.3	40.4	38.3	29.0	42.3
55 and over	WWI	51.2	36.3	35.0	27.0	29.0	45.7

Source: Public Use Sample.

than half the men (both U.S. born and foreign born) and U.S.-born women entered college. Among persons aged 25–34 in 1970 who entered college, between 40% and 50% completed at least 4 years. These proportions are about the same as those for non-Spanish whites.

With the exception of foreign-born women, the Central and South American population has had more schooling than has the Mexican, Puerto Rican, and Hispano populations and about the same amount of schooling as has the Cuban and U.S. non-Spanish white populations.

SCHOOL ATTENDANCE, 1970

Rates of school attendance for Central and South Americans are slightly below those for non-Spanish whites. Through the elementary and high school ages (7–17 years), the proportions of Central and South Americans attending school are slightly lower than those of non-Spanish whites, particularly for those 12 years of age (roughly seventh grade). For both groups, the proportions enrolled in high school decline at each grade level, dropping sharply between ages 17 and 18, presumably reflecting high school graduation (see Appendix Table G–7). The overall (standardized) attendance rate for ages 7–19 inclusive is 87%, as compared with 90.5% for the non-Spanish whites. Furthermore, more of the Central and South American youngsters are below the modal grade for their age, 13.1% versus 6.8% for the non-Spanish whites. On the other hand, perhaps slightly more Central and South Americans are above the mode, 4.9% versus 2.2%. In general, these Central and South American youngsters resemble the Cuban youngsters.

Among the college aged, the proportions enrolled in school are slightly higher for the Latin Americans. Whatever may be the reason for lower enrollment rates among Central and South Americans of elementary and high school age, they do not affect the proportions going to college. It may be, as we suggested previously, that the lower proportions attending high school reflect a dropout rate higher than that for the non-Spanish whites, whereas those who do remain in school are the more successful students who continue on through college.

FERTILITY

CHILDREN EVER BORN ALIVE

Central and South American women, whether U.S. or foreign born, have low fertility. The average number of children ever born alive to women of Central and South American stock aged 15–44 years is 1.4.

This is about 15% fewer children than are born to non-Spanish white women, who averaged about 1.6 children. Among other Spanish groups, only Cuban women had lower fertility, about 1.3 children per woman. Puerto Rican–origin women averaged 2.1, and Mexican-origin women, 2.2 children.[9]

Standardization of these rates by age, years of schooling, marital status, and employment reduced the average number of children ever born to Central and South American women to 1.3, to Cuban women to 1.2, to Puerto Rican women to 1.7, and to Mexican-origin women to 2.0 children. The average for non-Spanish white women remains unchanged—1.6.[10]

The influence of schooling on fertility behavior is slight, holding other factors constant. Central and South American women (aged 15–44) who had completed high school averaged slightly more than 1.25 children, whereas those with less than a high school education averaged 1.5 children (holding marital status and employment constant).

Another important influence on fertility is marital status. All other things being equal, it is expected that married women living with their husbands would be more likely to have higher fertility compared with other women (widowed, divorced, separated, and never married). Among Central and South American women, the influence of marital status on fertility is considerable. The average number of children ever born to married women with spouses present is 2 births, compared to slightly more than .66 child among other women (holding schooling and employment constant). Employed women had, on the average, 20% fewer children than did women who were not employed. The average number of children ever born to employed women aged 15–44 years was 1.2, compared with 1.5 among the latter.

It is clear that in 1970 the fertility of Central and South American women was fairly close to replacement level. If we compare women aged 35–44 in 1970 to non-Spanish white women, the average number of children ever born to Central and South American women is between 15% and 20% less than that of non-Spanish white women. The fertility of these women is virtually complete; it is unlikely that many of these women will have more children. The average number of children ever born alive per woman for Central and South American and non-Spanish white women aged 35–44 years is as shown on the following page.

---

[9] See Appendix Table G–15.
[10] See Table 3.6.

Years of schooling	Central and South American	Non-Spanish white
Total population	2.4	2.9
Under 12	2.5	3.1
12 or more	2.2	2.7

Central and South American women have, on the average, one-half child less than do non-Spanish white women, even when controlling for schooling. We may apportion the influence of the three factors in reducing fertility as follows:

Factor	Influence (%)
Increased schooling	19
Employment	17
Married and living with spouse	38
Joint influences	26

CHARACTERISTICS OF WOMEN IN THE REPRODUCTIVE AGES, 1970

With the exception of the youngest women, Central and South American women among both the lesser and more schooled have significantly lower proportions married and living with their husbands and significantly higher proportions of employed than do non-Spanish white women. The differences are greatest among the lesser schooled, which may help to explain their lower total fertility relative to non-Spanish white women. As is noted in the following discussion, the migrant status of these women may also be a factor in explaining their lower fertility, offsetting the effect of less schooling. (Table 9.4 presents characteristics of Central and South American and U.S. non-Spanish white women in the reproductive ages, by age and years of schooling.)

THE FUTURE

Whether Central and South American women will continue to have fewer children in the future cannot be predicted with any certainty. Sizable numbers of these women are recent migrants, and their lower fertility may well be influenced by their migrant status. We do not know to what extent future migration from Central and South America will continue to have an influence on the fertility of these women. Continued migration of fairly large numbers of women in their childbear-

TABLE 9.4

Selected Characteristics for Women of Central and South American–Origin in the Reproductive Years: U.S. 1970

Age and characteristics	Central & South American origin[a]		Non-Spanish white Total U.S.	
	Years of schooling		Years of schooling	
	Under 12	12 & over	Under 12	12 & over
15 to 19 years				
% married, spouse present	6.6	13.8	6.9	16.0
% employed	18.2	43.9	19.3	49.1
Av. no. children ever born per woman	.08	.11	.08	.10
20 to 24 years				
% married, spouse present	54.4	45.1	68.0	53.9
% employed	48.0	54.6	33.6	57.6
Av. no. children ever born per woman	.83	.46	1.38	.50
25 to 29 years				
% married, spouse present	65.3	70.1	79.2	80.7
% employed	44.4	50.4	32.3	44.8
Av. no.children ever born per woman	1.43	1.15	2.39	1.51
30 to 34 years				
% married,spouse present	63.1	75.1	81.2	84.6
% employed	52.7	51.7	37.3	41.9
Av. no. children ever born per woman	1.99	1.81	3.01	2.36
35 to 44 years				
% married, spouse present	60.9	71.0	81.7	84.8
% employed	54.8	57.1	44.0	49.1
Av. no. children ever born per woman	2.48	2.24	3.09	2.73

[a]Foreign born plus native of foreign parentage.

Source: Public Use Sample.

ing years could contribute to maintaining lower fertility, assuming the characteristics of these migrants were similar to those of earlier ones. However, if there should be a large increase in the numbers of little-schooled migrants, fertility could increase. As of the early 1970s, the characteristics of migrants favor lower fertility.

Central and South American–origin women who were residing in the United States in 1970 have fairly high levels of schooling. As well, they are more likely to be employed and have lower proportions married and living with their husbands in comparison with non-Spanish white women (Table 9.4). If in the future the characteristics of these women become more similar to those of the general population, we can expect their fertility to approach that of non-Spanish white women. Whatever the case, this would mean (at least in the next generation) only slightly higher levels of fertility than at present.

THE ECONOMIC PICTURE

LABOR FORCE AND EMPLOYMENT

Men. Central and South American men at all age levels were in the labor force in 1970 in about the same proportions as were U.S. non-Spanish white men (Table 9.5). The only exception was the larger proportions of older Central and South American men (55 years and older). Of the total population aged 16 years and over, about 82% of Central and South American men were in the labor force, compared with 77% of the general population.

For these men, the extent of schooling bears little relationship to labor force behavior. About the same proportions were in the labor force at all school-completion levels, and about the same proportions had worked full time during the census week.

Among men in the prime working ages of 20–64, 9 in 10 were in the labor force, a proportion that corresponds precisely to that of non-Spanish white men. This age group also shows little variation by years of schooling. Most of the Central and South American–origin men had also worked full time—slightly under 9 in 10. This extent of full-time work also corresponds closely to that of the non-Spanish whites.

Unemployment, however, decreases with increased schooling. Almost 1 in 20 of the men aged 20–64 who had not completed high school was unemployed; this compares with about 1 in 50 of the college graduates. In comparison with the non-Spanish white men, the Latin Americans had higher unemployment rates at all levels of education. The rates are as follows:

Years of schooling	Central and South American origin (%)	Non-Spanish white (%)
Under 12	4.7	4.1
12	3.8	2.7
13–15 years	3.7	2.8
16 and over	2.2	1.4
Total population	4.2	3.0

TABLE 9.5
Labor-Force-Participation and Employment Rates, Central and South American-Origin Population, by Sex, Age, and Years of Schooling: 1970

Age	Total			Under 12 years			12 years			13 to 15 years			16+ years		
	% in labor force	a/	b/	% in labor force	a/	b/	% in labor force	a/	b/	% in labor force	a/	b/	% in labor force	a/	b/
MEN															
Total	82.1	83.7	4.8	76.3	82.3	5.8	86.4	86.4	5.3	82.5	79.0	4.1	90.7	87.9	2.2
16 to 19 years	41.4	37.7	14.5	36.8	35.8	15.4	53.5	53.2	9.7	58.7	15.4	19.2	-	-	-
20 to 24 years	74.7	73.5	6.4	84.5	84.6	5.7	76.5	76.0	9.0	63.0	55.2	3.1	72.9	68.4	10.5
25 to 34 years	91.5	88.9	3.1	93.5	89.6	3.6	92.4	91.2	3.4	89.8	84.0	3.9	88.3	89.3	0.9
35 to 44 years	95.0	89.6	3.7	92.3	87.4	4.8	97.6	92.8	4.3	95.3	91.0	3.2	96.6	89.0	1.6
45 to 54 years	94.4	88.7	4.9	93.7	87.7	5.2	93.4	85.9	6.0	94.4	89.3	4.8	97.8	94.7	3.0
55 years and over	63.6	79.9	6.4	51.7	78.3	8.2	75.6	81.7	6.5	76.9	82.5	4.8	84.8	79.1	3.0
20 to 64 years	89.6	86.8	4.2	90.5	87.7	4.7	90.8	88.1	3.8	84.3	81.2	3.7	91.2	88.1	2.2
WOMEN															
Total	51.0	75.1	5.7	46.8	75.7	6.9	54.2	77.7	5.2	55.3	71.7	4.2	58.1	67.8	4.2
16 to 19 years	32.0	43.2	10.0	24.7	39.7	10.6	53.4	50.0	11.7	38.3	39.1	*	-	-	-
20 to 24 years	55.2	75.1	4.7	51.4	82.4	6.2	60.3	79.4	4.3	52.6	60.7	2.9	57.6	57.9	5.2
25 to 34 years	52.8	80.3	5.4	51.0	80.9	5.2	49.9	82.5	4.6	61.6	82.1	6.6	56.6	68.4	6.0
35 to 44 years	59.4	75.8	6.1	59.5	77.9	8.2	59.8	76.9	4.7	55.3	69.7	5.0	63.8	68.0	2.1
45 to 54 years	61.4	76.9	5.3	61.6	77.5	6.7	61.3	80.5	5.4	58.5	72.5	0.0	64.9	70.8	4.2
55 years and over	30.5	73.3	5.2	26.9	70.2	6.8	36.1	78.2	4.6	38.2	*	*	38.0	*	*
20 to 44 years	55.5	77.6	5.5	54.1	80.0	6.6	55.6	79.8	4.6	57.1	73.0	5.1	59.2	66.8	4.5

a/ Percentage of civilian labor force employed full time.

b/ Percentage of civilian labor force unemployed.

*Under 25 cases in sample.

In summary, except for slightly higher unemployment rates, there was little difference in the labor force picture between the Central and South American men and the non-Spanish white men in the United States.

Women. Half of the women of Central and South American origin aged 16 and over were in the labor force, a rate substantially above that of two in five for total U.S. non-Spanish white women. The participation rate increases somewhat with increased schooling, from 47% of those who had not completed high school to 58% of the college graduates. At each age group there is also a moderate increase from the least-schooled to the most-schooled groups.

Among women in the childbearing ages of 20–44, about 55% were in the labor force in 1970, as compared with close to 50% of the non-Spanish white women. With increased years of schooling for this age group, there is but a slight increase in labor force participation, from 54% of the high school dropouts to 59% of the college graduates (Table 9.5). On the other hand, the proportion who had worked full time during the census week—approximately three in four—decreased somewhat with increased schooling.

CLASS OF WORKER

Most employed persons worked for private concerns. Less than 1 in 10 of the men of Central and South American origin was self-employed, and 1 in 10 worked for a government agency. Among the women, 3% were self-employed, and 1 in 10 was a government worker. In comparison with the non-Spanish white population, significantly fewer of the Latin-origin workers were self-employed or government employees.[11]

The small proportion of government workers probably reflects the fact that many are not citizens of the United States. Another factor may be the nature of the job markets in which these people live. As we saw, the Latin Americans are not randomly distributed over the total United States, and it is possible that there are fewer government jobs in the areas where most of the Central and South Americans live. This question is outside the scope of our study, however, and we shall pursue it no further.

---

[11] See Appendix Table G–30.

FAMILY INCOME

Average (median) income in 1969 of families in which the head was of Central or South American origin was $8920, or a little less than $1200 below that of the non-Spanish white families (Appendix Table G–36). Income varied considerably in accordance with the number of earners in the family and the sex of the head. The more earners, the higher the average income was, and families headed by men had higher incomes than did those headed by women, as follows:

Number of earners	Head	
	Men ($)	Women ($)
Total population	9480	5110
None	1720	2000
1	8000	4620
2 or more	11,180	9150

The Central and South American families had about the same distribution of numbers of earners as did the non-Spanish white families, as follows:

Number of earners	Central and South American origin (%)	Non-Spanish white (%)
None	6	9
1	40	40
2 or more	54	51

On the other hand there were more women heads among the Latins, 17%, versus 9% among the non-Spanish whites. All in all, though, median family income of the Central and South Americans is not unduly influenced by the greater prevalence of women heads. If these families had the same distribution by number of earners and sex of head as did the non-Spanish white, their family income would have been close to that initially observed, about $8900.

That more of these Latin-origin families are headed by women than are non-Spanish white families is, in part at least, attributable to the larger proportion of women among the former. Among all Central and South American–origin persons aged 20 and over, 55% were women, as compared with 52% of the latter. In this respect, the Central and South Americans resemble those of Cuban origin.

INDIVIDUAL EARNINGS

Men. Those of Central and South American origin averaged about $6100 in 1969 (Table 9.6); this is the median amount received from wages, salaries, and self-employment income. This amount is $300–400 more than that earned by Cuban or Hispano men but is significantly less than that earned by non-Spanish white men, which amounted to $7290 (Appendix Table G–35). Many factors account for this difference, as reviewed in Chapter 3.

Earnings increase with increased schooling. For example, consider ages 35–44 and 45–64, as follows:

Years of schooling	35–44 ($)	45–64 ($)
Under 12	6000	6050
12	7600	7610
13–15 years	9190	7820
16 and over	13,100	13,540

Men who had completed college earned more than double that earned by those who had not completed high school.

Youth averaged considerably less than did older men, as a result, in large part, of working less during 1969 and, in smaller part, of their lower occupational status. With respect to weeks worked in 1969, only 4 in 10 of those under age 25 had worked a full year (48 weeks or more), whereas among the older men (excluding those aged 65 and over) close to 8 in 10 had worked a full year.

Within each age and educational group, there was considerable variation in earnings; some high school dropouts earned more than did some college graduates. This is indicated in the line marked "variation" in Table 9.6. Between the ages of 25 and 64, the variation index is smallest, indicating that most men tend to earn around average amounts. At the younger and older ages, however, the variation is considerably greater; this probably results from the greater prevalence of part-time work during 1969, as we discussed earlier, so that the median earnings for the age group do not indicate fairly the general level of earnings of all members.

TABLE 9.6
Earnings in 1969, Central and South American Descent by Sex, Age, and Years of Schooling

Years of schooling	MEN						WOMEN					
	14 & over	14-24 years	25-34 years	35-44 years	45-64 years	65+ years	14 & over	14-24 years	25-34 years	35-44 years	45-64 years	65+ years
Total U.S.												
1st quartile	$3,780	870	4,340	5,310	5,110	2,110	1,630	790	2,000	2,250	2,280	1,000
Median	6,140	2,470	6,480	7,810	7,490	5,060	3,470	2,180	3,720	3,920	3,740	2,130
3rd quartile	9,240	4,680	9,080	11,400	10,710	8,170	5,180	4,190	5,440	5,620	5,440	3,900
Variation*	.89	1.54	.73	.78	.75	1.20	1.02	1.56	.92	.86	.84	1.36
Under 12 years												
1st quartile	2,910	670	3,890	4,350	4,380	1,610	1,440	650	1,770	1,940	2,120	910
Median	5,050	1,940	5,500	6,000	6,050	3,250	3,090	1,750	3,250	3,440	3,380	1,930
3rd quartile	7,290	4,160	7,430	8,270	8,570	6,040	4,360	3,480	4,500	4,590	4,540	3,300
Variation	.87	1.80	.64	.65	.69	1.36	.94	1.62	.84	.77	.72	1.24
12 years												
1st quartile	4,070	1,540	4,630	5,640	5,620	2,670	2,020	1,170	2,150	2,920	2,790	1,310
Median	6,530	3,400	6,610	7,600	7,610	7,000	3,960	3,090	4,100	4,500	4,140	2,830
3rd quartile	9,050	5,820	8,890	10,130	10,200	10,000	5,530	4,780	5,570	6,180	5,800	4,440
Variation	.76	1.26	.64	.59	.60	1.05	.89	1.17	.83	.72	.73	1.10
13 to 15 years												
1st quartile	3,160	1,040	5,020	6,630	4,830	†	1,290	750	1,930	2,080	2,110	†
Median	6,630	2,340	7,320	9,190	7,820		3,600	1,820	4,500	4,860	4,650	
3rd quartile	9,520	4,520	9,480	12,230	10,890		5,880	4,110	6,450	6,340	6,870	
Variation	.96	1.49	.61	.61	.77		1.28	1.85	1.00	.88	1.02	
16+ years												
1st quartile	6,100	990	4,940	8,710	8,340	†	2,170	850	2,390	2,590	2,390	†
Median	10,360	3,060	8,360	13,100	13,540		4,660	2,500	4,200	5,950	6,440	
3rd quartile	15,930	6,210	12,500	19,760	20,680		7,830	5,210	7,570	8,430	8,950	
Variation	.95	1.71	.90	.84	.91		1.21	1.74	1.23	.98	1.02	

*Interquartile range divided by median.
†Too few cases in sample, under 500 inflated population.

Source: Special Census tabulation.

Women. The income of women averaged slightly over half of that of men, $3470 compared with $6140. However, direct comparisons are not possible, since many more women worked part-time during the year, and women are more likely to be in occupations and industries different from those of men. The median earnings of women as a percentage of that of men are as follows:

Years of schooling	Age		
	25–34 (%)	35–44 (%)	45–64 (%)
Under 12	59	57	56
12	62	59	54
13–15	61	53	59
16 and over	50	45	48

In general, women average between 50% and 60% of men's earnings. Neither age nor years of schooling appear to be major factors in differentiating the earnings of men and women.

In all groups between the ages of 25 and 64, the index of variation for women is greater than that for men. This reflects the greater prevalence of part-time work for women, as shown in the following proportions among all those who had worked in 1969 of those who had worked 48 weeks or more:

Age	Women (%)	Men (%)
25–34	51	75
35–44	59	81
45–64	65	78

OCCUPATIONS

Men. The occupational distribution of Central and South American men in 1970 was similar to that for all U.S. non-Spanish white men. Among upper-white-collar workers (professional, technical and kindred workers, and managers and administrators), proportionately more Central and South American men were classified in professional and technical occupations and proportionately fewer managers and administrators than were all men. Central and South American men were more highly represented than were all men in the clerical and kindred workers category and had fewer classified as sales workers (Table 9.7).

There were fewer craftsmen, higher proportions of transportation workers, lower proportions classified as laborers, and substantially more service workers among Central and South Americans. There were virtually no Latin men engaged in agricultural occupations in 1970.

When the occupational distribution is weighted using the Census Bureau's Socio-Economic Status (SES) scores, Central and South American men had a value of 59, the same as that for all non-Spanish white men. Central and South Americans ranked higher in SES than did all other Spanish-origin groups; Cuban men were next with 57; Hispanos, with 53; Puerto Ricans, with 50; and Mexican-origin men, with 46.

It is clear that levels of schooling and occupations are highly associated. In general, the more years of schooling an individual has achieved, the greater are his chances of obtaining a higher-level occupation.[12] Using the SES score as a basis for comparison, it is clear that for Central and South American men, as for U.S. men and other Spanish-origin groups, the higher the level of schooling, the higher the SES score. The SES score for Central and South American men completing less than 12 years of schooling was 49; those completing high school scored 57; those with some college, 65; and those completing 4 or more years of college had a score of 82. (The higher the SES score, the greater the proportions in the latter occupations, especially professional and managerial.) A comparison of the proportions of those in three broad occupational categories by years of schooling completed shows these differences clearly, as follows:

Class of occupation	Less than 12 years (%)	12 years (%)	Some college (%)	College graduates (%)
Upper white-collar	6	14	31	80
Lower white-collar	12	20	25	10
Manual	82	66	44	10

Among the college graduates, 8 in 10 were employed in upper-level white-collar jobs. At the opposite end of the scale, the least schooled were overwhelmingly concentrated in the manual occupations—more than 8 in 10 had jobs so classified, with more than half of these in operative and service-worker categories.

Obviously, this discussion draws on very broad categories of oc-

---

[12] The jobs that we refer to as upper-white-collar occupations tend to be filled by college graduates.

TABLE 9.7

Major Occupational Groups, by Years of Schooling, Age, and Sex, Men of Central and South American Descent: 1970

| | TOTAL | | | | | 14-34 | | | | |
| | Years of schooling | | | | | Years of schooling | | | | |
	Total	-12 years	12 years	13-15 years	16+ years	Total	-12 years	12 years	13-15 years	16+ years
Total	100.0	100.0	100.0	100.0	100.0	100.0	100.0	100.0	100.0	100.0
Professional, total	17.8	(2.4)	7.8	21.8	65.2	16.3	2.2†	(7.8)	21.4	66.1
Modern science	10.0	0.9†	2.6*	(10.0)	42.9	8.7	0.8†	2.9†	(9.5)	41.4
Classical	5.3	1.1†	2.5*	(6.0)	18.8	5.0	1.2†	1.5†	6.1*	(21.1)
Semiprofessional	2.5	0.5†	2.7*	(5.8)	3.4*	(2.6)	0.2†	3.3†	5.9*	3.6†
Manager, nonfarm, total	6.7	(3.4)	(6.3)	(9.2)	12.7	4.6	2.4*	3.7*	7.0*	9.1*
Employee	5.1	(2.4)	(4.5)	(7.3)	(10.6)	4.1	2.1†	3.1†	6.6*	8.1*
Self-employed	(1.6)	1.0†	1.8†	1.9†	2.1†	0.5†	0.4†	0.7†	0.4†	1.0†
Sales	5.4	(4.4)	(5.9)	(8.6)	4.1*	6.1	(5.2)	(7.1)	9.1*	2.6†
Clerical	10.5	7.4	14.4	16.4	(6.2)	12.3	(8.4)	16.5	(17.0)	8.7*
Craftsmen	18.9	21.8	24.8	16.7	5.1*	17.4	19.7	22.9	(13.8)	5.2†
Operatives (excl. transp.)	19.7	30.8	19.2	(10.3)	3.3*	21.2	33.3	18.7	(11.4)	4.4†
Transportation	3.0	(3.5)	(4.4)	2.3†	0.6†	(3.3)	3.9*	4.3*	2.3†	1.3†
Laborer, nonfarm	4.6	7.1	(3.9)	3.6*	0.5†	4.9	(6.9)	4.3*	4.9*	0.3†
Farm manager	0.2†	0.1†	0.4†	-	-	0.1†	-	0.3†	-	-
Farm laborer	0.3†	0.3†	0.3†	0.3†	-	0.2†	0.4†	0.1†	0.2†	-
Service, total	13.0	18.8	12.5	(10.8)	2.4†	13.7	17.6	14.3	(12.9)	2.1†
Household	0.1†	0.3†	-	-	0.1†	0.2†	0.5†	-	-	-
Protective	0.8*	0.7†	1.2†	1.2†	C.1†	0.9	1.1†	1.2†	0.8*	-
Other	12.1	17.8	11.3	(9.5)	2.2†	12.6	16.1	(13.0)	(12.1)	2.1†
	59.3	49.2	56.6	64.6	81.9	58.2	49.2	56.2	63.0	81.4

() 50-99 cases.
* 25-49 cases.
† fewer than 25 cases.

cupations and can provide only summary measures for purposes of comparison. It is beyond the scope of this study to examine specific occupations in any great detail, particularly for Central and South Americans who come from such extremely diverse backgrounds. However, if we examine only those with some college and college graduates in professional occupations, we gain some insight into the importance of education in providing entrance into upper-level occupations in contemporary U.S. society. We divided the broad category of professional occupations into three subdivisions:[13] (a) modern scientific, engineer, physicist, and so on; (b) classical, lawyers, artists and so

---

[13] See Appendix F.

| | 35-44 Years of Schooling | | | | | 45+ Years of Schooling | | | |
Total	-12 years	12 years	13-15 years	16+ years	Total	-12 years	12 years	13-15 years	16+ years
100.0	100.0	100.0	100.0	100.0	100.0	100.0	100.0	100.0	100.0
21.0	2.6†	6.3†	(23.4)	68.3	17.1	2.8†	10.0*	20.7*	58.2
13.3	0.6†	1.5†	12.6*	49.5	(8.9)	1.3†	3.1†	7.9†	(35.6)
(5.3)	1.1†	2.1†	6.1†	15.5*	(6.2)	0.9†	5.8†	5.7†	19.6*
2.4*	0.9†	2.7†	4.7	3.3†	2.1†	0.6†	1.1	7.1	3.1
8.1	4.1†	8.1*	12.2*	12.2*	10.3	4.8†	11.2*	12.9†	20.6*
(6.0)	3.3†	5.4†	8.9†	9.2*	(6.8)	1.9†	7.3†	7.1†	17.5*
2.1*	0.7†	2.7†	3.3†	3.0†	3.5*	2.8†	3.8†	5.7†	3.1†
(3.9)	3.2†	3.3†	5.6†	4.6†	(5.8)	3.9†	5.8†	11.4†	6.2†
9.1	6.1*	13.8*	16.8*	4.0†	(7.8)	6.5*	9.2†	13.6†	4.6†
21.4	25.1	(29.6)	21.5*	5.6†	19.3	22.9	(23.8)	20.0*	4.1
18.8	31.0	(21.0)	7.9†	2.3†	17.0	24.5	18.5*	10.0†	2.6†
3.0*	3.9†	4.8†	2.3†	-	2.2†	1.9†	4.2†	2.1†	-
3.2*	5.6*	2.4†	1.9†	1.0†	(5.6)	9.5*	5.0†	1.4†	-
-	-	-	-	-	0.6†	0.6†	1.2†	-	-
0.1†	0.2†	0.3†	-	-	0.6†	0.4†	0.8†	1.4†	-
11.3	(18.2)	10.5*	8.4†	2.0†	13.7	22.1	10.4*	6.4†	3.6†
0.1†	-	-	-	0.3†	0.1†	0.2†	-	-	-
0.5†	-	0.6†	2.3†	-	1.0†	0.6†	1.9†	1.4†	0.5†
10.7	(18.2)	9.9*	6.1†	1.7†	12.6	(21.2)	8.5†	5.0†	3.1†
61.4	49.9	57.2	67.1	82.6	59.1	49.1	57.5	66.5	81.5

on; and (c) semiprofessional, largely technicians and the paraprofessional occupations.

Of those men with some college, about half were in the first category, with the remainder about equally divided in the other two subdivisions. Among college graduates, two-thirds were in the modern scientific category, slightly more than one-fourth were in classical professions, and the remainder—about one-tenth—were semiprofessionals. Of the U.S. non-Spanish white men with some college, their distribution among the three subdivisions is similar to that of Central and South American men with the same amount of schooling. Non-Spanish white graduates, however, have roughly equal proportions in the modern scientific and classical professions, and a few are classified as semiprofessional.

Women. Unlike their male counterparts, the occupational distribution of Central and South American women is significantly different from that of non-Spanish white women. Although the educational attainment of both populations was similar, and Central and South Americans were more likely to be employed, they are underrepresented in white-collar occupations and are overrepresented in blue-collar ones, relative to all women. See Table 9.8 and as follows:

Class of occupation	Central and South American (%)	Non-Spanish white (%)
White-collar	45.4	65.4
Upper level	12.6	20.6
Lower level	32.8	44.9
Blue collar	56.6	34.6

Central and South American women at every level of schooling were more highly concentrated in blue-collar occupations, specifically operatives and services. The relative disadvantage of Central and South American women shows most clearly among the college graduates. Virtually all non-Spanish white women in this group were in white-collar occupations, with the vast majority in the professions. Central and South American women, on the other hand, even among the white-collar occupations, had higher proportions in the clerical category with fewer professionals, as well as slightly more than 10% in the operative and service-worker categories.

As we noted with respect to Cuban women, one possible explanation for the lower proportion of white-collar workers among Central and South American women may be English-language problems. Many, if not most, of these women are recent migrants and may not have the facility in English required for white-collar jobs. Women in white-collar occupations are concentrated in such occupations as teaching and secretarial and clerical jobs. Some 6 out of 10 women in the female labor force are white-collar workers and should have a good command of the English language. If lack of proficiency in English is the case, then we may expect their occupational distribution to become more similar to that of all women as their English-language skills improve.

Despite the disadvantaged position of Central and South American women relative to all non-Spanish white women, education attainment strongly influences their occupational structure, as it does for men. The following data summarize the proportions of least and best schooled by type of occupation:

Class of occupation	Did not complete high school (%)	Some college (%)	College graduates (%)
Upper white-collar	3	23	65
Lower white-collar	16	52	22
Manual	81	25	13

Latin women with some college who were in professional occupations were about equally divided between the modern scientific and classical occupations, whereas college graduates were concentrated primarily in the classical professions. Those women who had not completed high school were overwhelmingly concentrated in manual occupations, principally operative and service-worker categories.

THE SEVERAL REGIONAL POPULATIONS

INTRODUCTION

The total Central and South American foreign stock is a heterogeneous population in terms of country of origin. Furthermore, the only data we have for a regional analysis are from the census category "other Central and South America."[14] This grouping is not identical to ours, since the Census Bureau includes Brazil. Whether these two groupings otherwise contain the identical countries, we cannot tell, because we cannot ascertain exactly which countries are included in the census category. We can say only that the two groupings are largely the same. Finally, we must note that the Census Bureau has not provided all the desired statistics—there are far fewer than are available for the Mexican, Puerto Rican, and Cuban populations. Hence our regional analysis must be abbreviated.

DEMOGRAPHIC CHARACTERISTICS

Nativity and Mother Tongue. The largest proportions of U.S.-born are found outside of the two large metropolitan areas, Los Angeles, and

---

[14] Census Bureau, PC(2)–1A, *National Origin and Language.*

TABLE 9.8

Major Occupational Groups, by Years of Schooling, Age, and Sex, Women of Central and South American Descent: 1970

	Total	-12 years	12 years	13-15 years	16+ years
			Total Years of schooling		
Total	100.0	100.0	100.0	100.0	100.0
Professional, total	10.7	2.3*	(5.9)	19.3	61.4
Mod. science	3.9	1.1†	3.1*	7.5*	(16.2)
Classical	5.4	0.8†	1.8†	8.5*	39.9
Semiprofessional	(1.4)	0.3†	1.0†	3.3†	5.3†
Manager, nonfarm, total	(1.9)	1.1†	1.9†	3.3†	3.4†
Employee	(1.6)	0.8†	1.5†	3.1†	3.4†
Self-employed	0.3†	0.3†	0.4†	0.2†	–
Sales	3.7	(3.3)	(4.7)	3.1†	3.1†
Clerical	29.1	12.4	45.7	49.7	(18.7)
Craftsmen	(2.1)	2.1*	2.4*	1.6†	1.6†
Operatives (excl.transp.)	30.4	48.3	21.0	(10.4)	5.0†
Transportation	0.2†	0.4†	0.1†	–	–
Laborer, nonfarm	0.7*	1.2†	0.5†	0.2†	–
Farm managers	0.1†	0.1†	0.2†	–	0.3†
Farm laborer	0.1†	0.1†	0.1†	0.2†	–
Service,total	20.9	28.7	17.5	(12.3)	6.5†
Household	7.3	12.6	3.8*	1.6†	1.9†
Protective	0.1†	–	0.2†	–	–
Other	13.5	16.1	13.5	(10.8)	4.7†
SES	56.7	47.3	59.7	67.4	78.9

( ) 50-99 cases.
* 25-49 cases.
† fewer than 25 cases.

New York (Table 9.9). Whether this pattern indicates selective internal migration to the smaller cities and metropolitan areas around the country, we cannot tell. It is confusing, however, that English mother tongue is no more prevalent in the "all other areas" than in the New York metropolitan area, even though fewer U.S.-born are reported in the latter area. Ordinarily, we would conclude that U.S.-born were more likely to report English as their mother tongue. In the Los Angeles metropolitan area, many fewer people report English as their mother tongue than do the residents of New York, but both report about the same proportion of U.S.-born.

Age and Sex. There are no large differences in age among the inhabitants of the several areas. The median age of the New York residents is the highest and is close to that of the U.S. non-Spanish

TABLE 9.8 (cont.)

	14-34 Years of schooling					35+ Years of schooling			
Total	-12 years	12 years	13-15 years	16+ years	Total	-12 years	12 years	13-15 years	16+ years
100.0	100.0	100.0	100.0	100.0	100.0	100.0	100.0	100.0	100.0
10.4	2.1†	5.3*	18.2*	(59.0)	11.1	2.4†	6.7*	21.2*	63.8
(3.7)	0.9†	2.7†	7.2*	14.3†	(4.2)	1.2†	3.6†	7.9†	18.1*
5.3	0.9†	1.3†	9.1*	(37.3)	5.6	0.8†	2.4†	7.4†	(42.5)
1.4*	0.2†	1.3†	1.9†	7.5†	1.4*	0.4†	0.7†	5.9†	3.1†
1.7*	1.3†	1.7†	2.1†	3.1†	2.1*	1.0†	2.1†	5.4†	3.8†
1.6*	1.0†	1.6†	2.1†	3.1†	1.6*	0.7†	1.4†	4.9†	3.8†
0.1†	0.2†	0.1†	-	-	0.4†	0.3†	0.7†	0.5†	-
(3.7)	5.2*	3.1†	2.1†	1.9†	(3.7)	1.5†	6.6*	4.9†	4.4†
35.9	16.0	53.8	55.0	21.1*	21.4	(8.8)	35.9	(39.9)	16.3*
1.8*	1.8†	2.0	1.3†	1.2†	2.5*	2.4†	2.9†	2.0†	1.9†
27.1	47.9	15.7	9.1*	6.2†	34.2	48.8	27.4	12.8*	3.8†
0.2†	0.6†	-	-	-	0.2†	0.2†	0.2†	-	-
0.7†	1.0†	0.7†	0.3†	-	0.8†	1.3†	0.3†	-	-
0.1†	-	0.3†	-	-	0.1†	0.1†	-	-	0.6†
0.1†	0.2†	-	0.3†	-	0.1†	-	0.2†	-	-
18.2	23.9	17.3	11.5*	7.5†	23.9	33.3	17.8	13.8*	5.6†
5.6	(9.9)	3.4†	0.8†	2.5†	9.2	15.2	4.1†	3.0†	1.3†
-	-	-	-	-	0.2†	-	0.5†	-	-
12.7	14.0	(13.9)	10.7*	5.0†	14.5	18.1	(13.1)	10.8†	4.4†
58.5	49.2	60.8	67.5	77.6	54.7	45.3	58.1	66.9	80.0

whites—about 28 years. The people living in "all other areas" are the youngest.

Women's ages are, on the average, 2 or 3 years above those of men. The regional differences for the two sexes parallel each other.

There is a preponderance of women in all the areas. Of the total population in each region, 53% are women; of the adult population (aged 18 and over), 55% are women.

Extent of Schooling. Considerable differences in levels of schooling exist by region of residence, primarily between residents of the New York and New Jersey SMSAs and other metropolitan areas in the country. New York and New Jersey have the lowest proportions of high school graduates among both men and women compared with other SMSAs. Why these differences exist is largely a matter for speculation.

TABLE 9.9

Selected Demographic Characteristics of the Central and South American–Origin Population by SMSA of Residence: 1970

	U.S.	Los Angeles–Long Beach, Calif.	New York	All other areas
Total population (thousands)	577.9	86.3	148.7	342.9
Nativity				
% born in U.S.	36	30	29	41
Mother tongue				
% reporting English	17	9	18	18
Age				
% of total under age 18	37	39	33	38
% of total 45 and over	16	14	18	16
% of all women aged 18 to 44	48	48	44	48
Median age, years: Men	23.5	23.0	26.6	22.2
Women	26.3	26.0	28.2	25.4
Sex				
Men as % of total	47	47	47	47
Men 18 and over as % of total 18 and over	45	45	45	45
Schooling				
<u>Men</u>, aged 25 and over				
% completed high school	63	65	56	67
% high school graduates entered college	59	58	48	64
% college graduates	20	16	13	25
Median school years completed	12.5	12.6	12.2	12.7
Women, aged 25 and over				
% completed high school	56	54	49	59
% high school graduates entered college	43	40	32	43
% college graduates	9	8	7	11
Median school years completed	12.3	12.1	11.9	12.3

One possible explanation, however, may be the following: New York draws a substantial proportion of its Spanish-origin population from the Spanish-speaking Caribbean, where levels of schooling, at least among migrants, are lower than they are in South American countries such as Argentina and Chile. Unfortunately, we do not have information on specific country of origin of the foreign stock by standard metropolitan statistical area and can only speculate that differences in school attainment among the various SMSAs might be explained by differences in country of origin of the populations residing in them.

The proportions of those aged 25 and over who had completed high school in selected SMSA's in 1970 illustrate these differences, as follows:

Region	Men (%)	Women (%)
Total United States	63	56
New York SMSA	56	49
New Jersey SMSA	52	46
Miami	67	54
Washington, D.C.	81	64
Los Angeles	65	54

In the Washington, D.C.–Maryland–Virginia SMSA, the highest proportion of high school graduates and also the highest proportion of college graduates are noted—38% of the men and 12% of the women. These rates probably reflect the selection due to government employment. The proportions employed in 1970 who worked for a government were 23% of the men and 20% of the women; these rates are about double those for the entire U.S. Central and South American stock.

ECONOMIC CHARACTERISTICS

Labor Force Participation. Of the men aged 16 and over living in the Los Angeles–Long Beach metropolitan area, 84% were in the labor force. Of those living in the New York metropolitan area, some 8 in 10 were in the labor force in 1970, about the same as for all Central and South American stock in total United States. The minimum participation rate, 78%, was observed in "all other areas."

Among women aged 16 and over, the regional pattern is slightly different. The highest participation rate, 54%, was observed in these two metropolitan areas (Los Angeles–Long Beach and New York). The lowest rate, 46%, was reported in "all other areas." To what extent these differences among the regions reflect real differences in rates and to what extent they reflect varying age composition is difficult to say.

Family Income. Average (median) family income in 1969 in the New York metropolitan area and in "all other areas" was about the same as that for all families of Central and South American stock in the U.S., about $9500. In the Los Angeles metropolitan area, however, it was significantly less, about $8800; this occurred despite that larger proportions of both men and women were in the labor force. Whether this lesser family income in the Los Angeles area reflects the nature of economic opportunities there or the particular type (i.e., country of origin) of the Central and South American stock, we do not know. It is apparent, however, that the Latin population in this area is not so little schooled that their lower family income can be attributed to this factor (see preceding section).

Occupations. When discussing variations in levels of school attainment, we noted that there were significant differences in the proportions of Central and South Americans who had completed 12 or more years of schooling. Those living in the New York and New Jersey SMSAs were, by and large, less well schooled than were those living in other metropolitan areas of the nation. Since levels of schooling to a large extent determine occupational status, one would expect similar variations in the occupational distributions of Central and South Americans depending on where they were living in 1970. There are such variations, but they were not in the expected direction (Table 9.10). The SES score of Central and South American males in the New York SMSA was 59, compared with 56 for Los Angeles, both of which were below the national value of 61. On the basis of level of schooling alone as a predictor of overall occupational level, Los Angeles should have ranked higher than did New York. We suspect that differences in the respective labor markets of these two SMSAs may be a factor. Males in the New York SMSA have higher proportions in the clerical and service occupations, and those in Los Angeles are found more frequently in the crafts and operatives categories. The higher proportion of operatives and lower proportion of clerical workers in Los Angeles, relative to New York, account for the differences in overall SES levels.

Since the men in both of these metropolitan areas had SES scores lower than that for all Central and South Americans in the total United States, it is obvious that the SES score in the "all other areas" must be significantly higher. The estimated SES score of 63 for "all other areas" is in line with the previous observations that there were more U.S.-born

TABLE 9.10

Occupational Distribution of Employed Central and South American–Origin Persons, by Sex and Area of Residence: U.S. 1970 (population aged 16 and over)

| | | MEN | | | WOMEN | |
	Total	New York SMSA	Los Angeles SMSA	Total	New York SMSA	Los Angeles SMSA
Total	100.0	100.0	100.0	100.0	100.0	100.0
Professional, technical & kindred workers	19.5	14.7	15.0	12.5	11.1	9.2
Managers & administrators	7.8	7.4	5.6	2.2	1.8	1.8
Sales	5.3	4.4	5.9	4.2	2.9	3.4
Clerical	11.0	16.2	10.3	31.9	34.9	29.0
Subtotal	16.3	20.6	16.2	36.1	37.8	32.4
Craftsmen	19.8	19.8	23.4	2.1	1.9	2.0
Operatives ex. transport	16.9	15.6	24.0	24.5	26.0	34.2
Transport	3.1	3.6	3.2	0.2	0.2	0.2
Subtotal	20.0	19.2	27.2	24.7	26.2	34.4
Laborers, ex. farm	4.9	4.0	4.3	0.7	0.6	0.7
Service	11.3	14.2	8.3	21.7	20.7	18.9
Farmers & managers	.02	–	–	0.0	–	–
Farm workers	.03	–	–	0.0	–	–
SES score	61	59	56	60	58	56

living outside these two large metropolitan areas and that these men had significantly more schooling.

Of the women in the two SMSAs with the highest concentrations of Central and South Americans, those in the New York SMSA are somewhat more likely to be employed in white-collar occupations than are those in Los Angeles. Over one-third of the women living in New York were employed in white-collar jobs, compared with slightly under one-third in Los Angeles. Fewer New York residents were classified as operatives and somewhat more as service workers, when compared with Los Angeles. These SES scores were 58 and 56, respectively. Both scores were lower than the national value, indicating that Central and South American women in other parts of the country had a somewhat better occupational distribution. We remind our readers that New York and Los Angeles also contain sizable numbers of other Spanish groups—Puerto Ricans in New York and Mexicans in Los Angeles— that may affect their opportunities in these labor markets.

Two factors, English-language difficulty and proximity to other large Spanish minority groups, may well explain the relatively disadvantaged position of Central and South American women in New York and Los Angeles. To what extent they may also play a role in other areas of the country, we can only speculate that it is presumably to a somewhat lesser degree.

SUMMARY

Central and South Americans are, for the most part, the nation's newest immigrants. Most have been in the United States not much longer than a decade; hence their cultural heritages are undoubtably a major influence in their lives. Unlike other Spanish groups, such as Mexicans, Cubans, and Puerto Ricans, we cannot assume a common cultural heritage. This diversity, as well as the presumed selected characteristics of these migrants, undoubtedly contributes to their heterogeneity as a population. Statistically, they have been reported as one population by the Census Bureau, but, as we pointed out in the introduction to this chapter, they are in fact many groups, demographically and culturally.

Despite these differences in cultural origin, we can characterize Central and South Americans, at least as a statistical aggregate, as fairly similar in their demographic and economic characteristics to the non-Spanish white population in the United States. Of the other Spanish-origin groups, they are most similar to the Cubans, who themselves are tending to be similar to the non-Spanish white population. And both the Cuban- and Central and South American–origin populations are more similar to the general population than to either the Mexicans, Hispanos, or possibly the Puerto Ricans.

Although we do not have information regarding the rate of outmarriage among Central and South Americans, as we have for other Spanish-origin groups, we expect that in the future, if they are not already doing so, Central and South Americans born in the United States will marry into the non-Spanish population at least to the same extent as do other Spanish groups. The children of these marriages, we presume, will be demographically indistinguishable from the general population. To what extent they will retain their cultural identification, we cannot say, any more than we can predict the strength of ethnic identification among those who do not marry out.

Since those Central and South Americans who have come to the United States are already fairly similar to the U.S. non-Spanish white population, we can expect that over time they will not become less so. Whether they will disappear entirely as a culturally distinguishable group, or several groups, is another question.

10

The Late 1970s

INTRODUCTION

Our analysis of Spanish Americans has to this point been based largely on data from the 1970 Census of Population. Subsequent to this census and prior to the 1980 Census, we have only scattered information, most of which was obtained from the sample surveys conducted by the Census Bureau. These sample data are highly deficient for our purposes for a number of reasons; therefore, the following analysis should be regarded as preliminary. Once the 1980 Census results become available, perhaps in 1982, a more definitive analysis can be undertaken. Even the 1980 Census data will be deficient, as we shall describe subsequently.

The sample survey data collected by the Census Bureau during the 1970s are deficient and almost useless for our analytical purposes mainly because so few Spanish-American families and individuals are interviewed. This means that it is not possible to examine separately the several important components of the Spanish-American population. As mentioned previously, this is not a monolithic population. It is clear from our previous analysis that the five groups that we studied individually all differ significantly from one another and that each has its own set of problems. Combining them into one Spanish-American population results in meaningless figures that tell us nothing of any practical or theoretical value. Each group must be studied separately if we are to gain a maximum of useful knowledge. Indeed, if information had been available for additional groups such as the populations from the Dominican Republic, Colombia, or Spain, we would have studied them also. Unfortunately, the 1970 Census did not provide usable statistics for groups other than the five we analyzed.

Insofar as the sample surveys during the 1970s did report data for individual groups to a limited extent, we utilized that information. To do so, however, and in order to minimize the chance of errors inherent in the small numbers obtained from sample surveys, we averaged the annual reports for 3 years, 1976–1978. In the following analysis, all results that we present for "1977" are actually the average of these 3 years, unless otherwise specified.

A second deficiency in these post-1970 census data, and one that is as important as the first, is that no data exist for those born abroad (or on the island of Puerto Rico) and those born in the United States (including Puerto Rican descent who were born on the mainland). Throughout our previous analysis, it was demonstrated and emphasized that large differences in demographic characteristics occurred between the foreign-born and the native components of the Spanish Americans. For example, in each population the natives had significantly more formal education than did the foreign born, as of 1970. Since 1970, as we shall see subsequently, the sample data indicate that there was an increase in the amount of formal schooling when both nativity groups are combined. How should this be interpreted? It could mean simply that in 1977 the proportion of natives increased over 1970 but that each individual continued to receive the same amount of schooling as in former years. Or, it could mean that more persons were actually receiving more schooling. We cannot tell what actually happened when the two nativity groups are combined.

In many respects data derived from the 1980 Census will be deficient in comparison with that for 1970. This is because the 1980 Census, unlike that of 1970, omits the questions on place of birth of parents for those born in the United States. For certain populations this omission is not important; we can obtain statistics for the total population subdivided by nativity for those of Mexican, Puerto Rican, Cuban, and "all other" origin combined. However, if we wish to have information about those of Dominican Republic descent, for example, only data for the foreign born are available. It is impossible to determine any characteristics of their children who were born in the United States, unless these natives live in a household in which the head is reported as having been born in the Dominican Republic. Many of these natives of Dominican descent are living in their parents' homes. Many are not, however, and these latter individuals are irrevocably lost for analytical purposes. One result, of course, is that there are many more persons of Dominican Republic descent living in the United States in 1980 than are reported by the 1980 Census. This will result in an outcry that the census enumerators missed many of them, followed by debates on how many there *really* are.

Another Hispanic subpopulation about whom we have no further information are the Hispanos in the Southwest. In our previous analysis, we approximated their characteristics by assuming that those persons who reported in 1970 "Other Spanish" and were natives of native parentage were mostly Hispanos. Since place of birth of parents is not asked in the 1980 Census, it is no longer possible to distinguish these people from all "Other Spanish." With these admonitions and warnings in mind, let us now turn to an analysis of the existing information for the late 1970s.

INCREASE IN NUMBERS

In 1977 there were about 11.5 million Spanish Americans living in the United States. This is an increase of almost 3.5 million over the 1970 number and represents an average annual growth rate of 5%. Persons of Mexican descent, 6.8 million, constituted the largest group by far, about 60% of all, and also the fastest growing population, averaging close to 6% per year (Table 10.1). Those of Puerto Rican descent, 1.8 million, constituted the second largest group, about one-quarter as numerous as the Mexican-descent population; these people increased at the slowest rate, slightly above 3% per year.

The "Other Spanish" were almost as numerous as were the Puerto Rican components, 1.4 million, and increased at over 4% per year since 1970. There were about 800,000 persons of Central or South American descent, and they had increased in numbers over 5% per year. The smallest group were the Cubans, who comprised about 700,000 persons,[1] or 6% of all Spanish Americans in 1977; their annual growth rate was slightly above that of the Puerto Rican population.

The above estimates of the 1977 population and the rates of growth since 1970 derived from them are as "official" as can be had. Shall we accept them at their face value? How likely is it that the average annual growth rate of the Spanish-American population was 5%? The Census Bureau commented as follows:

> Growth of the Spanish population is another reason why the 1970 census estimate of the number of persons of Spanish origin differs from that of the March 1978 CPS [Current Population Survey]. Although birth, death, and migration data on persons of Spanish origin are not available nationally, nor

---

[1] The influx of tens of thousands of Cuban refugees in 1980 obviously increases the count well above 700,000. Since these people arrived after April 1, 1980 they will not be included in the 1980 Census.

TABLE 10.1

Numbers of Spanish Americans by Descent and Sex: 1970 and 1977 (numbers in thousands)

	1977			1970			Av. Annual % Change
Descent	Total	Men	Women	Total	Men	Women	Total
Total	11,477	5593	5884	8141	4006	4135	5.0
Mexican	6762	3347	3416	4532	2245	2287	5.9
Puerto Rican	1773	828	945	1429	705	724	3.1
Cuban	686	327	359	545	258	287	3.3
Central and South Americans[a]	829	393	436	578	274	304	5.3
Other Spanish	1427	699	728	1057	524	533	4.4

[a]1970 data include only the foreign born and native of foreign parentage.

can these data be, at present, precisely estimated, rough computations in-dicate an approximate rate of natural increase (excess of births over deaths) of about 1.8 percent per year or 14.4 percent for the period between 1970 and 1978. Furthermore, net immigration from abroad could also have con-tributed significant growth. For example, in the 8-year period ending June 30, 1978, an estimated 860,000 immigrants were admitted to the United States from all Spanish-speaking countries as permanent residents.

Thus, all told, population growth for the period from April 1970 to March 1978 may account for most of the difference between the 1970 census and the March 1978 figures; the balance in the difference can be accounted for by the other reasons noted above.[2]

We may evaluate the increase in population between 1970 and 1977 using information from the above census quote as follows:

1. Total population growth reported[3] was 3.3 million.
2. Excess of births over deaths[4] was 1.3 million.
3. Net immigration from abroad was .9 million.

[2] U.S., Bureau of the Census, *Population Characteristics,* ser. P–20, no. 339, *Persons of Spanish Origin in the United States: March 1978* (Washington, D.C.: Government Printing Office, 1979), p. 15. Virtually the identical statement is published each year.

[3] See Chapter 9, Footnote 5, for a discussion of overreporting of persons from Central and South America in the 1970 Census. We corrected for this in our analysis.

[4] A rate of natural increase of 1.8% per year provides this estimate of the probable ex-cess of births over deaths.

4. Sum of excess births and net immigration was 2.2 million.
5. The difference from the total reported growth amount that can be accounted for is − 1.1 million.

In essence, we are short by 1.1 million Spanish Americans who cannot be accounted for. The Census Bureau interprets this shortage as resulting from "the other reasons noted above." These reasons are as follows:

1. The procedures for collecting the data were somewhat different in the sample surveys than they had been in the 1970 Census.
2. The number of categories for Mexican origin were increased from one in 1970 to four in 1978.
3. In the 1970 Census the respondents themselves reported whether their children under 14 years of age were or were not of Spanish origin. In the sample surveys children under 14 years of age were classified as of Spanish origin if either the household head or his wife was of Spanish descent.

A fourth reason given for the discrepancy in growth is that each sample survey has considerable variability. Since we used a 3-year average instead of relying on the estimate of any single year, the size of the sample error should be reduced considerably.

It is our opinion that natural increase and recorded net immigration do not account "for most of the difference" between the 1970 Census figures and the subsequent sample survey returns. They account for a "considerable," but not "most," part. We suspect, instead, that the change in census procedures had much more impact on increasing the number of Spanish Americans than is admitted by the Census Bureau.

It may be asked whether the shortfall of 1.1 million could have resulted from the counting of additional illegal immigrants in the sample surveys of the 1970s. Since there is no way of knowing how many illegal aliens may have been counted in the 1970 Census and how many in the sample surveys, there is no point in speculating further on the possible number of illegal aliens.

AGE AND SEX COMPOSITION

By and large, there was little change in the age and sex composition between 1970 and 1977, except that the populations aged slightly, as measured by the average (median) age (Table 10.2). The Mexican- and Puerto Rican-descent groups continued to be the youngest, averaging only about 21 years in 1977; this median is from 1 to 2 years higher

TABLE 10.2

Percentage Distribution by Age and Sex: 1970 and 1977

Age	1977 Total	Men	Women	1970 Total	Men	Women
			Mexican Descent			
Total	100.0	49.5	50.5	100.0	49.6	50.4
Under 15	37.4	19.0	18.5	40.1	20.1	20.0
15 to 44	47.0	23.0	24.0	43.7	21.5	22.2
45 and over	15.6	7.5	8.0	16.2	8.0	8.2
Median age	20.9	20.5	21.0	19.3	19.0	19.6
			Puerto Rican Descent			
Total	100.0	46.7	53.3	100.0	49.3	50.7
Under 15	39.6	19.9	19.7	40.3	20.7	19.7
15 to 44	46.1	20.1	25.9	47.2	22.8	24.3
45 and over	14.3	6.7	7.6	12.5	5.8	6.7
Median age	20.7	18.3	22.8	19.8	19.0	20.7
			Cuban Descent			
Total	100.0	47.7	52.3	100.0	47.4	52.6
Under 15	21.0	11.1	9.9	27.2	13.9	13.3
15 to 44	41.1	19.1	22.0	44.9	21.0	23.9
45 and over	37.9	17.5	20.4	27.9	12.5	15.4
Median age	37.0	35.7	38.1	31.7	30.8	32.5
			Central and South American Descent			
Total	100.0	47.4	56.6	100.0	47.5	52.5
Under 15	31.0	16.3	14.7	33.8	17.3	16.5
15 to 44	55.0	25.3	29.7	50.1	23.4	26.7
45 and over	14.0	5.8	8.2	16.1	6.8	9.3
Median age	26.0	24.1	27.0	24.9	23.4	25.6
			Other Spanish Descent			
Total	100.0	49.0	51.0			
Under 15	37.8	19.9	17.9			
15 to 44	42.0	20.2	21.8		NA	
45 and over	20.2	8.9	11.3			
Median age	20.5	18.5	22.5			

TABLE 10.2 (cont.)

Age	Total	1977 Men	Women	Total	1970 Men	Women
			White Total U.S.			
Total	100.0	48.9	51.1	100.0	49.1	50.9
Under 15	22.8	11.7	11.1	27.4	14.0	13.4
15 to 44	45.0	22.6	22.4	41.3	20.7	20.6
45 and over	32.2	14.6	17.6	31.3	14.4	16.9
Median age	30.2	29.0	31.6	28.8	27.4	30.1

than in 1970. Those of Central and South American descent were somewhat older, having a median age of 26 years in 1977, or 1 year more than in 1970. Individuals of Cuban origin averaged 37 years in 1977, as compared to 32 years in 1970. Presumably, this rapid increase in median age resulted from the influx of older immigrants either directly from Cuba or via Spain or other countries. The miscellaneous group of "Other Spanish" was also relatively young, having a median age of 20.5 years.

In comparison with the total white population of the United States, all the groups except the Cubans were much younger, in some cases 10 years younger, judging from the average ages. The aging of the Spanish-origin groups between 1970 and 1977 parallels that of the total U.S. white population; this suggests that the same basic forces may be operating on all the groups. Such basic forces could include a declining birth rate and increasing length of life.

The sex composition remained virtually unchanged for all groups except that of Puerto Rican origin. In all the groups, there was a slight preponderance of women both in 1977 and 1970. Among the Puerto Ricans, however, the proportion who were women for all ages combined increased from almost 51% in 1970 to over 53% in 1977. Whether this resulted from underenumeration of Puerto Rican men, return of more men than women to the island, or more women than men migrants from the island to the U.S. mainland, we have no way of knowing.

EDUCATION

Increased education is an important key to improved socioeconomic position, as we emphasized in preceding chapters. The Spanish Americans have higher birth rates than does the total white population of the

United States, or earn less, or have employment on lower rungs of the occupational ladder, and a large part of such straitened circumstances stems from their lack of sufficient formal education. As noted earlier, Spanish Americans who completed college held jobs about as high on the occupational ladder as did non-Spanish white persons. It was also noted that many more of the native Spanish-origin persons were high school graduates and even college graduates as compared with the foreign-born component. Because of their higher education, more of the natives had better socioeconomic positions, tended to have lower fertility, and were more likely to marry out of their ethnic group, compared with those with fewer years of formal schooling. Hence it is of the utmost importance that we try to determine any changes in extent of formal schooling that may have occurred between 1970 and 1977.

Between 1970 and 1977 the number of years of schooling completed by the younger adult (20–24 years) Mexican- and Puerto Rican–origin persons increased significantly. No information is available for the other origin groups. Of Mexican-descent women aged 20–24, for example, 58% had completed 12 years or more of school in 1977, as compared with 50% in 1970 (Table 10.3).

Among Puerto Rican women of this age group, the proportion increased from 43% to 49%. Similarly, increased proportions of high school graduates went to college. Among Mexican women, the college entrance rate rose from 26% to 36%, and among Puerto Rican women, from 22% to 35%.

Among men, also, there were significant statistical increases in schooling. Among Puerto Rican men aged 25–34, for example, high school completion (12 years or more) rose from 30% to 51%.

Despite these large increases, however, the educational achievements of both groups lagged considerably behind the total white population of the United States. Among men aged 30–34 in 1977, 84% had completed high school, as compared with only 47% of Mexican-origin males and under 50% of Puerto Rican–origin men.

It is difficult to interpret these increases in reported numbers of years of schooling completed. On the one hand, we expect that as the 20–24-years-olds in 1970 aged 7 years (to 1977), their higher high-school-completion rate (in comparison with the older ages) would manifest itself in higher rates for those aged 25–29 and 30–34 in 1977. For example, among Mexican youth aged 20–24 in 1970, 53% had completed high school. In 1977 these young men were now aged 27–31; if no more youth had finished high school subsequent to 1970, we expect that in this age group (27–31), 53% would have reported having com-

TABLE 10.3

Years of School Completed, Mexican and Puerto Rican Descent: 1970 and 1977

Age and descent	Percentage who completed 12 or more years				College attendance[a]			
	Men		Women		Men		Women	
	1977	1970	1977	1970	1977	1970	1977	1970
Mexican								
20 to 24	58	53	58	50	39	35	36	26
25 to 29	56	45	54	41	42	36	36	22
30 to 34	47	36	45	33	46	36	32	23
Puerto Rican								
20 to 24	NA	42	49	43	NA	28	35	22
25 to 29	NA	33	46	26	NA	26	37	27
25 to 34	51	30	46	26	35	24	31	24
White Total U.S.								
20 to 24	85	81	85	81	51	53	46	45
25 to 29	88	76	86	76	59	50	49	39
30 to 34	84	71	82	71	59	47	44	34

[a]Percentage of those who completed high school who also completed 1 or more years of college.

pleted high school. This figure of 53% is close to the 1977 estimates of 56% for the 25–29-year-olds and 47% for the 30–34-year-olds. We conclude that there probably was no further schooling after 1970 for those persons aged 20–24 in 1970. This "wave motion" effect continues throughout all the older age classes and produces the increased schooling shown in Table 10.3.

On the other hand, that at ages 20–24 there were significant increases in the proportions graduating from high school indicates that more teenagers continued in school during the 1970s. The same can be said about entering college; the higher rates at the youngest age indicate that more high school graduates entered college. However, we saw previously that many more of the native than of the foreign born (or island born in the case of the Puerto Ricans) completed 12 years or more of school. Hence if in 1977 the natives constituted a significantly

TABLE 10.4

Percentage Enrolled in School, Mexican Descent: 1970 and 1977

| | Mexican descent | | White[c] |
	1977[a]	1970[b]	1977[a]
Age			
3 to 6	59	40	65
7 to 13	99	95	99
14 to 17	87	85	94
18 to 24	24	21	29

[a]Average of 1976–1978. U.S. Bureau of the Census, ser. P-20.

[b]PC(2)-16.

[c]White includes Spanish descent.

larger proportion of each age group than was the case in 1970, that in itself could account for the increase in the high-school-completion rate. Until we have data on number of years of completed schooling by nativity, the answer to this question will remain illusive. It can be stated only that the younger adult men and women have reached higher educational levels during the 1970s than they did in previous years. Whether this results from changes in the proportion of persons who are natives as opposed to being foreign born is not known. Nevertheless, these two Spanish-American groups lag far behind the general white population and to that extent will continue to have lower socioeconomic positions.

The conclusion that more youth are receiving more education is borne out by the data on school attendance for persons of Mexican origin (Table 10.4). There were significant increases in school attendance at all ages between 1970 and 1977. Among those of high school age, 14–17, the percentage attending school rose from 85% to 87%. This suggests that in another decade or so the Mexican-origin youth will have increased their school levels considerably. They appear to be on the road to higher socioeconomic status. Unfortunately, similar information about other Spanish-American groups is not available, but we suspect that they may be experiencing similar tendencies.

FERTILITY

Fertility varies greatly from one Spanish American–origin group to another, as we saw in Chapter 3. Those of Mexican descent had a rate that was 60% higher than that of the Cubans in 1970. Indeed, women of Cuban and Central and South American descent had fertility rates in 1970 below that of the non-Spanish white population of the United States. Those of Mexican and Puerto Rican origin and the Hispanos, on the other hand, had fertility rates (defined as the number of children ever born after taking into account age, education, marital status, and employment of women) considerably above that of the non-Spanish white women.

Since 1970, fertility may have decreased among women of Puerto Rican, Cuban, and Central and South American origin. The only measure of the birth rate that is available for 1977 is the child–women ratio, or the number of children under 5 years of age per 1000 women aged 15–44. For women of Mexican origin, the decrease, if any, is negligible, and for the "Other Spanish" we have no information for 1970 (Table 10.5).

The ratio of children to women for those of Mexican origin was almost double that of all white women in the United States in 1977: 56 per 1000 as compared to 30. Women of Cuban descent, however, had a ratio of only 23, or substantially below that of white women.

Once it has been noted that the birth rate of the Spanish American–descent women probably decreased during the 1970s, all has been said that the available data permit. More refined measures of reproduction are needed before we can specify more precisely how closely the Spanish Americans may be approaching the non-Spanish white population of the United States.

A possible indicator of future fertility—within the next decade or two—is provided by the estimates of lifetime number of births expected. Among all white women in 1977 (average of 1976–1978) aged 18–34, the average number of lifetime births expected is 2.2 per woman. this expectation decreases rapidly with increases in schooling, being 2.6 for women who have not completed high school and 2.0 for women who have completed 1 or more years of college (Table 10.5).

Among all Spanish-American women (no information is available separately for the several origin groups) the expected number is 2.6 per woman, or 18% above that of the white women. Fertility decreases with advanced schooling for the Spanish-American women also; among those who were not high school graduates, the average number of children expected is 2.9, and for those who have completed 1 or more years of college, it is 2.3 children.

Since the Spanish-American women have less schooling than do the white women, we can ask: If they had the same amount of schooling as did all the white women in the United States, what would the average number of expected lifetime births be? The answer is only 2.4 children, or 9% above that of the white women.

TABLE 10.5
Fertility of the Spanish-American Women: 1970 and 1977

Descent	Ratio: children under age 5 per 1000 women 15–44	
	1977	1970
Mexican	56	58
Puerto Rican	47	59
Cuban	23	32
Central and South American	39	43
Other Spanish	59	NA
All white women	30	39

	Lifetime number of births expected, 1977[b]		
	All Spanish	White[a]	Spanish as % of white
Total	255	222	155
Not a high school graduate	287	257	112
High school graduate	233	221	105
College, 1 year or more	227	204	111
Standardized[c]	241	222	109

[a]Includes Spanish descent.

[b]Average of 1976–1978; women 18–34 years of age; ratio per 100 women. Source: U.S. Bureau of the Census, ser. P–20, *Fertility of American Women.*

[c]Standardized on educational distribution of white women.

We may speculate as follows with regard to the future fertility of the Spanish-American women. First, probably most of their higher rate is accounted for by the women of Mexican descent, since this group constitutes close to two-thirds of all the Spanish Americans and since they have significantly higher fertility than do the other origin groups. The "Other Spanish" also have high fertility, but they are not numerous. Together with the Mexican-origin women, however, the two groups likely account for all of the fertility that is above that of the white women.

Second, the extent of formal schooling is increasing among the

Spanish Americans, including those of Mexican descent. Hence we expect Spanish-American fertility to be close to that of all white women in the United States in another decade or two. Only if vast numbers of poorly educated women immigrate to the United States will fertility remain high.

THE ECONOMIC PICTURE

With the extensive public interest shown in equal employment opportunities during the 1970s, the question may be raised of whether there are any visible changes in the economic characteristics of the Spanish Americans since the beginning of the decade. Due in large measure to the paucity of the data for the late 1970s, we can report only in a limited manner. Indeed, it is difficult even to explain the few results that seem to have emerged. One important element to note is that when economic change does occur, it comes about slowly. Economic levels of a population are raised—if they are raised—only over a period of a generation or longer. In a period as short as one or two decades, only cyclical changes, that is, changes due to variations in business and employment conditions, are visible. The long-run generation trends are detectable only over a 30-year period, or longer. Hence in 7 years—1970 to 1977—we expect to find little change, except possibly that of a cyclical nature.

LABOR FORCE PARTICIPATION

There may have been a small increase between 1970 and 1977 in the proportion of Mexican men aged 16 and over who were in the civilian labor force (from 77% to 79%). Among Mexican-origin women, there was clearly a significant increase in the proportion in the labor force, from 36% to 44%. Even in 1977 relatively fewer Mexican women as compared with all white women were in the labor force, but the data indicate that the gap is narrowing. Among Puerto Rican men, for a reason not yet determined, the proportion in the civilian labor force decreased from 76% to 71%, and that for women remained virtually unchanged: 32% in 1970 and 31% in 1977. The labor force rates for Cuban men may have increased slightly from 84% in 1970 to 86% in 1977. For women, there was virtually no change: 51% in 1970 and 52% in 1977. No information for the late 1970s is available for other origin groups.

Unemployment is a function of the business cycle, and hence changes in the unemployment rate can be interpreted only in cyclical terms.

Between 1970 and 1977 reported unemployment rates increased for all segments of the population including the whites, blacks, Spanish Americans, and all other segments of the population. The reported unemployment rates for the three groups in 1977 were as follows:

Descent group	Men (%)	Women (%)
Mexican origin	9.5	12.7
Puerto Rican origin	13.7	14.6
Cuban origin	10.5	9.2

All of these rates are higher than those for the total white population of the United States, as was also the case in 1970.

OCCUPATIONS

The shifts in occupational composition between 1970 and 1977 are so small that they are difficult to interpret.[5] Whether these shifts are any more than the historical difference between the decennial census information and that derived from the sample surveys cannot be determined at this time.

Among both men and women in all three origin groups—Mexican, Puerto Rican, and Cuban—there were small reported increases in the proportions of employed persons in professional and managerial occupations. This shift also occurred, however, in the total U.S. labor force between 1970 and 1977 (Table 10.6).

For clerical and sales personnel, there were decreases in the percentages for all three origin groups of men; simultaneously, there were increases among the women in each group.

The proportion of men who were skilled workers remained virtually unchanged among the Mexican component and may have decreased slightly among Puerto Rican and Cuban men. The proportion of men who were lower-level manual workers changed little, if at all. The Mexican origin is the only group with enough farm workers to warrant

---

[5] One of the problems is that the census coding and classification of occupations may have been slightly altered between these two dates. Also, we do know that statistics taken from the decennial censuses and the monthly population surveys never agree precisely. In addition, there is the problem of sampling variability.

TABLE 10.6

Occupational Distribution*, by Sex, Mexican, Puerto Rican, and Cuban Descent: 1970 and 1977

Sex and Occupation	Mexican		Puerto Rican		Cuban		Total U.S.[a]	
	1977	1970	1977	1970	1977	1970	1977	1970
MEN	100.0	100.0	100.0	100.0	100.0	100.0	100.0	100.0
Professional and managerial	10.8	9.3	12.8	8.9	24.1	20.4	28.5	25.4
Sales and clerical	7.0	9.0	12.4	14.1	12.9	16.3	12.3	14.6
Total white collar	17.8	18.3	25.2	23.0	37.0	36.7	40.8	40.0
Craftsmen	21.5	21.0	15.3	16.6	16.5	18.1	20.9	21.1
Operatives, laborers, service workers	53.3	50.9	57.7	58.9	46.5	45.2	34.1	34.4
Farmers and farm workers	7.4	9.8	1.8	1.5	--	--	4.2	4.5
WOMEN	100.0	100.0	100.0	100.0	100.0	100.0	100.0	100.0
Professional and managerial	9.9	8.3	12.2	8.6	14.8	9.8	21.8	19.4
Sales and clerical	33.5	31.6	38.5	33.6	33.6	31.3	41.4	42.4
Total white collar	43.4	39.9	50.7	42.2	48.4	41.1	63.2	61.8
Total manual including service	54.4	56.1	49.3	57.8	51.6	58.9	35.5	37.5
Farmers and farm workers	2.2	4.0	--	--	--	--	1.3	0.7

[a]Source: 1977, Employment and Earnings, January 1978. 1970, Census PC(1)-01, Table 222.

*Of employed persons.

323

mention; the proportion in this occupation may have decreased slightly since 1970.

Among the women, the proportion in manual work decreased for all three origin groups as a corollary of the increases in the proportions of white-collar workers.

One conclusion that can be drawn is that the previously discussed tendency for increased schooling since 1970 may be evincing itself in somewhat better jobs, perhaps for men as well as for women.

EARNINGS

Information for 1977 by level of education is available only for all the Spanish-American groups combined and for persons aged 25 and over. Spanish-American men averaged $10,500 in 1977, compared with $14,700 for all men in the United States. Spanish-American women averaged $5100, and all women, $6400. These differences, however, occur largely because the Spanish Americans have less schooling than does the total population of earners; at each educational level the differences are much less, as follows:

	Men		Women	
Years of schooling	Spanish American ($)	All ($)	Spanish American ($)	All ($)
Total population	10,500	14,700	5100	6400
Under 8	7500	7800	3300	3500
8–11	9600	10,900	4700	4600
12–15	12,300	14,400	6300	6400
16 and over	16,900	21,300	9200	9300

The average earnings for all Spanish-American men was about 29% below that of all men in 1977. Let us consider the amount of schooling, however, and ask: If the Spanish American men had the same amount of schooling as did all men, what would their average earnings have been? We find that their earnings would have been $12,500, or only 15% less than that of all men.

If we make the same kind of calculations for women, we find that the difference in earnings disappears. If Spanish-American women had the same educational levels as did all women, their average earnings would have been about $6300. This is virtually the same as the $6400 average for all women.

How does the situation in 1977 compare with that in 1970? This question cannot be answered to our statistical satisfaction, since all the required data for 1970 are not available. On the basis of the partial data that can be had,[6] it appears that in 1970 the Spanish American's average earnings were significantly below that of the total population, even after taking education into account. How much lower, we cannot say.

---

[6]The data in Appendix Tables G–32 and G–33 show that at each age and educational level, all of the Spanish-American groups earned significantly less than did the non-Spanish white population in 1970. This held for men and women.

Bibliography

Amaro, Nelson, and Portes, Alejandro. "Una sociologia del exilio; Situacion de los grupos Cubanos en Estados Unidos." *Aportes,* no. 23 (January 1972): 23–24.

Anderson, Jeanne L. "Trends in Expected Family Size in the United States." *New York Statistician* 26 (March–April 1975): 1ff.

Arriaga, Eduardo E. *New Life Tables for Latin American Populations in the Nineteenth and Twentieth Centuries.* Population Monograph Series, no. 3. Berkeley: Institute of International Studies, University of California, 1968.

Baldwin, Gordon C. *Indians of the Southwest.* New York: Capricorn Books, 1973.

Baldwin, S. E., and Daski, R. S. "Occupational Pay Differences among Metropolitan Areas." *Monthly Labor Review* 99 (May 1976).

Barnett, Larry D. "Research on International and Interracial Marriage." *Marriage and Family Living* 24 (February 1963): 105–107.

Barron, Milton H. "Research on Intermarriage: A Survey of Accomplishments and Prospects." *American Journal of Sociology* 59 (November 1951): 249–255.

Beegle, J. Allan, Goldsmith, Harold F., and Loomis, Charles Y. "Demographic Characteristics of the United States–Mexican Border." *Rural Sociology* 25 (March 1960): 106–162.

Besanceney, Paul H. "On Reporting Rates of Intermarriage." *American Journal of Sociology* 70 (May 1965): 721–730.

Bogue, Donald F. *Principles of Demography.* New York: John Wiley & Sons, 1969.

Bolton, Herbert E. *The Spanish Borderlands: A Chronicle of Old Florida and the Southwest,* Chronicles of America Series, vol. 23. New Haven: Yale University Press, 1921.

Bonacich, Edna. "A Theory of Middleman Minorities." *American Sociological Review* 38 (October 1973): 583–594.

Boswell, Thomas D. "The Growth and Proportional Redistribution of the Mexican Stock Population in the United States: 1910–1970." *The Mississippi Geographer,* in press.

———. "Residential Patterns of Puerto Ricans Living in the United States." *Geographical Review* 66 (January 1976): 92–94.

———. "Inferences concerning the Distribution of the Mexican American Population: 1910 to 1970." *Revista Geografica* 83 (December 1975): 67–86.

Boswell, Thomas D., and Jones, Timothy C. "A Data Resource Base for Studying Persons of Spanish Origin in the United States." *The Professional Geographer* 49 (May 1978): 201–203.

Bradshaw, Benjamin S., and Bean, Frank D. "Trends in the Fertility of Mexican Americans, 1950–1970." *Social Science Quarterly* 53 (March 1973): 688–696.

Bravo, Enrique R. ed. and comp. *An Annotated Selected Puerto Rican Bibliography.* Translated by Marcial Cuevas. New York: The Urban Center, Columbia University, 1972.

Broom, Leonard, and Shevky, E. "Mexicans in the United States." *Sociology and Social Research* 36 (January 1952): 150–158.

Browning, Harley L., and McLemore, S. Dale. *A Statistical Profile of the Spanish-Surname Population of Texas.* Austin: Population Research Center, University of Texas, 1964.

Buechley, Robert W. "A Reproducible Method of Counting Persons of Spanish Surname." *Journal of the American Statistical Association* 56 (March 1961): 88–97.

Bullock, Paul. "Employment Problems of the Mexican-American." *Industrial Relations* 3 (May 1964): 37–50.

Bumpass, Larry. "Age at Marriage as a Variable in Socio-Economic Differentials in Fertility." *Demography* 6 (January 1969): 45–54.

Bumpass, Larry L., and Sweet, James A. "Differentials in Marital Instability: 1970." *American Sociological Review* 37 (December 1972): 754–766.

Burch, Thomas K. "The Fertility of North American Catholics: A Comparative Overview." *Demography* 3 (1966): 174–187.

Burchinal, Leo, and Chancelor, Loren E. "Ages at Marriage, Occupations of Grooms, and Interreligious Marriage Rate." *Social Forces* 40 (1961): 348.

Burma, John. "The Civil Rights Situation of Mexican-Americans and Spanish-Americans." In *Race Relations: Problems and Theory,* edited by Jitsuichi Masouka and Preston Valien. Chapel Hill: University of North Carolina Press, 1961.

———. "Interethnic Marriages in Los Angeles, 1948–1959." *Social Forces* 42 (December 1963): 156–165.

———. "Research Note on the Measurement of Interracial Marriage." *American Journal of Sociology* 57 (May 1952): 587–589.

———. "Spanish-speaking Children." In *The Nation's Children,* edited by Eli Ginzberg. New York: Columbia University Press, 1960.

———. *Spanish-speaking Groups in the United States.* Durham, N.C.: Duke University Press, 1954.

Carlson, Alvar W. "Seasonal Farm Labor in the San Luis Valley." *Annals of the Association of American Geographers* 63 (March 1973): 97–108.

———. "Mexican-Americans and a Bibliography of the Geographical Literature, 1920–1971." *Revista Geografica* 75 (December 1971): 154–161.

Chavez, Fray Angelico. *My Penitente Land, Reflections on Spanish New Mexico.* Albuquerque: University of New Mexico Press, 1974.

———. *Origins of New Mexico Families.* Albuquerque: University of Albuquerque in collaboration with Calvin Horn, Publishers, 1973.

——— "Genizaros" In *Handbook of the North American Indians.* vol. 9, edited by Alfonso Ortiz. Washington, D.C.: Smithsonian Institution, 1979, pp. 198–200.

Coles, Robert. *The Old Ones of New Mexico.* Albuquerque: University of New Mexico Press, 1973.

Cutright, Phillips; Hout, Michael; and Johnson, David R. "Structural Determinants of Fertility in Latin America: 1800–1970." *American Sociological Review* 41 (June 1976): 511–527.

Dagodag, W. Tim. "Source Regions and Composition of Illegal Mexican Immigration to California." *International Migration Review* 9 (Winter 1975): 499–511.

Davis, Kingsley, and Senior, Clarence. "Immigration from the Western Hemisphere." *Annals of the American Academy of Political and Social Science* 262 (March 1949): 70–81.

Day, Lincoln H. "Natality and Ethnocentrism: Some Relationships Suggested by an Analysis of Catholic–Protestant Differentials." *Population Studies* 22 (March 1968): 27–50.

de la Vega, Garcilasco. *The Florida of the Inca*. Translated by John and Jeannette Varner. Austin: University of Texas Press, 1951.

de Smyrna, Ajax. "The Zhopa Principle." *New York Statistician* 23 (January–February, 1972): 1.

Dominguez, Fray Francisco Atanasio. *The Missions of New Mexico, 1776*. Translated and edited by Eleanor B. Adams and Fray Angelico Chavez. Albuquerque: University of New Mexico, 1956.

Dublin, Louis H., Lotka, Alfred J., and Spiegelman, Mortimer. *Length of Life*. Ronald Press, N.Y. 1949.

Duncan, Beverly, and Duncan, Otis Dudley. "Minorities and the Process of Stratification." *American Sociological Review* 33 (June 1968): 356–364.

Eichelberger, F. Pierce. "The Cubans in Miami: Residential Movements and Ethnic Group Differentiation." Master's thesis, University of Cincinnati, 1974.

Facts About Israel, 1969. Tel Aviv: Ministry for Foreign Affairs, 1969.

Featherman, David L. "The Socioeconomic Achievement of White Religio-ethnic Subgroups: Social and Psychological Explanations." *American Sociological Review* 36 (April 1971): 207–222.

Fitzpatrick, Joseph P. "Intermarriage of Puerto Ricans in New York City." *American Journal of Sociology* 71 (January 1966): 395–406.

———. *Puerto Rican Americans: The Meaning of Migration to the Mainland*. (Englewood Cliffs, N.J.: Prentice-Hall, 1971.

Fitzpatrick, Joseph P., and Gurak, Douglas T. *Hispanic Intermarriage in New York City: 1975*. Hispanic Research Center of Fordham University, Monograph no. 2. New York: Fordham University, 1979.

Glover, James W. *United States Life Tables, 1890, 1901, 1910, and 1901–1910*. Pt. 2. Washington, D.C.: Government Printing Office, 1921.

Goldscheider, Calvin, and Uhlenberg, Peter R. "Minority Group Status and Fertility." *American Journal of Sociology* 74 (January 1969): 361–372.

Grebler, Leo *Mexican Immigration to the United States: The Record and Its Implications*. Mexican American Study Project, Advance Report 2. Los Angeles: Division of Research, Graduate School of Business Administration, University of California, 1966.

———. "The Naturalization of Mexican Immigrants in the United States." *International Migration Review* 1 (Fall 1966): 17–32.

Grebler, Leo, Moore, Joan W., and Guzman, Ralph C. *The Mexican-American People: The Nation's Second Largest Minority*. New York: Free Press, 1970.

Hajual, John. "Analysis of Changes in the Marriage Pattern by Economic Group." *American Sociological Review* 19 (1954): 295–303.

———. "Differential Changes in Marriage Patterns." *American Sociological Review* 19 (April 1954): 148–154.

Hatt, Paul K. *Background of Human Fertility in Puerto Rico*. Princeton: Princeton University Press, 1952.

Heer, David M. "The Marital Status of Second Generation Americans." *American Sociological Review* 26 (1961): 233–241.

Hutchinson, E. P. *Immigrants and Their Children, 1850–1950.* New York: John Wiley & Sons, 1956.

Jaffe, A. J. *Handbook of Statistical Procedures for Long-Range Projections of Public School Enrollment.* Technical Monograph Project. Washington, D.C.: Government Printing Office, 1969.

———. "The Middle Years." *Industrial Gerontology,* special issue (September 1971).

———. *People, Jobs and Economic Development.* Glencoe, Ill.: Free Press, 1959.

———. "Urbanization and Fertility." *American Journal of Sociology* 48 (July 1942): 48–52.

Jaffe, A. J., and Carleton, R. O. *Occupational Mobility in the United States, 1930–1960.* New York: King's Crown Press, 1954.

Jaffe, A. J., and Ridley, Jeanne Clare. "Lifetime Employment of Women in the United States." *Industrial Gerontology* 3 (Winter 1976).

Jaffe, A. J., and Rios, R. J. "Demographic and Related Developments in Latin America during the 1960s." Paper presented at the Annual Meeting of the Latin American Studies Association, 1973, Madison, Wisconsin.

Keely, Charles B. "Effects of the Immigration Act of 1965 on Selected Population Characteristics of Immigrants to the United States." *Demography* 8 (May 1971): 157–169.

———. "Effects of U.S. Immigration Law on Manpower Characteristics of Immigrants." *Demography* 12 (May 1975): 179–191.

Kennedy, Robert E., Jr. "Minority Group Status and Fertility: The Irish." *American Sociological Review* 38 (February 1973): 85–96.

Kennedy, Ruby Jo Reeves. "Single or Triple Melting Pot? Intermarriage Trends in New Haven, 1870–1950." *American Journal of Sociology* 58 (July 1952): 56–69.

———. "Single or Triple Melting Pot? InterMarriage Trends in New Haven, 1870–1940." *American Journal of Sociology* 49 (1944): 331–339.

Kessell, John L. *Kiva, Cross, and Crown: the Pecos Indians and New Mexico, 1540–1840.* Washington, D.C.: National Park Service, Department of the Interior, 1979.

Kibbe, Pauline R. *Latin Americans in Texas.* Albuquerque: University of New Mexico Press, 1946.

Lamb, Ruth S. *Mexican Americans: Sons of the Southwest.* Claremont, Calif.: Ocelot Press, 1970.

Laytner, Rabbi Anson. "Chinese Jews Survive." *The National Jewish Monthly,* vol. 79, No. 4 (December 1979): 6ff.

Lewis, Robert A.; Rowland, Richard H.; and Clem, Ralph S. *Nationality and Population Change in Russia and the USSR.* New York: Praeger Publishers, 1976.

Linder, Forrest E., and Grove, Robert D. *Vital Statistics Rates in the United States, 1900–1940.* Washington, D.C.: Government Printing Office, 1943.

Locke, Harvey J.; Sabagh, Georges; and Thomas, Mary. "Interfaith Marriages." *Social Problems* 4 (April 1957): 329–333.

Long, Larry H. "Poverty Status and Receipt of Welfare among Migrants and Nonmigrants in Large Cities." *American Sociological Review* 39 (February 1974): 46–56.

Macisco, John J., Jr. "Assimilation of the Puerto Ricans on the Mainland: A Socio-Demographic Approach." *International Migration Review* 2 (Spring 1968): 21–38.

Macisco, John J., Jr., Bouvier, Leon F., and Renzi, Martha Jane. "Migration Status, Education and Fertility in Puerto Rico, 1960." *Milbank Memorial Fund Quarterly* 47 (April 1969): 167–187.

Maldonado, Rita M. "Why Puerto Ricans Migrated to the United States in 1947–73." *Monthly Labor Review* 99 (September 1976): 7ff.

Martinez, John. *Mexican Emigration to the U.S., 1910–1930.* Reprint. San Francisco: R and E. Research Associates, 1971.

McWilliams, Carey. *Brothers under the Skin.* Boston: Little, Brown & Co., 1964.

Meier, Matt S. and Feliciano Rivera. *The Chicanos.* New York: Hill and Wang, 1972.

Meinig, D. W. *Southwest: Three Peoples in Geographical Change, 1600–1970.* London: Oxford University Press, 1971.

Moore, Joan W., and Pachon, Harry. *Mexican Americans.* Englewood Cliffs, N.J.: Prentice-Hall, 1976.

Moquin, Wayne, ed. *A Documentary History of the Mexican Americans.* New York: Bantam Books, 1971.

Morison, Samuel Eliot. *The European Discovery of America, The Southern Voyages, 1492–1616.* New York: Oxford University Press, 1974.

Nam, Charles B. "Nationality Groups and Social Stratification in America." *Social Forces* 37 (May 1959): 328–333.

Nostrand, Richard L. "The Borderlands in Perspective." In *International Aspects of Development in Latin America: Geographical Perspectives,* edited by Gary S. Elbow. Muncie, Ind.: CLAG Publications, Ball State University, 1977.

——. "Mexican American and Chicano: Emerging Terms for a People Coming of Age." *Pacific Historical Review* 42 (August 1973): 389–406.

——. "Mexican Americans Circa 1850." *Annals of the Association of American Geographers* 65 (September 1975): 378–390.

——. "The Hispanic-American Borderland: Delimitation of an American Culture Region." *Annals of the Association of American Geographers* 60 (December 1970): 638–661.

Orleans, Leo A. *Every Fifth Child.* Stanford: Stanford University Press, 1972.

Ortmeyer, Carl E. "Educational Attainment as a Selective Factor in Marital Status Transitions in the U.S." *Demography* 4 (1967): 108–125.

Penalosa, Fernando. "The Changing Mexican-American in Southern California." *Sociology and Social Research* 51 (July 1967): 405–417.

Penalosa, Fernando, and McDonagh, Edward C. "Social Mobility in a Mexican-American Community." *Social Forces* 44 (June 1966): 498–505.

Powers, Mary G., and Macisco, Jr. John J., "Colombians in New York: 1970." Unpublished MS. New York: Fordham University, 1976.

Preuss, J. *Chinese Jews of Kaifeng-Fu.* Tel Aviv: Museum Haartiz.

Prohias, Rafael J., and Casal, Lourdes. *The Cuban Minority in the U.S.: Preliminary Report on Need Identification and Program Evaluation.* Boca Raton, Fla.: Cuban Minority Planning Study, 1973.

Raushenbush, Carl. "A Comparison of the Occupations of the First and Second Generation Puerto Ricans in the Mainland Labor Market." In *Puerto Rican Population of New York City.* New York: Bureau of Applied Social Research, Columbia University, 1954.

Richman, Irving Berdine. *California under Spain and Mexico,* 1911. Reprint. New York: Cooper Square Publishers, 1965.

Roberts, Robert E. "Mortality and Morbidity in the Mexican American Population." Paper presented at the Mexican American Population Conference, Austin, Tex., May 1973.

Roberts, Robert E., and Askew, C., Jr. "A Consideration of Mortality in Three Subcultures." *Health Services Reports* 87 (March 1972).

Roberts, Robert E., and Lee, Eun Sul. "Minority Group Status and Fertility Revisited." *American Journal of Sociology* 80 (September 1974): 503–523.

Rosen, Bernard C. "Race, Ethnicity, and the Achievement Syndrome." *American Sociological Review* 24 (February 1959): 47–60.

Rosenwaike, Ira. *Population History of New York City.* Syracuse: Syracuse University Press, 1972.

Ryder, Norman B. "Notes on Fertility Measurement." *Milbank Memorial Fund Quarterly* 49, pt. 2 (October 1971): 109–127.

Samora, Julian, ed. *La Raza: Forgotten Americans.* Notre Dame, Ind.: University of Notre Dame Press, 1966.

Sanchez, George I. *Forgotten People.* Albuquerque: University of New Mexico Press, 1940.

Schmitt, Robert C. "Demographic Correlates of Interracial Marriage in Hawaii." *Demography* 2 (1965): 463–473.

Shannon, Lyle W., and Krass, Elaine M. "The Urban Adjustment of Immigrants: The Relationship of Education to Occupation and Total Family Income." *Pacific Sociological Review* 4 (Spring 1963): 37–42.

Shibutani, Tamotsu, and Kwan, Kian M. *Ethnic Stratification.* New York: Macmillan Company, 1965.

Siegal, Jacob S. "Estimates of Coverage of the Population by Sex, Race, and Age in the 1970 Census." *Demography* Vol. II, No. 1 (February 1974): 1–24.

Simpson, George E., and Yinger J. Milton. *Racial and Cultural Minorities,* 3d. ed. New York: Harper & Row, 1965.

Sly, David F. "Minority Group Status and Fertility: An Extension of Goldscheider and Uhlenberg." *American Journal of Sociology* 76 (November 1970): 443–459.

Smith, M. Estelle. "The Spanish Speaking Population of Florida." In *Spanish Speaking People in the United States* edited by June Helm. Proceedings of the 1968 Annual Spring Meeting of the American Ethnological Society. American Ethnological Society; distributed by the University of Washington Press, Seattle and London, 1968.

Solé, Carlos A. "Spanish Spoken Here." *Americas* 28 (April 1976).

Sowell, Thomas, "Ethnicity in a Changing America." *Daedalus* Vol. 107, No. 1 (Winter 1978): 213ff.

Statistical Abstract of the United States. U.S. Census Bureau, Washington, D.C.: Government Printing Office.

Steward, Julian H., ed. *Handbook of South American Indians.* Bureau of American Ethnology Vol. 4. Washington, D.C.: Smithsonian Institution, 1945.

Taeuber, Alma F., and Taeuber, Karl E. "Recent Immigration and Studies of Ethnic Assimilation." *Demography,* vol. 4 (1968): 798–808.

Terrell, John Upton. *Journey into Darkness.* New York: William Morrow & Co., 1962.

U.S., Bureau of the Census. "Data on the Spanish Ancestry Population." Data Access Descriptions, no. 41. May 1975.

———. *Fifteenth Census of the United States: 1930. Population.* Vol. 2, *General Report, Statistics by Subjects.* Washington, D.C.: Government Printing Office.

———. *Language Usage in the United States: July 1975.* Ser. P–23, no. 60. Washington, D.C.: Government Printing Office, 1976.

———. *Population Characteristics.* Ser. P–20, nos. 2, 3, *Persons of Spanish Origin in the United States: November 1969.* Washington, D.C.: Government Printing Office, 1971.

———. *Puerto Ricans in Continental United States.* P–E., no. 30. Washington, D.C.: Government Printing Office, 1950.

———. *Thirteenth Census of the United States Taken in the Year 1910.* Vols. 2 and 3, *General Report and Analysis.* Washington, D.C.: Government Printing Office, 1913.

————. *Thirteenth Census of the United States Taken in the Year 1910.* Vol. 2 and 3, *Reports by States, with Statistics for Counties, Cities, and Other Civil Divisions.* Washington, D.C.: Government Printing Office, 1913.

————. Census of Population: 1950. *Special Reports.* P–E no. 31, *Nativity and Parentage.* Washington, D.C.: Government Printing Office, 1952.

————. Census of Population: 1970. *Subject Reports.* Final Report PC(2)–1A, *National Origin and Language.* Washington, D.C.: Government Printing Office, 1973.

————. Census of Population: 1970. *Subject Reports.* Final Report PC(2)–1C, *Persons of Spanish Origin.* Washington, D.C.: Government Printing Office, 1973.

————. Census of Population: 1970. *Subject Reports.* Final Report PC(2)–1D, *Persons of Spanish Surname,* Washington, D.C.: Government Printing Office, 1973.

————. Census of Population: 1970. *Subject Reports.* Final Report PC(2)–1E, *Puerto Ricans in the United States.* Washington, D.C.: Government Printing Office, 1973.

————. Census of Population: 1970. *Subject Reports.* Final Report PC(2)–3A, "Women by Number of Children Ever Born." Washington, D.C.: Government Printing Office, 1973.

————. "Methodology and Scores of Socioeconomic Status." Working Paper No. 15. (1963).

Van Heck, F. "Roman Catholicism and Fertility in the Netherlands: Demographic Aspects of Minority Status." *Population Studies* 10 (November 1956): 125–138.

Wagley, Charles, and Harris, Marvin. *Minorities in the New World.* New York: Columbia University Press, 1958.

Westoff, Charles F. "The Yield of the Imperfect: The 1970 National Fertility Study." *Demography* 12 (November 1975): 373–580.

Zeleny, Carolyn. *Relations between the Spanish Americans and Anglo Americans in New Mexico, 1944.* Thesis. New York: Arno Press, 1974.

Sources of Statistics on the Spanish-Origin Populations in the United States

All of the statistics of the various Spanish-origin populations utilized in this study have been provided by the Census Bureau. They comprise three types: (a) published statistics from the decennial censuses dating back to 1850; (b) Public Use Sample (PUS) tape files for 1960 and 1970; and (c) special tabulations of the 1970 Census of Population prepared by the Census Bureau. The purpose of this appendix is to discuss those identifiers of "Spanishness" developed by the Census Bureau[1] that bear most directly on the present research. Historical data on Mexican Americans are treated in a separate appendix[2] and will not be treated in this appendix.

In 1970 the Census Bureau introduced an innovation, namely, self-identification, into the 5% sample questionnaire. Anyone who checked one of the five Spanish groups listed in this question is considered to be a member of that group. This question, along with four others on birth and parentage, country of origin, and language, provided the basis for developing indicators of Spanish ancestry. It should be stressed that no one indicator gives a uniquely "perfect" definition of *Spanish*. Rather, the different indicators are intended to provide a choice for the analyst, depending on the nature of the research question under investigation.[3] Nor do the indicators developed by the Census Bureau exhaust all

---

[1] For a description of the statistics on Spanish ancestry, available in the 1970 Census, see U.S., Bureau of the Census, "Data on the Spanish Ancestry Population," Data Access Descriptions, no. 41 (May 1975).

[2] Appendix B, "Observation on the Historical Data about the Mexican-American Population."

[3] Census Bureau, "Data on the Spanish Ancestry Population," p. 2.

possible definitions of *Spanish*. The development of additional identifiers of Spanish ancestry is, however, limited to the information obtained from the following questions asked in the U.S. Census of 1970.

Identification of persons of Spanish ancestry was developed from several questions on the 5% and 15% sample questionnaires in the 1970 Census: (a) on place of birth, in the 5% and 15% samples; (b) on place of birth of parents, in the 15% sample; (c) on language spoken in the home as a child, in the 15% sample; and (d) on Spanish origin, asked in the 5% sample. Facsimiles of these questions appear in Figure A.1. These four questions provided the major identifiers of Spanish: (a) birth and parentage; (b) Spanish language; and (c) Spanish origin. In addition, two composite identifiers were developed: Spanish surname[4] (used also in the 1950 and 1960 Censuses) and Spanish heritage.[5]

Of the published statistics, most of the detailed characteristics on Spanish populations are contained in three subject reports: PC(2)–1E, *Puerto Ricans in the United States;* PC(2)–1C, *Persons of Spanish Origin;* and PC(2)–1D, *Persons of Spanish Surname.* In addition, limited information is available on persons of Central and South American birth and parentage in the Subject Report PC(2)–1A, *National Origin and Language.*[6] For the purposes of this research, published statistics are of limited utility, since comparable data are not available for all five Spanish-origin groups enumerated in the 1970 Census. Therefore, the PUS files and special tabulations of the five 5% and 15% samples were the major sources of data on Spanish Americans.

As was noted, the question on Spanish origin in the 5% sample inquired specifically about five Spanish populations living in the United States: Mexicans, Puerto Ricans, Cubans, Central and South Americans, and "Other Spanish," from which it is possible to derive statistics on the Hispanos.[7] By combining such information with that of country of birth of the foreign born and country of birth of parents for the natives of foreign parentage, it was theoretically possible to study foreign born, natives of foreign parentage, and natives of native paren-

---

[4] A detailed explanation of how Spanish surname persons were identified appears in Census Bureau, PC(2)–1C, *Persons of Spanish Surname.*

[5] See Census Bureau, "Data on the Spanish Ancestry Population," p. 4, for an explanation of this identifier. Spanish heritage provides the basic definition used for the Spanish American re-code in the PUS and for special tabulations, discussed in this appendix.

[6] This group is limited to foreign stock, because of apparent misinterpretation of this question by an unknown number of non-Spanish-origin persons in the central and southern United States who reported themselves as of Central or South American origin. See Census Bureau, PC(2)–1C, *Persons of Spanish Origin,* p. ix.

[7] Data are obtained by subtracting foreign stock (5% and 15%) from total origin (5%). The remainder (natives of native parentage) are primarily Hispanos.

13a. Where was this person born? *If born in hospital, give State or country where mother lived. If born outside U.S., see instruction sheet; distinguish Northern Ireland from Ireland (Eire).*

○ This State

OR

_____
(Name of State or foreign country; or Puerto Rico, Guam, etc.)

b. Is this person's origin or descent— *(Fill one circle)*

○ Mexican   ○ Central or South American
○ Puerto Rican   ○ Other Spanish
○ Cuban   ○ No, none of these

14. What country was his father born in?

○ United States

OR

_____
(Name of foreign country; or Puerto Rico, Guam, etc.)

15. What country was his mother born in?

○ United States

OR

_____
(Name of foreign country; or Puerto Rico, Guam, etc.)

17. What language, other than English, was spoken in this person's home when he was a child? *Fill one circle.*

○ Spanish   ■   ○ Other—
○ French   *Specify* _____
○ German   ○ None, English only

FIGURE A.1 *Questions from the 1970 Census 5% and 15% sample questionnaires.*

tage according to specific origin. Thus, it was theoretically possible to generate data on 15 Spanish-nativity groups. In actuality, we limited our analysis for the most part to the natives and foreign born. Puerto Ricans and Cubans were limited to birth and parentage, since there are too few natives of native parentage to permit detailed analysis. Central and South Americans, as was noted in Footnote 6, were limited by necessity to foreign stock. By definition, Hispanos are limited to "Other Spanish" who are natives of native parentage.

The original intention was to rely on the special tabulations for information on Spanish-origin populations and to use the PUS to prepare cross-tabulations on non-Spanish whites for comparative purposes. Table shells for the tabulations were prepared in two parts. The first part was designed to provide cross-tabulations on the numbers of children ever born to women of the five Spanish-origin groups by age, nativity, years of schooling, family income, employment, and marital status. These same cross-tabulations were also to be provided for areas of residence (inside and outside Standard Metropolitan Statistical Areas (SMSAs), inside and outside central cities) and by language spoken in home as a child. All of these tabulations were to be provided for total United States. In addition, the same tabulations were to be provided for Mexican-origin persons in the five southwestern states of Arizona, California, Colorado, New Mexico, and Texas. For the Puerto Rican population, additional tabulations were to be provided for New York City and the New York–New Jersey SMSAs outside New York City. Part II of the tabulations were to contain cross-tabulations of selected socioeconomic characteristics for each of the five Spanish-origin groups, for the same nativity groups, areas of residence, and language requested for the Part I tabulations. These characteristics included occupation, median family income, family income by sex of head and numbers of earners, employment, and weeks worked in 1969. All of these were to be cross-tabulated by age, sex, and years of schooling. The final table provided information on school attendance by single years of age.

An inordinate delay was experienced in receiving the special tabulations that the Census Bureau undertook to prepare, and even then some were not completed.[8] As far as we can determine, much of the delay resulted from the combination of definitions of *Spanish* used to prepare the census computer tapes, as well as difficulties in combining items from the 5% and 15% samples to meet our specifications. For example, we requested both 5% and 15% data on country of birth of the foreign born, whereas published reports were limited to 15% sample items.

As we noted earlier in this appendix, the bureau had developed five different identifiers of "Spanishness" for the 1970 Census. These identifiers were used to prepare various published materials. In addition, they were also used to prepare a "Spanish American Re-code" for the PUS[9] and, for special tabulations, a "Spanish American sub-file," which was essentially the same definition as the PUS re-code and the composite indicator "Spanish Heritage."

The most important definition, since it provides the basis from which the Spanish subfile was created, is that of "Spanish Heritage." The Census Bureau defines this category as follows:

Spanish heritage was created to consolidate data for Spanish ancestry persons in various parts of the United States. The Spanish heritage population, therefore, is specifically termed when reference is made to particular areas. For example, in the five Southwestern States . . . the population of Spanish

---

[8] Part II tabulations were not prepared for Puerto Ricans in New York City, and areas of residence were mislabeled.

[9] See U.S., Bureau of the Census, Description and Technical Documentation, Public Use Samples of Basic Records from the 1970 Census, p. 121.

heritage is specified as the population of Spanish language or surname; in the three Middle Atlantic States . . . , as the population of Puerto Rican Birth or Parentage; and in the remaining 42 States and the District of Columbia, as the population of Spanish language. The information for the population of Spanish heritage was obtained from the 15% sample of census question- naires.[10]

Note that the Spanish heritage definition is limited to the 15% sample, as is the Spanish-American re-code in the PUS, and presumably, the Spanish subfile created for special tabulations. But, it is also based on geographical criteria, which further complicate the problem of defining Spanish-origin groups, particularly in areas outside sizable concentrations of such persons. In addition, "Spanish Heritage" identifies only specific groups in certain areas. For example, in the Middle Atlantic states, Puerto Ricans are designated as the Spanish heritage population. This excludes a substantial number of Cubans and Central and South Americans.[11] In the five southwestern states, Spanish heritage is a combination of language and surname and would include both Mexicans and Hispanos. Most important, for our purposes, identification of Spanish outside the five southwestern states and the three Middle Atlantic states is limited to the single identifier of language. By definition, therefore, an unknown number of persons who identified themselves as Spanish origin would be excluded from this category, particularly if they lived outside areas of large concentrations of Spanish-origin populations. With the continued delay in delivery of the tabulations, we decided to prepare our own tabulations from the PUS, but without using the recode.

The definition of Spanish we used differs considerably from the Spanish-American re-code used by the Census Bureau. Using the complete files from the PUS, we took all related members in every family in which: (a) any one or more members reported being of Spanish origin; (b) of those left over, families in which any member was born in one of the specified Spanish countries; (c) of those left over, anyone reporting Spanish mother tongue; and (d) of those left over, anyone with Spanish surname. Most of the Spanish Americans were identified under a and b. When tabulating the data for any particular group, those persons who reported that group, or the relevant country of birth of self or parents, were counted as members of that group.

The two definitions do not give large differences in total numbers for

---

[10] Census Bureau "Data on the Spanish Ancestry Population," p.4.

[11] In preparing the special tabulations, the bureau inadvertently omitted non-Puerto Rican Spanish in these three states when preparing the fertility tabulations.

total U.S. population. Our definition, being more inclusive, gives somewhat larger numbers; this is especially so in those states where the Spanish Americans are scattered outside of their main areas of concentration (e.g., Mexican origin who live outside the five southwestern states). Nevertheless, from the analytical viewpoint, these discrepancies cause problems in attempting to reconcile numbers from the special census tabulations with the diverse assortment of published totals—"totals" of what? Remember that our only check of a special tabulation (whether from census or our own PUS) is how the totals compare with published census data. Or, are we naive in believing—or supposing—that the published totals are correct? We compiled the following data from the PUS of the proportions of Spanish Americans in the five southwestern states who do not have Spanish surnames and the proportions of Mexicans who do not have Spanish language:

Groups	Spanish surname (%)	Non-Spanish surname (%)
Mexican	84.1	15.9
Cuban	72.5	27.5
Puerto Rican	59.9	40.1
Other Spanish	68.4	31.6
Central and South American	47.9	52.1

U.S. Mexicans	Spanish language (%)	All other languages (%)
Foreign born	98.0	2.0
Native, foreign parentage	92.0	8.0
Total U.S. Mexican population	94.2	5.8

In the tabulations prepared by the Census Bureau, family members who had *not* checked Spanish American, or were not foreign stock in the specified Spanish countries, were excluded. We have therefore only a small number of tables derived from our tabulations of the PUS, in which we get some information about these non-Spanish family members, that is, persons who themselves are not Spanish but are living with relatives who are.

The problems encountered in the use of such a varied assortment of definitions of *Spanish* resulted in some changes in our research goals. We placed less reliance on the special census tabulations, particularly for Central and South Americans, and relied more heavily on our own PUS tabulations. However, in terms of the final accomplishment of our research goals, only minor adjustments had to be made in the analysis of the five populations. Of the analysis contained in this report, possibly one-quarter comes from published volumes, one-quarter from the special tabulations prepared by the Census Bureau, and one-half from our own PUS tabulations.

Observation on the Historical Data about the Mexican-American Population

We have discussed previously the innovation introduced into the 1970 U.S. Census of Population, namely, self-identification. We are quite willing to accept as Mexican Americans any persons who so identify themselves. This item was not used in any previous census, however, except that for 1930, when an analogous but not identical procedure was used. Therefore, we are forced to piece together various published bits of information that will provide, at least, the major outlines of the historical picture.

COUNTRY OF BIRTH

Since 1850 the United States decennial censuses have collected data on persons of foreign origin. Until 1870 the figures pertained solely to the numbers of persons born in foreign countries. Country of origin of the foreign born is shown for each census from 1850 to date.

Beginning in 1870 and continuing through 1970, the censuses included natives of foreign parentage. However, the 1870 Census did not list this nativity group by individual country of origin of parents. The 1880 Census did list country of origin but did not cover the entire United States. The 1910 Census was the first to cover the entire country and to list Mexico as a country of birth of parents.

Together, the foreign born and natives of foreign and mixed parentage constitute what the Census Bureau calls "foreign stock." An individual is so designated if either he was born in some country other than the United States or one of its possessions or he was a native of the

343

United States, but one or both of his parents were foreign born. Thus, a person who is categorized as being of Mexican stock was either born in Mexico or had a mother and/or father who was so born.[1]

We used the data published by the decennial censuses for: (a) country of the foreign born for the period 1850–1900; and (b) country of origin for the total foreign stock for the period 1910–1970, separately for the Mexico born and the natives of Mexican parentage.

There is at least one major problem involved in using these data. We can study only the first generation Mexican immigrants to the United States in the latter half of the nineteenth century and the first and second generations of the Mexican stock, separately, in the twentieth century. However, third and subsequent generations of Mexican Americans will be missed. Thus, the grandson of an immigrant from Mexico may consider himself to be a Mexican American, but the censuses, except that of 1970, cannot distinguish him as such.

IMMIGRATION STATISTICS

The recorded immigration statistics, particularly for the earlier decades, are of little if any use for our purposes. Table B–1 displays data collected by the United States Bureau of Immigration and Naturalization Service and its predecessors on immigration to the United States from Mexico by decades for the 1850–1970 period. It also contains the increases in the numbers of Mexico-born persons living in the United States during each decade, based on the various decennial population censuses for the same period.

If both the immigration and the increase in Mexico born statistics are correct, the immigration figures should be considerably larger than the former. This is because significant numbers of Mexico-born persons return to Mexico, and of those who do not, some die in each intercensal period. Unfortunately, there is no information about return migration or deaths.

A quick glance at the table indicates that 1920–1929 was the first decade in which the immigration figures were greater than those for the increase of the Mexico-born persons. It has, therefore, been concluded that the Mexican immigration data for the period prior to

---

[1] The 1970 Census did not coin the phrase "foreign stock." This first appeared in the 1880 Census. However, the 1870 Census did classify the nativity of white individuals according to their place of birth and that of their parents. Thus, it is possible to determine the number of persons of white foreign stock in 1870 in compliance with the 1880 definition. See Hutchinson, *Immigrants and Their Children*, pp. 266–271.

TABLE B–1

Immigration from Mexico to the United States and Increase in the Total
Number of Mexico-Born Persons Living in the United States: 1850–1969

Decade	Immigration numbers* (thousands)	Increase in number of persons born in Mexico and living in U.S.† (thousands)
1850–1859	3.4	14.2
1860–1869	2.0	14.9
1870–1879	5.1	26.0
1880–1889	N.A.	9.5
1890–1899	N.A.	25.5
1900–1909	31.2	116.4
1910–1919	185.3	264.5
1920–1929	498.9	155.1
1930–1939	32.7	−264.1
1940–1949	56.2	73.2
1950–1959	273.8	125.3
1960–1969	441.8	183.8

* By country of last residence

† These figures have been calculated using the total number of Mexico-
born persons residing in the United States and thus are not quite
identical to the figures shown in Chapter 6, Table 31, p. 138.

N.A. Data not available.

Sources:

For immigration:

A. 1850–1959: U.S. Bureau of the Census. Historical Statistics
for the United States: Colonial Times to 1957.
Washington, D.C. 1960. pp. 58–59.

B. 1958–1961: U.S. Bureau of the Census. Statistical Abstract
of the United States: 1962. Washington, D.C. p. 98.

C. 1962–1966: U.S. Bureau of the Census. Statistical Abstract
of the United States: 1967. Washington, D.C. p. 96

D. 1967–1969: U.S. Bureau of the Census. Statistical Abstract
of the United States: 1970. Washington,D.C. p. 93.

1920 are not of acceptable quality for this study. How accurate the immigration figures since 1920 may be is still open to question. These
observations are in line with the conclusions of others.[2]

Some indication of the possible volume of the pre-1920 migration
stream is given by Martinez,[3] who speaks of the "continuous flow of

[2] For instance, see Grebler et al., Mexican-American People, pp. 61–81; and Wayne
Moquin et al., eds., A Documentary History of the Mexican-Americans (New York: Bantam Books, 1971), p. 334.

[3] John Martinez, Mexican Emigration to the U.S., 1910–1930 reprint ed., San Francisco: (R and E Research Associates, 1971), pp. 1, 10.

Mexicans back and forth across the border before 1910." Apparently no one paid any attention to the border, least of all the U.S. Immigration authorities. Between 1910 and 1917, while the Mexican revolution was still going on, perhaps a total of close to 400,000 persons crossed into the United States. Compare this with the fewer than 200,000 reported by U.S. Immigration for the entire decade.

THE 1930 CENSUS

At the time of the 1930 Census, it was decided to enumerate the "Mexican population" as a separate ethnic group, similar to the Negroes, American Indians, Chinese, and so on. The instructions to the enumerators read:

> 150. Color or race.—White "W" for White . . ."Mex" for Mexican.
>
> 154. Mexicans.—Practically all Mexican laborers are of a racial mixture difficult to classify, although usually well recognized in the localities where they are found. In order to obtain separate figures for this racial group, it has been decided that all persons born in Mexico, or having parents born in Mexico, who are not definitely white, Negro, Indian, Chinese, or Japanese, should be returned as Mexican ("Mex").[4]

These instructions seem to suggest that the traditional place of birth is the important factor in assigning ethnicity and that the statistics ought to be reasonably comparable with those of earlier decades. Nevertheless, the 1930 Census reported 264,000 Mexicans as natives of native parentage![5] How this figure could be obtained from the instructions to the enumerators is difficult to imagine. This observation leads us to believe that the enumerators by and large simply reported as Mexican anyone whom they considered to be Mexican, with only little regard to the census instructions.

The numbers reported in the 1930 Census were: born in Mexico, 617,000; born in the United States of Mexican-born parents, 806,000. An increase in the number of natives of foreign parentage from 252,000 in 1920 to 806,000 in 1930 is impossible. The 1940 Census reported a revised number of natives of Mexican parentage as 583,000. This latter number is close to the original (806,000) minus the 264,000 Mexicans categorized as natives of native parentage in 1930. We feel that

---

[4] U.S., Bureau of the Census, *Fifteenth Census of the United States: 1930.* Vol. 2, *General Report, Statistics by Subjects* (Washington, D.C.: Government Printing Office), pp. 1398, 1399.

[5] *Ibid.*, p. 34, Table 9.

583,000 is still too large as it indicates an increase of over 300,000, or more than double, in the decade 1920–1930. Accordingly, we arbitrarily reduced the 1930 estimate of natives of Mexican-born parents to 450,000.

The basic problem with the 1930 Census was that it tried to create a special minor race category that it called "Mexicans." As it turns out, most of these individuals would have been classified as white persons of Mexican stock in all the other censuses. However, all persons who were born in Mexico or were natives of Mexican parents were excluded from the 1930 "Mexican" classification if they were considered to be "white" rather than "Mexican" in appearance.[6] Thus, the data from the 1930 Census do not represent a population that is strictly comparable to that of the other censuses in regard to their Mexican-stock classifications. Fortunately, even though the 1930 "Mexican" rubric enumerated some persons who were third and subsequent generation Mexican Americans, it still managed to miss most of the Hispanos living in New Mexico.[7]

ESTIMATING POPULATION CHARACTERISTICS FOR 1910

The 1910 Census provided little direct information concerning the demographic characteristics of the Mexican-American population. What little data there were dealt primarily with the total Mexican-born and white Mexican stock populations and offered figures only for such characteristics as absolute numbers living in the major divisions and states, numbers living in urban and rural residences, numbers living in large cities, and mother tongue.[8] In addition, the number of males and females was given for the total Mexican-born population, and the number of Mexican-born whites was given on a county scale for certain selected states.[9]

---

[6] The number of persons who were thus classified was relatively small, 65,968. This represented about 4.4 % of what the "Mexican" category would have been if the "White" Mexican stock had been included with it. U.S., Bureau of the Census. *Fifteenth Census of the United States: 1930, Population,* vol. 2 (Washington, D.C.: Government Printing Office, 1933), pp. 27, 268.

[7] See U.S., Bureau of the Census. Census of Population: 1950. Vol. 4, *Special Reports,* pt. 3, chap. C, "Persons of Spanish Surname" (Washington, D.C.: Government Printing Office, 1953), p. 5.

[8] See U.S., Bureau of the Census, *Thirteenth Census of the United States Taken in the Year 1910, Population,* vol. 1. *General Report and Analysis* (Washington, D.C.: Government Printing Office, 1913), chap. 7–9.

[9] The county scale data for the white Mexican-born population is found in *ibid.,* vol. 2 and 3, *Reports by States, with Statistics for Counties, Cities, and Other Civil Divisions* (Washington, D.C.: Government Printing Office, 1913).

As a result of this scarcity of direct information, it became necessary to develop a set of surrogate data using an array of estimating procedures. We now explain how these estimates were achieved.

We selected a group of counties in the five southwestern states that contained largely Mexican-origin populations.[10] The demographic characteristics of these counties, in the aggregate, were then taken as approximations of the same characteristics of the total Mexican-American population in the United States.

Unfortunately, there were difficulties in separating the Hispano and Mexican-American populations in New Mexico and Colorado. In addition, California contained only one county that could be considered as containing a predominantly Mexican-origin population. Hence it was decided to further restrict the selection of counties to the states of Arizona and Texas.[11] The criteria for the selection of these counties were as follows:

1. Less than 50% of the total population was native of native parentage.
2. Indians, Chinese, and Japanese made up less than 15% of the total population.
3. Mexican-born persons accounted for at least 10% of the total population and represented the most numerous of the foreign-born groups.
4. Blacks made up less than 10% of the total population.

On the basis of these criteria, 4 counties from Arizona and 15 from Texas were selected to represent the Mexican-American population. These counties are listed in Table B–2 and shown in Figures B–1 and B–2.

The county data were aggregated for each of the two states. These consolidated figures were then viewed as representing the Mexican-American population for Arizona and Texas. Unfortunately, some of the data listed in the census volumes had to be processed and refined so that they could be more easily and meaningfully compared with other populations. The data presented in the text of this report contain aggregated figures, many of which are based on numbers directly ex-

---

[10] In 1910, 94.4% of the white Mexican stock lived in the five southwestern states of Arizona, California, Colorado, New Mexico, and Texas. All of the raw county data were taken from the sources listed in Footnote 9.

[11] These two states contained 74.4% of the total white Mexican stock population living in the United States in 1910.

TABLE B–2
Counties Selected as Containing Predominantly Mexican-American Populations in Arizona and Texas in 1910*

Arizona	Texas	
1. Cochise	1. Brewster	9. Medina
2. Graham	2. Cameron	10. Presidio
3. Santa Cruz	3. Duval	11. Starr
4. Yuma	4. El Paso	12. Terrell
	5. Frio	13. Val Verde
	6. Hidalgo	14. Webb
	7. LaSalle	15. Zapata
	8. Maverick	

*See p. 348 of text for a list of the criteria used in making this selection.

tracted from the Census of 1910. However, the figures dealing with percentage of illiteracy, age structure, and the child–woman ratio have been, at least in part, estimated. Most of the remaining portion of this appendix will be an elaboration of the procedures utilized in fabricating these estimates.

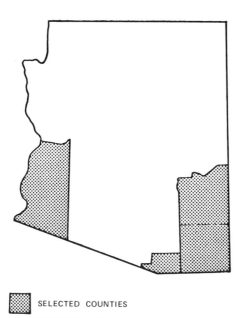

SELECTED COUNTIES

FIGURE B.1. *Mexican-American counties in Arizona, 1910.*

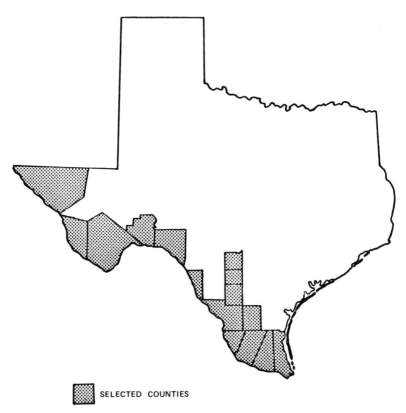

SELECTED COUNTIES

FIGURE B.2. *Mexican-American counties in Texas, 1910.*

ESTIMATES OF PERCENTAGE ILLITERATE

On a county scale the 1910 Census of Population published the following information on illiteracy: (a) the number and percentage of the total population aged 10–20 years who were illiterate; (b) the number and percentage of males 21 years and older who were illiterate; and (c) the number and percentage of the total population 10 years and older who were illiterate. In addition, it was possible to obtain either direct figures from the census or estimated figures from the age estimates (to be explained in the following discussion) for the following age groups: (a) males and females separately aged 10–20 years of age; and (b) the number of males and females who were 21 years of age or older.

If it is assumed that the males and females were characterized by the

same illiteracy rates in the 10–20-year age groups,[12] then by multiply-
ing both the number of males and females in the 10–20-year category
by the percentage of the total population in this same age group that
was enumerated as being illiterate, we obtain a count of the number of
males and females aged 10–20 years who were illiterate. The number
of females 21 years of age and over who were illiterate can now be
estimated as follows: Subtract from the total number of persons 10
years of age or older who were illiterate the sum of the total population
aged 10–20 years who were illiterate and the number of males 21 years
of age and older who were illiterate. Thus, we now have a set of figures
on the number and percentage of both males and females who were illiterate for the following age groups: (a) 10–20 years; (b) 10 years and
over; and (c) 21 years and over.

ESTIMATES OF AGE STRUCTURE

Table B–3 illustrates the age-group data that are obtainable on a
county scale from the published results of the 1910 Census of Population. The classes accompanied by an X are directly obtainable,
whereas the groups followed by numbers in parentheses must be calculated in the manner shown. The steps at which these calculations can
be carried out most conveniently are listed in the right-hand column.
Several examples illustrate how Table B–3 is to be interpreted. The X
for segment number 2 indicates that the total-male-population figure
can be directly copied from the published census figures. The figure for
the total population less than 10 years of age is calculated by subtracting segment number 7 from segment number 1 at the first step. The
estimating factor in segment number 13 is achieved by dividing segment 11 by segment 10 at the fifth step. This estimating factor is then
used to approximate the number of males in segments 15, 18, 21, 24,
and 27 through multiplication.[13]

For ease of comparison it was found desirable to combine or convert
the age figures in Table B–3 into the groups listed in the text. However,
to achieve this end it was necessary to convert the 0–5- and 18–20-year
age groups of Table B–3 into 0–4- and 18–19-year groups. The years
that were subtracted from each of the two age groups in Table B–3

---

[12] In 1930, of males 10–20 years of age, 15% were reported to be illiterate, and among
females, 16%. These data suggest that in 1910 as well, the two sexes may have had more
or less the same illiteracy rates.

[13] Thus, an assumption is made that the same male–female proportions that prevailed
for the aggregate 0–20-year group also obtained for each of its listed subgroups.

TABLE B–3. *Diagram of Age Data Available from the 1910 Census of Population on a County Scale*

Segment of population	How obtained	Step calculated
1. Total population	X [a]	
2. Males	X	
3. Females	X	
4. Total population 21 + years	(5) + (6) [b]	7 [c]
5. Males	X	
6. Females	(3) − (12)	6
7. Total population 10 + years	X	
8. Total population less than 10 yrs.	(1) − (7)	1
9. Total population 10–20 yrs.	X	
10. Total population 0–20 yrs.	(8) + (9)	2
11. Males	(2) − (5)	3
12. Females	(10) − (11)	4
13. Estimating factor	$\dfrac{(11)}{(10)}$	5
14. Total population 0–5 yrs.	X	
15. Males	(13) (14)	8
16. Females	(14 − (15)	9
17. Total population 6–9 yrs.	X	
18. Males	(13) (17)	10
19. Females	(17) − (18)	11
20. Total population 10–14 yrs.	X	
21. Males	(13) (20)	12
22. Females	(20) − (21)	13
23. Total population 15–17 yrs.	X	
24. Males	(13) (23)	14
25. Females	(23) − (25)	15
26. Total population 18–20 yrs.	X	
27. Males	(13) (26)	16
28. Females	(26) − (27)	17

[a] X = copied from census.

[b] Figures in parentheses represent the population segments that were arithmetically manipulated to yield the desired figure.

[c] Figures in the far right column represent the steps at which the calculations took place.

were then added to their adjacent higher age groups. Thus, the 6–9-year group became the 5–9-year class, and the year subtracted from the 18–20-year group was included in a new 20–44-year age class. In making these adjustments, it was necessary to estimate the number of persons (by sex) that were in the 5.000–5.999 and 20.000–20.999 age categories. These estimates were obtained by using Sprague Multipliers

on the total native white of foreign parentage population (by sex) for
Texas and the total population (by sex) for Arizona.[14] A correction factor was achieved, which was then multiplied by the numbers in the
0–5- and 18–20-year age groups in Table B–3 for both the selected
Arizona and Texas populations.

Finally, it was necessary to estimate the 20–44-year age groups for
both Arizona and Texas. In the case of Arizona, the total state population aged 20–44 years was divided by the total state population 20
years of age or older. This fraction was then multiplied by the number
of persons in the 20 years of age and older class in Table B–3 for
Arizona. The same procedure was used for the Texas Mexican-American counties, except that the total native of foreign parentage population for the state was used as a basis for estimating the proportion of
the over-20-year age group that was in the 20–44-year class. Thus, each
of the age categories shown has been obtained through the procedures
described in the preceding discussion.

CHILD–WOMAN RATIO ESTIMATES

The child–woman ratio approximations for the selected Arizona and
Texas populations were calculated by dividing the estimates of the
number of children in the 0–4-year age group by the number of women
in the 15–44-year age category. These figures have been further refined
by taking into account child mortality levels that were characteristic of
(a) the total white U.S. population; (b) the total black U.S. population;
and (c) the total Mexican population (residing in Mexico) for 1910.
Thus, four estimates of fertility were obtained. The first was the
child–woman ratio that was uncorrected for child mortality.

As far as we could determine, there are no data on mortality for the
Mexican-American population in 1910. However, in his excellent sum-
mary of the literature, Roberts[15] refers to a paper by himself and
Askew, in which they calculate that in 1950 in Houston, Texas, the
Chicanos had higher mortality than did the blacks, who in turn had

---

[14] The use of Sprague Multipliers in making similar estimates is illustrated in A. J.
Jaffe, *Handbook of Statistical Procedures for Long-Range Projections of Public School
Enrollment*, Technical Monograph Project (Washington, D.C.: Government Printing Of-
fice, 1969), app. B, pp. 79–85.

[15] Robert E. Roberts, "Mortality and Morbidity in the Mexican American Population"
(Paper presented at the Mexican American Population Conference, Austin, Texas, May
1973). See also Robert E. Roberts and C. Askew, Jr., "A Consideration of Mortality in
Three Subcultures," *Health Services Reports* 87 (March 1972).

higher mortality than did the Anglos. This gives us confidence that the life tables for the country of Mexico that we used, and which showed higher mortality than either the white or black U.S. life tables, were most appropriate for converting the census count on number of children under age 5 to an estimate of the number of births (without any allowance for census undercounts).

As a means of estimating the effects of child mortality for 1910, life tables were used.[16] In each of the three mortality cases, the probabilities of a male and female child surviving to an age of 2.5 years were averaged to produce a combined figure. This was taken as being the best estimate of the mortality rate for the 0–4-year age group. Each of these refined estimates was then divided into the uncorrected child–woman ratio. Since the Mexicans (resident in Mexico) had the highest mortality rate, they conversely had the lowest survival probability rate. Thus, when the Mexican survival probability was divided into the uncorrected child–woman ratio, it resulted in the highest refined fertility estimate. A similar use of the figures from the black and white life tables produced the second and third highest fertility estimates, respectively. Obviously, the uncorrected child–woman ratio provided the lowest fertility estimate of the four.

COMBINING THE ARIZONA AND TEXAS FIGURES

The final step in producing the estimates of the demographic characteristics of the Mexican-American population was obtained by combining the aggregate figures for the selected Arizona and Texas counties. Up to this point we had one set of figures for Arizona and a second set for Texas. The combination of the two was achieved by weighting both sets of figures and then simply adding them together. The weights were figured on the basis of the respective proportion that each state contained of their combined white Mexican stock population. Thus both states together included 284,022 white persons of Mexican stock. Since 232,920 of these individuals lived in Texas, its weight was .82, whereas for Arizona the weight was .18.

---

[16] The life-table figures used for the total white and black U.S. populations for 1910 came from James W. Glover, *United States Life Tables, 1890, 1901, 1910, and 1901–1910,* pt. 2 (Washington, D.C.: Government Printing Office, 1921), pp. 68, 74, 80, 86. The figures used for Mexican population residing in Mexico were taken from Eduardo E. Arriaga. *New Life Tables for Latin American Populations in the Nineteenth and Twentieth Centuries,* Population Monograph Series, no. 3 (Berkeley: Institute of International Studies, University of California, 1968), pp. 174, 175.

As an example of how this procedure was carried out, we can calculate the combined uncorrected child–woman ratio as follows:

1. The child–woman ratio for the Arizona population (62 per 100 women) was multiplied by .18 to produce 11.2.
2. The child–woman ratio for the selected Texas population (56 per 100 women) was multiplied by .82 to yield a figure of 45.9.
3. When 11.2 and 45.9 were added together, the result was 57.1, which was rounded to 57. This was the final estimate for the uncorrected child–woman ratio for the combined Arizona and Texas figures.

Weights Used for Calculating Standardized Fertility Rates

The 1970 State, 5% Public Use Sample was tabulated for non-Spanish white women as shown in Table C–1.

TABLE C–1

Characteristics	Total U.S. non-Spanish White women	Characteristics	Total U.S. non-Spanish White women
15 to 19 years	76,116	*25 to 29 years*	56,461
-12 years school	54,630	-12 years school	12,563
Employed	10,569	Employed	4,053
Married, spouse present	768	Married, spouse present	2,779
Other	9,801	Other	1,274
Not employed	44,061	Not employed	8,510
Married, spouse present	3,016	Married, spouse present	7,174
Other	41,045	Other	1,336
12+ years school	21,486	12+ years school	43,898
Employed	10,552	Employed	19,652
Married, spouse present	1,484	Married, spouse present	12,836
Other	9,068	Other	6,816
Not employed	10,934	Not employed	24,246
Married, spouse present	1,964	Married, spouse present	22,582
Other	8,970	Other	1,664
20 to 24 years	68,810	*30 to 34 years*	47,795
-12 years school	12,071	-12 years school	12,764
Employed	4,053	Employed	4,760
Married, spouse present	2,150	Married, spouse present	3,524
Other	1,903	Other	1,236
Not employed	8,018	Not employed	8,004
Married, spouse present	6,056	Married, spouse present	6,846
Other	1,962	Other	1,158
12+ years school	56,739	12+ years school	35,031
Employed	32,682	Employed	14,667
Married, spouse present	14,671	Married, spouse present	10,506
Other	18,011	Other	4,161
Not employed	24,057	Not employed	20,364
Married, spouse present	15,928	Married, spouse present	19,118
Other	8,129	Other	1,246

(Continued)

TABLE C–1 (cont.)

Characteristics	Total U.S. non-Spanish White women	Characteristics	Total U.S. non-Spanish White women
35 to 44 years	97,998	*Total, 15 to 44 years*	347,180
-12 years school	32,231	-12 years school	124,259
Employed	14,168	Employed	37,603
Married, spouse present	10,795	Married, spouse present	20,016
Other	3,373	Other	17,587
Not employed	18,063	Not employed	86,656
Married, spouse present	15,538	Married, spouse present	38,630
Other	2,525	Other	48,026
12+ years school	65,767	12+ years school	222,921
Employed	32,319	Employed	109,872
Married, spouse present	24,559	Married, spouse present	64,056
Other	7,760	Other	45,816
Not employed	33,448	Not employed	113,049
Married, spouse present	31,237	Married, spouse present	90,829
Other	2,211	Other	22,220

Source: Special tabulation of PUS, State, based on 5% sample.

Estimating the Population Characteristics of the Hispanos in 1910

The procedure used for processing the census data for the Hispanos in 1910 was the same as that used for the Mexican-American population, described in Appendix B. Accordingly, here we shall limit ourselves to specifying the counties studied and explaining why they were selected as representative of the total Hispano population. The counties are shown in the following table:

New Mexico	Colorado
Guadalupe	Archuleta
Mora	Conejos
Rio Arriba	Costilla
San Miguel	
Santa Fe	
Socorro	
Taos	

The basis for selecting these counties was as follows.

NEW MEXICO

We began with data found in *Forgotten People* by George I. Sanchez (1938). The author supplies a table showing the estimated population of Spanish descent in each county in 1930 and the percentage that this was of the total population. We first selected out those counties in which he estimated that at least two-thirds of the population was of

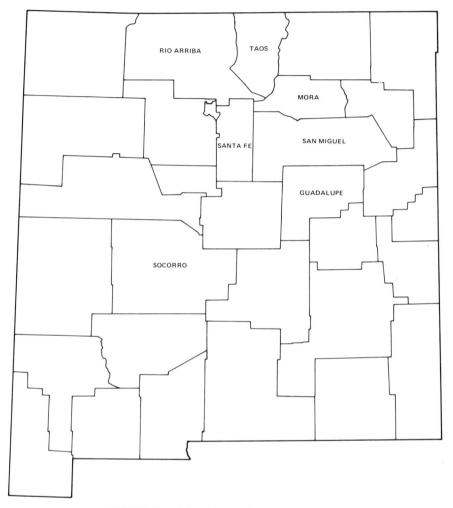

FIGURE D.1. *Selected counties of New Mexico.*

Spanish descent. This list included the above counties plus Sandoval and Valencia.

We then checked against the 1910 Census data for those who had been reported as native white of native parentage and eliminated Sandoval and Valencia, since they contained too many persons returned as Indian and/or Chinese or Japanese. In Sandoval, 33% of the total population fell into this category, and in Valencia, 18%. The counties we finally used contained at least 85% white of native parentage and few who were born in Mexico.

COLORADO

No estimates of the population of Spanish descent were available for this state. Accordingly, we examined the counties close to New Mexico and on the upper Rio Grande, knowing that this was the area settled by the Hispanos. Within each county we examined the names of the precincts and rejected those in which the names were not predominantly Spanish. We reason that the Hispanos would have given Spanish names to the geographic subdivisions. If many of the names were non-Spanish, we reasoned that they were probably settled by an Anglo population. Finally, we eliminated any counties that had a large Indian and/or Chinese or Japanese population. Thus, the three counties finally used contained populations of which 87% or more were reported as native white of native parentage, had Spanish-name precincts, had virtually no Indian population, and were along the Rio Grande and close to New Mexico.

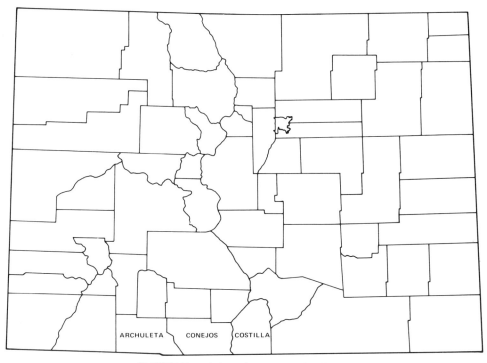

FIGURE D.2. *Selected counties of Colorado.*

Methodology for Estimating Individual and Combined Influences of Employment, Marital Status, and Education on Fertility

It is the purpose of this appendix to describe the logic and methodology we used to estimate the relative influence of the several factors—marital status, employment, and amount of schooling—both individual and joint, in reducing fertility.

We are looking for the answers to these questions: Does the simple addition of the influence of each factor taken separately overestimate its influence on fertility? Is there an influence exerted by the interaction of these factors that might reduce (or increase) the influence of the factors considered separately?

We know that completing high school, being employed, and being other than married with spouse present exerts the greatest influence on fertility levels, that is, results in fewest number of children ever born. Conversely, not completing high school, not being employed, and being married with spouse present, results in the greatest number of children ever born. We know that no one factor alone accounts for these differences in fertility levels, but we do not know the relative contribution of each factor toward the total reduction in fertility. Nor do we know if the total reduction of fertility is equal to the sum of its parts, that is, the simple addition of the influence of each of the three factors taken separately. Analytically, we can view these factors as acting independently on one another, whereas in reality they are much interrelated, and the very interaction of these factors can itself produce an effect that would further reduce (or increase) levels of fertility.

These procedures are illustrated in Table E–1. For this illustration we chose women who had been born in Puerto Rico, were 35–44 years

TABLE E–1
Island Born Women Aged 35–44 Years Living in New York City, 1970

Characteristic	Children per 100 women		Observed	Adjusted	% distribution of adjusted column
		Influence of:			
Employed		education	18	13	24
1) −12 years school	267	employment	36	27	48
2) 12+ years school	233	marital status	9	7	13
Not employed		Sub-total	63	47	–
3) −12 years school	370	Joint effect	8	8	15
4) 12+ years school	310	Remainder	55	–	–
		Final total		55	100
Employed					
5) −12 years school	221				
6) 12+ years school	167				
Not employed					
7) −12 years school	393				
8) 12+ years	319				
INFLUENCE OF:					
Education					
Line 2 + line 1	87				
Line 4 + line 3	84				
Line 6 + line 5	76				
Line 8 + line 7	81				
average	82				
100 minus average	18				
Employment					
Line 1 + line 3	72				
Line 2 + line 4	75				
Line 5 + line 7	56				
Line 6 + line 8	52				
average	64				
100 minus average	36				
Marital status					
Line 5 + line 1	83				
Line 6 + line 2	72				
Line 7 + line 3	106				
Line 8 + line 4	103				
average	91				
100 minus average	9				

of age, and were living in New York City in 1970. The same procedures, of course, can be applied to any other population.

Using the rate, number of children ever born per 100 women, by employment and marital status, cross-tabulated by education, we first estimated the separate influences of education (under 12 or 12 or more years of schooling completed), employment (employed or not employed, including not in the labor force), and marital status (married and spouse present versus all other statuses). We then adjusted the sum of these individual influences to the combined influence of all three factors.

The total or combined influence of all three factors is measured by dividing Line 6 by Line 3—167 by 370. Line 3 is highest fertility—under 12 years of school, not employed, and married with spouse present. Line 6 is the opposite and has lowest fertility. The division gives an answer of 45%; 100 minus this equals 55%, or the total amount that fertility is reduced by the operation of all three factors.

The individual influences of education, employment, and marital status are calculated as in the following table and turn out to be, respectively: 18%, 36%, and 9%, for a total of 63%. But the actual combined effect is only 55%. Presumably, 8% represents the joint effect of all three factors. We then adjust the individual influences as in the table.

Subdivisions of the 1970 Census Major Occupational Group, "Professional, Technical, and Kindred Workers"

Census code	"Modern Scientific" category
001	Accountants
002	Architects
	Computer specialists
003	Computer programmers
004	Computer systems analysts
005	Computer specialists, not elsewhere classified (n.e.c.)
	Engineers
006	Aeronautical and astronautical engineers
010	Chemical engineers
011	Civil engineers
012	Electrical and electronic engineers
013	Industrial engineers
014	Mechanical engineers
015	Metallurgical and materials engineers
020	Mining engineers
021	Petroleum engineers
022	Sales engineers
023	Engineers, n.e.c.
024	Farm management advisors
025	Foresters and conservationists
026	Home management advisors
	Mathematical specialists
034	Actuaries

(continued)

Census code	"Modern Scientific" category (cont.)
035	Mathematicians
036	Statisticians
	Life and physical scientists
042	Agricultural scientists
043	Atmospheric and space scientists
044	Biological scientists
045	Chemists
051	Geologists
052	Marine scientists
053	Physicists and astronomers
054	Life and physical scientists, n.e.c.
055	Operations and systems researchers and analysts
056	Personnel and labor relations workers
	Physicians, dentists, and related practitioners
061	Chiropractors
062	Dentists
063	Optometrists
064	Pharmacists
065	Physicians, medical and osteopathic
071	Podiatrists
072	Veterinarians
073	Health practitioners, n.e.c.
	Nurses, dietitians, and therapists
074	Dietitians
075	Registered nurses
076	Therapists
	Social scientists
091	Economists
092	Political scientists
093	Psychologists
094	Sociologists
095	Urban and regional planners
096	Social scientists, n.e.c.
	Teachers, college and university
102	Agriculture teachers
103	Atmospheric, earth, marine, and space teachers
104	Biology Teachers
105	Chemistry teachers
110	Physics teachers

(continued)

Census code	"Modern Scientific" category (cont.)
111	Engineering teachers
112	Mathematics teachers
113	Health specialties teachers
114	Psychology teachers
115	Business and commerce teachers
116	Economics teachers
120	History teachers
121	Sociology teachers
122	Social science teachers, n.e.c.

	"Classical" category
	Lawyers and judges
030	Judges
031	Lawyers
	Librarians, archivists, and curators
032	Librarians
033	Archivists and curators
	Religious workers
086	Clergymen
090	Religious workers, n.e.c.
	Social and recreation workers
100	Social workers
101	Recreation workers
	Teachers, college and university
123	Art, drama, and music teachers
124	Coaches and physical education teachers
125	Education teachers
126	English teachers
130	Foreign language teachers
131	Home economics teachers
132	Law teachers
133	Theology teachers
134	Trade, industrial, and technical teachers
135	Miscellaneous teachers, college and university
140	Teachers, college and university, subject not specified
	Teachers, except college and university
141	Adult education teachers
142	Elementary school teachers
143	Prekindergarten and kindergarten teachers

(continued)

Census code	"Classical" category (cont.)
144	Secondary school teachers
145	Teachers, except college and university, n.e.c.
174	Vocational and educational counselors
	Writers, artists, and entertainers
175	Actors
180	Athletes and kindred workers
181	Authors
182	Dancers
183	Designers
184	Editors and reporters
185	Musicians and composers
190	Painters and sculptors
191	Photographers
192	Public relations persons and publicity writers
193	Radio and television announcers
194	Writers, artists, and entertainers, n.e.c.
195	Research workers, not specified
196	Professional, technical, and kindred workers—allocated

Census code	"Technician" category
	Health technologists and technicians
080	Clinical laboratory technologists and technicians
081	Dental hygienists
082	Health record technologists and technicians
083	Radiologic technologists and technicians
084	Therapy assistants
085	Health technologists and technicians, n.e.c.
	Engineering and science technicians
150	Agriculture and biological technicians, except health
151	Chemical technicians
152	Draftsmen
153	Electrical and electronic engineering technicians
154	Industrial engineering technicians
155	Mechanical engineering technicians
156	Mathematical technicians
161	Surveyors
162	Engineering and science technicians, n.e.c.
	Technicians, except health, engineering, and science
163	Airplane pilots

(continued)

Census code	"Technician" category (cont.)
164	Air traffic controllers
165	Embalmers
170	Flight engineers
171	Radio operators
172	Tool programmers, numerical control
173	Technicians, n.e.c.

Statistical Tables

LIST OF TABLES

TABLE G-1
Highest Year of School Completed, Mexican Descent, by Age, Sex, and Nativity: U.S. 1970

	No. of years school completed						% distribution					Percentages				
Native	Total	-8	8-11	12	13-15	16+	-8	8-11	12	13-15	16+	8+	12+	13+	a	b
Men																
20-24	157,564	20,831	48,457	57,765	27,632	2,878	13.2	30.8	36.7	17.5	1.8	86.8	56.0	19.3	34	9
25-29	124,655	20,243	42,394	40,207	16,482	5,328	16.2	34.0	32.3	13.2	4.3	83.8	49.8	17.5	35	25
30-34	99,752	24,004	35,072	26,390	8,936	5,349	24.1	35.2	26.4	9.0	5.3	75.9	40.7	14.3	35	37
35-44	191,579	71,322	62,424	35,295	14,722	7,816	37.2	32.6	18.4	7.7	4.1	62.8	30.2	11.8	39	35
45-54	123,388	59,316	39,163	16,687	5,115	3,105	48.1	31.8	13.5	4.1	2.5	51.9	20.1	6.6	33	38
55+	101,868	72,112	20,799	5,703	2,227	1,028	70.8	20.4	5.6	2.2	1.0	29.2	8.8	3.2	36	31
Women																
20-24	171,442	25,505	54,458	67,367	21,879	2,233	14.9	31.8	39.2	12.8	1.3	85.1	53.3	14.1	26	9
25-29	132,694	25,526	47,400	47,577	8,039	4,152	19.2	35.7	35.9	6.1	3.1	80.8	45.1	9.2	20	34
30-34	104,510	27,593	36,996	31,077	5,762	3,083	26.4	35.4	29.8	5.5	2.9	73.6	38.2	8.4	22	35
35-44	197,028	80,267	67,530	39,499	6,832	2,899	40.8	34.2	20.0	3.5	1.5	59.2	25.0	5.0	20	30
45-54	130,866	70,795	38,905	17,327	2,627	1,210	54.1	29.7	13.3	2.0	0.9	45.9	16.2	2.9	18	31
55+	102,841	73,633	19,596	7,103	1,672	836	71.6	19.1	6.9	1.6	0.8	28.4	9.3	2.4	26	33
Foreign Born																
Men																
20-24	30,098	10,557	8,036	7,131	3,749	625	35.0	26.7	23.7	12.5	2.1	65.0	38.3	14.6	38	14
25-29	33,362	16,567	7,495	5,644	2,651	1,005	49.6	22.5	16.9	8.0	3.0	50.4	27.9	11.0	39	27
30-34	31,170	17,980	6,347	3,964	1,722	1,156	57.7	20.4	12.7	5.5	3.7	42.3	21.9	9.2	42	40
35-44	57,683	38,703	10,150	4,847	1,728	2,255	67.1	17.6	8.4	3.0	3.9	32.9	15.3	6.9	45	56
45-54	48,949	31,667	8,891	4,895	2,173	1,324	64.7	18.2	10.0	4.4	2.7	35.3	17.1	7.1	42	38
55+	98,252	77,054	12,334	4,971	2,368	1,524	78.4	12.5	5.1	2.4	1.6	21.6	9.1	4.0	44	40
Women																
20-24	33,384	14,015	8,661	8,031	2,285	392	42.0	25.9	24.1	6.8	1.2	58.0	32.1	8.0	25	15
25-29	37,153	19,158	8,302	6,842	1,984	867	51.6	22.4	18.4	5.3	2.3	48.4	26.0	7.6	29	30
30-34	36,615	22,427	7,118	5,016	1,266	788	61.2	19.4	13.7	3.5	2.2	38.8	19.4	5.7	29	39
35-44	60,555	40,663	9,768	7,011	1,901	1,212	67.2	16.1	11.6	3.1	2.0	32.8	16.7	5.1	31	39
45-54	45,482	30,255	8,098	4,918	1,615	596	66.5	17.8	10.8	3.6	1.3	33.5	15.7	4.9	31	27
55+	105,518	84,072	12,376	5,814	1,978	1,278	79.7	11.7	5.5	1.9	1.2	20.3	8.6	3.1	36	39

Col. a: Percentage of high school graduates who entered college.
Col. b: Percentage of college entrants who completed 4 years.

TABLE G-2

	Total	Number years school completed					% distribution					8+	12+	13+	Percentages	
		-8	8-11	12	13-15	16+	-8	8-11	12	13-15	16+				a	b
Men																
20-24	33,650	2,100	8,650	12,750	8,400	1,750	6.2	25.7	37.9	25.0	5.2	93.8	68.1	30.2	44	17
25-29	25,100	2,700	6,950	9,750	3,600	2,100	10.8	27.7	38.8	14.3	8.4	89.2	61.5	22.7	37	37
30-34	22,350	2,850	7,000	7,450	3,150	1,900	12.8	31.3	33.3	14.1	8.5	87.2	55.9	22.6	40	38
35-44	37,150	7,500	13,350	8,950	3,600	3,750	20.2	35.9	24.1	9.7	10.1	79.8	43.9	19.8	45	51
45-54	29,600	8,050	9,850	7,100	2,250	2,350	27.2	33.3	24.0	7.6	7.9	72.8	39.5	15.5	39	51
55+	36,450	19,300	10,050	3,800	1,650	1,650	53.0	27.6	10.4	4.5	4.5	47.0	19.4	9.0	46	50
Women																
20-24	41,400	2,550	11,200	18,750	7,800	1,100	6.2	27.1	45.3	18.8	2.7	93.8	66.8	21.5	32	13
25-29	28,600	2,450	9,950	12,250	2,550	1,400	8.6	34.8	42.8	8.9	4.9	91.4	56.6	13.8	24	36
30-34	23,650	2,600	9,050	9,250	1,850	900	11.0	38.3	39.1	7.8	3.8	89.0	50.7	11.6	23	33
35-44	41,050	8,750	15,800	12,200	2,950	1,350	21.3	38.5	29.7	7.2	3.3	78.7	40.2	10.5	26	31
45-54	30,250	8,850	11,500	6,900	2,050	950	29.3	38.0	22.8	6.8	3.1	70.7	32.7	9.9	30	31
55+	38,700	17,900	11,800	6,300	1,600	1,100	46.3	30.5	16.3	4.1	2.8	53.7	23.2	6.9	30	41

Col. a: Percentage of high school graduates who entered college.
Col. b: Percentage of college entrants who completed 4 years.

378

TABLE G-3
Highest Year of School Completed, Puerto Rican Descent, by Age, Sex, and Place of Birth, U.S. 1970

Mainland born	No. of years school completed						% distribution					Percentage				
	Total	-8	8-11	12	13-15	16+	-8	8-11	12	13-15	16+	8+	12+	13+	a	b
Men																
20-24	13,842	1,023	4,680	5,293	2,464	382	7.4	33.8	38.2	17.8	2.8	92.6	58.8	20.6	35	14
25-29	7,461	942	2,468	2,774	718	559	12.6	33.1	37.2	9.6	7.5	87.4	54.3	17.1	31	44
30-34	5,479	689	1,752	1,989	731	318	12.6	32.0	36.3	13.3	5.8	87.4	55.4	19.1	34	30
35-44	9,356	1,568	3,491	2,554	1,001	742	16.7	37.3	27.3	10.7	7.9	83.3	45.9	18.6	41	42
45-54	3,391	827	1,388	742	210	224	24.4	40.9	21.9	6.2	6.6	75.6	34.7	12.8	37	52
55+	2,585	1,695	584	190	97	19	65.6	22.6	7.4	3.7	0.7	34.4	11.8	4.4	37	16
Women																
20-24	15,098	1,104	4,282	7,025	2,271	416	7.3	28.4	46.5	15.0	2.8	92.7	64.3	17.8	28	16
25-29	8,336	1,086	2,764	3,324	689	473	13.0	33.2	39.9	8.3	5.7	87.0	53.9	14.0	26	41
30-34	5,810	843	1,953	2,601	253	160	14.5	33.6	44.8	4.4	2.8	85.5	52.0	7.2	14	39
35-44	9,489	1,329	3,754	3,385	576	445	14.0	39.6	35.7	6.1	4.7	86.0	46.5	10.8	23	44
45-54	3,387	1,148	1,008	801	280	151	33.9	29.8	23.6	8.3	4.5	66.1	36.4	12.8	35	35
55+	2,712	1,557	726	313	79	36	57.4	26.8	11.6	2.9	1.3	42.6	15.8	4.2	27	31
Island born																
Men																
20-24	51,135	10,611	21,541	14,381	3,885	717	20.8	42.1	28.1	7.6	1.4	79.2	37.1	9.0	24	16
25-29	49,363	13,070	21,885	10,936	2,040	1,432	26.5	44.3	22.2	4.1	2.9	73.5	29.2	7.0	24	41
30-34	44,543	14,069	20,219	8,379	1,326	550	31.6	45.4	18.8	3.0	1.2	68.4	23.0	4.2	18	29
35-44	69,798	28,935	25,881	11,008	2,437	1,537	41.5	37.1	15.8	3.5	2.2	58.5	21.5	5.7	27	39
45-54	42,405	20,158	14,109	5,687	1,459	992	47.5	33.3	13.4	3.4	2.3	52.5	19.1	5.7	30	40
55+	35,170	21,438	9,600	2,615	697	820	61.0	27.3	7.4	2.0	2.3	39.0	11.7	4.3	37	53
Women																
20-24	57,056	13,138	22,780	17,154	3,265	719	23.0	39.9	30.1	5.7	1.3	77.0	37.1	7.0	19	19
25-29	54,279	16,329	22,326	12,462	2,137	1,025	30.1	41.1	23.0	3.9	1.9	69.9	28.8	5.8	20	33
30-34	47,952	19,202	17,685	8,704	1,571	800	40.0	36.9	18.1	3.3	1.7	60.0	23.1	5.0	22	34
35-44	74,567	35,326	23,807	10,940	2,288	1,206	47.4	33.3	14.7	3.1	1.6	52.6	19.4	4.7	24	34
45-54	46,057	25,600	13,663	4,701	1,168	925	55.6	29.7	10.2	2.5	2.0	44.4	14.7	4.5	31	44
55+	45,312	31,029	9,846	2,977	960	500	68.5	21.7	6.6	2.1	1.1	31.5	9.8	3.2	33	34

Col. a: Percentage of high school graduates who entered college.
Col. b: Percentage of college entrants who completed 4 years.

TABLE G–4
Highest Year of School Completed, Cuban Descent, by Age, Sex, and Nativity: U.S. 1970

Native	No. of years of school completed						% distribution					Percentage				
	Total	-8	8-11	12	13-15	16+	-8	8-11	12	13-15	16+	8+	12+	13+	a	b
Men																
20–24	1,796	52	275	565	694	210	2.9	15.3	31.5	38.6	11.7	97.1	81.8	50.3	61	23
25–29	1,493	126	213	561	356	236	8.4	14.3	37.7	23.8	15.8	91.6	77.3	39.6	51	40
30–34	1,415	133	315	576	221	171	9.4	22.3	40.7	15.6	12.1	90.6	68.4	27.7	41	44
35–44	2,246	219	527	588	371	541	9.8	23.5	26.1	16.5	24.1	90.2	66.7	40.6	61	49
45–54	1,777	363	628	373	242	171	20.4	35.3	21.0	13.6	9.6	79.6	44.2	23.2	52	41
55+	2,771	1,601	767	287	96	20	57.8	27.7	10.3	3.5	0.7	42.2	14.5	4.2	29	17
Women																
20–24	1,900	78	281	776	651	114	4.1	14.8	40.9	34.3	6.0	95.9	81.2	40.3	50	15
25–29	1,539	33	360	607	281	258	2.1	23.4	39.4	18.3	16.8	97.9	74.5	35.1	47	48
30–34	1,329	79	376	647	129	98	5.9	28.3	48.7	9.7	7.4	94.1	65.8	17.1	26	43
35–44	1,874	190	557	691	232	204	10.1	29.7	36.9	12.4	10.9	89.9	60.2	23.3	39	47
45–54	2,141	535	756	503	232	114	25.0	35.3	23.5	10.8	5.3	75.0	39.6	16.1	41	33
55+	2,708	1,267	893	314	116	118	46.8	33.0	11.6	4.3	4.4	53.2	20.3	8.7	43	50
Foreign born																
Men																
20–24	12,039	788	2,785	3,605	3,809	1,052	6.6	23.1	30.0	31.6	8.7	93.4	70.3	40.3	57	22
25–29	14,752	1,967	3,031	3,919	3,631	2,203	13.3	20.5	26.7	24.6	14.9	86.7	66.2	39.5	60	38
30–34	16,692	4,450	4,278	3,294	2,582	2,088	26.7	25.6	19.7	15.5	12.5	73.3	47.7	28.0	59	45
35–44	42,093	11,823	11,189	8,257	5,229	5,595	28.1	26.6	19.6	12.4	13.3	71.9	45.3	25.7	57	52
45–54	32,530	9,193	8,138	6,312	3,299	5,588	28.3	25.0	19.4	10.1	17.2	71.7	46.7	27.3	58	63
55+	30,902	10,893	7,330	6,224	1,932	4,523	35.3	23.7	20.1	6.2	14.6	64.7	40.9	20.8	51	70
Women																
20–24	15,381	1,771	3,541	6,108	3,195	765	11.5	23.0	39.7	20.8	5.0	88.5	65.5	25.8	39	19
25–29	18,452	3,803	3,960	6,489	2,717	1,483	20.6	21.5	35.2	14.7	8.0	79.4	57.9	22.7	39	35
30–34	20,470	6,049	5,552	4,536	2,837	1,496	29.6	27.1	22.2	13.9	7.3	70.4	43.4	21.2	49	35
35–44	46,152	12,428	12,308	12,154	4,384	4,878	26.9	26.7	26.3	9.5	10.6	73.1	46.4	20.1	43	53
45–54	34,172	10,156	9,584	8,914	1,839	3,678	29.7	28.0	26.1	5.4	10.8	70.3	42.3	16.2	38	67
55+	44,817	21,436	12,244	7,526	1,562	2,050	47.8	27.3	16.8	3.5	4.6	52.2	24.9	8.1	33	57

Col. a: Percentage of high school graduates who entered college.
Col. b: Percentage of college entrants who completed 4 years.

TABLE G-5

Highest Year of School Completed, Central and South American Descent, by Age, Sex, and Nativity: U.S. 1970

Native	Total	Numbers					% distribution					Percentage				
		-8	8-11	12	13-15	16+	-8	8-11	12	13-15	16+	8+	12+	13+	a	b
Men																
20-24	6,607	209	904	2,503	2,017	974	3.2	13.7	37.9	30.5	14.7	96.8	83.1	45.2	54	33
25-34	7,981	581	1,318	2,526	1,364	2,192	7.3	16.5	31.7	17.1	27.5	92.7	76.3	44.6	58	62
35-44	7,766	700	1,469	2,169	1,749	1,679	9.0	18.9	27.9	22.5	21.6	91.0	72.0	44.1	61	49
45-54	4,172	410	1,026	1,505	479	752	9.8	24.6	36.1	11.5	18.0	90.2	65.6	29.5	45	61
55+	2,945	879	365	737	491	473	29.9	12.4	25.0	16.7	16.1	70.1	57.8	32.8	57	49
Women																
20-24	6,948	300	838	2,456	2,755	599	4.3	12.1	35.3	39.7	8.6	95.7	83.9	48.6	58	18
25-34	8,103	398	1,426	3,227	1,518	1,534	4.9	17.6	39.8	18.7	18.9	95.1	77.4	37.6	49	50
35-44	8,042	416	1,560	3,950	1,391	925	5.1	18.9	47.9	16.9	11.2	94.9	76.0	28.1	37	40
45-54	5,042	654	1,698	1,602	772	316	13.0	33.7	31.8	15.3	6.3	87.0	53.4	21.6	40	29
55+	3,516	1,082	631	1,172	448	183	30.8	18.0	33.3	12.7	5.2	69.2	51.2	17.9	35	29
Foreign born																
Men																
20-24	17,040	1,727	4,112	4,930	4,976	1,295	10.1	24.1	28.9	29.2	7.6	89.9	65.7	36.8	56	21
25-34	44,180	4,470	9,007	12,225	9,707	8,771	10.1	20.4	27.7	22.0	19.8	89.9	69.5	41.8	60	47
35-44	30,779	5,070	5,966	7,978	4,750	7,015	16.5	19.4	25.9	15.4	22.8	83.5	64.1	38.2	60	60
45-54	14,977	2,959	3,504	3,853	1,807	2,854	19.8	23.4	25.7	12.1	19.1	80.2	56.9	31.2	55	61
55+	16,937	5,335	4,415	3,097	1,738	2,352	31.5	26.1	18.3	10.3	13.9	68.5	42.5	24.2	57	57
Women																
20-24	21,739	3,060	5,962	7,753	3,944	1,020	14.1	27.4	35.6	18.1	4.7	85.9	40.9	22.8	56	21
25-34	51,453	8,431	11,927	17,988	8,112	4,995	16.4	23.2	35.0	15.8	9.7	83.6	60.5	25.5	42	38
35-44	36,827	7,734	8,849	12,322	4,495	3,427	21.0	24.0	33.5	12.2	9.3	79.0	55.0	21.5	39	43
45-54	21,173	5,690	5,059	6,435	2,301	1,688	26.9	23.9	30.4	10.9	8.0	73.1	49.3	18.9	38	42
55+	24,178	8,855	6,558	6,400	1,285	1,080	36.6	27.1	26.5	5.3	4.5	63.4	36.3	9.8	27	46

Col. a: Percentage of high school graduates who entered college.
Col. b: Percentage of college entrants who completed 4 years.

TABLE G-6
Highest Year of School Completed, Non-Spanish Whites, by Age and Sex: U.S. 1970

	Numbers (000) Number years school completed						% distribution								Percentages	
	Total	-8	8-11	12	13-15	16+	-8	8-11	12	13-15	16+	8+	12+	13+	a	b
Men																
20-24	6,452	198	959	2,444	2,148	703	3.1	14.9	37.9	33.2	10.9	96.9	82.0	44.1	54	25
25-29	5,490	211	1,010	2,126	957	1,187	3.8	18.4	38.7	17.4	21.7	96.2	77.8	39.1	50	56
30-34	4,649	248	1,012	1,787	654	947	5.3	21.8	38.4	14.1	20.4	94.7	72.9	34.5	47	59
35-44	9,499	742	2,613	3,171	1,148	1,824	7.8	27.5	33.4	12.1	19.2	92.2	64.7	31.3	48	61
45-54	9,716	1,021	3,225	3,080	1,072	1,318	10.5	33.2	31.7	11.0	13.6	89.5	56.3	24.6	44	55
55+	15,250	3,857	6,249	2,707	1,165	1,271	25.3	41.0	17.8	7.6	8.3	74.7	33.7	15.9	47	52
Women																
20-24	6,848	158	1,046	3,096	1,917	631	2.3	15.3	45.2	28.0	9.2	97.7	82.4	37.2	45	25
25-29	5,594	160	1,099	2,645	878	813	2.8	19.6	47.4	15.7	14.5	97.2	77.6	30.2	39	48
30-34	4,761	183	1,092	2,289	648	547	3.9	22.9	48.1	13.6	11.5	96.1	73.2	25.1	34	46
35-44	9,827	524	2,687	4,486	1,193	937	5.3	27.4	45.7	12.1	9.5	94.7	67.3	21.6	32	44
45-54	10,369	836	3,380	4,226	1,148	778	8.1	32.6	40.8	11.0	7.5	91.9	59.3	18.5	31	40
55+	19,153	4,125	7,865	4,234	1,726	1,203	21.5	41.1	22.1	9.0	6.3	78.5	37.4	15.3	41	41

Col. a: Percentage of high school graduates who entered college.
Col. b: Percentage of college entrants who completed 4 years.

TABLE G-7

School Attendance and Relative Progress in School,* by Descent, 1970 (Age as of date of census)

	Mexican descent				Puerto Rican descent				
	% attending		Below		Above	% attending		Below		Above
Age	school	Total	mode	Mode	mode	school	Total	mode	Mode	mode
7	94.8	100.0	1.8	93.4	4.8	84.4	100.0	2.4	86.8	10.8
8	94.6	100.0	9.2	87.9	2.9	87.2	100.0	4.5	85.8	9.7
9	95.1	100.0	11.5	85.2	3.3	86.8	100.0	7.5	84.3	8.2
10	94.5	100.0	15.6	81.8	2.6	87.5	100.0	12.4	80.6	7.0
11	95.0	100.0	16.7	80.9	2.4	86.5	100.0	15.2	77.9	6.9
12	94.7	100.0	19.9	77.9	2.2	87.0	100.0	19.9	74.7	5.4
13	94.9	100.0	19.7	77.9	2.4	87.0	100.0	18.2	75.3	6.5
14	93.1	100.0	22.9	75.2	1.9	86.0	100.0	21.6	72.5	5.9
15	90.5	100.0	25.8	72.1	2.1	86.0	100.0	23.5	72.7	3.8
16	82.6	100.0	25.0	73.4	1.6	76.6	100.0	26.8	69.4	3.8
17	72.4	100.0	26.0	73.0	1.0	58.2	100.0	26.4	72.1	1.5
18	48.4	100.0	30.5	68.7	0.8	42.3	100.0	32.9	66.2	0.9
19	33.3	100.0	50.1	48.6	1.3	23.8	100.0	59.5	38.5	2.0
Stand-ardized	84.1	100.0	19.4	78.2	2.4	76.0	100.0	18.6	75.5	5.9
20-24	11.5	-	-	-	-	6.9	-	-	-	-
25-34	3.7	-	-	-	-	2.7	-	-	-	-

	Cuban descent				Hispanos				
	% attending		Below		Above	% attending		Below		Above
Age	school	Total	mode	Mode	mode	school	Total	mode	Mode	mode
7	88.9	100.0	0.9	93.3	5.8	93.3	100.0	1.0	94.0	5.0
8	90.6	100.0	5.0	90.1	4.9	92.8	100.0	4.8	92.9	2.3
9	88.1	100.0	4.9	91.4	3.7	93.5	100.0	9.6	87.1	3.3
10	89.8	100.0	10.4	84.8	4.8	92.5	100.0	10.9	83.8	5.3
11	91.0	100.0	9.4	88.5	2.1	93.6	100.0	11.4	84.6	4.0
12	88.3	100.0	10.7	84.9	4.4	95.2	100.0	11.9	84.2	3.9
13	89.9	100.0	15.6	80.6	3.8	92.5	100.0	9.2	88.4	2.4
14	87.7	100.0	14.0	81.3	4.7	93.2	100.0	12.5	84.5	3.0
15	90.7	100.0	16.6	80.0	3.4	92.6	100.0	12.6	85.8	1.6
16	88.8	100.0	19.3	77.7	3.0	83.7	100.0	15.4	82.4	2.2
17	76.9	100.0	24.3	71.4	4.3	71.6	100.0	14.0	84.3	1.7
18	64.6	100.0	31.3	66.1	2.6	49.0	100.0	19.8	78.0	2.2
19	42.6	100.0	34.8	62.3	2.9	33.4	100.0	35.2	63.9	0.9
Stand-ardized	83.4	100.0	13.6	82.4	4.0	83.6	100.0	11.7	85.3	3.0
20-24	26.8	-	-	-	-	14.0	-	-	-	-
25-34	4.4	-	-	-	-	4.4	-	-	-	-

*Progress of those attending school, calculated according to the measure of relative progress as presented in U. S. Census of Population, 1960, PC(2)5A, p. IX

TABLE G-7 (cont.)

	Central and South American descent				Non-Spanish white, total U.S.				
	% attending		Below		Above	% attending		Below		Above
Age	school	Total	mode	Mode	mode	school	Total	mode	Mode	mode
7	95.2	100.0	2.5	92.0	5.5	96.9	100.0	1.3	95.9	2.8
8	95.2	100.0	4.9	89.2	5.9	97.4	100.0	3.0	94.9	2.1
9	93.7	100.0	5.7	89.2	5.0	97.6	100.0	4.4	93.6	2.0
10	92.7	100.0	6.4	88.8	4.8	97.4	100.0	5.6	92.2	2.2
11	96.1	100.0	9.6	85.1	5.3	97.8	100.0	6.0	91.9	2.1
12	91.0	100.0	13.9	82.9	3.2	97.8	100.0	6.8	91.1	2.1
13	94.2	100.0	10.9	86.0	3.1	97.6	100.0	7.2	90.6	2.2
14	92.6	100.0	14.1	79.7	6.2	96.6	100.0	8.1	89.6	2.3
15	90.5	100.0	16.8	78.6	4.5	96.1	100.0	8.4	89.5	2.1
16	84.5	100.0	22.6	73.5	4.0	90.1	100.0	8.6	89.4	2.0
17	83.6	100.0	21.3	73.1	5.6	87.7	100.0	8.3	90.2	1.5
18	65.9	100.0	23.1	71.3	5.6	67.3	100.0	10.1	87.6	2.3
19	49.5	100.0	38.8	55.6	5.6	48.8	100.0	19.1	77.8	3.1
Stand-ardized	87.0	100.0	13.1	82.0	4.9	90.5	100.0	6.8	91.0	2.2
20–24	25.2	–	–	–	–	22.7	–	–	–	–
25–34	8.2	–	–	–	–	6.2	–	–	–	–

TABLE G-8

Distribution of Women in the Republic of Mexico by Age, Years of Schooling Completed, and Urban–Rural Residence: 1970

			Years of schooling completed				
			1 to 5	6	7+	6+	
	Total	None	years	years	years	years	a/
URBAN							
15 to 19 years	100.0	9.1	27.9	36.2	26.7	62.9	42
20 to 24 years	100.0	12.7	30.2	34.7	22.4	57.1	39
25 to 29 years	100.0	15.2	33.1	33.9	17.9	51.8	35
30 to 34 years	100.0	17.5	38.7	30.0	13.9	43.9	32
35 to 39 years	100.0	22.5	40.5	25.5	11.5	37.0	31
40 to 44 years	100.0	24.3	39.4	25.2	11.1	36.3	31
RURAL							
15 to 19 years	100.0	21.0	43.2	23.2	12.6	35.8	35
20 to 24 years	100.0	26.9	45.0	18.5	9.6	28.1	34
25 to 29 years	100.0	33.8	44.7	14.8	6.6	21.4	31
30 to 34 years	100.0	34.7	46.8	12.8	5.7	18.5	31
35 to 39 years	100.0	41.8	43.2	11.1	3.9	15.0	26
40 to 44 years	100.0	46.0	41.2	8.7	4.1	12.8	32

a/ 7+ years as a percentage of 6+ years; that is, the proportion of primary school graduates who went on to secondary school.

Source: Special tabulation of the 1% sample of the 1970 Mexican census of population.

TABLE G-9
Children Ever Born per 100 Hispano Women, 1970, United States

Age and characteristics	Years schooling				
	Total	Under 8 years	8-11 years	Under 12 years	12+ years
15-19 total	14	30	12	14	14
Married spouse present	76	121	88	94	42
Employed	43	147	55	77	18
Not employed	85	116	92	97	54
Other marital status	5	9	4	4	7
Employed	8	19	6	8	7
Not employed	4	6	3	4	7
20-24 total	101	171	158	161	69
Married spouse present	129	199	183	186	95
Employed	88	154	156	156	67
Not employed	151	209	191	196	116
Other marital status	59	129	109	115	33
Employed	37	83	74	76	24
Not employed	90	155	132	139	50
25-29 total	210	270	264	265	162
Married spouse present	229	288	280	282	183
Employed	186	217	255	248	153
Not employed	251	304	288	293	203
Other marital status	146	215	206	208	98
Employed	92	215	143	162	56
Not employed	220	214	259	246	185
30-34 total	304	357	354	355	251
Married spouse present	319	385	362	368	319
Employed	274	256	351	332	229
Not employed	344	425	368	384	298
Other marital status	245	295	316	307	173
Employed	189	243	254	250	138
Not employed	314	333	379	359	236
35-44 total	372	447	402	419	308
Married spouse present	396	468	430	444	331
Employed	347	424	377	393	301
Not employed	427	491	459	470	356
Other marital status	293	394	293	338	226
Employed	237	293	265	275	202
Not employed	380	465	326	396	318

TABLE G-10

Children Ever Born per 100 Women of Mexican Descent, 1970, United States

Age and characteristics	Total							Foreign born			Native foreign parentage			Native native parentage		
	Total	Under 8 years	8-11 years	Under 12 years	12 years	13+ years	12+ years	Total	Under 12 years	12+ years	Total	Under 12 years	12+ years	Total	Under 12 years	12+ years
15-19 total	14	28	12	14	15	12	14	15	15	16	13	13	12	15	15	15
Married spouse present	78	103	79	85	48	56	49	83	87	57	90	99	54	73	80	46
Employed	68	119	78	89	34	28	33	65	69	50	66	86	32	69	95	32
Not employed	80	100	79	84	56	94	59	87	90	61	96	101	66	74	77	56
Other marital status	6	12	4	6	8	7	8	5	5	8	4	4	5	7	6	9
Employed	8	15	7	8	8	5	8	6	5	8	5	7	2	10	10	10
Not employed	5	12	4	5	8	9	8	5	5	8	4	4	9	6	6	8
20-24 total	107	158	147	151	68	37	60	107	130	59	98	153	55	111	161	64
Married spouse present	153	212	182	193	105	75	99	151	171	101	152	184	100	153	203	97
Employed	109	174	164	167	78	42	70	115	140	78	109	178	73	107	174	67
Not employed	171	219	188	201	122	106	119	162	178	112	171	205	120	176	211	121
Other marital status	47	72	84	79	27	10	22	37	51	16	42	82	19	54	90	26
Employed	29	48	60	55	20	9	17	25	35	15	26	61	11	32	66	19
Not employed	73	91	102	98	46	14	37	55	71	20	69	102	35	80	105	41
25-29 total	233	289	263	275	181	122	166	230	255	155	223	251	161	241	287	166
Married spouse present	261	326	288	305	203	150	191	257	280	185	256	316	192	267	319	193
Employed	207	287	256	268	162	122	151	208	237	146	209	290	152	206	277	151
Not employed	284	336	298	316	228	178	218	272	291	203	279	325	218	297	333	227
Other marital status	141	167	179	173	111	56	95	119	146	50	132	185	75	159	182	129
Employed	104	118	147	133	89	52	78	76	99	34	82	121	56	135	169	110
Not employed	198	218	207	212	172	81	156	183	202	96	212	245	138	194	193	199
30-34 total	344	402	361	383	277	222	264	346	367	254	333	381	261	356	401	271
Married spouse present	371	438	374	409	304	256	293	369	391	274	364	414	293	381	422	302
Employed	317	391	337	361	270	209	255	337	364	251	318	372	262	305	348	246
Not employed	396	452	392	426	326	293	319	379	399	284	388	430	315	421	453	345
Other marital status	235	259	303	278	161	103	146	228	245	148	225	276	140	252	311	152
Employed	177	200	241	219	141	86	125	176	190	125	156	200	106	209	291	148
Not employed	312	310	359	331	225	190	218	299	312	204	330	352	252	300	322	168
35-44 total	431	498	416	466	329	277	318	439	462	315	424	462	319	438	474	317
Married spouse present	458	531	435	492	456	321	349	469	494	338	451	489	349	462	495	356
Employed	396	463	402	433	321	302	317	405	431	304	394	433	323	392	434	309
Not employed	490	555	455	517	384	341	376	492	516	356	482	515	372	503	524	408
Other marital status	329	385	339	368	217	127	196	310	328	206	322	364	201	356	407	181
Employed	249	294	282	289	170	132	159	237	249	184	186	286	170	269	344	121
Not employed	420	454	408	439	320	101	294	412	428	265	418	438	294	428	446	305

TABLE G-11

Children Ever Born per 100 Women of Mexican Descent, by Residence, 1970, United States

Column groups **Total**, **Foreign born**, **Native foreign parentage**, and **Native native parentage** fall under *Residence in five southwestern states*. The last group falls under *Residence outside five southwestern states*.

Age and characteristics	Total: Total years	Under 8 years	8-11 years	12 years	13+ years	12+ years	Foreign born: Total years	Under 12 years	12+ years	Native foreign parentage: Total years	Under 12 years	12+ years	Native native parentage: Total years	Under 12 years	12+ years	Residence outside: Total years	Under 12 years	12+ years
15-19 total	14	27	12	14	11	14	14	14	15	13	13	12	15	15	14	14	13	18
Married spouse present	80	101	81	50	60	51	83	85	62	91	99	55	64	83	49	66	76	37
Employed	65	106	81	32	19	31	68	72	57	66	86	31	65	93	29	81	94	50
Not employed	83	100	81	62	115	65	86	88	67	96	101	70	78	81	64	62	70	31
Other marital status	6	12	5	7	6	7	5	5	6	4	4	5	7	7	8	6	5	13
Employed	8	15	7	8	3	7	5	5	6	6	8	2	10	10	9	8	6	12
Not employed	5	11	4	7	9	7	5	5	7	4	4	9	6	6	7	5	5	15
20-24 total	106	154	147	68	38	60	108	131	58	98	154	53	110	157	64	109	160	61
Married spouse present	153	209	185	104	77	98	154	172	103	153	201	100	153	203	97	150	190	100
Employed	108	165	163	79	45	71	120	144	83	108	176	73	105	166	68	113	188	63
Not employed	172	218	191	121	107	118	164	178	113	173	207	121	175	213	118	166	191	126
Other marital status	47	70	83	28	11	23	38	53	17	43	86	19	53	85	28	43	88	17
Employed	22	44	59	20	9	17	26	36	16	27	64	13	31	56	20	30	80	15
Not employed	74	91	104	47	16	38	56	73	21	70	107	33	81	103	45	65	94	25
25-29 total	234	291	264	180	122	165	235	258	158	224	283	159	240	286	175	224	266	172
Married spouse present	263	328	287	202	152	191	262	283	190	260	319	192	266	316	191	250	299	191
Employed	209	289	254	162	132	154	212	241	149	212	289	153	206	274	156	199	273	131
Not employed	286	338	299	227	172	217	277	295	208	281	330	217	294	329	221	273	308	225
Other marital status	143	170	183	111	55	96	124	151	52	133	187	75	160	185	128	125	149	92
Employed	106	123	149	90	54	79	79	101	36	83	126	54	137	167	113	83	109	64
Not employed	200	222	212	169	61	150	187	207	95	212	243	138	197	201	184	184	180	201
30-34 total	346	402	361	278	222	265	349	369	258	334	381	261	357	401	272	333	379	257
Married spouse present	374	440	374	305	262	296	374	394	280	366	413	295	382	422	303	355	400	280
Employed	317	388	330	273	220	261	340	365	261	319	373	265	300	335	255	320	384	218
Not employed	400	454	394	327	294	320	385	403	289	391	429	317	422	456	339	374	408	314
Other marital status	235	256	308	160	92	142	228	245	141	227	278	141	251	309	143	230	276	169
Employed	174	193	245	134	75	116	175	192	109	158	205	106	197	266	132	194	239	164
Not employed	313	310	368	228	175	217	299	311	212	326	348	248	308	336	175	300	305	234
35-44 total	432	494	417	332	278	321	464	496	322	422	460	316	440	472	333	424	477	299
Married spouse present	459	528	437	358	325	351	474	519	345	450	487	346	464	494	366	450	497	335
Employed	394	455	402	321	300	316	406	423	316	390	428	323	392	435	305	406	453	318
Not employed	492	552	457	386	353	381	498	519	360	481	513	366	506	521	434	479	521	350
Other marital status	337	383	337	227	129	204	316	332	214	322	363	200	361	401	206	305	378	151
Employed	248	287	278	176	130	163	244	255	192	244	284	169	259	312	128	256	344	143
Not employed	425	456	410	333	120	310	414	427	273	414	434	293	446	462	344	374	411	180

TABLE G-12

Children Ever Born per 100 Puerto Rican-Origin Women Born on Island and Living on Mainland, 1970

Age and characteristics	Residence 1970									Residence 1965					
	Total			New York City			Elsewhere			Mainland			Island		
	Total	Under 12 years	12+ years	Total	Under 12 years	12+ years	Total	Under 12 years	12+ years	Total	Under 12 years	12+ years	Total	Under 12 years	12+ years
15-19 total	33	35	19	35	37	19	31	33	19	30	32	18	39	41	28
Married spouse present	93	99	57	97	102	63	89	95	50	96	102	59	80	84	40
Employed	61	68	39	63	76	38	60	64	41	65	75	36	45	50	27
Not employed	101	105	67	102	105	75	99	104	55	104	108	72	87	90	48
Other marital status	15	16	8	18	19	8	12	12	6	14	15	6	17	18	8
Employed	9	12	3	10	15	4	7	9	6	9	13	2	4	5	-
Not employed	17	17	13	19	20	12	13	13	16	15	16	12	20	20	15
20-24 total	136	172	71	137	172	73	134	171	69	139	177	73	126	152	73
Married spouse present	152	179	99	151	176	104	152	183	94	156	183	104	133	153	92
Employed	95	127	65	79	106	60	109	140	71	99	132	68	86	108	60
Not employed	172	191	122	172	187	131	172	198	110	177	196	129	148	165	108
Other marital status	111	160	33	118	166	37	96	145	25	114	167	33	114	149	38
Employed	34	63	18	31	59	18	36	61	18	38	78	18	26	38	13
Not employed	164	191	65	168	191	74	157	191	44	167	193	67	170	196	73
25-29 total	237	268	160	230	258	155	250	286	167	240	269	164	223	268	120
Married spouse present	240	268	177	229	253	175	254	264	179	244	271	181	221	270	130
Employed	168	199	131	151	175	128	185	218	135	176	206	139	122	170	75
Not employed	261	284	199	249	266	198	279	313	201	264	286	202	244	287	151
Other marital status	232	267	111	230	264	112	238	275	109	231	265	116	226	264	88
Employed	94	129	59	88	122	60	106	141	56	96	127	66	79	113	29
Not employed	285	297	194	278	289	193	305	321	196	284	295	198	282	303	154
30-34 total	310	331	236	297	316	223	333	361	253	308	329	235	301	323	227
Married spouse present	369	331	246	291	271	233	336	365	262	309	330	245	307	323	249
Employed	213	269	211	214	226	192	283	306	231	251	272	209	215	257	206
Not employed	329	348	263	310	325	251	360	391	278	328	347	262	325	341	265
Other marital status	311	333	203	308	328	199	320	346	211	307	328	202	290	321	185
Employed	178	197	145	167	185	140	197	216	155	172	187	148	182	216	138
Not employed	358	367	279	349	356	274	389	402	290	351	359	274	340	353	255
35-44 total	348	365	274	332	345	266	377	408	284	346	363	274	387	417	277
Married spouse present	351	369	283	333	345	279	379	413	288	349	366	284	396	425	309
Employed	292	307	252	258	267	233	327	353	268	295	312	250	295	299	285
Not employed	380	395	308	362	370	310	415	350	305	376	390	310	431	465	320
Other marital status	340	357	243	331	347	238	369	392	260	339	356	242	373	406	197
Employed	227	244	180	207	221	167	271	297	206	233	249	185	191	225	125
Not employed	397	404	330	385	393	319	439	446	370	394	401	324	436	452	284

TABLE G-13
Children Ever Born per 100 Puerto Rican–Origin Women Resident on Island, 1970

Age and characteristics				*Years of schooling*					
				Urban			Rural		
	Total	Under 12 years	12+ years	Total	Under 12 years	12+ years	Total	Under 12 years	12+ years
15–19 total	15	16	4	11	12	4	17	18	5
Married spouse present	88	94	30	73	80	24	94	99	35
Employed	56	70	29	36	57	0	63	75	40
Not employed	91	96	31	76	82	31	97	101	32
Other marital status	6	6	2	5	5	3	6	7	2
Employed	6	8	2	8	11	2	4	6	2
Not employed	6	6	2	5	5	3	6	7	2
20–24 total	96	150	41	79	141	39	107	154	43
Married spouse present	169	212	97	142	188	90	184	223	102
Employed	109	175	78	93	143	73	120	193	81
Not employed	188	218	111	161	196	102	201	226	118
Other marital status	38	74	13	33	80	15	41	71	12
Employed	20	59	9	21	67	13	20	55	6
Not employed	49	77	18	43	83	17	52	75	18
25–29 total	222	287	134	192	264	132	241	297	136
Married spouse present	270	334	176	235	308	173	292	345	179
Employed	186	276	143	180	307	143	190	263	144
Not employed	308	346	212	265	309	204	333	362	222
Other marital status	119	175	53	100	167	48	131	178	57
Employed	67	124	42	67	138	42	67	114	41
Not employed	160	192	76	137	180	63	171	197	86
30–34 total	312	372	207	264	329	202	344	391	214
Married spouse present	346	407	237	291	356	229	379	429	246
Employed	259	318	219	232	294	204	279	329	233
Not employed	384	430	255	322	374	250	420	352	263
Other marital status	213	267	120	191	256	129	229	272	106
Employed	152	230	93	125	191	93	181	254	91
Not employed	262	283	182	265	290	213	260	279	137
35–44 total	396	453	252	323	377	249	448	491	256
Married spouse present	433	490	283	347	402	277	489	530	293
Employed	318	392	250	266	310	241	367	437	262
Not employed	476	512	318	388	427	312	526	548	330
Other marital status	293	344	165	267	324	166	316	359	164
Employed	224	293	144	204	268	148	249	318	137
Not employed	340	366	207	327	355	215	349	374	200

TABLE G-14

Children Ever Born per 100 Puerto Rican–Origin Women, Mainland Born and Living on Mainland, 1970

Age and characteristics		Total			New York City			Elsewhere	
	Total	Under 12 Years	12+ Years	Total	Under 12 years	12+ years	Total	Under 12 years	12+ years
15–19 total	12	11	17	12	11	13	13	11	26
Married spouse present	73	85	51	73	86	47	73	83	57
Employed	54	61	43	48	65	18	59	57	63
Not employed	80	93	54	79	92	55	80	97	54
Other marital status	6	6	7	6	6	6	6	6	11
Employed	4	5	2	4	5	2	5	6	0
Not employed	7	6	13	7	7	9	7	6	25
20–24 total	94	154	57	97	158	57	88	146	58
Married spouse present	126	180	89	130	177	94	121	188	79
Employed	70	117	57	72	109	60	67	138	53
Not employed	154	194	113	156	192	118	151	197	104
Other marital status	60	121	29	65	136	26	47	75	35
Employed	26	60	18	27	66	19	25	52	15
Not employed	107	154	54	112	161	43	90	113	78
25–29 total	195	231	158	208	240	168	171	209	145
Married spouse present	210	244	182	214	235	192	205	266	169
Employed	149	194	128	137	159	123	164	250	131
Not employed	234	257	210	239	251	223	225	272	192
Other marital status	169	215	112	198	248	126	108	129	89
Employed	79	96	71	82	89	79	74	105	58
Not employed	231	249	181	262	282	198	144	141	148
30 to 34 total	259	284	229	247	260	224	282	342	234
Married spouse present	272	303	240	251	267	228	304	374	254
Employed	232	257	217	203	213	198	263	304	238
Not employed	292	317	257	269	279	250	330	411	265
Other marital status	226	246	183	239	248	214	189	241	125
Employed	171	189	155	173	172	173	167	228	129
Not employed	269	270	261	277	274	296	227	251	103
35–44 total	278	309	235	261	296	205	300	330	267
Married spouse present	294	322	260	273	304	227	317	344	288
Employed	273	302	250	249	281	216	295	328	275
Not employed	308	331	269	286	314	236	332	352	302
Other marital status	239	283	163	241	284	163	236	282	164
Employed	180	214	144	179	205	152	183	234	126
Not employed	304	334	206	229	338	189	298	324	236

TABLE G-15

Children Ever Born per 100 Women of Central and South American Descent, 1970, United States (top); Children Ever Born per 100 Women of Cuban Descent, 1970, United States (bottom)

Central and South American Descent

Age and characteristics	Years schooling		
	Total	Under 12 years	12+ years
25-29 total	127	143	115
Married spouse present	152	168	142
Employed	120	137	110
Not employed	171	184	163
Other marital status	73	98	53
Employed	60	83	45
Not employed	105	122	82
30-34 total	190	199	181
Married spouse present	220	235	209
Employed	183	193	175
Not employed	247	265	233
Other marital status	121	139	97
Employed	95	106	83
Not employed	200	221	157
35-44 total	236	248	224
Married spouse present	272	290	257
Employed	256	274	243
Not employed	284	302	269
Other marital status	165	183	142
Employed	154	167	138
Not employed	208	228	163

Cuban Descent

Age and characteristics	Years schooling		
	Total	Under 12 years	12+ years
15-19 total	9	8	11
Married spouse present	56	60	48
Employed	35	30	40
Not employed	64	69	11
Other marital status	5	4	5
Employed	7	7	8
Not employed	4	4	3
20-24 total	61	83	46
Married spouse present	97	120	80
Employed	74	95	60
Not employed	112	132	94
Other marital status	26	40	18
Employed	24	37	17
Not employed	29	46	20
25-29 total	143	164	128
Married spouse present	169	184	157
Employed	135	147	127
Not employed	196	209	184
Other marital status	42	103	55
Employed	54	71	46
Not employed	123	140	94
30-34 total	183	191	173
Married spouse present	204	210	198
Employed	178	184	171
Not employed	227	230	222
Other marital status	102	122	80
Employed	71	79	65
Not employed	170	182	141
35-44 total	197	201	192
Married spouse present	212	210	213
Employed	197	195	199
Not employed	229	225	237
Other marital status	137	159	117
Employed	126	144	112
Not employed	174	191	143

TABLE G–16

Children Ever Born per 100 Non-Spanish White Women, by Residence, 1970, United States

Age and characteristics	Total U.S.			Inside N.Y. & N.J. S.M.S.A.'s			All other states		
	Total	Under 12 years	12+ years	Total	Under 12 years	12+ years	Total	Under 12 years	12+ years
15–19 total	8	8	10	5	4	6	9	8	10
Married spouse present	58	74	41	62	83	40	58	73	40
Employed	39	70	23	27	48	18	40	71	24
Not employed	66	74	53	81	99	60	65	73	53
Other marital status	3	3	4	2	2	3	3	3	4
Employed	4	4	4	2	2	3	4	3	3
Not employed	3	2	4	2	2	3	3	2	4
20–24 total	66	138	50	46	101	38	68	141	52
Married spouse present	98	165	80	86	144	75	99	167	80
Employed	55	135	43	34	82	29	56	138	44
Not employed	131	176	113	126	162	115	131	177	113
Other marital status	24	79	16	14	44	10	102	157	83
Employed	18	66	13	8	21	7	20	71	14
Not employed	35	91	22	28	72	19	37	93	23
25–29 total	170	239	151	142	200	128	173	242	153
Married spouse present	190	258	171	171	223	159	192	261	172
Employed	139	224	121	99	168	87	143	228	124
Not employed	217	272	199	201	239	190	218	275	200
Other marital status	90	162	67	56	131	38	94	166	71
Employed	66	136	53	36	93	28	71	142	57
Not employed	152	188	123	127	174	92	154	188	126
30–34 total	253	301	236	222	255	212	256	305	238
Married spouse present	272	319	255	252	274	246	273	323	256
Employed	239	293	220	205	249	191	241	296	222
Not employed	290	332	274	270	284	266	292	337	275
Other marital status	159	221	131	107	185	81	165	224	139
Employed	126	195	106	67	117	56	135	204	114
Not employed	231	248	215	223	261	190	231	246	217
35–44 total	285	309	273	249	257	245	289	315	276
Married spouse present	303	326	292	276	280	275	306	330	294
Employed	277	297	268	245	241	246	270	302	270
Not employed	323	346	311	297	304	294	325	350	313
Other marital status	193	234	169	131	163	115	202	243	177
Employed	171	217	152	108	136	99	180	226	159
Not employed	245	258	231	193	200	186	253	265	238

TABLE G–17

Children Ever Born per 100 Non-Spanish White Women, Residence in Five Southwestern States and Outside Five Southwestern States, 1970

Age and characteristics	Five Southwestern States Total							Outside Five Southwestern States		
	Total	8 years	8-11 years	Under 12 years	12 years	13+ years	12+ years	Total	Under 12 years	12+ years
15-19 total	9	20	7	8	14	5	12	8	7	9
Married spouse present	54	103	72	73	39	28	38	59	74	41
Employed	37	150	69	72	23	27	23	40	70	23
Not employed	62	96	72	73	50	28	48	67	75	55
Other marital status	3	10	2	2	6	2	5	3	3	4
Employed	5	40	4	5	6	2	5	4	3	4
Not employed	3	4	2	2	7	2	5	3	2	4
20-24 total	65	100	145	140	75	27	50	66	137	50
Married spouse present	92	192	164	166	94	47	74	99	165	81
Employed	50	114	129	128	56	24	40	56	136	43
Not employed	123	207	176	178	122	74	104	132	176	115
Other marital status	28	31	97	84	39	10	21	23	78	15
Employed	24	30	87	78	34	8	18	17	64	12
Not employed	53	32	108	90	51	14	25	35	91	21
25-29 total	164	185	252	245	176	109	145	172	237	152
Married spouse present	183	255	264	263	191	131	164	192	258	172
Employed	134	207	230	228	154	85	120	140	223	121
Not employed	210	271	276	275	210	166	192	218	271	201
Other marital status	96	89	205	183	110	48	75	88	159	65
Employed	75	89	181	165	94	40	62	64	131	51
Not employed	154	89	230	199	160	86	126	151	185	122
30-34 total	241	271	296	293	247	198	226	256	302	238
Married spouse present	257	331	305	307	258	221	243	275	321	258
Employed	226	329	286	290	230	182	211	241	294	223
Not employed	274	332	314	316	274	244	262	293	335	277
Other marital status	169	136	205	236	186	107	147	156	218	127
Employed	149	217	241	239	166	91	128	121	187	101
Not employed	220	79	276	233	242	171	213	233	250	215
35-44 total	271	300	303	303	267	245	259	288	310	277
Married spouse present	285	335	313	316	279	266	274	306	328	296
Employed	264	326	292	295	258	245	253	279	298	271
Not employed	302	339	328	330	295	283	291	327	348	315
Other marital status	204	203	254	245	207	165	188	191	233	164
Employed	190	230	247	244	191	152	172	167	212	146
Not employed	242	173	268	246	253	218	239	246	260	229

393

TABLE G–18

Selected Characteristics for Women of Mexican Descent in the Reproductive Years, by Years of Schooling Completed: U.S. 1970

Age and characteristics	Mexican descent					
	0–7 years	8–11 years	12 years	13+ years	–12 years	12+ years
15 to 19 years						
% married, spouse present	17.1	9.6	16.7	10.7	10.9	15.8
% employed	18.2	14.8	51.3	53.2	15.3	51.4
Av. no. children ever born per woman	.28	.12	.15	.12	.14	.14
20 to 24 years						
% married, spouse present	61.7	64.1	52.8	41.0	63.2	49.9
% employed	27.5	31.1	54.6	61.5	29.7	56.3
Av. no. children ever born per woman	1.58	1.47	.68	.37	1.51	.60
25 to 29 years						
% married, spouse present	76.7	77.8	76.4	69.8	77.3	74.9
% employed	27.4	30.6	46.2	60.5	29.2	49.5
Av. no. children ever born per woman	2.89	2.63	1.81	1.22	2.75	1.66
30 to 34 years						
% married, spouse present	79.8	81.2	80.6	77.9	80:4	79.9
% employed	27.6	35.2	46.3	52.5	31.1	47.8
Av. no. children ever born per woman	4.02	3.61	2.77	2.22	3.83	2.64
35 to 44 years						
% married spouse present	77.8	80.0	80.4	77.2	78.7	79.8
% employed	29.7	39.8	49.3	59.4	33.7	51.8
Av. no. children ever born per woman	4.98	4.16	3.29	2.77	4.66	3.18

TABLE G–19

Selected Characteristics for Women of Mexican Descent in the Reproductive Years, Residing in Five Southwestern States, by Years of Schooling Completed: U.S. 1970

Age and characteristics	Mexican descent					
	0–7 years	8–11 years	12 years	13+ years	−12 years	12+ years
15 to 19 years						
% married, spouse present	16.9	9.5	16.1	9.0	10.8	15.1
% employed	18.1	14.0	50.7	52.4	14.7	51.0
Av. no. children ever born per woman	.27	.12	.14	.11	.14	.14
20 to 24 years						
% married, spouse present	60.1	63.3	52.2	40.5	62.1	49.3
% employed	27.5	31.5	54.5	61.2	30.0	56.2
Av. no. children ever born per woman	1.54	1.47	.68	.38	1.50	.60
25 to 29 years						
% married, spouse present	76.6	77.7	75.4	68.9	77.2	73.9
% employed	29.2	30.4	47.0	60.8	28.9	50.4
Av. no. children ever born per woman	2.91	2.64	1.80	1.22	2.76	1.65
30 to 34 years						
% married, spouse present	79.5	80.6	81.0	76.2	80.0	79.9
% employed	27.1	34.4	46.3	53.0	30.4	47.8
Av. no. children ever born per woman	4.02	3.61	2.78	2.22	3.84	2.65
35 to 44 years						
% married, spouse present	77.1	79.8	80.5	76.2	78.1	79.7
% employed	29.3	39.2	48.4	61.0	33.2	50.9
Av. no. children ever born per woman	4.94	4.17	3.32	2.78	4.64	3.21

TABLE G–20

Selected Characteristics of Mexican Women in Reproductive Years, by Residence, by Years of Schooling Completed: U.S. 1970

| Age and characteristics | FIVE SOUTHWESTERN STATES | | | | ALL OTHER STATES | |
| | Inside SMSAs | | Outside SMSAs | | | |
	-12 years	12+ years	-12 years	12+ years	-12 years	12+ years
15 to 19 years						
% married, spouse present	10.7	14.9	11.1	16.4	11.6	20.9
% employed	15.0	52.6	13.1	40.5	20.2	54.7
Av. no. children ever born per woman	.15	.13	.13	.17	.13	.18
20 to 24 years						
% married, spouse present	62.6	49.8	60.1	46.1	70.7	53.4
% employed	30.7	57.1	27.2	50.5	28.1	57.0
Av. no. children ever born per woman	1.49	.59	1.52	.65	1.60	.61
25 to 29 years						
% married, spouse present	77.0	73.9	78.0	73.7	78.4	80.5
% employed	29.6	50.8	26.4	47.2	30.8	44.7
Av. no. children ever born per woman	2.71	1.64	2.96	1.82	2.66	1.72
30 to 34 years						
% married, spouse present	79.4	80.0	82.3	79.0	83.5	80.0
% employed	31.0	48.3	28.1	44.6	35.5	47.4
Av. no. children ever born per woman	3.72	2.62	4.28	2.86	3.79	2.57
35 to 44 years						
% married, spouse present	77.5	79.6	80.9	80.1	82.7	80.3
% employed	34.1	51.6	29.0	46.0	38.1	53.7
Av. no. children ever born per woman	4.54	3.18	5.09	3.42	4.77	2.99

TABLE G–21.

Selected Characteristics of Mexican Women in the Reproductive Years, Residing in Five Southwestern States, by Years of Schooling Completed: U.S. 1970

Age and characteristics	Native						Foreign born	
	0–7 years	8–11 years	12 years	13+ years	–12 years	12+ years	–12 years	12+ years
15 to 19 years								
% married, spouse present	15.8	9.8	16.3	9.8	10.6	15.4	11.9	15.8
% employed	15.1	13.4	51.0	53.8	13.6	51.4	19.5	52.8
Av. no children ever born per woman	.25	.12	.13	.10	.14	.13	.14	.15
20 to 24 years								
% married, spouse present	55.3	64.5	52.4	39.8	61.6	49.2	65.4	48.0
% employed	28.1	30.7	55.3	62.2	29.9	57.1	30.9	53.1
Av. no. children ever born per woman	1.64	1.55	.69	.36	1.58	.60	1.31	.58
25 to 29 years								
% married, spouse present	71.7	77.2	75.1	68.4	75.3	73.6	81.1	76.8
% employed	27.9	30.1	48.9	63.3	29.3	52.2	26.9	44.5
Av. no. children ever born per woman	3.14	2.72	1.79	1.22	2.87	1.66	2.35	1.58
30 to 34 years								
% married, spouse present	76.0	79.6	80.4	74.5	78.0	79.1	82.9	83.8
% employed	26.2	35.0	47.8	56.5	31.2	49.7	28.1	38.3
Av. no. children ever born per woman	4.27	3.67	2.79	2.15	3.93	2.65	3.69	2.58
35 to 44 years								
% married, spouse present	75.7	79.4	80.0	74.8	77.4	79.0	80.2	81.7
% employed	28.6	39.3	15.3	64.3	33.6	52.3	30.6	40.0
Av. no. children ever born per woman	5.04	4.22	3.30	2.73	4.67	3.19	4.64	3.22

TABLE G–22

Selected Characteristics for Non-Spanish White Women *in the Reproductive Years, by Years of Schooling Completed: U.S. 1970*

Age and characteristics	0–7 years	8–11 years	12 years	13–15 years	16+ years	–12 years	12+ years	13+ years
15 to 19 years								
% married, spouse present	10.4	6.8	18.3	8.0	9.1	6.9	16.0	8.0
% employed	15.4	19.5	50.9	42.5	100.0	19.3	49.1	42.6
Av. no. children ever born								
per woman	.16	.07	.11	.05	.18	.08	.10	.05
20 to 24 years								
% married, spouse present	45.1	71.5	64.8	37.7	48.9	68.0	53.9	40.6
% employed	32.8	33.7	55.6	53.8	77.7	33.6	57.6	60.1
Av. no. children ever born								
per woman	1.03	1.43	.72	.26	.18	1.38	.50	.24
25 to 29 years								
% married, spouse present	60.8	81.8	83.6	78.9	73.2	79.2	80.7	76.1
% employed	32.4	32.2	40.1	45.1	59.3	32.3	44.8	52.2
Av. no. children ever born								
per woman	2.00	2.44	1.77	1.39	.79	2.39	1.51	1.09
30 to 34 years								
% married, spouse present	68.1	83.4	86.1	83.3	79.9	81.2	84.6	81.7
% employed	32.6	38.1	40.6	40.6	48.4	37.3	41.9	44.3
Av. no. children ever born								
per woman	2.67	3.06	2.53	2.31	1.75	3.01	2.36	2.04
35 to 44 years								
% married, spouse present	73.0	83.3	86.3	83.8	79.2	81.7	84.8	81.8
% employed	36.1	45.5	48.4	46.8	55.6	44.0	49.1	50.7
Av. no. children ever born								
per woman	3.03	3.10	2.81	2.74	2.35	3.09	2.73	2.57

TABLE G–23

Selected Characteristics for Non-Spanish White Women in the Reproductive Years, Residing in New York and New Jersey, by Years of Schooling Completed: U.S. 1970

Age and characteristics	New York and New Jersey							
	0–7 years	8–11 years	12 years	13–15 years	16+ years	–12 years	12+ years	13+ years
15 to 19 years								
% married, spouse present	3.5	3.3	9.4	4.6	25.0	3.3	8.2	4.7
% employed	19.7	20.0	55.8	42.5	100.0	20.0	52.4	42.9
Av. no. children ever born per woman	.08	.04	.07	.03	.00	.05	.06	.03
20 to 24 years								
% married, spouse present	35.5	62.2	54.9	30.3	41.6	58.4	44.7	33.8
% employed	36.8	34.6	59.5	53.1	78.8	34.9	60.2	61.1
Av. no. children ever born per woman	.68	1.14	.61	.22	.13	1.07	.41	.20
25 to 29 years								
% married, spouse present	57.6	78.9	79.9	74.8	68.3	76.0	76.3	71.2
% employed	36.4	29.1	35.7	46.3	59.1	30.1	43.0	53.4
Av. no. children ever born per woman	1.70	2.16	1.60	1.26	.76	2.09	1.34	.98
30 to 34 years								
% married, spouse present	72.1	79.4	83.6	79.4	76.4	78.2	81.5	77.7
% employed	29.8	35.2	34.9	39.3	46.8	34.3	38.0	43.4
Av. no. children ever born per woman	1.97	2.79	2.40	2.18	1.60	2.65	2.21	1.86
35 to 44 years								
% married, spouse present	72.9	81.6	84.6	80.8	77.5	80.2	82.8	79.1
% employed	38.8	43.2	44.5	44.8	58.9	42.4	46.9	52.2
Av. no. children ever born per woman	2.31	2.75	2.64	2.52	2.18	2.67	2.54	2.34

TABLE G-24

Selected Characteristics for Non-Spanish White Women in the Reproductive Years, by Residence, by Years of Schooling Completed: U.S. 1970

Age and characteristics	All states except New York and New Jersey							
	0-7 years	8-11 years	12 years	13-15 years	16+ years	-12 years	12+ years	13+ years
15 to 19 years								
% married, spouse present	11.1	7.2	19.4	8.6	–	7.4	17.1	8.6
% employed	14.9	19.5	50.3	42.5	–	19.3	48.7	42.6
Av. no. children ever born								
per woman	.16	.07	.12	.05	.29	.08	.10	.05
20 to 24 years								
% married, spouse present	46.2	72.4	66.1	41.4	50.2	68.9	55.2	41.7
% employed	32.3	33.6	55.1	53.9	77.5	33.4	57.2	60.0
Av. no. children ever born								
per woman	1.07	1.46	.73	.27	.18	1.41	.52	.25
25 to 29 years								
% married, spouse present	61.2	82.2	84.1	79.4	74.0	79.6	81.3	76.8
% employed	31.9	32.6	40.7	45.0	59.3	32.5	45.0	52.0
Av. no. children ever born								
per woman	2.04	2.47	1.79	1.41	.80	2.42	1.53	1.11
30 to 34 years								
% married, spouse present	67.5	83.8	86.4	83.8	80.5	81.6	85.0	82.3
% employed	33.0	38.4	41.4	40.8	48.7	37.6	42.4	44.4
Av. no. children ever born								
per woman	2.76	3.09	2.54	2.32	1.77	3.05	2.38	2.07
35 to 44 years								
% married, spouse present	73.0	83.6	86.5	84.2	79.5	81.9	85.1	82.2
% employed	35.7	45.8	49.0	47.1	55.0	44.2	49.5	50.5
Av. no. children ever born								
per woman	3.12	3.15	2.84	2.77	2.38	3.15	2.76	2.60

TABLE G–25

Selected Characteristics for Non-Spanish White Women in the Reproductive Years, Residing in Five Southwestern States, by Years of Schooling Completed: U.S. 1970

Age and characteristics	0–7 years	8–11 years	12 years	13–15 years	16+ years	–12 years	12+ years	13+ years
15 to 19 years								
% married, spouse present	10.7	7.1	22.7	11.7	–	7.2	20.2	11.7
% employed	15.4	16.4	47.4	46.1	–	16.3	47.1	46.2
Av. no. children ever born per woman	.20	.07	.14	.05	– ·	.08	.12	.05
20 to 24 years								
% married, spouse present	41.9	71.7	66.5	44.2	50.4	68.4	55.8	45.7
% employed	28.1	32.1	52.7	55.0	73.1	31.6	56.2	59.4
Av. no. children ever born per woman	1.00	1.45	.75	.30	.18	1.40	.50	.27
25 to 29 years								
% married, spouse present	57.7	79.6	81.9	76.2	71.1	77.3	78.2	73.9
% employed	32.5	30.8	41.8	48.0	60.0	31.0	47.3	53.5
Av. no. children ever born per woman	1.85	2.52	1.76	1.38	.75	2.45	1.45	1.09
30 to 34 years								
% married, spouse present	69.1	81.5	84.5	80.5	79.1	80.3	82.5	79.8
% employed	33.7	38.1	42.7	43.6	50.5	37.7	44.4	46.7
Av. no. children ever born per woman	2.71	2.96	2.47	2.22	1.68	2.93	2.26	1.98
35 to 44 years								
% married, spouse present	73.8	82.7	84.3	81.3	77.3	81.5	82.5	79.6
% employed	38.4	46.0	49.4	48.0	56.2	45.0	50.2	51.3
Av. no. children ever born per woman	3.00	3.03	2.67	2.58	2.28	3.03	2.59	2.45

TABLE G-26

Selected Characteristics for Non-Spanish White Women in the Reproductive Years, Residing Inside SMSAs in Five Southwestern States, by Years of Schooling Completed: U.S. 1970

Age and characteristics	0-7 years	8-11 years	12 years	13-15 years	16+ years	-12 years	12+ years	13+ years
15 to 19 years								
% married, spouse present	12.1	6.9	22.0	11.0	–	7.0	19.5	10.9
% employed	13.5	16.6	48.8	47.5	–	16.5	48.5	47.6
Av. no. children ever born per woman	.20	.07	.14	.06	.05	.07	.12	.06
20 to 24 years								
% married, spouse present	42.1	70.4	66.2	43.8	49.5	67.5	55.3	45.2
% employed	28.0	33.3	53.8	56.7	73.1	32.7	57.4	60.8
Av. no. children ever born per woman	.98	1.42	.74	.29	.18	1.38	.49	.26
25 to 29 years								
% married, spouse present	57.9	79.0	81.6	75.1	70.1	76.7	77.4	72.8
% employed	36.0	31.8	42.2	48.8	60.8	32.3	47.9	54.3
Av. no. children ever born per woman	1.86	2.50	1.76	1.34	.72	2.43	1.43	1.06
30 to 34 years								
% married, spouse present	71.9	81.1	83.6	79.7	78.8	80.2	81.7	79.3
% employed	31.5	39.2	43.2	43.9	49.6	38.5	44.6	46.5
Av. no. children ever born per woman	2.49	2.92	2.44	2.17	1.68	2.88	2.23	1.96
35 to 44 years								
% married, spouse present	73.3	82.2	83.9	80.7	76.4	81.1	81.9	78.9
% employed	40.3	46.6	49.5	48.0	55.7	45.9	50.2	51.2
Av. no. children ever born per woman	2.93	3.00	2.66	2.57	2.26	2.99	2.26	2.44

TABLE G–27

Selected Characteristics for Non-Spanish White Women in the Reproductive Years, Residing Outside SMSAs in Five Southwestern States, by Years of Schooling Completed: U.S. 1970

Age and characteristics	0–7 years	8–11 years	12 years	13–15 years	16+ years	–12 years	12+ years	13+ years
15 to 19 years								
% married, spouse present	5.3	8.2	27.0	16.8	–	8.1	24.8	16.8
% employed	22.8	15.1	38.6	36.6	–	15.5	38.2	36.6
Av. no. children ever born								
per woman	.21	.08	.16	.01	–	.09	.13	.01
20 to 24 years								
% married, spouse present	41.0	78.2	68 9	47.9	59.6	73.4	60.1	50.3
% employed	28.2	25.6	45.2	41.1	73.1	25.9	46.4	47.7
Av. no. children ever born								
per woman	1.08	1.59	.81	.36	.14	1.53	.58	.31
25 to 29 years								
% married, spouse present	56.7	82.8	84.9	86.4	81.0	80.1	84.6	84.1
% employed	13.3	25.6	38.9	40.4	51.4	24.3	41.4	42.1
Av. no. children ever born								
per woman	1.80	2.60	1.81	1.76	.99	2.51	1.65	1.44
30 to 34 years								
% married, spouse present	57.1	83.9	90.6	87.7	81.9	80.6	88.8	85.4
% employed	42.9	32.3	39.7	41.1	60.6	33.6	42.8	48.8
Av. no. children ever born								
per woman	3.63	3.14	2.66	2.68	1.70	3.20	2.53	2.30
35 to 44 years								
% married, spouse present	75.7	85.1	87.3	86.2	85.6	83.7	86.8	86.0
% employed	29.9	42.6	49.2	47.9	60.2	40.8	50.4	52.7
Av. no. children ever born								
per woman	3.32	3.18	2.77	2.60	2.49	3.20	2.70	2.56

TABLE G–28

Selected Characteristics for Non-Spanish White Women *in the Reproductive Years, Residing in All States Except Five Southwestern States, by Years of Schooling Completed: U.S. 1970*

Age and characteristics	0–7 years	8–11 years	12 years	13–15 years	16+ years	–12 years	12+ years	13+ years
15 to 19 years								
% married, spouse present	10.4	6.7	17.5	7.3	–	6.9	15.2	7.3
% employed	15.4	20.1	51.6	41.8	–	19.9	49.5	41.9
Av. no. children ever born								
per woman	.15	.07	.11	.05	–	.07	.09	.04
20 to 24 years								
% married, spouse present	45.6	71.4	64.5	36.0	48.6	67.9	53.5	39.4
% employed	33.5	34.0	56.1	53.4	78.7	33.9	57.7	60.3
Av. no. children ever born								
per woman	1.04	1.42	.71	.25	.18	1.37	.50	.23
25 to 29 years								
% married, spouse present	61.2	82.2	83.9	79.8	73.7	79.6	81.2	76.7
% employed	32.4	32.5	39.8	28.9	59.1	32.5	44.2	51.8
Av. no. children ever born								
per woman	2.02	2.43	1.77	1.40	.80	2.87	1.52	1.09
30 to 34 years								
% married, spouse present	68.0	83.7	86.3	84.2	80.1	81.4	85.0	82.2
% employed	32.5	38.0	40.2	39.7	47.9	37.2	41.3	43.6
Av. no. children ever born								
per woman	2.66	3.08	2.54	2.33	1.76	3.02	2.38	2.06
35 to 44 years								
% married, spouse present	72.9	83.5	86.6	84.6	79.7	81.7	85.3	82.4
% employed	35.8	45.4	48.2	46.5	55.5	43.8	48.9	50.5
Av. no. children ever born								
per woman	3.03	3.12	2.84	2.80	2.36	3.10	2.77	2.60

TABLE G-29
Labor-Force Participation and Employment Rates, Non-Spanish White Population, by Sex, Age, and Years of Schooling: 1970

Age	Total			Under 12 years			12 years			13 to 15 years			16+ years		
	% in labor force	a/	b/	% in labor force	a/	b/	% in labor force	a/	b/	% in labor force	a/	b/	% in labor force	a/	b/
MEN															
Total	77.4	82.9	3.5	65.4	77.3	4.9	88.6	88.0	3.1	80.1	80.7	2.9	90.7	88.4	1.4
16 to 19 years	50.0	34.8	10.0	44.6	25.1	11.2	65.2	57.0	8.2	50.3	30.3	6.7	0.0	0.0	0.0
20 to 24 years	81.4	73.9	6.1	84.3	77.6	9.2	92.5	84.3	5.7	67.3	57.3	5.4	82.0	71.6	3.5
25 to 34 years	95.0	89.0	2.8	91.5	85.6	4.9	97.4	91.4	2.7	94.3	89.3	2.1	95.2	88.3	1.4
35 to 44 years	95.8	91.2	2.2	92.6	88.3	3.5	97.3	92.6	1.9	97.1	92.5	1.9	98.4	92.4	1.0
45 to 54 years	93.5	90.5	2.4	90.3	88.0	3.4	95.5	92.1	1.9	95.3	92.7	1.8	97.6	92.7	1.1
55 and over	53.6	80.6	3.3	46.8	77.7	4.0	66.7	85.3	2.6	65.5	83.5	2.3	70.1	84.1	1.6
20 to 64 years	90.4	87.7	3.0	86.7	86.2	4.1	94.8	90.6	2.7	85.4	83.2	2.8	94.4	89.1	1.4
WOMEN															
Total	41.0	66.2	4.9	30.5	60.5	6.9	47.7	70.0	4.4	46.7	63.9	3.8	58.0	71.6	2.1
16 to 19 years	36.9	38.4	10.2	27.7	19.8	12.6	55.9	60.5	8.4	45.3	35.9	6.1	0.0	0.0	0.0
20 to 24 years	56.9	70.6	5.8	38.3	65.8	12.2	59.2	77.5	5.8	56.5	59.5	4.5	80.4	73.0	2.8
25 to 34 years	43.5	67.5	4.7	37.8	65.3	7.9	42.2	67.9	4.4	44.9	66.8	3.5	56.5	69.5	2.6
35 to 44 years	49.4	66.8	3.8	46.5	67.8	5.5	50.1	66.5	3.3	48.6	65.2	3.4	57.0	67.2	2.2
45 to 54	52.6	71.9	3.6	46.4	70.1	5.1	55.3	72.3	3.1	55.9	72.2	2.8	66.7	76.2	1.3
55 and over	24.5	67.3	4.2	19.3	63.3	5.3	32.2	71.4	3.8	30.7	68.9	3.3	41.8	73.6	1.5
20 to 44 years	49.0	68.2	4.7	41.9	66.7	7.3	49.2	70.2	4.4	50.7	63.0	3.9	62.0	69.9	2.5

a/ Percentage of civilian labor force employed full time.

b/ Percentage of civilian labor force unemployed.

405

TABLE G–30
Class of Worker* by Sex and Nativity. Population Aged 25 and Over: 1970

	Total	Employees Private	Govt.	Self-emp.	Total	Employees Private	Govt.	Self-emp.
Non-Spanish white	100.0	70.2	14.4	15.4	100.0	74.0	20.1	5.9
Mexican origin, total	100.0	80.0	13.5	6.6	100.0	82.7	14.0	3.3
Native	100.0	76.6	16.8	6.6	100.0	80.0	16.4	3.6
Foreign born	100.0	87.6	5.7	6.7	100.0	89.2	7.2	3.6
Puerto Rican origin, total	100.0	83.7	11.4	4.9	100.0	83.4	14.0	2.6
Mainland born	100.0	77.8	16.8	5.4	100.0	77.6	20.0	2.4
Island born	100.0	84.5	10.7	4.8	100.0	84.3	13.1	2.6
Hispanos	100.0	70.8	20.4	8.8	100.0	73.8	21.9	4.3
Cuban origin, total	100.0	84.4	5.9	9.7	100.0	90.0	6.8	3.2
Native	100.0	64.3	24.3	11.4	100.0	81.1	14.2	4.7
Foreign born	100.0	85.6	4.9	9.5	100.0	90.5	6.4	3.1
Central and South American origin	100.0	82.6	9.7	7.7	100.0	87.0	10.3	2.7

*Data from special tabulation of the PUS. "Self-employed" includes all persons who reported self-employment, whereas in the published U.S. Census volumes those self-employed who reported themselves as having an incorporated enterprise were included with private employees.

TABLE G-31

Percentage Distribution by Class of Worker, Employed Persons Aged 25 and Over, by Type of Spanish-American Origin, Nativity, and Sex: 1970

	MEN				WOMEN			
	Total	Private	Govern- ment	Self- employed	Total	Private	Govern- ment	Self- employed
Non-Spanish white	100	71	14	15	100	74	20	6
Mexican, total	100	80	13	7	100	83	14	3
Foreign born	100	87	6	7	100	89	7	4
Native	100	76	17	7	100	80	16	4
Puerto Rican, total	100	84	11	5	100	83	14	3
Island born	100	84	11	5	100	84	13	3
Mainland born	100	78	17	5	100	78	20	2
Hispano	100	71	20	9	100	74	22	4
Cuban, total	100	84	6	10	100	90	7	3
Foreign born	100	85	5	10	100	91	6	3
Native	100	65	24	11	100	81	14	5
Central and South American	100	82	10	8	100	87	10	3

TABLE G–32

Median 1969 Earnings, Men of Spanish-American Descent, as Percentage of Non-Spanish White Men, by Type of Descent, Age, and Years of Schooling

Age and descent	*Years of schooling*			
	Under 12 years	12 years	13–15 years	16+ years
Age 25 to 34				
Mexican	78	86	87	81
Native	80	87	88	83
Foreign born	73	80	80	73
Southwestern states	75	85	87	82
Other states	93	89	84	80
Puerto Rican	78	79	88	97
Mainland born	88	91	100	106
Island born	78	79	85	84
Hispano	87	91	92	89
Cuban	86	81	88	100
Central & South American	80	81	85	83
Age 35 to 44				
Mexican	77	85	84	78
Native	80	86	86	78
Foreign born	71	79	74	80
Southwestern states	74	84	84	75
Other states	93	91	88	88
Puerto Rican	74	77	75	90
Mainland born	78	83	88	91
Island born	72	71	71	79
Hispano	85	86	87	66
Cuban	73	71	71	65
Central & South American	77	82	85	92
Age 45 to 64				
Mexican	72	86	81	77
Native	75	81	83	77
Foreign born	69	80	78	79
Southwestern states	71	83	80	74
Other states	83	90	89	77
Puerto Rican	76	76	78	89
Mainland born	88	91	NA	NA
Island born	75	75	77	86
Hispano	82	96	93	81
Cuban	69	65	65	57
Central & South American	83	84	74	91

TABLE G-33

Median 1969 Earnings, Women of Spanish-American Descent, as Percentage of Non-Spanish White Women, by Type of Descent, Age, and Years of Schooling

Age and descent	*Years of schooling*			
	Under 12 years	12 years	13-15 years	16+ years
Age 25-34 years				
Mexican	81	97	106	95
Native	78	99	108	97
Foreign born	89	96	93	72
Southwestern states	82	99	106	97
Other states	59	98	102	91
Puerto Rican	139	118	125	98
Mainland born	156	132	133	120
Island born	136	116	121	102
Hispano	63	99	111	99
Cuban	122	103	108	81
Central & South American	135	120	116	71
Age 35-44 years				
Mexican	73	104	116	79
Native	73	105	120	110
Foreign born	73	91	95	82
Southwestern states	70	102	108	110
Other states	96	113	128	NA
Puerto Rican	115	120	134	128
Mainland born	122	123	NA	NA
Island born	116	119	118	125
Hispano	74	100	95	108
Cuban	104	104	107	78
Central & South American	110	125	126	97
Age 45-64 years				
Mexican	69	92	97	86
Native	70	93	100	90
Foreign born	68	90	90	63
Southwestern states	66	90	98	88
Other states	92	95	117	NA
Puerto Rican	111	101	130	87
Mainland born	109	89	NA	NA
Island born	109	107	108	101
Hispano	82	90	121	94
Cuban	96	86	83	59
Central & South American	102	99	98	85

TABLE G–34

Puerto Rican Descent, *Median Earnings in 1969 of Island Born, as Percentage of Mainland Born, by Sex, Age, and Years of Schooling*

	AGE		
	25–34 years	35–44 years	45–64 years
Men			
Under 12 years	88	92	85
12 years	87	86	82
13–15 years	85	81	NA·
16+ years	79	86	NA
Women			
Under 12 years	87	95	100
12 years	88	97	119
13–15 years	91	NA	NA
16+ years	85	NA	NA

TABLE G-35

Earnings in 1969, Non-Spanish White, by Sex, Age, and Years of Schooling

	MEN						WOMEN					
Years of schooling	14 & over	14-24 years	25-34 years	35-44 years	45-64 years	65+ years	14 & over	14-24 years	25-34 years	35-44 years	45-64 years	65+ years
Total U.S.												
1st quartile	$3,440	800	5,980	6,900	5,880	2,400	$1,070	650	1,320	1,570	2,020	900
Median	7,290	1,940	8,260	9,550	8,600	3,170	3,090	1,550	3,480	3,560	3,960	1,790
3rd quartile	10,660	4,490	10,860	13,090	11,930	7,430	5,270	3,700	5,690	5,660	6,050	4,240
Variation*	.99	1.90	.59	.65	.70	1.59	1.36	1.97	1.25	1.15	1.02	1.86
Under 12												
1st quartile	1,930	600	4,830	5,540	4,900	1,120	800	400	920	1,410	1,650	750
Median	5,850	900	6,900	7,790	7,260	2,400	2,230	750	2,410	3,140	3,310	1,550
3rd quartile	8,400	2,500	9,200	10,210	9,670	6,090	4,170	1,510	4,080	4,710	4,880	3,240
Variation	1.10	2.11	.63	.60	.66	2.08	1.51	1.48	1.31	1.05	.98	1.60
12 years												
1st quartile	4,790	1,540	6,270	7,120	6,660	1,610	1,390	920	2,360	1,620	2,220	1,090
Median	7,730	3,320	8,180	9,320	9,100	4,680	3,400	2,460	3,420	3,600	4,200	2,230
3rd quartile	10,510	5,930	10,310	11,860	11,880	8,630	5,270	4,260	5,310	5,540	6,050	4,950
Variation	.74	1.32	.49	.51	.57	1.50	1.14	1.36	.86	1.09	.91	1.73
13 to 15 years												
1st quartile	2,560	1,130	6,300	8,110	7,470	1,640	1,000	650	1,470	1,490	2,410	960
Median	7,290	2,070	8,630	10,780	10,570	5,170	2,870	1,490	3,870	3,870	4,760	2,000
3rd quartile	11,150	3,940	11,120	14,220	14,720	10,000	5,430	3,490	6,000	6,230	6,860	5,330
Variation	1.18	1.36	.56	.57	.69	1.62	1.54	1.90	1.17	1.22	.93	2.18
16+ years												
1st quartile	7,340	1,730	7,150	10,480	10,140	2,450	2,370	1,750	2,430	2,110	4,300	1,340
Median	11,620	3,510	10,090	14,200	14,890	8,440	6,000	3,580	5,920	6,150	7,550	3,880
3rd quartile	18,250	6,250	13,430	21,220	22,910	16,560	8,470	6,200	7,860	9,110	10,140	8,020
Variation	.94	1.29	.62	.76	.86	1.67	1.02	1.24	.92	1.14	.77	1.72

*Interquartile range divided by median.

Source: Special Census tabulation.

411

TABLE G-36
Family Income by Number of Earners in Family, by Type of Spanish-American Population: 1969 (numbers in hundreds)

| | MEXICAN | | | | PUERTO RICAN | | | | HISPANO | | | |
| | Number earners | | | | Number earners | | | | Number earners | | | |
Total	Total	None	1	2 or more	Total	None	1	2 or more	Total	None	1	2 or more
	18,454	1,425	7,639	9,390	7,123	1,472	3,066	2,585	3,275	289	1,384	1,600
Under $1,000	804	436	303	65	526	409	101	16	113	69	34	10
$1,000 to 1,999	951	347	443	161	301	175	101	25	172	82	67	23
2,000 to 2,999	1,264	299	675	290	537	352	151	34	171	45	84	42
3,000 to 3,999	1,553	180	907	466	658	308	292	58	246	47	128	71
4,000 to 4,999	1,550	75	858	617	678	119	458	101	242	21	139	82
5,000 to 5,999	1,596	34	849	713	707	55	497	155	241	3	146	92
6,000 to 6,999	1,573	18	800	755	665	23	428	214	261	7	134	120
7,000 to 7,999	1,504	12	723	769	583	10	344	229	250	6	114	130
8,000 to 9,999	2,595	7	1,006	1,582	854	12	358	484	493	4	210	279
10,000 to 11,999	1,895	11	567	1,317	644	5	182	457	404	2	146	256
12,000 to 14,999	1,6 0	3	298	1,339	493	1	76	416	352	2	99	251
15,000 to 24,999	1,335	1	158	1,176	410	2	60	348	267	1	68	198
25,000 and over	194	1	52	141	67	1	18	48	63	0	17	46
Median	6,960	1,800	5,740	9,090	6,230	2,430	5,870	9,900	7,770	1,920	6,700	9,650

(continued)

412

TABLE G-36 (cont.)

| | CUBAN | | | | CENTRAL & SOUTH AMERICAN | | | |
| | Number earners | | | | Number earners | | | |
	Total	None	1	2 or more	Total	None	1	2 or more
Total	3,023	182	998	1,843	2,665	168	1,055	1,442
Under $1,000	111	69	32	10	97	65	24	8
1,000 to 1,999	95	43	39	13	73	21	41	11
2,000 to 2,999	107	29	54	22	88	25	39	24
3,000 to 3,999	153	18	95	40	141	24	88	29
4,000 to 4,999	177	7	110	60	167	10	102	55
5,000 to 5,999	209	6	113	90	195	8	120	67
6,000 to 6,999	229	3	97	129	190	3	98	89
7,000 to 7,999	275	2	116	157	206	3	96	107
8,000 to 9,999	453	2	131	320	380	2	156	222
10,000 to 11,999	411	0	76	335	326	2	90	234
12,000 to 14,999	355	2	64	289	354	2	85	267
15,000 to 24,999	366	1	45	320	360	3	79	278
25,000 and over	82	0	24	58	88	0	37	51
Median	8,690	1,510	6,580	10,480	8,920	1,880	7,160	10,930

413

TABLE G-37

Numbers of Families by Number of Earners and Sex of Head, for Spanish-Origin Groups: 1970 (numbers in hundreds)

	MEXICAN				PUERTO RICAN				HISPANO			
	Total	Distribution			Total	Distribution			Total	Distribution		
	nos.	Total	Men	Women	nos.	Total	Men	Women	nos.	Total	Men	Women
Total	18,454	100.0	86.3	13.7	7,123	100.0	75.0	25.0	3,275	100.0	85.6	14.4
No earners	1,425	7.7	4.0	3.7	1,472	20.7	5.9	14.8	290	8.9	4.8	4.1
1 earner	7,639	41.4	35.3	6.1	3,066	43.1	36.3	6.8	1,385	42.3	36.2	6.1
2+ earners	9,390	50.9	47.0	3.9	2,585	36.2	32.8	3.4	1,600	48.8	44.6	4.2

	CUBAN				CENTRAL & SOUTH AMERICAN				NON-SPANISH WHITE			
	Total	Distribution			Total	Distribution			Total a/	Distribution		
	nos	Total	Men	Women	nos.	Total	Men	Women	nos.	Total	Men	Women
Total	3,023	100.0	88.0	12.0	2,665	100.0	82.7	17.3	43,730	100.0	91.3	8.7
No earners	182	6.0	3.8	2.2	168	6.3	3.2	3.1	3,795	8.7	7.0	1.7
1 earner	998	33.0	27.6	5.4	1,055	39.5	31.5	8.0	17,635	40.3	36.2	4.1
2+ earners	1,843	61.0	56.6	4.4	1,442	54.2	48.0	6.2	22,300	51.0	48.1	2.9

a/ Numbers in thousands.

Occupational Groups, by Years of Schooling and Sex, Non-Spanish White: 1970

| | MEN | | | | | WOMEN | | | | |
| | (Years of schooling) | | | | | (Years of schooling) | | | | |
	Total	-12 years	12 years	13-15 years	16+ years	Total	-12 years	12 years	13-15 years	16+ years
Total	100.0	100.0	100.0	100.0	100.0	100.0	100.0	100.0	100.0	100.0
Professional, total	15.3	2.2	7.9	21.2	59.0	16.5	3.1	7.5	24.1	78.0
Modern science	7.5	0.8	3.2	10.0	31.5	5.1	1.3	4.3	10.8	11.9
Classical	5.7	0.9	1.9	6.1	25.8	10.3	1.5	2.3	11.2	64.2
Semiprofessional	2.1	0.6	2.8	5.2	1.7	1.0	0.4	0.9	2.2	1.9
Managers	12.2	6.7	12.3	18.3	20.3	4.0	3.1	4.1	5.0	4.7
Employees	9.4	4.3	9.4	14.7	17.6	3.3	2.4	3.4	4.1	4.3
Self-employed	2.8	2.3	2.9	3.6	2.8	0.7	0.7	0.7	0.9	0.5
Sales	7.8	5.7	7.9	12.8	8.6	8.1	9.9	8.6	7.4	2.4
Clerical	7.5	5.3	9.6	11.9	4.9	36.8	20.8	51.9	48.1	11.8
Craftsmen	21.7	26.7	27.3	14.5	3.1	1.9	2.8	1.8	1.1	0.4
Operatives excl. transp.	12.7	18.5	14.1	6.2	0.9	12.9	26.0	9.8	2.4	0.4
Transportation	5.5	8.3	5.6	2.7	0.4	0.5	0.7	0.5	0.3	0.0
Laborers	5.6	9.2	4.7	3.3	0.5	0.9	1.7	0.7	0.4	0.1
Farm managers	3.1	4.5	3.0	1.7	0.8	0.3	0.4	0.2	0.2	0.1
Farm laborers	1.4	2.6	0.9	0.7	0.2	0.4	0.8	0.3	0.2	0.1
Total service and household	7.3	10.4	6.8	6.6	1.4	17.8	30.7	14.7	10.7	1.9
Protective service	1.9	1.8	2.6	2.2	0.5					
Other services	5.4	8.6	4.1	4.4	0.9					

Index

STUDIES IN POPULATION

Under the Editorship of: H. H. WINSBOROUGH

Department of Sociology
University of Wisconsin
Madison, Wisconsin

David L. Brown and John M. Wardwell (Eds.). **New Directions in Urban–Rural Migration:** *The Population Turnaround in Rural America.*

A. J. Jaffe, Ruth M. Cullen, and Thomas D. Boswell. **The Changing Demography of Spanish Americans**

Robert Alan Johnson. **Religious Assortative Marriage in the United States.**

DATE DUE

GAYLORD			PRINTED IN U.S.A.